CLUB SOCCER 101

ALSO BY LUKE DEMPSEY

Monty Python's Flying Circus:
Complete and Annotated (essays and annotations)

A Supremely Bad Idea:
Three Mad Birders and Their Quest to See It All

CLUB SOCCER 101

THE ESSENTIAL GUIDE TO THE STARS, STATS, AND STORIES OF 101 OF THE GREATEST TEAMS IN THE WORLD

LUKE DEMPSEY

W. W. NORTON & COMPANY

NEW YORK   LONDON

For information about permission to reproduce selections from this book,
write to Permissions, W. W. Norton & Company, Inc.,
500 Fifth Avenue, New York, NY 10110

For information about special discounts for bulk purchases, please contact
W. W. Norton Special Sales at specialsales@wwnorton.com or 800-233-4830

Manufacturing by Courier Westford
Book design by Daniel Lagin
Production manager: Anna Oler

ISBN 978-0-393-34930-6 (pbk.)

W. W. Norton & Company, Inc.
500 Fifth Avenue, New York, N.Y. 10110
www.wwnorton.com

W. W. Norton & Company Ltd.
Castle House, 75/76 Wells Street, London W1T 3QT

1 2 3 4 5 6 7 8 9 0

CONTENTS

Soccer fans around the globe have just lived through a month they never quite believed they'd see: finally, a World Cup that lived up to its billing. The 2014 tournament, held in Brazil, saw goals upon goals—many of them last-minute—and games that will live on in football souls for a generation. It was probably the best World Cup ever played.

It was about time. For decades, international soccer—that is, games played between nations rather than between clubs within nations—has become a pale imitation of club soccer. The real game, the global game, the one that compels so many millions across the world, is played every weekend in vibrant, thrilling leagues: the Premier League in Britain (or the league of the same name in Egypt); Serie A in Italy (or the league of the same name in Brazil); Spain's La Liga; the German Bundesliga; the Primera Division in Argentina; Major League Soccer in the U.S. On top of that, the best clubs in these leagues regularly play each other in knockout competitions, like the Champions League in Europe or the Copa Libertadores in South America.

The reason club soccer is now often more interesting is this: playing for your national team means getting together with colleagues a few times a year—many of whom you actually play against each week in your club league—and attempting to forge a team identity. Naturally, the soccer that gets played tends to be disjointed if not downright poor. (Spot the England fan.)

Club football, on the other hand, is vibrant because now that players are free to ply their trade anywhere, the best leagues are melting pots (and are filled with gallons of money), pitting African or Japanese playmakers in midfield driving forward against stolid Serbian or Brazilian center backs marshaling brilliant little Argentine or Spanish strikers. Crucially, these groups of men play together week in week out, train together constantly, and are backed by hordes of completely committed and generally unhinged fans. In short, though soccer fans eagerly await the World Cup every four years, now they also tune in with a similar passion to the final eight games of a Champions League tournament in Europe, or they watch the Copa Libertadores in South America, or they watch teams from Europe play friendly matches against South American or African or Asian teams between seasons, filling stadiums in the United States and elsewhere with fans hungry for 90 minutes of top-class soccer.

The love of these teams may be driven by the cult of superstars. I recently noticed a young woman on the subway in New York with a Lionel Messi cover for her iPhone; soccer moms of my acquaintance in my part of New Jersey like Manchester United. But it may be predicated on stranger prejudices: There are teams for intellectuals (Arsenal, because of their professor-like manager, Arsene Wenger), for the brain-dead (Lazio, in Italy, beloved of fascists everywhere), and for people with strange, personal afflictions (one soccer-mad American I know for some reason supports Doncaster Rovers, a small team from Yorkshire in England who sadly won't feature in this book except as a comic foil for Leeds United, their nearest rival).

It wasn't always thus. When I moved to the U.S. in 1995, club soccer was still very much a minority interest. In New York City, where I made my new home, it came down to Mexicans cheering on teams like Cruz Azul in restaurant kitchens, or a bunch of ex-pat Brits getting together on Saturday mornings at pubs like McCormack's and Nevada Smith's on 3rd Avenue in Manhattan to peer at a usually-balky satellite feed. In May 1995, I sat almost alone in McCormack's watching the final game of the English Premier League season . . . but just one year later, I squeezed in to that same pub and found myself one of hundreds keening at the denouement of the 1996 season.

Since then, with the rise of the Champions League in Europe especially, club soccer has become a fashionable thing to follow for many Americans, seemingly akin to knowing a great organic butcher or having an acquaintance who plays Meyer Lansky in *Boardwalk Empire*. (In fact, Anatol Yusuf, the actor who plays Meyer Lanksy in *Boardwalk Empire*, is a rabid Arsenal fan; we have sometimes watched games together in Mr. Dennehy's on Carmine Street, McCormack's having sadly closed.) The game, with its shiny NBC TV deal and regular coverage in all the major newspapers—not to mention stirring USMNT and USWNT performances in World Cups and Olympic Games—has cornered a mass media obsession that has brought it front and center to many American homes.

Club Soccer 101 is an attempt to provide a historical guide to the teams whose names are no longer strange to American ears. Soccer—"association football"—has been around a long time, and many of the teams that appear in the book have histories that stretch back a century or more. (Note to those—usually British—who scoff at the word "soccer": its history rivals that of the word "football," and until very recently y'all were fine with it [ask your fathers]. So hush.) Most have won a slew of major trophies and have featured superstars of their day, from Pele and Eusebio, to Johann Cruyff and Maradona and Dennis Bergkamp, to Lionel Messi and Ronaldo the plump Brazilian and Ronaldo the Portuguese pinup.

But more than just history, *Club Soccer 101* is an account of what these storied teams stand for, the trophies they've won (and lost), the great players who've graced their line-ups, what their fans remember and sing about and wish had never happened and were glad they witnessed. It's about the unforgettable games, the last-minute goals, the terrible refereeing, the unbeaten seasons, the bankruptcies, the managers who changed a club and the great teams they built. From each team's founding, whether in the nineteenth century or just a decade ago, through their early years, their first trophies, their growing fan base, through wars and reconstructions of countries, to the explosion of TV money and the new, mega-game we all somehow still love, the book tracks the development of 101 of the world's top teams.

Throughout I've tried to go beyond the game itself to capture the ways club history has intertwined with larger events. There is the club whose entire side was wiped out in a terrible air disaster; another who dominated a decade of European football but whose history has since been plagued by tragedy; a team in South America who are ever the bridesmaid and never the bride, and one that should have won for a generation and more, but who quit to concentrate on exhibition games instead. From Asia, through Africa and Europe, to North, Central, and South America, *Club Soccer 101* tells the story of a world obsessed with a sport in which 11 players face 11 players, the ball their only focus.

Where teams are included that haven't won much (here's looking at you, Notts County, Torino, and the New York Red Bulls, to name just three), it's because their stories offer something central either to the history of the sport, or an important geographical area of growth for the game. Any account of soccer's rich narrative would be incomplete without the stories of the oldest team in the world (Notts County), the Superga disaster (which befell Torino), or the rise of soccer in the U.S. (my suprisingly-good-to-watch New York Red Bulls). It was difficult to keep to just 101 clubs, of course. To help make decisions about which teams to include or leave out, I've relied on their record in international games—the Champions Leagues finals they've reached, the Copa Libertadores trophies they've won—as well as how they've fared in their respective domestic leagues. I realize I've left out some strong candidates—sorry Fulham and Fluminense fans—but check out the online presence of *Club Soccer 101* for essays about teams that didn't make it into the book itself.

A few years ago, I was lucky enough to become friends with a man from Buffalo, NY. Robert Rich Jr., aka, Lord Bedlington, aka, Lord

Bubba, is a brilliant yet avuncular businessman who's made his moolah—and there's a ton of it—from non-dairy toppings and the like. His dear wife, Mindy, wondering what you buy a billionaire for Christmas, purchased for him the deed to the title of the Lordship of Bedlington, a small town just north of Newcastle, in the UK. Being a sports fan, and wanting to do something nice for his newly-adopted town, Bob decided to fund the local soccer team, the Bedlington Terriers, who play in the Northern League (the ninth level of soccer in England). Bob even brought the team over to the U.S. and Canada to play a couple of exhibition games.

In the first such game, in Canada, for reasons best known to Bob and Bob alone, he convinced the Bedlington Terriers to put little old me on the bench. The kit-man gave me a Bedlington Terriers shirt (with #42 on the back, for my then-age), and the players gave me quizzical glances. And there I sat, waiting for my big chance.

With about four minutes to go in the game, I was summoned to stand next to the linesman, handshakes were shared with the departing Terrier, and suddenly I found myself running out onto the Canadian turf, heading for the right wing. I saw Bob and Mindy Rich in the crowd, beaming with what I thought could either have been amusement or the sudden realization that they'd made a terrible mistake.

I say I ran out onto turf, but it felt more like clouds. I had been obsessed with this sport since my very earliest moments. Growing up in a British household where everything stopped for an hour and a half each Saturday afternoon, football, as I called it then, was the barometer by which we assessed the weather of our lives. When our team won, we lived in a land of milk and honey; when we lost, we moped and moaned, even though my mother would remind my father that, referring to the Manchester United players who regularly failed us in the 1970s and 1980s, "Vincent, *they've* never heard of *you.*"

For those four minutes in Canada, I played at the ninth level of English football, albeit in a non-regulation friendly, and named, on the official teamsheet, as "Trialist." With about a minute to go, Bedlington got a throw-in, and for some reason, the right back hurled the ball my way. I don't know how it happened, but I controlled the ball on my thigh, and flicked it around an approaching opponent, into the path of a surging Bedlington midfielder. Off he ran, away from me, as I stood there, dumbfounded at my luck, that I had, from an early age, lived for this sport, had somehow been placed on this team, and had just not entirely sucked at football for a second or two. On such filigree moments life turns; I've seldom been happier. And then the referee blew the final whistle, and I came back to earth.

The previous day, in a pre-match training session, I had been so utterly terrible that one of the Bedlington players had reminded me that I was nothing more than a "f***ing book writer." This book, then, is for all those players, on so many different teams, from Bedlington to Barcelona, who've given me and so many millions of others so much joy across the years—this "f***ing book writer" salutes you.

A NOTE ABOUT CLUB SOCCER

Most major soccer-playing nations have a domestic league (such as the Premier League in England or Serie A in Italy), many of which employ a system of relegation and promotion: a set number of teams with the worst records in a higher league may move down, or be relegated, while teams with the best records from the league below may replace them, or be promoted.

In addition to domestic leagues, there are numerous domestic cup competitions (such as the FA Cup in England or Copa del Rey in Spain), in which club teams play each other in knockout games to reach a single final. These competitions are played concurrently with the domestic league season.

There are also a slew of international tournaments (such as the UEFA Champions League in Europe or the Copa Libertadores in South America), in which club teams from various nations play against one another.

A list of the main domestic leagues and domestic cup competitions may be found in Appendix 1. A list of the main international club competitions, along with historical results, may be found in Appendix 2.

Finally, the statistics at the head of each chapter that denote stadium capacity, leading goal-scorer, and player with most appearances have been collected from the clubs themselves wherever possible. In the case of goals and appearances, they reflect all competitive games through the end of each club's 2013–2014 season.

THE 101 CLUBS

Location	Milan, Italy
Established	1899
Nicknames	*I Rossoneri* ("The Red and Blacks"), *Il Diavolo* ("The Devil"), *Casciavit* (Lombard for "Screwdrivers")
Current stadium	San Siro, Milan; officially Stadio Giuseppe Meazza (capacity 80,018)
Home colors	Red and black
Leading goal-scorer	Gunnar Nordahl (1949–56), 221 goals
Most appearances	Paolo Maldini (1984–2009), 902 appearances

They wear red for the devil, and black for fear; they are the club of both Kilpin and Colombo, an organization that has stretched from bored British businessmen all the way to the "bunga bunga" of Silvio Berlusconi; they have been christened *Gli Immortali* ("The Immortals"), *Gli Invicibili* ("The Invincibles"), *I Meravigliosi* ("The Glorious Ones"). And of the two major teams in the same city, only one can go by the city's name alone: Milan.

Let's begin with Herbert Kilpin—*Il Lord*—who in 1891, at the age of 21, moved from Nottingham, England, to Torino (Turin) to work in the textile business (he'd been a lacemaker's assistant in the English Midlands). But lace wasn't entirely his thing, and eventually Kilpin started turning out for the local football team, Internazionale Torino—no relation to either Inter Milan, or Torino—making him, according to many, the first foreign export from British soccer. Then, as legend has it, alcohol intervened when, a year before the turn of the century, he and a bunch of other British expats inhaled the contents of Fiaschetteria Toscana bar in Milan—the fashion capital of the world had been Kilpin's home since 1897—and in their drunken stupor decided they missed cricket enough to create the Milan Cricket and Foot-ball Club. (The A.C. Milan crest still features the date 1899.)

As so often in the establishment of sports teams by British expats, the cricket soon fell by the wayside and football became the predominant game. In this case, Kilpin seems to have been a key member of the British contingent, as by 1901 he had helped deliver a national championship, scoring the winning goal in a semifinal against Juventus, and one of the three goals that beat Genoa in the final. John Foot, writing in *Calcio: A History of Italian Football*, notes that both success *and* drink followed Kilpin throughout his Milan career (in nine years he played just 27 games for the fledgling club); there is even a claim that Kilpin kept a bottle of whiskey behind the goal so that he could drown his sorrows when the other team scored. This portly utility player was quite a character, even claiming he missed his wedding night as he was on the soccer field—and getting his face kicked "unrecognizable"—in Genoa.

Drunkard or not, Kilpin—who as a player with Milan won the national championship three times and as their coach twice—helped establish a side that has since become one of the most successful to ever play club soccer. Once Inter Milan split away from A.C. in 1908 (a number of reasons are posited, usually centering around Inter's desire to hire foreign players), A.C. Milan set out to conquer Italian soccer and pretty much succeeded. The list of their achievements is one of the best compiled in any league, on any continent: 18 times Italian champions, 17 times runners-up; winners of the Coppa Italia five times, seven times losers in the final; six times winners of the Supercoppa Italiana, three times losers in the final. (There is no MegaSupercoppa Italiana, yet.) Their European exploits are second only to those of Real Madrid—A.C. Milan have won the European Cup/Champions League seven times, including back-to-back at the end of the 1980s, and have appeared in three consecutive finals (1993, 1994, and 1995, though they only won the middle one). They've also won the

Cup Winners' Cup twice and the UEFA Super Cup five times. The only major tournament they've never won is the UEFA Cup.

Internationally they have excelled, too, winning three Intercontinental Cups, from seven appearances in the final, and one FIFA Club World Cup in 2007.

Pitted against this astonishing record, however, is A.C. Milan's ability to provide some of the true low points in soccer history, either off the field, through high-level corruption and sometimes deadly violence; or on the field, via losses at key moments. It sometimes feels that for every Paolo Maldini that Milan produced—their extraordinary defender played 902 times for the club and never seemed to attract even a talking-to from a referee, let alone a red card—there is a Vincenzo Spagnolo, a 24-year-old Genoa fan who on January 29, 1995, was stabbed to death outside the Genoa stadium in a riot involving some 20 Milan "ultras" (organized fan groups that rely on chants, banners, flares, and intimidation, all in order to rabidly support their team). (Maldini actually received one red card in his career—and that was in a friendly—but even that extraordinary fact is bettered by a stat Simon Kuper recounts in the *Financial Times*: Kuper quotes Mike Forde, former Director of Football Operations for Chelsea, as saying that research proved that Maldini was so talented and position-aware on the field that he made "one tackle every two games.")

Paolo Maldini's father, Cesare, also played for A.C. Milan—some 347 games—including as captain during their first European Cup triumph in 1963. That victory came at Wembley Stadium in London against a Benfica side, from Portugal, that boasted the world's best player at the time, Eusébio, who in the 19th minute ghosted past the entire Milan defense to give Benfica the lead. That defense included a statuesque Maldini *père,* as well as Giovanni Trapattoni, who would later win everything as coach of Juventus, and lose everything as coach of Italy and then Ireland. But two goals in the space of nine second-half minutes by José Altafini gave Milan, and Italy, its first European Cup triumph.

That great 1960s team was matched, if not bettered, by probably the greatest Milan side ever put together, that of the late 1980s. The 1989 European Cup final lineup is worth listing in full, as it's hard to imagine a greater set of eleven players. In goal was Giovanni Galli, who played for Italy in the 1986 World Cup. At the back was surely the best defense who ever played together: the aforementioned Maldini *fils*, then only 22 years of age; Alessandro Costacurta; Mauro Tassotti; and the great/scary center back Franco Baresi, he of the long Milan/Italy shirt that gave him the appearance of a man who had forgotten to wear shorts. In midfield, the riches were manifold: future New York/New Jersey MetroStar Roberto Donadoni was at the height of his powers; marauding Dutch masters Frank Rijkaard and Ruud Gullit ran games; and rounding out the midfield was Carlo Ancelotti, the future manager of Milan, Chelsea, and Real Madrid. These ten would probably have been enough to beat most teams, but spearheading their fearful lineup was one of the greatest center forwards ever to play the game, Dutchman Marco van Basten (his career was cut short by an ankle injury in 1993).

In that 1989 tournament, Milan eviscerated a fine Real Madrid side in the semifinal, 5–0—their first goal was probably the pick of the bunch, a dark-haired Ancelotti slipping past two defenders before he hit a 25-yard screamer into the roof of the net, though both van Basten and Donadoni scored beauties, too. Donadoni shouldn't have even been alive to score—in the second round of the tournament his life was saved by a quick-thinking Red Star Belgrade physio who broke Donadoni's jaw to help him unswallow his tongue after a collision.

In the final, Milan devastated Steaua Bucharest, led by Georghe Hagi and Marius Lacatus, 4–0; the Romanian goalkeeper, Silviu Lung, must have needed oxygen at half-time as his team was already three down. This Milan team for the ages won the competition the following year, too, though it was much more hard-fought—a tight extra-time, away-goals win over Bayern Munich in the semis was followed by a dull, 1–0 defeat of a Sven-Göran Eriksson-coached Benfica in the final.

How different it had been just a decade earlier. In 1980, while archrivals Inter Milan won the Scudetto (Italy's top tier champion-ship)—and also beat A.C. "home" and "away" (they share a stadium)— A.C. Milan reached their lowest point, being forcibly relegated to Serie B after it was revealed that players and officials had bet on games. Felice Colombo, A.C. Milan's then president, was barred from the game for life for his involvement in what came to be known as Totonero 1980 (the year was added later as there was another Totonero scandal in 1986, though not involving Milan). Though A.C. went straight back up to Serie A the next season, in 1983 they spent another season in the second tier. Something had to be done; the club was as low on inspiration and confidence as it had ever been. By 1986, and finally back in Serie A for good, Milan came under the spell of a man who has changed the club, not to mention his entire country, forever: Silvio Berlusconi.

It's quite a résumé: convicted tax evader; media tycoon; Musso-lini apologist; the man who has said black people (including President Obama) have "nice tans" and are happy to dance the "bunga bunga"; four-time Italian prime minister; and, since 1986, the owner of A.C. Milan. It was he who brought the Dutch triumvirate of Gullit, Rijkaard, and van Basten to Milan, as well as the cream of Italian play-ers; he who oversaw eight Scudettos, five Champions League victo-ries (but three final defeats), two Intercontinental Cups and a FIFA Super Cup victory. His 1991–92 team—*Gli Invicibili*—went unbeaten behind 25 van Basten goals, and began a run of three consecutive Serie A victories, matched by those three consecutive Champions League final appearances. The first, against Olympic Marseille in 1993, ended in a dull 1–0 defeat. It would be the last game in which van Basten appeared.

The second Champions League final, in 1994, featured a perfor-mance to match that of 1989 against Bucharest. Gone were the Dutch players, and missing through suspension were Baresi and Costacurta. In had come Marcel Desailly, Dejan Savićević, Zvonimir Boban, Demetrio Albertini, and Christian Panucci, though the then-enforced rule against more than three foreign-born players meant no place for superstars Jean-Pierre Papin and Brian Laudrup. Instead, playing up front was Daniele "Saint" Massaro, so called for his ability to score important goals in key games. Opposing them was a Barcelona club teeming with brilliance: Zubizarreta, in goal, was probably the best in the world for a decade; add to him Ronald Koeman at sweeper, crazy/brilliant Hristo Stoichkov and Romário up front, and midfielder Pep Guardiola, who would one day lead the greatest ever Barcelona team of Messi et al. Brian Laudrup's brother, Michael, had been similarly denied a spot in the Barcelona team because of the three-foreigner limit rule. Along the bench sat Johan Cruyff, the Netherlands' finest ever player and now a talented coach for the Barcelona team. Everyone expected a closely fought game.

What happened instead was a master class of Milanese football—staunch defense matched by the best finishing possible. Barcelona started strongly, but were unable to convert any chances. On 22 minutes, the ball fell to "Saint" Massaro who made no mistake for 1–0. On the stroke of half-time Massaro smashed the ball across the Barcelona keeper and into the far corner for a second. Cruyff's face on the bench said it all: a mixture of annoyance and confusion.

The second half was all Milan, and began with one of the most audacious goals ever scored in the Champions League final. Chasing down a hopeful ball, Savićević, with just the hint of a high boot, charged down Nadal's clearance, and then lobbed Zubizarreta from a tight angle. The icing on the cake was a finely-curved shot from Marcel Desailly just before the hour mark, and the final half hour was a procession: Milan had trampled over a hugely talented Barcelona team.

The following year, Milan lost to Ajax, a team filled with Dutch players including former Milan stalwart Frank Rijkaard, alongside Marc Overmars, two de Boers, Clarence Seedorf, Edgar Davids, and a young Patrick Kluivert, who came off the bench to score the winner with six minutes to play.

On the home front, A.C. Milan again won the Scudetto in 1994—their third in a row. And Inter Milan? They avoided relegation by a single point, having lost both of that season's games against their archrivals by a score of 2–1. The rivalry remained white-hot, despite A.C.'s dominance. The Derby della Madonnina, as it's called in Italy, has raged since its inception in 1908; in its early years it was a middle-class (Inter) vs. working class (A.C.) rivalry, but these days it has transcended politics to become merely one of the most intense derbies anywhere in the world. With both teams having won 18 Serie A titles, seasons can often come down to the head-to-head games; but it is in international competition that A.C. Milan has the edge.

Except when it doesn't.

The Champions League final loss in 1995 was eclipsed a decade later by perhaps Milan's worst moment on the football field. Playing Liverpool in the 2005 Champions League final, Milan were facing a team that had had to navigate a qualifying round to even make the tournament, and who had scored a single, is-it-over-the-line goal in two semifinal legs against Chelsea. Given Liverpool's obvious limitations, it was no surprise that Milan were a goal up after 50 seconds, thanks to a fine finish from Paolo Maldini. They added two more from Hernán Crespo to go into the break three ahead—British commentator Alan Green had even said, at 2–0, that "this final is over," so dominant were the Italian side. The *Guardian* website's minute-by-minute guide to the game commented at the end of the first half that "if the Liverpool team was a dog, you'd shoot it at this stage."

Then it all changed. Milan somehow managed to let in three goals in the first 15 minutes of the second half—the last of which came via a horrendous dive by Liverpool's Steven Gerrard to "earn" a penalty. A double save by Liverpool keeper Jerzy Dudek—the second of which still defies a number of physical laws—three minutes before the end of extra time kept the British team in the tie, which they went on to win on penalties.

For that first half of the 2005 final one could imagine that all the excesses of Milan's history—Kilpin's bottle behind the goal, the death of Vincenzo Spagnolo, Felice Colombo's corruption, and Berlusconi's . . . well, just Berlusconi—had been wiped away by the beauty of their third goal: Pirlo intercepting a Steven Gerrard pass then knocking it forward to Kaká, who spins Gerrard like he's a beginner before curving a 50-yard pass into the path of an onrushing and onside Crespo, who dinks a sand wedge over the approaching Dudek, wheeling away as the Italian commentator wails about "*musica*" and "*magica*." It is surely the high point of Milan's existence.

Two hours later, it was forgotten.

Location	Amsterdam, Netherlands
Established	1900
Nicknames	*De Godenzonen* ("The Sons of the Gods"), *Ajacieden*, *De Joden* ("The Jews"), *De Amsterdammers* ("The Amsterdammers"), *I Lancieri* ("The Lancers"), Lucky Ajax
Current stadium	Amsterdam ArenA (capacity 53,052)
Home colors	Red and white
Leading goal-scorer	Piet van Reenen (1929–42), 273 goals
Most appearances	Sjaak Swart (1956–73), 603 appearances

Their Total Football team was a team to rival any, built from a new kind of soccer, one where each outfield player was expected to be able to contribute in pretty much any position. Gone were the traditional and often rigid formations of defender, midfielder, attacker. They came at you from every angle, throwing their opponents' formation around like riders on a rollercoaster. Not since the Real Madrid teams of the late 1950s did a club side so dominate European football. When the dust settled, they had won three European Cups in a row; in fact, UEFA gave them the actual cup to keep. It was as if Europe said, "Here, we can't get the ball off of you, so you may as well keep the trophy, too."

Who could have imagined in March 1900, when Ajax was formed, that one day they'd be the greatest club side in the world, at least for a brief time? Ajax—pronounced "EYE-ax," in the Dutch style—were named after the Greek hero who killed himself; the club's first chairman, Floris Stempel, died in an altogether too classical-legend way, in a shipwreck, in 1910. The team adopted its shirt, boasting a single, broad red stripe, the following year and joined the Eredivisie. By the 1930s, Ajax were dominating the Dutch league, winning it five times, before war arrived in the Netherlands.

Simon Kuper recounts what happened to Ajax, to Amsterdam, and to the Netherlands generally during World War II in his book *Ajax, the Dutch, the War: The Strange Tale of Soccer During Europe's Darkest Hour*. Kuper describes the devastation wrought upon all, and the collaborations with, and resistance to, the occupying Nazi forces. The Nazis wanted no Jewish players or officials on Dutch teams; some were sent to death camps. Kuper's powerful rewriting of Dutch wartime history reveals that collaboration was as damaging in the Netherlands as in other countries more usually associated with it, and the subsequent idea that Ajax is a "Jewish club" remains problematic, too, just as it does with regard to Tottenham Hotspur in England.

At the end of World War II, a striker named Rinus Michels turned out for the newly liberated Ajax, having recently returned from duty with the Dutch army. In his first game for the club, Michels scored five of the eight goals they managed that day, but he wasn't considered a cultured player, which makes what happened two decades later even more remarkable. Done on the field, Michels took over as manager of Ajax in 1965, and it's not too much to say that he transformed not only the club, but how football was conceived in continental Europe.

Michels' idea was an expansion of one initially conceived by the great British coach Jack Reynolds, who had led Ajax three separate times (1915–25, 1928–40, and 1945–47). The idea, which had also seen partial expression in the great Hungarian national team of the 1950s, was in part to make sure that outfield players were comfortable playing in different positions, but also to compress the field by bringing the back line way up, close to the midfield, so that midfielders didn't have to come and get the ball and make it travel long distances to attackers. This was as important as the interchangeability of players, and in Michels' Ajax side, it found its fullest expression.

But Michels was also lucky, in that when he started as coach in

Amsterdam, a young player called Johan Cruyff was beginning to establish himself in the team. By Michels' first full season, Cruyff was scoring 25 goals for Ajax; and in the next six seasons, his lowest tally was 27 in 1971, the only time his goal return slipped under 30. It wasn't just goals, however—Johan Cruyff, a slender, tall man, played with an upright authority and balance that has seldom been equaled. Total Football? When you're as good as Johan Cruyff, it's not as hard as it sounds.

Success in the Netherlands came relatively easily, Ajax winning the title three years in a row (1966–68), which led them to their first European Cup final, and the first European Cup final any Dutch side had reached. But it came too early for the club—the 1969 European Cup final saw Ajax hammered by A.C. Milan, 4–1.

Michels knew that for his theory to work on the European and world stage, he'd need different players, so in came Johan Neeskens, Nico Rijnders, and the amusingly named Dick van Dijk. The team now purred, players flitting about and switching around like fireflies. Goals rained down on opponents: in the 1970–71 season Ajax scored 90 of them, though they still finished second to Feyenoord. That was the season, however, when Ajax reached the pinnacle in Europe, a pinnacle they wouldn't leave for three seasons.

The 1971 European Cup final featured Ajax approaching their interchangeable best, and though their opponents, Panathinaikos, had staged an amazing comeback in their semifinal against Red Star Belgrade, they went a goal down after five minutes to a Dick van Dijk header and never recovered. Ajax were champions of Europe, and they weren't done being so.

But Rinus Michels *was* done, leaving in the off-season for Barcelona. His team didn't seem to notice. The following season, Ajax scored 104 goals in winning the Dutch league by eight points, and made it back to the European Cup final, though their road there was a tough one, in which they squeezed past Benfica by a single goal in the semifinals. Inter Milan, their opponents in the final, struggled, too, in their semifinal against Celtic, neither team scoring in two legs except during the deciding penalty shootout.

In that 1972 Ajax–Inter final, Cruyff was irresistible, with a first-half, mazy run past most of the Inter defense putting fear into Italian hearts. Two minutes into the second half, a cross evaded defenders and keeper and found its way to Cruyff, on his own at the back post. Cruyff's control killed the ball in an instant. All that was left to do was sweep the ball into the open net, and perform his trademark leap-with-one-arm-punching-the-air celebration. With 12 minutes to go, Cruyff scored again, a bullet header from a corner; cue the same celebration. Could Ajax complete the "threepeat" in 1973?

Yes, they could, but first they went off to become world champions. After a tense 1–1 draw in Argentina against Independiente in the Intercontinental Cup, in the second leg, in Amsterdam, Ajax swarmed all over the South American side to win 3–0. Ajax had won every single tournament they'd entered that season: Dutch league, Dutch cup, European Cup, Intercontinental Cup. There may never have been a single-season team in history better than the 1972 Ajax side.

Perhaps those exertions in 1972 lead to Ajax only winning the league in 1973 by two points, and shockingly, scoring two fewer goals, reaching a mere 102. In the European Cup, they would face their sternest test yet, having to play CSKA Sofia, Bayern Munich, and Real Madrid in the knockout stages. But Ajax put six past Sofia in two legs, five past Bayern Munich, and three past Real Madrid. Perhaps most illustrative of the brilliance of the Dutch team was the fact that when the great Gerd Müller scored twice for Bayern in the second leg against Ajax, those were his 11th and 12th goals of the tournament, but by that point in the tie, Bayern were 5–0 down on aggregate.

In the 1973 final, Ajax faced a strong Juventus side who had had a much easier ride, facing the small-time English side Derby County (even so, led by the legendary Brian Clough) in the semifinal. Clough maintained that Juventus had bribed the officials, calling them "cheating bastards"—whatever the truth, Juventus now faced one of the greatest club sides ever assembled.

Wearing all red that night (Juventus got to keep their stripes), Ajax went ahead after just four minutes, when Johnny Rep scored a looping header over Dino Zoff at the far post. Brian Moore, the British commentator, noted that the game was being played at walking pace, but that "A-jacks," as he called them, were in control. It was all A-jacks, so much so that coach Stefan Kovacs had time to smoke on the bench. Arie Haan had a number of good chances, and Rep could have scored a hat-trick—Neeskens was running the entire game from midfield, though in truth it was a game that never really came alive. Rep's was the only goal, which Ajax won 1–0.

Cruyff and Neeskens left to join Michels at Barcelona, and Ajax's domination was over. CSKA Sofia, whom Ajax had knocked out of the 1973 European Cup, repaid the favor the next year, and all that was left was for Michels to translate his Total Football for the Dutch national side, who should have won the 1974 World Cup final but lost to a stultifying German side led by Gerd Müller.

The next great Ajax team was created in the mid-1980s, under their new coach, a man called Johan Cruyff, and featuring the brilliant center forward Marco van Basten. That Ajax side reached two, back-to-back Cup Winners' Cup finals, winning the first on a van Basten goal over East German side Lokomotive Leipzig, but losing the following year to obscure Belgian side Mechelen, after van Basten had moved to A.C. Milan. Once again, Cruyff would run off to Barcelona—this time, like Michels, to be their manager—and Ajax fell back, only to resurge in the mid-1990s on the back of their third superb squad.

The mid-nineties squad had started to come together a few years earlier under new coach Louis van Gaal, when Ajax won the 1992 UEFA Cup over Torino. That team had featured Frank de Boer at the back and Dennis Bergkamp just behind the front two; on the bench, a young keeper called Edwin van der Sar awaited his turn. By 1995, van der Sar was in goal, and Frank de Boer had been joined by his center forward brother Ronald. In midfield, Frank Rijkaard, Clarence Seedorf, Edgar Davids, and Jari Litmanen were a brilliant quartet, and Marc Overmars had joined Bergkamp, with Patrick Kluivert on and off the bench. It was a side that should have won more than a single Champions League, though they made the final two years running.

In 1995, Ajax faced A.C. Milan, but it took until five minutes before the end for substitute Kluivert to win the game with a messy goal. A subsequent Intercontinental Cup victory over Grêmio featured a dull 0–0 draw and a Kluivert penalty miss in the shootout, but even worse penalties taken by the Brazilian side.

In the 1996 Champions League final, another penalty shootout followed a 1–1 draw, once again against Juventus. But Edgar Davids set the tone by missing the first kick, and Ajax never recovered. Once again, Ajax lost its coach, van Gaal, to Barcelona, and most of that great team was gone by the turn of the century.

Since then, Ajax have won six more domestic titles, but have become just another perfectly fine European team, without playing either Total Football or even winning football.

When Barcelona starlet Neymar performed a kind of Cruyff turn (a move Cruyff perfected, in which in one move the attacker spins and drags the ball with the wrong foot past the defender) against Sevilla in September 2013, Ajax fans must have felt a twinge. Though they will always have Cruyff and Michels and Neeskens as their own, Cruyff's time as coach at Barcelona laid the groundwork for the football we now marvel at: when Busquets, Iniesta, Xavi, Messi, Neymar, et al., interchange positions, fill in for each other, pass with precision, take on defenders, Cruyff-turn themselves inside out, and score hatfuls of beautiful, Catalan—not Dutch—goals.

Location	Cairo, Egypt
Established	1907
Nicknames	National Club, Century Club, Red Devils
Current stadium	Cairo International Stadium (capacity 75,000)
Home colors	Red and white
Leading goal-scorer	Mahmoud El Khatib (1972–88), 154 goals
Most appearances	Hady Khashaba (1991–2006), 436 appearances

They traveled 125 miles across their country to watch their team. In a year of turmoil, there was still this: a football match. Not just any match, of course—how could any game in this place at this point in history be just any old 90 minutes? But it still held out hope: it was soccer, and sometimes the frenetic excitement of a great game can make people forget their troubles, if only for a brief time.

And what a team they supported, these happy travelers: the great Al-Ahly! Thirty-six times champions of Egypt, eight times champions of their continent, and the first team ever to twice reach the finals of FIFA's World Club Cup, a competition in which they excelled. In 2006, they narrowly lost to the eventual winner, Internacional of Brazil, in a semifinal; Internacional were the reigning Copa Libertadores champions and went on to beat Barcelona in the final, so they weren't too shabby. Al-Ahly even won the third-place playoff against a top Mexican side, Club America, causing consternation: "The only thing left for me to do now is to apologize to our supporters for having failed to meet their expectations," Club America's coach, Luis Fernando Tena, said. The reality was that America had been beaten by a better team, and there was no shame: just because the name Al-Ahly didn't trip off the tongue like Barcelona or Internacional didn't mean they weren't an excellent and storied club.

Politics is never far away in Egyptian sports. After the Anglo-Egyptian War of 1882, Britain took control of the country and, more importantly for their global interests, the Suez Canal (which had been allowing a much shorter passage to the east since its completion in 1869). The Denshawai Incident of 1906, in which British soldiers behaved like goons in a small village by killing the locals' pet pigeons and shooting a woman dead, led to a deepening of nationalist and anti-British feelings, especially after summary and blatantly biased trials (of the Egyptians, naturally—the Brits got off scot-free). By the next year, cresting a wave of this new sentiment, the students of Cairo had established a sporting club, Al-Ahly, as a focus for their anticolonial aspirations.

Few could have foreseen how Al-Ahly would grow into the premier soccer club in Africa, attracting a massive fan base in Egypt and beyond and accruing more than 100 trophies. The great mid-century team led by their greatest ever player, Saleh Selim, won the league every year for nearly a decade, and yet 2005 was their greatest season: they went unbeaten in 46 matches, winning everything they entered (Egyptian league, cup, and Super Cup, as well as the African Champions League). The next year, they went to Japan and won a famous bronze at FIFA's Club World Cup.

By the time of Al-Ahly's centenary, Egypt was an utter mess: President Mubarak had given himself the power to dissolve parliament at will, Egyptians were struggling under his yoke, and the trail of sparks toward the powder keg was lit. On February 2, 2011, Mubarak-supporting thugs attacked protesters in Tahrir Square in the "Battle of the Camel"—a last-ditch, monsters-on-camelback effort that failed, after which Mubarak resigned and ran. In November that year, elections were held, bringing Mohamed Morsi and his Muslim Brotherhood to power. Then, on February 1, 2012—almost one year to the day after the Tahrir Square attack—fans of Al-Ahly, whose "ultras" had been in the square and who are thought to have significantly contributed to the end of Mubarak's rule, made the 125-mile trip northeast to Port Said, where the Suez Canal meets the Mediterranean, to watch a game against their archrival, Al-Masry.

The fans of Al-Masry, for their part, came with guns and knives and sticks and bricks and rocks—anything they could get their hands on. There were no security checks outside the stadium. Inside, the home team, one down at half-time, scored three second-half goals, which to any normal soccer fan would be cause for wild celebration and taunting of an inferior opponent. But this was Egypt during its bloody revolution; security forces, loyal to the deposed Mubarak, stood aside; Al-Masry fans, also said to be loyal to the old regime, attacked. The result was obscene: Al-Ahly fans were thrown from the stands, stabbed and shot, chased and murdered. There was carnage. In all, 79 Al-Ahly fans died and over a thousand were injured. Al-Ahly's coach, Manuel José of Portugal, who had taken the team to Japan to play in those famed Super Cups, ran for his life and somehow survived; their legendary playmaker Mohamed Aboutrika—a man who has scored the same number of goals (four) in the FIFA Club World Cup tournament as Lionel Messi—watched fans of his team die in their changing room (one is even said to have died in Aboutrika's arms). The fans had sought shelter with their beloved players because they couldn't flee—the doors leading out of the stadium had been locked—some claimed welded—shut.

On the back of the massacre, trials were held, death sentences passed down; the Egyptian league was canceled. Eventually, Morsi was jettisoned too, throwing the country into further turmoil. In 2012, Al-Ahly once again won the African Champions' League. Incredibly, they won it again the following year, the second leg of the final being the first game held in Cairo since the Port Said massacre.

Despite the horror, the soccer fan's mind struggles and turns back to the middle of last century, and to Saleh Selim, Al-Ahly's most storied player. "El Maestro," they called him, because he won nine successive Egyptian league titles with the Al-Ahly team he led and inspired, and because he loved Latin music above all other things: samba, rumba, tango. Saleh Selim played in midfield, then he managed the team, then he became its president; he was so popular, he even did an Elvis and made a bunch of movies.

At the end of his Al-Ahly playing career, Saleh Selim is said to have been happy to warm the bench and, according to one fan site, simply "[admire] the great crowds that filled the stadiums."

Location	Lima, Peru
Established	1901
Nicknames	*Aliancistas*, *Blanquiazules* ("White and Blues"), *Grones* ("Blacks"), *Los Intimos* ("The Beloved"), *El Equipo del Pueblo* ("The Village Team")
Current stadium	Estadio Alejandro Villanueva (capacity 35,000)
Home colors	Navy blue and white
Leading goal-scorer	Waldir Sáenz (1992–98), 167 goals
Most appearances	—

Since their founding in 1901, Alianza Lima have won the Peruvian League 23 times, but it will never be 24, not really. Because if and when this club wins its 24th title, it will never be their 25th; their 26th will never be their 27th; 27 can never be 28 . . . and on, ad infinitum. There will always be something missing for this top Peruvian side.

Soccer in Peru has Anglo roots, as British immigration spread across South America in the late nineteenth and early twentieth centuries. In Peru it quickly became a game of the masses, though much of its spectacle still revolved around the capital, Lima, the Amazonian interior being difficult to reach via road. By the 1980s, a movement to decentralize Peru politically and economically led to the establishment of regional soccer championships, but the decision would have tragic consequences.

On December 8, 1987, and with the end of the season fast approaching, Alianza Lima flew 400 miles inland to a town on the

Ucayali River called Pucallpa. There, they notched up a routine 1–0 victory over Deportivo Pucallpa on the way to surely clinching the championship, Alianza's first since 1978. They had been the best team that season, and after the win in Pucallpa they sat atop the table. That evening, the team boarded a navy plane and headed back to Lima (the military supplied air transport for soccer teams, as they struggled to afford flights around the country for these new regional matches).

It was 6:30 in the evening. The pilot, a navy man called Edilberto Villar, who had limited night-flying experience—and was doubtful about the condition of the plane, navy aircraft being notorious for lousy maintenance—asked the control tower at Lima airport to tell him if the landing gear was down. Assured that it was, despite there being no confirming light in the cockpit, Villar circled back toward the airport, but he had burned out his fuel. One wing clipped the sea, about seven miles offshore; the resulting crash was catastrophic.

The rescue boats never came that night—their gasoline had been corruptly siphoned off. It wasn't until the next morning that the search began, and by then it was too late—only one person survived: Edilberto Villar. Gone was the team, the coaching staff, some fans, some journalists—44 people in total. To the tragedies that befell Torino in 1949, Manchester United in 1958, Denmark's national team in 1960—victims all of plane crashes—now was added the name of Alianza Lima.

Los Potrillos del '87, they had been called: The '87 Colts. Among them was Luis Escobar, who first played for Alianza Lima on May 26, 1984, when he was 14 years old. His body was never found, though people rushed to the beaches to wait for corpses to wash up. At the other end of his career was José González Ganoza, a 33-year-old goalkeeper—he had played for the Peruvian national team and was about to win his first title. One player is said to have survived the night, but though he was a strong swimmer, a broken leg denied him any hope of survival.

There was no time to mourn, according to the football authorities; the Peruvian league continued. Lima borrowed players from Colo Colo of Chile, 2,000 miles away. But it was to no avail—Lima's archrivals, Universitario de Deportes, won the national title. It would be a decade before Alianza recovered enough to win the Peruvian title once again. They have won the Peruvian Primera División five times since 1992, but there will always be one title missing.

The navy, for their part, sent the secret report on what went wrong to a safety deposit box in Florida. It took 16 years to find out that the pilot was at fault, the plane a mess, the air traffic controllers blameless. In *The Ball Is Round*, David Goldblatt reports that there was even a conspiracy theory that the players had discovered cocaine on board and the navy, fearing exposure, had shot the players and brought the aircraft down. (Context is all: at the time, Peru was under attack from Shining Path, a Marxist guerrilla movement that terrorized the country, though many thought that it collaborated with the navy.)

Whatever the cause of the crash, tragedy has always seemed to stalk the team. On May 12, 1976, the day after beating Alianza 4–0, famed Cruzeiro player Roberto Batata died in a car accident. And having finally won the Peruvian championship in 1997 after a decade of sadness, Alianza's central defender, Sandro Baylon, died after drunkenly crashing *his* car into a wall and a light fixture in Lima—he was 22 years old. It was 5:45 am on January 1, 2000.

AMÉRICA DE CALI

Location	Santiago de Cali, Colombia
Established	1918 (as América Football Club); officially 1927
Nicknames	*Los Diablos Rojos* ("The Red Devils"), *Los Escarlatas* ("The Scarlets"), *La Mechita* ("The Fuse"), *La Pasión de un Pueblo* ("The Passion of a People")
Current stadium	Estadio Olímpico Pascual Guerrero (capacity 45,000)
Home colors	Red and white
Leading goal-scorer	Ántony de Ávila (1982–87, 1988–96, 2009), 203 goals
Most appearances	Alexander Escobar Gañán (1983–96), 505 appearances

The Curse of Garabato, the failure of a Smurf, four finals lost, and Executive Order 12978—it isn't easy to be an América de Cali fan.

Santiago de Cali, Colombia, is the country's second city behind the capital, Bogotá, though it has a reputation for being primary if you need plastic surgery. During the height of the cocaine wars of the 1980s and 1990s, Cali went head to head against more famous Medellín, to the north: the Cali Cartel vs. the Escobars, and not a shiny trophy in sight.

The rivalry did play out in the world of soccer, though, too—a kind of Coca Libertadores.

América de Cali had been around since 1927, and their first brush with curses came early when, in 1948, a member of the club, a local dentist called Benjamin Urrea, swore to God that they'd never be champions if they went professional. If he was referring to the Colombian championship, he was wrong: Cali won their first 31 years after the Curse of Garabato, as it's known, was uttered. But if Urrea meant the ultimate South American championship, the Copa Libertadores, then he was a powerful necromancer indeed.

With the advent of cocaine money, Colombian football sold much of its soul to the white-powder devil. By the 1980s, the country was awash with trafficking cash, and football profited wildly. Players were acquired from all over South America, and two teams prospered above all others: Atlético Nacional, from Medellín, and América de Cali.

Cali's first championship in 1979 was followed by five in a row starting in 1982. The Cali Cartel—men to chill the soul, like José Santacruz Londoño, and brothers Gilberto and Miguel Rodríguez Orejuela—supplied North America and Europe with drugs, and América de Cali's working-class fans with a team to cherish. It was blood money, but soccer fans seldom worry where the money's coming from. Manchester United fans may say they hate the Glazer family for loading the club with debt, but try getting a ticket to a game at Old Trafford; Cardiff City fans claim to loathe Malaysian businessman Vincent Tan for changing their colors from blue to red and firing their manager, but the club sold out its 2013–14 season tickets four months before the season started.

In Colombia, however, the money was of a different order from bored billionaires trying to make more billions. The lure of the coca leaf led to a spiral of violence, kidnappings, and murders, the like of which had never before been seen in the country. It may have been the Curse of Garabato or the red-tinged money, but the "Red Devils" of América de Cali found their way to four separate Copa Libertadores finals and lost them all.

The first of those finals, in 1985, featured three tight games against Argentinos Juniors, the club where both Riquelme and Maradona began their careers. The first two games ended 1–0, to Juniors and América respectively, and the third, played in Asunción, Paraguay, was 1–1 at full time. With the teams tied after four goals each in the penalty shootout, it was left to América de Cali's diminutive Ántony de Ávila—at 5 feet 2 inches, he was known as *"El Pitufo,"* or "the

Smurf"—to keep it that way. But the Smurf slowed his run at the end and hit a weak chip to the keeper's right. The result was a simple save, though the goalie was about 10 yards off his line when he put his hands out. Juniors scored their final kick via Mario Videla, and América de Cali were defeated.

The following year, Cali would lose to River Plate of Argentina, and in 1987, they lost a three-game series to Uruguayan outfit Peñarol. The final match that year was the closest game imaginable, causing the excitable commentator to shout, "*Bomba, bomba, bomba, ay, ay, ay, ay, ay, ay, ay, ay, ay, ay, ay, ay, ay, ay, ay, ay!*" when a shot narrowly went past América's post. The América de Cali team, featuring legends Willington Ortiz, Ávila the Smurf, and Julio Francioni in goal, was one of the best they ever put on the field. But against Peñarol in that third game, they succumbed to bad blood, with Roberto Cabañas being sent off (Herrera of Peñarol would walk, too). The blood spilled over in the 120th minute of the game, after Peñarol's Diego Aguirre got free on the left of the box and, with two seconds left in the game, hit a fabulous shot across Francioni and into the back of the net. América de Cali players sank to their knees or threw themselves down, holding their heads in pain; as Francioni lay with his face in the dirt, a Peñarol attacker ran past, slowed a bit, and spat on him.

Two years later, Pablo Escobar's beloved (and similarly well-funded) Atlético Nacional would win the Copa Libertadores, furthering the pain of the Cali fans. Escobar even gave the trophy a ride on his private plane. By 1993, Escobar had been terminated by a combination of Colombian and American operatives, and two years later, other principals of the Cali Cartel were arrested.

In 1995, Cali would come under the controlling auspices of Executive Order 12978, a.k.a. "La Lista Clinton," a list of "specially designated nationals and companies" whose assets are blocked and with whom the world may not do business without an American-issued permit.

The tide was turning. Cali would reach their fourth Copa Libertadores final in 1996, but once again they would face River Plate. Sadly, a massive goalkeeping blunder in the second leg by Óscar Córdoba led to Hernán Crespo heading home, and Cali had lost yet another final. The Smurf, now 33 years old, had scored in the first leg, but it was to no avail. Ávila would move to MLS in 1996 to play for the New York/New Jersey MetroStars; on July 20, 1997, while still a Metro-Stars player, he scored for the Colombian national team in a World Cup qualifier and dedicated the goal to the incarcerated Rodríguez Orejuela brothers. The MetroStars neither fined nor suspended him. In 1998, Ávila scored for Colombian side Barcelona in the Copa Libertadores final against Vasco da Gama, from Brazil, but was yet again on the losing team.

The Rodríguez Orejuela brothers were extradited to the United States, one in late 2004, the other in early 2005. They remain in jail, one in Memphis and one in Kentucky; their $2.1 billion assets were seized by the US government. In 2009, at the ripe old age of 46, the Smurf once again turned out for América de Cali before retiring. Two years later, and in great debt, América de Cali's fall was complete as they were relegated to Colombia's second-tier league, Primera B, though by April 2013 they were off the Clinton List, at least.

ANDERLECHT

Location	Brussels, Belgium
Established	1908
Nicknames	Dutch: *Paars-wit*; French: *Les Mauves et Blancs* ("The Purple and Whites"), Sporting
Current stadium	Constant Vanden Stock Stadium (capacity 26,361)
Home colors	Purple and white
Leading goal-scorer	Joseph Mermans (1942–57), 338 goals
Most appearances	Paul Van Himst (1960–75), 457 appearances

There's a joke that says it's impossible to name ten famous Belgians, and though in reality there may well be more than ten (or fewer), eleven have never coalesced at the same time for one of the country's most successful teams, Anderlecht. A club that has dominated the Belgian scene has merely done decently in the greater challenge of European football. The reasons for that are not entirely clear. Belgium is a soccer nation and has produced plenty of good players, but 33 league titles for Anderlecht has yielded nothing in the Champions League, only a couple of Cup Winners' Cup wins, and a UEFA Cup victory. Brugge, their closest rivals, have similarly under-achieved on the biggest stage, making Belgium the repository of second-tier club teams in European competition.

Anderlecht came into being in 1908 after a meeting at a café called the Concordia. (There is still a history to be written of the importance of drinking and restaurants in the formation of sporting clubs.) They started out in the third level of Belgian soccer—the mind boggles as to the standard of *that* in 1908—but by 1920 Anderlecht were in the top flight and a generation later were regularly winning the league.

On the wider European stage, Anderlecht's best performance was two European Cup semifinal appearances in the 1980s. The first of those, against Aston Villa, defined tight and tedious, especially the second leg in Belgium, which ended 0–0, with both sides lucky to get nil. The *Daily Mirror* in England commented, "The Belgian approach to the game became even more inexplicable when they brought on a defensive substitute." The only notable thing about the game were the riots during and after it, which briefly threatened to have Villa thrown out of the tournament—a Belgian police spokesman explained the lack of arrests of rioting Villa fans by saying, "We just want to get rid of them." Villa had nicked a goal in the first leg in Birmingham and so went on to the final, where they beat Bayern Munich with a goal that went in off Villa striker Peter Withe's shin.

The 1986 European Cup semifinal against Steua Bucharest was even less edifying. Anderlecht won the first leg 1–0, then conceded a tying goal after just four minutes in Bucharest. Steua went on to score two more unanswered goals.

Where Anderlecht have had success is in the Cup Winners' Cup—in fact, for three years they dominated the tournament, winning two finals either side of a loss. The first win, in 1976, came at the end of a fabulous tournament. Anderlecht's opponents in the final, London's West Ham United, had sneaked through the quarterfinals 5–5 on away goals and the semifinals 4–3; Anderlecht reached the final by knocking out an East German side with the fabulous name of BSG Sachsenring Zwickau.

The final lived up to the tournament that had preceded it. West Ham scored first by way of Holland—Pat Holland, that is, whose mere surname must have rankled the Belgians. Then disaster struck for the English side. Frank Lampard (father of the Chelsea and England great also called Frank Lampard), attempted a back pass to the keeper from the left back position and got it horribly wrong, leading to both the tying goal and, bizarrely, a torn stomach muscle. With

Frank Senior gone, the game went to 2–2 early in the second half, only for Anderlecht to get a penalty after a perfectly good tackle in the box by—you guessed it—Holland. Rob Rensenbrink had made a nifty Cruyff turn outside the box; he didn't dive, but the referee simply got it wrong. The penalty duly dispatched, Anderlecht scored another late goal from François Van der Elst—his second of the game, too—to win the cup.

Two years later they won again, having lost in the intervening season to two late goals from German side Hamburg. In 1978, they produced their best ever European performance, beating Austria Vienna 4–0, with two first-half goals from Rensenbrink—the first a brave foot in at the near post, the second a free kick that somehow squirmed under the body of Vienna's keeper, Hubert Baumgartner. Defender Gilbert Van Binst scored the other two goals, in a team featuring other wonderfully-named players such as Nico de Bree, Hugo Broos, Ludo Coeck, and Jean Dockx.

Baumgartner's work for that second Rensenbrink goal was so poor, and his reaction—an over-the-top, head-in-hands performance—so theatrical, that one wonders if the fix was in. It certainly would be a few years later, in 1984, when the chairman of Anderlecht, Constant Vanden Stock, bribed Spanish referee Emilio Guruceta Muro one million Belgian francs (about $35,000) to help them beat Nottingham Forest in the second leg of the semifinal of that year's UEFA Cup. Forest scored a perfectly good goal that Guruceta Muro disallowed, leaving Anderlecht to win via a dodgy penalty 3–0—making it 3–2 on aggregate—and head to the final, where they lost to another British team, Tottenham Hotspur, in a penalty shootout after both legs finished 1–1. Icelandic player Arnór Gudjohnsen, father of Eidur Gudjohnsen (notably of Bolton, Chelsea, and Barcelona—and now Anderlecht's great rivals, Brugge) missed the final penalty to hand the London club the trophy. Anderlecht had won the previous year's UEFA Cup legitimately, beating Benfica 2–1 on aggregate. But most fans who pause to think of Anderlecht remember instead 1984, and Guruceta Muro. (Anderlecht were finally, more than a decade later, banned for a year from European competition for their part in the bribery scandal.)

As for that corrupt Spanish referee? Well, he died in a car accident in 1987. And there is now a trophy named after him in Spain—Trofeo Guruceta—awarded to the best referee of the season.

ARSENAL

Location	London, England
Established	1886
Nicknames	The Gunners
Current stadium	Emirates Stadium (capacity 60,355)
Home colors	Red and white
Leading goal-scorer	Thierry Henry (1999–2007), 228 goals
Most appearances	David O'Leary (1975–93), 772 appearances

In the 1970s and 1980s, the English First Division was stuck in a rut of Merseyside domination. From 1976 to 1988, either Liverpool or their city mates Everton won the league every season except two. If you were from the city of Liverpool that was all well and good, but if you were a fan of competitive football—or if you hated Scousers—it was downright depressing. Thirteen seasons, from 1975–76 through 1987–88, won by: Liverpool, Liverpool, Nottingham Forest, Liverpool, Liverpool, Aston Villa, Liverpool, Liverpool, Liverpool, Everton, Liverpool, Everton, Liverpool.

Then came the last game of the 1988–89 season. No one knew at the time, but Merseyside domination was about to come to an end, and what a way to do it. Boring, boring Arsenal were about to become very interesting indeed.

Arsenal Football Club has its origins in 1886, when workers at the Woolwich Arsenal armament factory decided they needed a football team. They played at first as Dial Square, then became Royal Arsenal, adopting their red shirts from Nottingham Forest players who joined them, just as Independiente of Argentina would adopt Forest's red shirts in 1907; Juventus appropriated Notts County's black and white stripes in 1903, proving that if you're on the lookout for a new soccer kit, look no further than the city of Nottingham. (But then, Sparta Prague appropriated the design of Arsenal's shirts, so who knows?)

After they shocked the small-minded British football world by turning professional, Royal Arsenal became Woolwich Arsenal; by 1915 they were simply Arsenal and two years into their residence at their new home: Highbury, in north London. Henry Norris, who had taken over Woolwich Arsenal just before World War I, didn't want to move the team next to Tottenham Hotspur. Woolwich is just south of the River Thames, some 11 miles southeast of Highbury and, up the road, Tottenham's ground at White Hart Lane—but it was the only suitable place he could find.

Norris was not a man to argue with; pictures of him reveal a steely gaze emanating from either side of a nose whose svelte bridge suddenly widens like a river delta into what can only be described as a stonker. In 1919, Norris used that gaze to convince John McKenna, then chairman of Liverpool, to promote Arsenal instead of Spurs to the top division, a division they've graced ever since, a record for an English club in the top flight. If Spurs and Arsenal were destined to hate each other because of their proximity, this surely didn't help, though chants pointing out that Arsenal stole Spurs' place in the 1919 season are seldom heard these days at White Hart Lane. (Norris's later fall was a precipitous one—he was banned from football for his part in an illegal payments scam intended to contravene the Football League's attempts to institute a minimum wage.)

Whatever the origins of their league status—and it's as unconfirmed as why they wear white sleeves on their red shirts—Arsenal took time to establish themselves as serious contenders for the championship. It would take the arrival of one Herbert Chapman in 1925 to deliver Arsenal their first period of dominance. But Chapman did more than just change Arsenal; a visionary, he changed the game, too.

Chapman didn't win straight away. His successful years managing Huddersfield Town, where he'd won two league championships in a row, seemed a million miles away as Arsenal struggled in the latter part of the 1920s. Nevertheless, he held to the philosophy that would bring Arsenal to their peak in the 1930s: staunch defense matched by counterattacking, a philosophy that some would say lasted through the rest of the century. (In *The Ball Is Round*, David Goldblatt reports that he also suggested floodlit games, a white ball, squad numbers on shirts, and scouting of opponents, among many other ideas.) He brought Arsenal an FA Cup in 1930, and their first and second championships in 1931 and 1933. That these victories came after the offside rule changed from a limit of three players, including the keeper, between attacker and goal line, to just two, and Chapman (and others) moved the free-range midfielder back to be a defender, neatly presages Arsenal's later emphasis on tight defense and their reputation as boring merchants of 1–0 victories.

And then, midway through the 1933–34 season, Chapman died, a victim of pneumonia. He was just 55 years old. The team he had built went on to win their third, fourth, and fifth titles in the next four seasons, an incredible record.

For the next four decades, Arsenal peaked here and there, but delivered only three more championships, the third of which, in 1971, was matched by an FA Cup, bringing them the fabled double. The rest of the 1970s featured four FA Cup finals—three losses and one win, over Manchester United in 1979. That game presaged a more entertaining Arsenal; two up with four minutes to go, Arsenal allowed two goals in a minute past their legendary goalkeeper Pat Jennings, only for their perm-haired center forward, Alan Sunderland, to appear at the back post to slip home a cross by Graham Rix after a surging run by genius Irish playmaker Liam Brady. As he ran away, arms aloft, a careful reading of Sunderland's lips revealed his paean to his good fortune, namely, "you fucking bastard," a phrase Manchester United fans use about him to this day.

A decade later, George Graham created another team capable of winning trophies, but as the end of the 1988–89 season came to its climax, Arsenal had conspired to leave themselves with an impossible task—travelling to Anfield to face a Liverpool team whose name was on the trophy. Three points behind and with an inferior goal difference, the only way Arsenal could pip Liverpool was to beat them by two or more goals. Liverpool had conceded just 26 goals in 37 games, and only once that season had they let in three goals in game—a trip to Manchester United on New Year's Day had seen a team of Alex Ferguson-coached youngsters score three times in six second-half minutes—and they had only lost one game at home. There seemed little Arsenal could do to turn it around; yet another Liverpool championship awaited.

What happened next left all who witnessed it wide-eyed with wonder. There are some moments in the great sport of association football that are remembered as dream for supporters of one team; as nightmare for fans of the other; and, for neutrals, as the reason we tune into any game, any time, anywhere . . . just in case. This was one of those.

Before the game George Graham told reporters that "nobody really fancies us outside of Highbury, so we can come up here and relax and enjoy the game and get the goals that we need." As the players ran out onto the field, Arsenal's eleven, wearing their road yellows, took bouquets of flowers to all corners of Anfield in tribute to those who had died in the Hillsborough Stadium disaster six weeks earlier, in which a crush before an FA Cup semifinal killed 96 Liverpool fans. Then the football began.

It was a tense game. In the first half, Liverpool survived a couple of Arsenal chances. The footage is chilling to watch now, as massed ranks of Liverpool fans surge and crest behind the goal in the Kop stand (these would be the last throes of massed, unseated fans—the Taylor Report into the Hillsborough disaster mandated all-seater stadiums in the Premier League). Eight minutes into the second half, Alan Smith, Arsenal's free-scoring center forward, nicked a goal with a far-post header from a Nigel Winterburn free kick. The referee consulted with the linesman about whether Smith had actually headed the ball (if he had not, the goal should not have been awarded as the free kick had been an indirect one); but Smith clearly had got his head to it. That was pretty much it. Arsenal huffed and puffed but couldn't break through Liverpool's vaunted defense. Michael Thomas, a journeyman midfielder for Arsenal, had a very presentable chance to score a second but scuffed his shot straight at Liverpool's eccentric Zimbabwean keeper, Bruce Grobbelaar.

With the clock showing 89 minutes and change, cameras picked up Liverpool's central midfielder and all-round pantomime villain Steve McMahon raising a single finger at his teammates to signal that they merely had to hold out for one minute longer—he even points to the far left corner of the stadium, down by the swaying Kop, as if to say, "That's where you put the ball if you get the chance." Brian Moore, the TV commentator for the night, declared him "a real competitor . . . a man who really has earned a championship medal."

Sadly for McMahon and Liverpool, John Barnes, Liverpool's silky winger, didn't heed his teammate's advice and, with 90 minutes up, instead of heading to the corner flag he went on a mazy run into the Arsenal box and lost possession. The ball was funneled back to John Lukic, the Arsenal keeper—in 1989 you could still pass back to a goalkeeper and he could pick it up. Lukic threw the ball out to launch what was, in Moore's legendary words, "surely . . . [Arsenal's] last attack." Moore's tenor changed quickly: "A good ball by Dixon . . . Thomas, charging through the midfield . . . Thomas, it's up for grabs now. Thomas! Right at the end! An unbelievable climax to the season! Liverpool players are down, absolutely abject. Dalglish [Liverpool's manager] just stands there . . . We have the most dramatic finish maybe in the history of the Football League."

So much for "boring boring Arsenal." They had snatched a winner with no time left on the clock; they were applauded off the field by Liverpool fans already heartsick with real tragedy, let alone a sporting one.

Another league championship two years later didn't, however, herald a new era of Arsenal victories, though they borrowed a modicum of cool by being the subject of a popular memoir by Nick Hornby, *Fever Pitch*, published in 1992. That said, even Hornby noted that "we're boring, and lucky, and dirty, and petulant, and rich, and mean, and have been, as far as I can tell, since the 1930s . . . we are the Gunners, the Visigoths, with King Herod and the Sheriff of Nottingham as our twin centre-halves, their arms in the air appealing for offside." (And that's from the pen of a diehard fan.) George Graham would be gone in 1995 after it was revealed that he played fast and loose with what he called a "gift" of £425,000 from a player's agent, otherwise known as a "bung." Eventually, a new titan of Arsenal coaches would appear in the unlikely form of a man who looks like a tax inspector and has the charisma of one: the perfectly-named Arsène Wenger.

Studious, passionate when crossed, the utterly decent Wenger created probably the greatest team in Arsenal's history, the Invincibles of 2003–04. His emphasis on healthy living, intense training, and tactical sophistication was revolutionary in the British game, where players were more used to beer, pies, and a late night out. The results of Wenger's revolution were astonishing: In that 38-game league season of 2003–04, they drew 12 games and won all the others. They had celebrated a league victory two years earlier, in 2002, having won their last 13 games in that campaign, but this 2003 team, featuring Thierry Henry, Robert Pirès, Freddie Ljungberg, Dennis Bergkamp, Patrick Vieira, and the stingiest defense imaginable (they conceded just 26 goals), was unmatched. It was in Bergkamp that Arsenal fans finally found a player whose skills fully defied the "boring" tag. The Dutchman had impeccable control of the ball at all times and extraordinary vision, never more so than in one astonishing goal against Newcastle United. Running on to a Pirès pass, Bergkamp flicked the ball with his left foot around the front of Nikos Dabizas, the Newcastle defender, turned 360 degrees around the back of his bemused opponent, then slotted the ball home. Few players would attempt such a move, let alone know how to even imagine it.

Unmatched by other teams, and unmatched by Arsenal ever since—after 2003, they have won just two major trophies, the 2005 and 2014 FA Cups. In 2006, they finally reached the Champions League final—in Europe they have been particularly toothless, a single Cup Winners' Cup in 1994 their only major victory—only to lose 2–1 to Barcelona. Their cause that night was not helped by hapless German keeper Jens Lehmann getting himself sent off after 18 minutes, and though they scored first, Arsenal couldn't hold out.

Wenger's longevity—when Sir Alex Ferguson retired from Manchester United in 2013, he became the longest-serving manager in the Premiership—has tended to mask Arsenal's underachievement. Always challenging but never winning is not good enough for a club that has won the league 13 times, but not for a decade and counting. Letting stalwarts like Cesc Fabregas and Robin van Persie leave to archrivals (Barcelona and Manchester United respectively) has periodically made Arsenal fans wonder about the club's ambitions, though Gooners, as they are known, have furrowed their brows while happily sitting in a state-of-the-art £390 million stadium, the Emirates, which replaced Highbury in 2006.

They've gone unbeaten for a season, they've lost 8–2 at Old Trafford; they've won a last-minute thriller at Anfield to claim the league title, they've been knocked out of the FA Cup by lowly Wrexham. In 2013, Arsenal fans, including the journalist Piers Morgan, called for Arsène Wenger to be fired (#WengerOut) after they lost their first game to Aston Villa, only to watch him sign the German star Mesut Özil and make the team purr once more. Through it all, Wenger has retained a sense of decorum and reasonableness, except in the case of the large padded coat he sometimes wears to games. On at least four occasions TV cameras have caught him angrily trying—and failing—to zip it up while watching the game at the same time. Like a number of Arsenal teams across the years, and like loudmouths demanding that people lose their jobs, it's not a pretty sight.

Location	Birmingham, England
Established	1874
Nicknames	The Villans, The Lions, The Claret and Blue
Current stadium	Villa Park (42,788 capacity)
Home colors	Claret, sky blue, and white
Leading goal-scorer	Billy Walker (1920–33), 244 goals
Most appearances	Charlie Aitken (1959–75), 660 appearances

Triumph arrived for Aston Villa in the form of Peter Withe's shin and Nigel Spink's big foamy gloves.

Peter Withe: a center forward from central casting. Big, ungainly, not unskilled but hardly a man of finesse. Nigel Spink: the reserve team keeper, a baby thrust into action and having the game of his young life.

Peter Withe is the kind of player British teams regularly produce and help flourish, given the culture's penchant for long, low-percentage balls out of the defense: the theory goes, "Bang the ball up there, hope the big feller gets his nut to it, something might happen." Only in this crucial case Withe got some part of his leg to it, at the back post, a post he still managed to hit from two yards out. But the ball went in anyway, and in doing so brought his team, Aston Villa, the European Cup in the most unlikely of victories.

At the other end of the field, Nigel Spink, a 22-year-old tyro, was making saves like a veteran.

All in the service of Aston Villa: the biggest club in England's second biggest city. Villa is an old organization—established in 1874, the year Gladstone yielded the British prime ministership to Disraeli. The next year, the other Birmingham club, City, were formed. The local derby began in 1879 and continues to this day, at least when both teams are in the same league or drawn together in a cup competition. But being in the same league isn't a given, as both Villa and Birmingham have spent plenty of time in the lower divisions: for a city of more than 2 million people, Birmingham has consistently underachieved as a soccer hub.

For Villa, success came early, and then mostly not at all. They won the championship five times at the very end of the nineteenth century, once again in 1910, and then, apart from the odd FA Cup win, proceeded to fall like a stone—their first relegation to the Second Division was in 1936, and though they bounced up and down between the top two divisions, they found themselves, in 1970, in the Third Division, a disgrace for such a storied club.

One happy moment in all the gloom was the visit of Pelé and his Santos team to Villa Park. It was the time of power cuts in England—"1972, you know," as Morrissey puts it—and Villa paid £5,000 to rent an electrical generator so that the 54,000 people who turned up could actually see the game (or some of it—the generators barely ran four of the floodlights). Villa were unlikely winners, 2–1, and it was a brief moment of bright in all that darkness.

Then came a man called Ron Saunders. Taking over as manager of Villa in 1974, Saunders turned the team around, eventually leading them to the unlikeliest of First Division championships, in 1981. It had been more than 70 years since their last one, and the win brought Saunders his own trinket, the 1981 Manager of the Year Award. Almost always described as a "no-nonsense" coach, this moniker was sadly almost always untrue: Saunders littered his conversation with hilarious non sequiturs and gobbledygook, such as "If you're going to commit suicide, you don't do it yourself," and "Allegations are all very well, but I would like to know who these alligators are." By midway through the 1981–82 season, he would become famous for another statement: "If I'm going to manage, then I want to be a manager, not an office boy." At the time, Villa were struggling in the league—they were 15th, and had just been hammered 4–1 at Old Trafford—and Saunders was in dispute with Villa's chairman, Ron Bendall. The result was an epic strop that saw Saunders go home from training ill on February 9, 1982, and write his resignation letter propped up in bed.

By May 26, 1982, Aston Villa were in the European Cup final.

Saunders, of course, wasn't there (Villa were led by backroom coach Tony Barton), and the team Saunders had built almost didn't make it either. During the second leg of their semifinal in Belgium against Anderlecht their fans rioted, but UEFA decided against banning the team from the final.

On that final night in May, Villa faced a Bayern Munich side that featured superstars like Dieter Hoeness and Karl-Heinz Rummenigge; moreover, they lost their veteran keeper, Jimmy Rimmer, after just nine minutes (he'd been injured in training and tried to play but was in too much pain). On came Spink, a kid in huge gloves, who went on to make a handful of immaculate saves, including one in the second half against Rummenigge which defied the laws of time: the ball was basically past him and he clawed it back from the future (a goal) to the present (a brilliant save). Villa, who'd done nothing throughout the game, then went up field, and a mazy run and searching cross by winger Tony Morley led to the ball appearing at the back post where Peter Withe could not miss. Nevertheless, Withe did his best, shanking the ball sideways and against the inside of the post. Somehow it span into the back of the net, and 20-odd minutes later, Villa had their trophy. Withe, admitting Villa's underdog status, was later quoted using the age-old sporting cliché: "We were just looking forward to the day." Villa had had little hope of winning the European Cup, but there they were, holding aloft the big silver trophy in the warm air of a Rotterdam evening.

Next day, the *Daily Mirror* commented that the win would bring Aston Villa an Austin Powers/Doctor Evil-like windfall of—gasp!—"one million pounds!" Alas, the money brought Villa no more real success—since that win, they've notched a couple of League Cup wins and nothing else.

Their financial losses for the 2012 season alone equal more than 52 times what they won thirty years earlier. For almost the last forty years of the twentieth century, Doug Ellis was either chairman or majority shareholder of the club, and his name still invokes frustration at Villa Park—a club so vast should have won more than it has done, but Ellis was always loath to splash his cash.

Ellis finally relinquished control, and since 2006 Aston Villa has been owned by Randy Lerner, who also owns the Cleveland Browns. The last time the Browns won anything significant was the old NFL Championship in 1964; they have never made it to the Super Bowl. And even Lerner has now given up—in May 2014 he put Aston Villa up for sale.

Location	Bilbao, Spain
Established	1898
Nicknames	*Los Leones* ("The Lions"), *Rojiblancos* and *Zurigorri* ("Red and Whites" in Spanish and Basque respectively)
Current stadium	San Mamés (53,332 capacity)
Home colors	Red and white stripes, with black shorts
Leading goal-scorer	Telmo Zarra (1940–55), 336 goals
Most appearances	José Ángel Iribar (1962–80), 614 appearances

I t is tempting to think of countries as being made up of single peoples, nonvariegated unities where everyone is "English" or "Brazilian" or "Spanish." In the case of that last nationality, nothing could be further from the truth. Though Spain is a sovereign state with a clearly defined border and boasts a national, parliamentary government cake topped with the icing of a constitutional monarchy, as much as any country in Europe it is also a collection of disparate, sometimes competing peoples. In the northeast, centered around Barcelona and stretching up to France via Andorra, the Catalans have long been known for their fierce independence. The principality of Asturias is an autonomous region in northwest Spain. To its east lies Basque country, where at least 30 percent of people speak their local tongue, a language that is not of Spain nor even of the Indo-European set of languages. From this hotbed of Basque nationalism (and separatism), comes a team unique to Spain and, indeed, to the world: Athletic Bilbao.

In the late nineteenth and early twentieth century, the Basque people were beset by what Athletic Bilbao's official history calls "Anglo-mania." The city of Bilbao had morphed from a small town into an economic powerhouse, with iron and steel, mining, chemical plants, banking, and shipyards driving the growth of a well-to-do middle class. In turn, that middle class looked to greater Europe, and to Britain especially, as symbols of sophistication, sending their sons there to become experts in the industries driving Bilbao's growth. In turn, British workers in those Basque steel mills and shipyards wanted to play their favorite sport.

All these forces came together to form Athletic Club, a merging of a previous Athletic Club with Bilbao FC, at the start of the new century. Wearing a version of Southampton's kit, they were champions of Spain four times in their first decade (1903, 1904, 1910, and 1911). Money from wealthy Basques went toward the construction of San Mamés, Athletic Club's cathedral-like stadium, and as Basque separatist claims grew, so did La Cantera—the rule by which Bilbao players may only be Basque. It's a rule that continues to this day.

Success continued in regional championships and the Copa del Rey, but the country as a whole still awaited a truly national tournament. In 1928–29, La Liga came into being, and one year later the Rojiblancos, as the red-and-white-striped players came to be known, won this new league as well as the Copa del Rey; they repeated the same feat the next season. At the helm was a British manager named Fred Pentland, known as "*El Bombín*" for his habit of wearing a bowler hat.

It was the start of their greatest run of victories—in all, Athletic won four league titles, four Copas, and a bunch of regional and Basque competitions (along the way they beat Barcelona 12–1 in 1931, the Catalan giants' worst ever defeat). And then, as with all stories of Spanish football, the terrible civil war intervened. Athletic Bilbao would never be the same.

For a start, General Franco forced them to de-Anglicize their name, and they became, for a time, Atlético Bilbao. Though they won La Liga in 1943 and a few Copas in that same decade, once Real Madrid and Barcelona started using "foreign" players like Alfredo Di Stéfano, et al., Bilbao struggled to keep up. A single La Liga championship in 1956 (again backed by a Copa del Rey win) was scant reward for this most vibrant of Basque teams. Franco died in 1975; a year later, a Basque flag was raised in the center circle before a game against another Basque powerhouse, Real Sociedad. Bilbao had had to wait decades to get their original name back and to win more La Liga titles, but in 1983 they finally reached the summit of Spanish football and the following season they once again won the double.

But that was it. Athletic Bilbao have featured in two UEFA Cup finals and lost both—the latter, in 2012, to the team that owes its existence to Basque country, Atlético Madrid. (At about the same time as Bilbao FC and Athletic were coming together in the vibrant port on the Bay of Biscay, Basque students, homesick in Madrid, created Atlético Madrid as an homage to their homeland, 250 miles away.) On May 9, 2012, almost exactly 100 years after its birth, the child eclipsed the father in that all-Spanish Europa League final on two goals by Radamel Falcão and one by Diego. The starting lineup for Atlético Madrid that night—a team born out of Basque fervor, lest we forget—featured a Belgian, a Uruguayan, three Spaniards and one Asturian-Spaniard, a Turk, and three Brazilians.

Athletic Bilbao's team featured eleven Basques.

ATLÉTICO MADRID

Location	Madrid, Spain
Established	1903
Nicknames	*Los Colchoneros* ("The Mattress Makers"), *Los Rojiblancos* ("The Red and Whites"), *Los Indios* ("The Indians"), *El Atleti*
Current stadium	Vicente Calderón Stadium, Madrid (54,960 capacity)
Home colors	Red, white, and blue
Leading goal-scorer	Luis Aragonés (1964–74), 173 goals
Most appearances	Adelardo Rodríguez (1959–76), 551 appearances

Spare a thought for those with talent who nevertheless labor in the shadow of the greater: J. C. E. Bach, Anne Brontë, Cooper Manning, Vince DiMaggio, Tito Jackson, Patrick McEnroe. Fine performers, all, but paler than J. S., Charlotte and Emily, Eli and Peyton, Joe, Michael, and John.

Add to this poignant list Atlético Madrid. Imagine being the other team in the same town as Real. Imagine winning the league ten times, the Intercontinental Cup, the Europa League, and looking across town to the Bernabéu Stadium where your archrivals have won no less than 32 league titles and ten European Cups, the most recent over you in the 2014 final. O Atlético! We sing of thee, but sadly. (And we will sing of Hans-Georg Schwarzenbeck, and the away goals rule, or lack of it—and we are sorry for those things, too.)

The history of Spanish club soccer is so bound up with the politics of the twentieth century that to unravel it would take a full 90 minutes, extra time, and a penalty shootout. Suffice it to say that Atlético

Madrid began in 1903 when a group of Madrid-based Basque students—fans of Basque club Athletic Bilbao—formed a team. Once again, as in the cases of Independiente with Nottingham Forest, Juventus with Notts County, and others, there is some evidence that their original blue and white stripes were influenced by those worn by a British team, in this case Blackburn Rovers (though eight years later they are said to have changed to Southampton's red and white stripes, while maintaining Rovers' blue shorts). Such concerns were made inane by the horrors of the 1930s in Spain and its brutal civil war. After the end of the war on April 1, 1939, and with their team decimated by the conflict, they joined with Aviación Nacional—the jock section of Franco's air force—to become Athletic Aviación de Madrid, and as such managed to win the league in both 1940 and 1941.

But at heart they were a Republican-supporting team, and though Franco initially extolled their virtues, he jumped on the Real bandwagon once Real started winning all those European trophies. By 1947, Atlético Aviación had reverted to Club Atlético de Madrid (they celebrated by thrashing Real 5–0 that year, their greatest ever margin of victory over their city rivals), and a decade after their previous back-to-back titles they repeated the feat, in 1950 and 1951. That team was helmed by Helenio Herrera, the legendary Argentine coach who mixed an exacting personal style with multilanguage sayings (he spoke Spanish, English, French, and Italian), one of which exhorted his teams to avoid monotony in conversation, training sessions, and meals.

With Herrera gone, in 1959 Atlético nevertheless reached the semifinals of the European Cup. Their opponents? Real Madrid, of course. In the first leg, in front of an astonishing 120,000 fans at the Bernabéu Stadium, Real, featuring Hungarian master Ferenc Puskás and Argentine genius Alfredo Di Stéfano, squeaked a 2–1 victory, having gone a goal down. In the second leg, Atlético did just enough, winning 1–0 via a goal by their much-beloved center forward, Enrique Collar, who ended up playing nearly 500 games for Atlético. Given that away goals count double, Atlético rightfully took their place in the final . . . oh, wait—the away goals rule in the European Cup was still a decade away. Instead, a playoff was staged in neutral Zaragoza and once again Collar scored, but it wasn't enough: first-half goals by Puskás and Di Stéfano took Real to the final, where they beat French side Reims for their fourth European Cup win in a row.

Poor Atlético—this paradigm of being good, but not as good as Real, was firmly established. Atlético won the Cup Winners' Cup in 1962, but lost the same tournament the following year by the trouncing score of 5–1 to Tottenham Hotspur (Collar scored yet again, but it was for naught). They won La Liga four times in the sixties and seventies, but Real won it 14 times.

Perhaps Atlético's lowest point came in 1974, when they traveled to Glasgow to face Celtic in the first leg of a European Cup semifinal. Coaching them was the man who led Argentina in the 1966 World Cup, Juan Carlos Lorenzo. "*El Toto*," as he was known, had led a team branded "animals" by the manager of England's World Cup-winning team, Alf Ramsey. Eight years hadn't mellowed El Toto—Atlético's center back in that April 10, 1974 game, Panadero Diaz, has since described Lorenzo as a "monster" who abused his players to make them act like barbarians. Diaz admits he was being outplayed by Celtic's center forward, Jimmy Johnstone, so he kicked him in the ribs. Two other Madrid players were sent off and pretty much everyone else on the Spanish side was booked, as Atlético basically kicked Celtic out of the tournament. Surviving video of the game makes one's blood run cold: Johnstone is hacked somewhere near his knees, then Ayala goes through the back of a Celtic defender to get the first red card. There is still half an hour to play; Diaz takes his swipe at Johnstone and he goes, too (though in fairness, he merely kicked him just above the shins, rather than in the ribcage). Madrid gave up 51 free kicks, and their hugs at the end of the game prove they knew that the 0–0 draw might be enough to get them through—and so it was, two late goals back in Spain taking them to the final.

Perhaps there is a soccer god who dispenses soccer justice, as the final saw Madrid score with six minutes to go in extra time, only for

Bayern Munich's Hans-Georg Schwarzenbeck—a center back, no less—to nick an equalizer in the very last minute with a piledriver from 25 yards. The replay two days later was no contest: the twin Munich superstars Hoeness and Müller scored a couple each to thrash Atlético 4–0.

The same Atlético team represented Europe in the Intercontinental Cup that year, when Bayern withdrew because they had too much to do. They managed to win it, beating Independiente of Argentina 2–1 on aggregate. Since then they've won La Liga three times—including in 2014 when a last-day draw at Barcelona clinched the title over the Catalans—the Europa League twice, and the European Super Cup twice, and took Real to extra time in the 2014 Champions League final. But they are still Atlético Madrid, the Andrés or Andrea or Luisa or Rodrigo or Magdalena or Juan to Real Madrid's Miguel de Cervantes.

BARCELONA

Location	Barcelona, Spain
Established	1899
Nicknames	Barça, *Blaugrana* ("Blue and Red")
Current stadium	Camp Nou (99,354 capacity)
Home colors	Blue and scarlet
Leading goal-scorer	Lionel Messi (2004–), 253 goals
Most appearances	Xavi Hernández, known as Xavi (1998–), 628 appearances

*E*l Barcelona es algo mas que un club de futbol. "Barcelona," the club's motto goes, "is something more than a football club."

All football clubs in some ways aspire to be more than they are—who doesn't want to *stand* for something as well as win something? F.C. Barcelona seems to aspire *more* than any other club to more than football, be it through its deep Catalan pride, its anti-Franco stance, or its sponsorship deal with UNICEF. Yet any discussion of the club inevitably finds itself drawn back and back and back to the *futbol*, to Johan Cruyff and Josep Samitier, "the Locust Man," to Lionel Messi and László Kubala and the Xavi–Iniesta–Busquets triangle, where the ball disappears for hours at a time, and to Maradona—yes, even to Diego Maradona, even though he had hepatitis, and even though Andoni Goikoetxea broke his leg.

The club was founded by a man with a multitude of possible first names. We know his surname is Gamper, but various authorities call him Joan, some Hans, some Hans-Max. He was Swiss, for sure, and wanted to play soccer, so in October 1899 he put an ad in the newspaper, and was joined by another Swiss, a couple of Brits, a German, and a gaggle of Catalans in establishing Futbol Club Barcelona. There is some thought that he brought Basel F.C.'s kit with him, but what is clear is that the garnet and blue colors (known in Catalan as *blaugrana*) stuck early, as did the sense that Barça wasn't just about football. It was also about Catalan identity, and a kind of plurality and openness made possible by a part of Spain that welcomed non-Catalans, like Gamper, with open arms. Later, in the 1960s, more than a million people would move from the poverty-wracked south of Spain to Catalonia during the darkest days of Franco, but even at the turn of the century the place was inundated with immigrants desperate to ride Barcelona's bustling port to prosperity.

Gamper's club stood as a symbol of Barcelona's rise and Catalan pride. By the early 1920s this relatively new soccer team could afford to build Les Corts, a stadium that would eventually hold 60,000 people. (Barcelona's official website lists the cost of Les Corts at a pleasingly exact 991,984.04 pesetas.) But these were the days before La Liga, so Barça's trophies came in regional tournaments and the Copa del Rey—with Gamper as president, they won three Copas (he had scored 100 goals as a player). And then, dictatorships put paid to everything for Gamper.

The first Spanish dictator to have his way was the Fascist precursor Primo de Rivera. In 1925, when a band played the Spanish national anthem at Les Corts, the booing (of the music, and thereby of Primo de Rivera) by the Catalans only subsided when the band changed tack and played "God Save the Queen." Les Corts was closed down for six months and Gamper thrown out of the presidency of the club; five years later, he committed suicide. By then, Barcelona had a new rising star in its offices by the name of Josep Sunyol. This left-wing politician and newspaper owner would become president of the club in 1935, and he, like so many others, saw Barcelona in terms of what it stood for as much as for what happened on the field, commenting that "our club's popularity undeniably includes elements that are not related to sport." Sadly, his words were prophetic: a year later, as

Spain was wracked by the start of its civil war, Sunyol was executed by the Francoists.

So began a period of suppression of both F.C. Barcelona and Catalonia. Franco's Spain would be all about machismo and Spanish identity, and Catalonia's aspirations to independence, though never as fiercely held as those of the Basques, were deemed threatening to the regime. A tour of Mexico and the US by the team in 1937 led to a number of players refusing to return to Spain; once the civil war was over and Franco in power, F.C. Barcelona as a name was considered too Catalan and was changed to Barcelona Club de Futbol (the Catalan colors were removed from their crest, too). In 1942, Franco used Les Corts for a parade, in which 1,000 actual doves and 24,000 metaphorical hawks—a.k.a. Falangists—were loosed upon what should have merely been a soccer stadium. A year later, Barcelona beat Real Madrid at Les Corts in the first leg of the ridiculously named Copa del Generalísimo; the return leg, in Madrid, was rigged after a visit to the Barcelona dressing room by José Escrivá de Romaní, the Director of State Security. (This writer refuses to give credence to the final score of that game—and thereby the dictatorship that dictated it—by reporting it here.)

But *futbol* was too strong a force to be held down by a crazy regime. Enter Josep Samitier. *"Home Llagosta"* ("Locust Man," so called because of his ability to jump and contort on the field) had been the first real superstar Barça player, scoring 333 goals in 454 appearances in the 1920s—the David Beckham of his day, hobnobbing with celebrities. By the end of World War II he was back as coach, leading Barcelona to a Spanish championship in 1945, its first since its inaugural year in 1929. Barça would win the league again in 1948 and 1949, and then four times in the 1950s behind the goal-scoring feats of László Kubala, who had fled Communist Hungary hidden in a truck, and who shocked the world by "curling the ball." Coach for those legendary fifties' teams was Helenio Herrera, known as "HH," a man who liked to say things like "We'll win without getting off the bus," though his teams usually won by actually getting off the bus and play-

ing excellent football. Joining the fun was Luis Suárez—no relation to
the toothy Uruguayan—a goal-scorer who won the Ballon d'Or in
1960, the sole Spanish player ever to do so.

But despite the victories at home and a couple of Inter-Fairs Cups,
the seeds of demise had been sewn. Barcelona lost out in a tussle with
Real Madrid to sign the legendary Alfredo Di Stéfano, and they lost
the 1961 European Cup final to Benfica in what became known as the
Curse of the Square Posts. Played at the comically-named Wankdorf
Stadium in Bern, Switzerland, the final—the first to not feature Real
Madrid, who'd won the first five—featured a bizarre own goal by
Barça's keeper Antoni Ramaletts, who pushed the ball onto the post,
only for the sharp edges to angle the ball over the line. Worse was to
come: in the second half, as Barcelona saw a header come straight
back off the square post, and a long-range effort actually hit both posts
before bouncing away at right angles to the goal line. Benfica won 3-2,
and the victory signaled the start of Barça's true decline, which can in
part also be traced back to the building of the Camp Nou, the money
for which (288,088,143 pesetas, again to be precise; it opened in 1957)
meant that cash for player acquisitions was severely limited.

Barcelona won the league once in the seventies, and once in the
eighties, but had to settle for Copa del Rey victories, second-place finishes, and Cup Winners' Cup wins until the 1990s came around. Johan
Cruyff had excelled as a player for Barcelona for five years in the 1970s,
leading them to their La Liga win in 1974; now, as manager, he changed
the course of the team.

Cruyff took over the Barcelona job in 1988, inheriting a team that
had won La Liga just once in the decade since he'd won it with them
as a player. The master of Total Football, as the Dutch system of players being able to operate anywhere on the field was known, would
eventually morph into what is now known as tiki-taka, a pass-and-
move technique that can be dazzling to watch and impossible to beat.
Cruyff also brought in a galaxy of stars in their prime—gone were the
days of underachieving figures like Maradona, who sort of played for
Barcelona for two seasons, though he was mostly sick or injured.

Instead, Cruyff marshaled Hristo Stoichkov, Txiki Begiristain, Ronald Koeman, Michael Laudrup, and Romário into often unbeatable sides. They won La Liga four years in a row: 1991–94.

Cruyff's greatest triumph was to finally lead Barcelona to their first European Cup. In the 1992 final, they faced a typically drab Sampdoria team intent on not losing rather than on winning, and it took an extra-time free kick by Dutchman Koeman to break Italian resistance. The free kick had been harshly awarded, but with 112 minutes on the clock, Koeman stepped up and blasted the tapped indirect free kick into the far corner from 25 yards, past Gianluca Pagliuca in the Sampdoria goal. Barcelona's long, hard wait for European glory had come to an end.

Sixteen years later, Josep "Pep" Guardiola, a cultured defensive midfielder who was on the pitch in that 1992 European Cup final, would ascend to become coach of Barcelona at just 37 years of age. In the intervening years, another Dutchman, Frank Rijkaard, brought two La Ligas and another Champions League trophy to Barcelona, the latter via two late goals against ten-man Arsenal in the final in 2006. But those "*jogo bonito*" victories pale now when one considers what Pep Guardiola wrought.

It is no overstatement to say that the former Barcelona midfielder created probably the best club side the world has ever seen. Featuring a solid goalkeeper and defense, a midfield that pretty much never gave the ball away, and, in Lionel Messi, a talent up front to rival Pelé, Maradona, and all the other greats, the Barcelona team of Guardiola seemed to reinvent modern football. Their play was predicated upon intense triangular passing formations in which a player would knock a short pass and then move this way or that to form a new triangle, always giving the receiver of the pass two options: tiki-taka. Opposing teams were passed to death. Before the 2009 Champions League final, Manchester United boss Alex Ferguson warned his team against being swallowed by the Bermuda Triangle-like passing of Xavi–Iniesta–Busquets–Messi, et al., the phase of Barça's play Ferguson called a "carousel." With a few minutes to go in the first half and

United already a goal down, any fan could see Park Ji-Sung, United's hardworking midfielder, stuck on that very carousel as Barcelona players literally passed around him, over and over and over. Two years later, Barcelona would beat Manchester United again with a similar performance in the final of the same tournament—if anything, that game was even more one-sided, as Barcelona now also featured David Villa up front, a man who could score from any angle. The BBC called that performance a masterclass, and this writer, present at Wembley for the game, didn't even dare celebrate Wayne Rooney's equalizer for United just before half-time as it had been clear from the earliest minutes of the game that there would be only one team holding the trophy aloft.

They would hold aloft so many, that team—under Guardiola, they won three league titles, two Copa del Reys, three Super Cups, two Champions League titles, two UEFA Super Cups, and two FIFA Club World Cups. Barcelona, delighting the corporate-weary world by wearing the UNICEF logo on their *blaugrana* shirts (before 2006, their shirts were empty of a sponsor altogether), dominated every tournament in which they played. Everywhere one went in the world, Messi shirts could be found. But at the end of the 2012 season Guardiola left, citing exhaustion. Barcelona would go on to win La Liga the following season with a staggering 100 points—drawing four games, losing two, and winning all the others, with a goal difference of +75.

It had been incoming Barça president Narcís de Carreras who said, on January 17, 1968, *"El Barcelona es algo mas que un club de futbol."* On December 28, 1975, Barcelona faced Real Madrid at the Camp Nou. Five weeks earlier Franco had died and Madrid's legendary president, Bernabéu, had proudly talked about his time occupying Catalonia with the Fascists. In response to the new state of Spanish affairs, that night the Camp Nou was awash with a thousand Catalan flags—the first time they'd been seen there since 1939—and one could believe that a football team could stand for more than mere play when a last-minute long-range strike by Catalan player

Carles Rexach bounced over the Madrid keeper for a 2–1 win to Barcelona.

And yet, in 2012, UNICEF moved to the back of Barcelona's shirts, replaced on the front by the Qatar Foundation. Barcelona now stood for many things—for tiki-taka, for Catalonia, for UNICEF's aim "to save and improve children's lives," and for the furtherance of the aims of a small but rich Gulf state.

BAYER LEVERKUSEN

Location	Leverkusen, Germany
Established	1904
Nicknames	*Werkself* ("The Factory Workers"), Vizekusen ("Second-kusen"), Neverkusen (as in, never winning)
Current stadium	BayArena (30,000 capacity)
Home colors	Black and red
Leading goal-scorer	Ulf Kirsten (1990–2003), 181 goals
Most appearances	Rüdiger Vollborn (1982–99), 401 appearances

Before May 12, 1979, theirs had been a quiet history, notable only for their fealty to first a paint factory, then the succeeding Bayer AG pharmaceutical company. All that changed for Bayer 04 Leverkusen at the end of the 1970s, when Die Werkself—the team's nickname means "factory workers"—finally made it into the Bundesliga.

Bayer 04 Leverkusen have a number in the middle of their name to signal the date of their origin, which is reckoned to be July 1, 1904. A February 1903 letter signed by 170 employees of Bayer begged the right to establish sporting clubs in the company's name, which was then the fabulously tortured "Paint Factories Formerly Known as Friedrich Bayer & Co." (a formation coopted by Prince many years later, perhaps). More than a year later, Die Werkself finally got their gymnastics and sports club. It would be another four years before a football team broke out, and even then it was 1927 before they split off to create what was then called 04 Leverkusen Football Club. Everyone involved worked for Bayer.

Nothing much went right for the fledgling club, at least not at a national level. Sure, they won the Cologne district league, but big whoop. Once professional football came to Germany after World War II, the most prestigious league was the Oberliga West, which Bayer failed to reach a number of times before they made it in 1951. Five years later they were gone again, and when the Bundesliga was formed in 1963, there was still no sign of Bayer 04 Leverkusen. Five years into the league they almost reached the promised land, only to lose to that German "powerhouse," the Offenbacher Kickers (now of the fourth division of German soccer and a cool 9 million euros in the red).

It would be another decade before Bayer put together a team strong enough to get them to the Bundesliga, but get there they did in 1979. Some solid early seasons led to their qualification for the UEFA Cup in 1986—they were now a competent, if not spectacular, Bundesliga side.

Two years later, they were much better than competent.

In 1988, Bayer 04 were once again in the UEFA Cup, but this time—and just nine years after their ascension to top-flight football—they made it all the way to the final, where they faced Espanyol of Spain. It hadn't been an easy ride for either team—Espanyol had had to knock out both Milan teams to make it to the final, and Bayer 04 Leverkusen had faced a quarterfinal two-leg match-up against Espanyol's city-mates, Barcelona. The first leg in Germany had ended in a disappointing 0–0 draw, and few gave Bayer much hope back at the Camp Nou. But the Gary Lineker-led Spanish side played poorly at home (in front of just 20,000 fans, to boot), and Bayer scored the only goal halfway through the second half to go through. It was a famous victory for the relative newcomers, but better was yet to come: they knocked out fellow German team Werder Bremen, again 1–0 on aggregate, in the semifinal—and that Werder Bremen team would be German champions by the end of the season.

And so back to the city of Barcelona for the first part of the two-leg final against Espanyol. In that first leg, Leverkusen simply didn't show up, losing 3–0 to a trio of goals in 11 minutes around half-time.

The first half of the second leg was goalless, despite Bayer's Brazilian center forward Tita's efforts, which included heading the ball out of the Espanyol keeper's hands and passing it into the empty net, a goal that should have stood but didn't thanks to a fussy referee. One can imagine Die Werkself edging toward the exits of their Ulrich-Haberland-Stadion early that night, but those who stayed were glad. The game changed around the hour mark, when Tita pounced on comical Spanish defending to score for Bayer, making it 3–1 on aggregate. Six minutes later, Falko Götz made it 3–2 with a brilliant diving header after a jaw-slackeningly wonderful cross from Klaus Täuber, who had been on the field for only a minute. With just nine minutes to go—ba-dum-ching!—the wonderfully-named South Korean Cha Bum-Kun equalized the tie. Known to German fans—as well as the German commentator when his header hit the back of the net—as "Tscha Bum!" or "Cha-boom!", Cha is widely considered the greatest player to come out of South Korea. (He had previously won the UEFA Cup with Eintracht Frankfurt in 1980, making him a legend in Germany as a whole.)

But here, in 1988, the job was only partially done—the game required penalties to find a winner. At first everything went right for Espanyol, as they scored their first and Bayer's first was saved. Espanyol players started to celebrate on the halfway line, but they were premature—though they scored their next kick, that was the last one they netted, the remaining three hitting the bar, the Bayer keeper, and Die Werkself fans behind the goal. Bayer 04 Leverkusen scored theirs to win the UEFA Cup.

And that has been pretty much it. Michael Ballack scored an own goal on the last day of the 2000 season to deprive Bayer of their first Bundesliga title (all they had had to do was draw), but even that was better than 2002, when they lost a five-point lead to Borussia Dortmund to end second, lost the German Cup final, and were beaten in the Champions League final by Real Madrid—but that last defeat was no disgrace, given how it transpired. The winning goal, scored right on half time, is probably the best goal scored in any major final of any major tournament anywhere anytime ever. A looping, 50-feet-in-the-air cross—one commentator called it "aimless," which was being kind—by Roberto Carlos fell to Zinedine Zidane on the edge of the Bayer 04 Leverkusen box, and to say that Zidane sweetly curled a first-time left-footed volley into the top corner of the net undersells "sweetly," "first-time," "volley," and "top corner." The goal is a wonder, and if you're going to lose a European final, do it to a player like Zidane doing something like that.

Zidane wasn't even left-footed.

Location	Munich, Germany
Established	1900
Nicknames	*Der FCB* ("The FCB"), *Die Bayern* ("The Bavarians"), *Stern des Südens* ("Star of the South"), *Die Roten* ("The Reds")
Current stadium	Allianz Arena (71,137 capacity)
Home colors	Red and white
Leading goal-scorer	Gerd Müller (1964–79), 365 goals
Most appearances	Sepp Maier (1962–89), 473 appearances

For Bayern Munich, almost uniquely among major clubs, there is a sense of great highs butting up against deep lows—no great victory is ever without a corresponding painful defeat. This has been true throughout their history.

It's difficult to imagine a team like Bayern Munich not being part of every major German soccer narrative, but even in the 1960s they were still a small team in a distant corner of a large country. When the Bundesliga began in 1963, amalgamating five disparate German leagues, Bayern were overlooked in favor of the team that won the equivalent of the previous season's second division, 1860 Munich. There was plenty of history between the two rivals, but two moments stand out: one was the last ever game played under the Third Reich, a 3–2 victory for Bayern in a game played exactly a week before Hitler committed suicide. And the other, in which a young man named Franz Beckenbauer was assaulted, changed the course of German club soccer forever.

All that is to come; first, we must meet a magician.

Richard "Dombi" Kohn was an Austrian Jew who, after an undistinguished playing career, ended up bopping around a few German teams as coach before he took over at Bayern in 1931, and, the following year, brought them their first national championship. Kohn is still as much remembered for his Dutch nickname, *de Hongaarse wonderdokter*, thanks to his love of quack-like remedies for his players (and the fact that in 1888, when Kohn was born, his home country was actually Austria-Hungary). Gerard Meijer, Dutch team Feyenoord's physio (where "Dombi" later coached, hence the Dutch nickname) remembers one potion being made from "pure rubber milk ... heated to 100 degrees, mixed with paraffin." This burning *hete spul* (hot shit), as Meijer later called it, fixed players effectively and quickly, apparently, though not surprisingly they were said to be horribly afraid of it. Sadly, the wonder doctor had taken his magic to the Netherlands because the heat of prewar German racial politics was potentially deadly to a Jewish coach, no matter how great he was.

By the time World War II broke out, Bayern Munich was considered a "Jewish club" (it boasted a number of Jewish members and expected its players to be well-educated, neither of which endeared it to the Nazis). This effectively ended Bayern's hopes of capitalizing on their early 1930s' national success; players fled, and coaches did too. Munich's downswing continued throughout the postwar period, including that first Bundesliga season when they didn't even join the new national league. Eventually, however, one man dragged Bayern into national and international dominance: perhaps the greatest center back to ever play the game: "*der Kaiser*," Franz Beckenbauer.

Beckenbauer first appeared for Bayern before they were in the Bundesliga, though he had grown up an 1860 Munich fan. (He joined Bayern rather than the club he loved after getting hacked off the field—even being slapped in the face at one point—by an 1860 Munich youth team when he was 13 years old.) A center back when he helped Bayern reach the Bundesliga in his first full season, Beckenbauer grew as an all-round player, which changed Bayern's fortunes forever. Together with standout players Gerd Müller (center forward) and Sepp Maier (goalkeeper), the team won the German Cup in 1967 and the European Cup Winners' Cup the following year, but these were just preludes to the main event. By the start of the 1970s Bayern were the dominant team in Germany and Europe, achieving two separate "threepeats": the Bundesliga title in 1972–74 and the European Cup in 1974–76.

To call Beckenbauer a center back is like calling Lionel Messi a bit good at dribbling. Beckenbauer not only excelled as a defender; he managed to redefine the position, including inventing a new position on the field, that of libero, a free-floating defender/midfielder. The libero should be able to tackle, pass, and construe the defensive game not merely as a chance to stop the other team but as the place to begin creating attacking opportunities. (That said, there's only ever really been one libero who has fully lived up to the model: Franz Beckenbauer.)

It was at this golden time that a strange thing happened, something that would come back to haunt Bayern Munich in two of their most famous games post-Beckenbauer: fans and soccer pundits started to believe in magic—but not the "Dombi" kind, involving injuries and hot-shit potions. Instead, the casual viewer came to think that last-minute winning goals were specifically saved for Bayern by a higher power. The word *Bayerndusel* came to be employed to explain how it was that Bayern had all the *dusel* (luck) in the world (*Bayerndusel* is now used in Germany beyond the realm of soccer to denote a kind of unearned luck).

Shaking a fist at the gods can happen when a team wins a lot of games. In Britain, during the reign of coach Alex Ferguson at Manchester United, the mythical "Fergie time" came to denote something generally accepted but utterly without basis in fact—namely, that referees tacked on time to Manchester United games so that they could win. But in 1999, a mixture of "Fergie time" and *Bayerndusel* came together to bring Bayern its worst ever night on the soccer field.

The European Cup competition in the 1980s was unkind to Bayern Munich. Despite continued domination in the Bundesliga (they won the league seven times in the 1980s alone, and another five times in the 1990s), they managed only two final appearances, both of which they cruelly lost. The first, in 1982 to a very limited Aston Villa side, 1–0, was almost laughably embarrassing: Peter Withe, Villa's center forward, was two yards out and yet almost managed to miss his winning goal, scoring off the post when it was actually harder to miss. Five years later, Porto scored two late goals in a minute to nick the trophy from Bayern once again. But nothing comes close to 1999.

By 1999, Franz Beckenbauer was long gone from Bayern. In his place in the final of what was now called the Champions League was midfielder-turned-sweeper Lothar Matthäus, a man who managed to play with less finesse than *der Kaiser*, and even less class (Matthäus was universally loathed by all soccer fans save those of Bayern Munich, for his strutting self-aggrandizement). Matthäus had been Bayern's captain in the Porto defeat in 1987, and around him in 1999 a solid, if unexciting, Bayern team took an early 1–0 lead against the English champions, Manchester United. United that season featured attacking greats like Ryan Giggs and David Beckham, to name but two, but were failing to create much in the final. In the second half, Bayern conspired to hit both the post and the bar in separate attacks, but didn't manage to score a second goal.

With the regular 90 minutes already played, British TV commentator Clive Tyldesley commented, "Can Manchester United score? They always score," And then, *Bayerndusel* turned on Bayern and "Fergie time" was invoked. During time added on, Beckham whipped in a corner which somehow spun out to Giggs. Giggs managed to skew a horrible shot, spinning wide left—only for Teddy Sheringham, on as a desperate Ferguson substitution, to knock the ball home. Bayern defenders (not including Lothar Matthäus, who had himself been replaced and who watched the final 10 minutes with a look of triumph on his face as the championship beckoned) appealed for offside, but they were turned down. Tyldesley said, "Name on the trophy," and he was right: incredibly, not two minutes later, and with the very last kick of the game, another Beckham corner was nodded on by Sheringham at the near post and was then turned into the top of the Bayern goal by United supersub Ole Gunnar Solskjaer.

Delirium reigned; *Bayerndusel* had turned on the German team for a third time in a major final; "Fergie time" had found its most perfect expression (even though the extra minutes had been legitimately added). From leading 1–0 with regular time done, Bayern had contrived to lose the game and yet another Champions League final. For Samuel Kuffour, in particular, the turnaround was unbearable. Bayern's Ghanaian-born center back had been utterly brilliant (and modest) for 90 minutes, yet he and his teammates were going to lose the game and the trophy. Bald Italian referee Pierluigi Collina had to manhandle a sobbing Kuffour off the grass and stand him upright so that he could properly restart the game and then immediately blow for its conclusion. (A rabid Manchester United fan of my acquaintance who attended the game—okay, my brother—said two things in the aftermath: that he had been close enough to reach out and touch Beckham on the back before each historic corner kick, and that the vision of Kuffour's distress was so poignant as to affect his enjoyment of the win, if only for a millisecond.) As the medals were handed out, Matthäus immediately removed his runners-up trinket, an act for which many in the soccer world have yet to forgive him.

Fortunately for Kuffour, he had only to wait two seasons to feel the joy of winning the Champions League. Bayern beat Valencia on penalties in 2001, with Kuffour again having a terrific game for the German champions (along with Englishman Owen Hargreaves, a man who had grown up in Germany and who starred for Bayern before moving to—guess who—Manchester United). But there was no Lothar Matthäus—by 2001, he was playing a single dreadful season in New York for the execrable New York/New Jersey MetroStars, a team as bad as their name.

Highs and lows, though, are Bayern's way. Eleven years later, and after another decade of Bayern Bundesliga dominance, Munich came to yet another Champions League final brimming with confidence and replete with stylish players like Franck Ribéry, he of the medieval haircut, and Bastian Schweinsteiger, a tall, rangy player whose drive from midfield is as notable as his blond hair. Nevertheless, an out-played Chelsea team beat the Munich side on penalties, a result as baffling to German fans (and many others in the football world) as the ones in 1999 and 1987 and 1982.

The following season saw Bayern once again dominate in the Bundesliga and in Europe, thrashing "unbeatable" Barcelona 7–0 on aggregate in the Champions League semifinal. In the all-German final, they faced Borussia Dortmund, a prospect that filled many Bayern fans with excitement and dread in equal measure: they were clearly the best team in Europe this season, but which way would *Bayerndusel* fall? Would it be like the era of 1974–76, when they won the European Cup three times in a row and were able, therefore, to keep the trophy? Or would it be more like a cool October night in Munich, in 1993, when a tiny team called Norwich City came to the Olympic Stadium for a European game that Bayern Munich, and their captain, Lothar Matthäus, simply never imagined they'd lose?

The 2013 final was a classic, featuring a ton of great football, but the first half ended 0–0. After an hour, Bayern finally scored; then disaster struck, as Dortmund equalized with a penalty barely eight minutes later. It was 2012 all over again; the better team were being frustrated. If ever Bayern needed their trademark *dusel*, it was now. And then it happened: in the 89th minute, maverick Dutch winger Arjen Robben used some fancy footwork to come one-on-one with Roman Weidenfeller, the Dortmund keeper, and yet mishit his shot— it seemed to bang off his ankle. No matter—*Bayerndusel* caused the ball to skid past Weidenfeller and trickle into the net. Munich had their victory. No Bayern player needed to be picked up off the ground that night; they proudly walked the trophy around Wembley Stadium, basking in the power of *Bayerndusel*.

Location	Lisbon, Portugal
Established	1904
Nicknames	*Benfiquistas*, *As Águias* ("The Eagles"), *Os Encarnados* ("The Reds"), *Glorioso* ("Glorious One")
Current stadium	Estádio da Luz (65,200 capacity)
Home colors	Red and white
Leading goal-scorer	Eusébio (1960–75), 638 goals
Most appearances	Tamagnini Manuel Gomes Baptista, known as Nené (1968–86), 802 appearances

This is the story of two men: one, a goal-scoring genius who paused to laud a goalkeeper, the other, a dictator who didn't know he'd been deposed.

The first went by one name: Eusébio. He was born in 1942, in Portuguese East Africa (now Mozambique), a poor child in the capital, Lourenço Marques (now Maputo). For much of the 1960s, as Portugal rose to prominence as a soccer nation via its club teams and its national squad, many of its young men were sent to defend its colonial outpost on the Indian Ocean. Scouts were also sent to its colonies, to pick up players for its big three soccer teams: Sporting Lisbon, Porto, and Benfica. It was during this plundering that Eusébio was scouted and signed for Benfica, though he had initially played for Lisbon's feeder team.

The other man went by his full name, António de Oliveira Salazar. He was Portugal's prime minister—really, its dictator—for more than a third of a century. In the way of right-wing dictators, de Oliveira

Salazar restricted civil liberties, and other people's politics, and their rights to travel. It was he and his regime that attempted to keep Angola and Mozambique for Portugal, and it was he who wouldn't let his national treasure leave.

Eusébio was burly, strong, wide as a house, and had what many believed to be the strongest shot in the game. He first appeared for Benfica in 1961, the day after they had won the European Cup. It was a heady time for the team from Lisbon—established in 1904, by the time of Eusébio's debut they had already won ten Portuguese championships and were beginning to threaten the Spanish hold over the European scene. In that 1961 tournament they had beaten Barcelona 3–2, but with Eusébio on board they would win eleven more national championships and consolidate themselves into a European powerhouse.

In the 1962 final, Eusébio's Benfica came up against one of the strongest teams ever assembled, the Real Madrid side of Alfredo Di Stéfano, Ferenc Puskás, Pachín, et al. Two down to Puskás after just 23 minutes—the first a breakaway, the second a 30-yard screamer—Benfica managed to level the score after half an hour (both on assists by Eusébio), only for Puskás to complete his hat-trick before half-time with another fine finish. Would there be any way back for Benfica, faced with such a potent Real Madrid?

Another 30-yard screamer—for Benfica, this time, from Mário Coluna—tied the game five minutes into the second half, and then it was Eusébio's moment. Picking up the ball in his own half, he thundered down the right wing for 50 yards and into the Real Madrid box, where he was unceremoniously dumped to the ground. He buried the resulting penalty to give Benfica a 4–3 lead with 25 minutes to go. Five minutes later, Eusébio struck again, this time drilling home a tapped indirect free kick. At the end of the game, Di Stéfano handed his shirt to the 20-year-old from Mozambique in homage.

Eusébio, a Didier Drogba of his day (only without the need to slap opposing players in the face), had delivered a second European Cup victory in a row for Benfica, and this in his first full season. They would go on to notch three more final appearances in the sixties—in 1963, 1964, and 1968—though they would lose all three. In 440 appearances, Eusébio scored 638 goals, and yet he is perhaps remembered for one goal he didn't manage to bag and for the act of sportsmanship that followed.

By the late sixties, Portuguese domination was on the wane. The national team had made the semifinals of the 1966 World Cup only to lose to two goals by Bobby Charlton and the eventual winners England—a penalty by Eusébio, who else, not being enough to beat back the home country's run to the world title. Portugal sagged under the weight of repression and colonial wars. In 1968, Eusébio once again found himself at Wembley Stadium in London, this time playing for Benfica against Manchester United in the European Cup final.

The first half was short on action, except for an astonishing run by Eusébio and the subsequent shot, which curved and dipped and crashed against United's bar. Eight minutes into the second half Bobby Charlton once again scored at Wembley, this time for his club side, and Benfica's hearts must have turned to the 1965 European Cup, when United had gone to Benfica's extraordinary stadium, Estádio da Luz (which would eventually hold 135,000 fans), for a quarterfinal and had won 5–1, a performance often described as the best any United team had ever produced. Now, in 1968, Benfica were a goal down and seemingly overmatched. But they were a resilient team and a hugely skillful one, keeping the ball on the ground and passing past the more earthy United side. And any team with Eusébio leading the line had a chance. Sure enough, with just 11 minutes to go, Jaime Graça equalized from a tight angle, and a few minutes later a long ball over the United defense had Eusébio bearing down on United keeper Alex Stepney's goal.

Time stopped for United fans, for fans of English soccer. Here was the greatest center forward of his day with just the goalkeeper to beat, the ball bouncing up beautifully for him to score, in the last minute of a European final. Eusébio, the poor kid from southeast Africa, couldn't miss.

It's hard to describe the power of Eusébio's shot generally, and in this case, he can't have ever hit a ball harder. Crucially, though, he hit it straight at Stepney, who somehow clung on—grateful, perhaps, that the ball did not go right through him, cartoon-like, and into the back of the net. The force of the shot knocked Stepney back onto his derrière, and as he stood, winded and a bit dazed, something extraordinary happened: with a minute to go in the European Cup final, Eusébio patted Stepney on the shoulder and waited, trying to shake Stepney's hand. Stepney was all business, trying to get United going on an attack with a throw of the ball, and rebuffed Eusébio, but still the center forward waited, applauding the save that had cost him glory. Ken Wolstenholme, the legendary British broadcaster commentating on the game, said, "What a sportsman, Eusébio, when he could have won that match, to applaud Stepney like that!"

And so the Black Pearl, as Eusébio was known, fluffed his ultimate lines. The miss proved even more costly, as United went on to score three goals in extra time to clinch their first European victory.

The later history of Benfica has been one of similar disappointments: plenty of Portuguese championships (they now have the most by any team from Portugal, 33), but in Europe they have been runners-up in the European Cup twice, twice in the UEFA Cup. Worse, the building of a third tier of the Estádio da Luz, and profligacy in signing players, and manifold changes of coach, led to terrible financial difficulties at the end of the twentieth century. A new Estádio da Luz replaced the old, huge one in 2003, and since then Benfica has stabilized, even pushing a star-packed Chelsea side to extra time in the Europa League final of 2013 before losing 2–1 (extra time has never been kind to Benfica—they'd reach the Europa League final again in 2014 only to lose on penalties to Sevilla).

But nothing can bring back that moment for Eusébio, one on one with Stepney in London, except that it helped define him as one of the great gentleman footballers of his generation, of any generation. Who knows how high he could have flown—two offers for his services in the 1960s, from top Italian teams, were rebuffed by President Salazar himself, who said he was a national treasure, like a painting.

A few months after Eusébio's Stepney moment, Salazar had a brain hemorrhage. He was replaced as prime minister, though no one told him. From September 1968 until his death in July 1970, he spent his time signing papers and thinking he was running Portugal. Eusébio stayed at Benfica until 1975; for the last few years of his career, he played for two smaller Portuguese teams and in North America. His last ever game was for the Buffalo Stallions, in the Major Indoor Soccer League; he died in 2013.

BOCA JUNIORS

Location	Buenos Aires, Argentina
Established	1905
Nicknames	*Xeneizes* ("The Genoese"), *La Mitad Más Uno* ("Half Plus One")
Current stadium	La Bombonera ("The Chocolate Box"), officially Estadio Alberto J. Armando (capacity 49,000)
Home colors	Blue and gold
Leading goal-scorer	Martín Palermo (1997–00, 2004–11), 236 goals
Most appearances	Roberto Mouzo (1971–84), 426 appearances

In the words of the 1912 song, "It's a long way to Tipperary / It's a long way to go." But never mind the distance (some 7,000 miles)—from County Tipperary in the south of Ireland he came, a phys-ed teacher by the name of Paddy McCarthy, all the way to bustling Buenos Aires at the turn of the last century.

Once there, McCarthy boxed and played football. Employed as a teacher at the National School of Commerce, in the shadow of the Buenos Aires docks, he taught a small group of men from Genoa, Italy, how to play soccer. Their names were Esteban Baglietto, Santiago Sana, and Alfredo Scarpatti. Together with the brothers Juan and Teodoro Farenga, these five men, under the tutelage and influence of their pugilist teacher, formed a club for their barrio. In one of their meetings, the young men were making too much noise and got thrown out of the Farenga house; they repaired to La Plaza Solis, a stone's throw from the waterfront. There, in 1905, Boca Juniors came into being.

La Boca is the area that everyone who visits Buenos Aires heads to at some point. Nestled in the southeast corner of the city, this famous barrio is where you can find tango in the streets (they dance it for the tourists) and brightly painted houses. The port is gone, but not the soccer team, and it still feels like the right place for Boca Juniors, because it has always prided itself on being the people's club. It's true that archrivals River Plate also started here, but they soon moved north to a more affluent neighborhood. Boca stayed in La Boca, and it was from here that the team became one of the most famous and successful in the world.

At the center of La Boca life is a chocolate box, or at least a soccer stadium that is said to resemble one. Smallish for such a major sporting stadium (it currently holds just under 50,000 people), the construction of La Bombonera ("the Chocolate Box") started just before World War II, though it took a while to complete (its nickname comes from the tacked-on third tier). It is now one of the most famous places in the world to watch soccer, not just for the intensity of the fans it attracts, but also for its odd shape. Three sides of the stadium feature a dome of sloping sides, just like many other stadiums, but the fourth side is vertical so as to not overstep the property's footprint. It creates an odd scene, as the upright stand runs along one length of the pitch, as though the teams are being watched from the boxes of a theater. When the fans stamp their feet, as they're wont to do, everything shakes; La Bombonera is not for the faint of heart.

And what fans they are. "Semi-criminals," they were called by César Menotti—"El Flaco," "the slim one," the man who led Argentina to their 1978 World Cup triumph, and managed a host of clubs, including both Boca Juniors *and* River Plate—according to Simon Kuper in *Soccer Against the Enemy*. The Boca fans themselves self-identify as "*la mitad más uno*," or always "more than 50 percent" in terms of their support across Argentina, though the number is probably ten points lower than that. Still, it's a huge number, and the team has rewarded them with a lineup of trophies pretty much second to none in the world.

For a start, Boca Juniors have won the top division in Argentina 30 times. Their crest features 30 stars for all those wins, and is in the traditional blue and yellow, said to have been hijacked from the colors of a Swedish ship docked in the port in 1906 (the Swedish flag is blue and yellow). They are equal top winners of the Copa Ibarguren (Boca would lead that category of wins if they hadn't fielded ineligible players in the first final), named after Carlos Ibarguren, an academic and politician who thought that democracy was too welcoming to different points of view and should be curbed by a staunch adherence to right-wing policies.

Boca Juniors' real power comes from their international prowess, however. They attracted world attention when, in 1925, they toured Europe. Traveling across Spain, Germany, and France, they played 19 games and won 15 of them (it's worth bearing in mind that Argentine football didn't turn professional until 1931). On March 6, 1925, in the first game of that tour, they beat Celta Vigo 3–1, startling the soccer-mad Spanish with their play. With King Alfonso XIII—still six years shy of his ouster by the Second Spanish Republic—in attendance, Boca Juniors took on Real Madrid on March 22 and beat them 1–0.

It would be more than 50 years before further international victories arrived. In the meantime, Boca had some stellar decades—the 1960s saw them win four titles on the back of the staunch defensive play of Antonio Rattín, the man who was sent off in the 1966 World Cup against England, and was so angry that he sat on the red carpet laid out for the Queen in protest before two London bobbies picked him up.

In 1963 they made it all the way to the Copa Libertadores final, where they faced Pelé's Santos, of Brazil. In Rio de Janeiro's Maracanã Stadium in the first leg, Boca escaped with a creditable 3–2 defeat, creditable especially given that they were 3–0 down in under half an hour. A goal for Boca at the start of the second half of the second leg tied the tie, but almost immediately Pelé's strike partner Coutinho, who had scored the first two goals in the first leg, scored again to make it 4–3 on aggregate. Boca never recovered, and shipped one last goal to Pelé with eight minutes remaining.

Much worse was to come five years later. On Sunday, June 23, 1968, thousands of Boca Juniors fans went across town to the El Monumental Stadium to watch a midseason Superclasico against River Plate. This Superclasico is considered one of the most passionate derbies in the world, with streamers and songs and pyrotechnics and shaking stands making an unforgettable atmosphere. But on that day, the weather was cold—the game was played two days after the winter solstice—and the match itself was poor, ending 0–0 after much on-field rancor between the players and the officials. Boca fans naturally rushed to get home. There are some reports that the police harassed them, some that a lit River Plate flag rained down on the lower tiers. Whatever the case, when the fans reached a tunnel toward Gate 12, there was a crush and a stampede—the gate was locked, or partially blocked, or something. In the terrible scenes, 71 Boca fans died. La Tragedia de la Puerta 12, as it is known, is the worst disaster in Argentine sporting history. Two administrators from River Plate were convicted, then released. No one was ever found culpable. The average age of those killed was 19.

The lowest point for Boca on the field came in Buenos Aires on March 17, 1971, during a Copa Libertadores game against Sporting Cristal of Peru. Neither team had been up to much in the tournament, and with a few minutes to go the score was 2–2, a scoreline that neither team needed. The next few minutes would certainly not be what anyone wanted, either. A Boca midfielder, Roberto Rogel, was accused by Cristal players of diving in the box, and a fight started. Punches were thrown; one player was kicked so hard he needed multiple stitches; a corner flag was upended and brandished as a weapon. A full 19 players were sent off, with the two goalkeepers and Boca's Julio Meléndez left on the field (Meléndez was, oddly enough, Peruvian). Boca were thrown out of the tournament, but not before those from both sides not in hospital were taken to jail. There, they ate pizza together and helped a prostitute pay her fine. The 30-day jail sentences were commuted, and the players variously banned and exonerated. All remaining bans were rescinded on May 1 that year to celebrate Día del Trabajador—Labor Day in Argentina and around the world.

In 1977, Boca found themselves in another two-legged final against Brazilian opposition; this time, Cruzeiro. After two draws, a third game, played in neutral Montevideo, ended 0–0, and the dreaded penalties arrived.

The shootout almost started disastrously when Roberto Mouzo, who would play more than 400 times for Boca, hit the right post with the first penalty, only for the referee to order it retaken as the Cruzeiro goalkeeper had danced off his line. Few referees would have the *cojones* to make such a call, but Señor Llobregat of Venezuela was clearly a stickler. Mouzo scored at the second attempt.

No other Boca player missed, and neither did the first four Cruzeiro players. To tie the penalties and head to sudden death, Vanderley of Cruzeiro had to score, but he wandered to the ball as though not sure what to do, or maybe he was being cocky. Either way, he hit the ball to the keeper's left—and Hugo *"El Loco"* Gatti, known for sometimes joining in on defense and attack, stayed on his line and palmed it away, bringing Boca their first Copa Libertadores.

The next season, Boca would win it again. They once again faced River Plate in typically passionate affairs, with more sendings-off (three) than goals (two) across the two games. River Plate ended the second game at home with nine men and lost to two second-half goals. Boca headed to the final, where they walloped Deportivo Cali of Colombia 4–0 in the second leg to win it.

In between the two Copa Libertadores was the no-little-matter of the 1977 Intercontinental Cup, confusingly played in 1978. Usually a contest between the Libertadores winners and the European Cup winners, in 1978 Liverpool declined to play, as they had the previous year, leaving Borussia Mönchengladbach to face Boca in a two-leg final. In the first leg in March 1978, the German team led Boca 2–1 until Jorge Ribolzi equalized. Bizarrely, the second leg was not held until August 1. By then Borussia were in preseason mode, and not match-fit; Boca were three up at half-time and never looked back. It was the first of their three Intercontinental Cups: they would beat the Figo–Raúl–Guti–Roberto Carlos Real Madrid in 2000, and the Kaká–Seedorf–Shevchenko–Pirlo A.C. Milan side three years later.

But after that International Cup victory in 1978, Boca faced debts and sold a cadre of players, leading to a drought of trophies for the next 20 years. Eventually, though, there would be more Copa Libertadores victories—adding to 1977 and 1978 were four wins in the first seven years of the new century.

At the heart of so many of those triumphs was one of Boca's finest ever players, playmaker Juan Riquelme. In his first spell at the club he led them to back-to-back Copa Libertadores, in 2000 and 2001, scoring in penalty shootouts in both. Then tragedy struck for Riquelme—his 17-year old brother, Cristián, was kidnapped by armed thugs from the Buenos Aires suburb of Don Torcuato. Cristián's famous brother paid a ransom and the boy was released, but Riquelme had had enough of recession-rocked, new-century Argentina and signed for Barcelona in Spain. It didn't really work out and he was loaned to Villareal, where in 2006 he led them to the final four of the Champions League, only to have his penalty saved by Arsenal's Jens Lehmann two minutes from time in the second leg, thereby eliminating the Spanish side.

Eventually, Riquelme ended up back at Boca and in 2007 would lead them to yet another Copa Libertadores, scoring three times in the two-legged final as his team easily beat Brazilian side Gremio 5–0 on aggregate. It was Boca's sixth Copa Libertadores—a Carlos Tévez/Marcelo Delgado-led team had also won it in 2003, knocking off Robinho's Santos. The stars keep piling up for Boca—not just on their crest, but on the field. In their history they've seen the likes of Martín Palermo (236 goals), Roberto Mouzo (426 appearances), Riquelme, Tévez, Delgado, Rattín, and so many others—Roberto Cherro, Francisco Varallo, Ángel Rojas, Diego Maradona, Claudio Caniggia, Gabriel Batistuta, Rolando Schiavi—grace Boca Juniors' blue and yellow.

Yet despite all those legends of yore and millionaires of today, without six names—Paddy McCarthy, Esteban Baglietto, Santiago Sana, Alfredo Scarpatti, and Juan and Teodoro Farenga, none of this would have come to pass: a boxer from Tipperary, Ireland, and his eager students, dreaming of something.

Location	Dortmund, Germany
Established	1909
Nicknames	*Die Borussen, Die Schwarzgelben* ("The Black and Yellows"), *Der BVB*
Current stadium	Westfalenstadion, officially Signal Iduna Park (capacity 80,645)
Home colors	Black and yellow
Leading goal-scorer	Manfred Burgsmüller (1976–83), 135 goals
Most appearances	Michael Zorc (1981–98), 463 appearances

Lars Ricken: for Borussia Dortmund fans, his name is still whispered, as though a benevolent but unknowable deity once descended and touched the young man with a patina of pure grace, at just the perfect moment. It was 1997, in Munich. Running around the Olympicstadion field that day were holders Juventus and challengers Dortmund in the Champions League final. On the sleek Juve side, Zinedine Zidane was at the very height of his powers, as was Alessandro Del Piero. For Dortmund, later Aston Villa manager Paul Lambert was chasing Zidane like a dog chases a tennis ball, and Matthias Sammer and Andreas Müller, among others, did their best to upset the Italian champions.

Somehow at half-time it was 2–0 to Dortmund, and a historic upset was on the cards. Ottmar Hitzfeld, Dortmund's coach who had transformed the 1990s' Borussia side into a well-drilled and exciting team, had pulled off a masterstroke of management—Zidane had been marked out of the game by Lambert. Standing on the sidelines in a beige camelhair overcoat, collar up, Hitzfeld looked like a police detective: as Riedle scored the first of his two first-half goals, Hitzfeld calmly shook his fist like he'd just cracked a difficult case.

In the second half, though, blue-shirted Juventus (surely they'd never make that mistake again) turned on the pressure, bringing two great saves from Dortmund keeper Stefan Klos and a back-heeled goal via Del Piero. It was 2–1, and one-way traffic. How could Dortmund hold out?

In the greater scheme, though, this was just a football match: Borussia Dortmund had faced much worse. The Nazis fired Borussia's president before the war because he refused to join the party, and like many other clubs, prewar success was left behind as the club was disbanded by the triumphant Allies. It wasn't until 1948 that Borussia Dortmund reemerged—their 1907 beginnings as a breakaway club run by a too-strict Catholic priest, one Father Dewald, and their members' subsequent eff-you to Dewald and his type in renaming their club after a type of beer, were now mostly forgotten as Germany confronted its terrible recent past.

Borussia became one of the founding members of the Bundesliga in 1963. They regularly attracted huge crowds to their stadium in this industrial powerhouse town in the west of Germany. With steel and mining and beer—lots of beer *production*, that is—driving postwar growth, the team became the first German team to win a European trophy, beating Liverpool 2–1 to win the 1966 Cup Winners' Cup. But it was a false dawn for the team, and they even spent four years out of the Bundesliga in the early seventies. The eighties weren't much better, a time marked by financial strains and little success on the field. And then came Ottmar Hitzfeld.

Hitzfeld took over in 1991 and transformed the club. Though they lost the UEFA Cup final in 1993, Dortmund under Hitzfeld nevertheless won Bundesliga titles in 1995 and 1996, which led them to the Champions League final and the moment, at 2–1 and with Juventus (who had beaten them in the 1993 UEFA Cup final) pressing, that Borussia's charismatic coach called for 20-year-old Lars Ricken to join the fray.

The kid was Dortmund-born and bred, and had scored a couple of crucial goals in the games leading up to the Champions League final. Ricken said later, "I was disappointed I hadn't started—I'd been decisive for that team making it to the final." Here he was, finally, on 70 minutes, running onto the field. Ricken had spent those 70 minutes of benchwarming noticing that Juventus keeper Angelo Peruzzi came off his line a lot, far too far off his line, and less than 20 seconds after coming onto the field—"I wasn't nervous at all," Ricken later claimed—he was set free by a pass down the right-hand side of the field. Ricken swung a boot at the ball—his first touch of the game— and the ball took off into the Munich night. When it landed, it was in the back of the net, and 19 minutes later Borussia Dortmund had won the Champions League. It was a goal to grace any game, but a 20-year-old hometown kid, with his first touch, playing for a German team in Munich? Surely this was inspired by a higher power; it was Lars and the Real Goal.

In 2013, Dortmund would reach the Champions League final again, having won the double of German league and cup in 2012 (following a Bundesliga win in 2011, too). In that all-German final played in London, Dortmund would lose to Bayern Munich in a tense and often brilliant game, 2–1. But they had reestablished themselves as a top German team, under the guidance of their manager, Jürgen Klopp, a dapper and eccentric coaching wizard—he wrote his graduate degree thesis on race walking—and a man who in 2013 raged at a linesman in frustration during a Champions League game against Napoli, behavior he later said made him look "like a monkey."

Lars Ricken, for his part, was beset by injuries and up-and-down form after that final. He played 301 games for Dortmund and 16 for Germany, eventually heading to the States where he tried out for the Columbus Crew in the US, though the move didn't work out.

Lars Ricken had a replica of the Champions League trophy made, though, to commemorate his greatest moment, and he keeps it in his house.

BORUSSIA MÖNCHENGLADBACH

Location	Mönchengladbach, Germany
Established	1900
Nicknames	*Die Fohlen* ("The Foals")
Current stadium	Borussia-Park (capacity 54,010)
Home colors	White, green, and black
Leading goal-scorer	Jupp Heynckes (1963–67, 1970–78), 195 goals
Most appearances	Berti Vogts (1965–79), 419 appearances

They were famous in the 1970s because they were a great team, and because of that name: who didn't like to let the words "Borussia Mönchengladbach" roll around the mouth like a large ball bearing?

For much of their long history—they were founded in August 1900—Borussia Mönchengladbach moseyed along in obscurity, plying their trade in lower, regional divisions of German soccer. Mönchengladbach the town was hardly more celebrated. Nestled on the western edge of Germany, just 20 miles from the Dutch border, it is the birthplace of two famous Josephs, Pilates and Goebbels, but not much else of note. Once part of Prussia—hence, Borussia—Mönchengladbach sat quietly in the former German kingdom for much of the nineteenth century and the first quarter of the twentieth.

By the 1950–51 season, Borussia Mönchengladbach had made it to the Oberliga West, as high as West German teams could go before the founding of the Bundesliga. Their highest finish was sixth in 1961; otherwise, they never got above eleventh, making them a solidly mid-table team. By 1965–66, they had done enough to be accepted into the Bundesliga, along with Bayern Munich. This ascension would set the stage for a decade—the 1970s—in which the two teams set Germany and Europe alight with their football.

First it was Bayern's turn, winning three Bundesliga titles in a row—1972, 1973, and 1974—but a glance at the tables for those years is instructive: in 1972, Borussia finished third, 12 points adrift of Munich; next season, they slipped further off the pace, finishing fifth and 13 points away, and one might imagine at that point that they would settle back into mid-table safety going forward. But coach Hennes Weisweiler had created a team of young players—nicknamed "*Die Fohlen*," "the Foals"—who simply needed experience before they could truly excel. In 1974 they gained it, finishing just a point behind Bayern and, notably, winning one game more than the champions (they lost two games more, hence the second-place finish). What's more, their two games against each other that year produced 12 goals and were a pair of classic Bundesliga games.

In the first, on December 8, 1973, goals came early: after 23 minutes it was 3–2 to Bayern, though if Franz Beckenbauer's 40-yard missile at 2–1 down hadn't been turned around the post the game might have been out of reach for Mönchengladbach. Twenty minutes into the second half Bayern scored again. The final score of 4–3 highlighted the growing rivalry, and how far Mönchengladbach had come in just a few years.

In the second classic of the season, played on the final day—and after Franz Beckenbauer had received the German Footballer of the Year award right before the game (the Mönchengladbach crowd had honored him with a rousing "hip, hip, hooray!")—Mönchengladbach announced that they were ready to take over from Bayern. It's true that Munich had already won the league, but no one expected Mönchengladbach to be 4–0 up at half-time. The second goal in particular was instructive, with Allan Simonsen dancing past a stationary and starting-to-look-a-bit-past-it Beckenbauer as though he wasn't there before squeezing the ball home for 2–0. (That said, Beckenbauer seldom deigned to muddy his shorts by attempting something as gauche and low-class as a tackle.) A few minutes later, the clearest penalty in the history of all football was denied by a referee who must have been watching a different game—legendary Munich keeper Sepp Maier almost removed both legs of Borussia's Jupp Heynckes in a sliding tackle, but nothing was given. No matter—by half-time Heynckes had added to Rainer Bonhof's volley to make it 4–0.

The game ended 5–0, and the following season, Bayern found themselves languishing in tenth place. Borussia Mönchengladbach won the Bundesliga by a solid six-point margin (in the two-points-for-a-win era). On the back of their second-place finish the previous season, they entered the 1975 UEFA Cup full of confidence.

Confident enough to win it, too, while scoring freely and often. Their aggregate wins included 6–2 over Olympic Lyonnais, 9–2 over Real Zaragoza, 4–1 over Banik Ostrava, 4–1 over fellow German side F.C. Köln in the semifinals, and after a 0–0 draw in the first leg of the final against F.C. Twente of the Netherlands, Mönchengladbach drove 100 miles north for the second leg in Enschede. F.C. Twente probably wished they hadn't: Twente were 4–0 down at home after an hour, and the game ended 5–1 to the German champions. Once again Heynckes netted, this time a hat-trick, and Simonsen scored the other two.

It was a devastating performance, which set Mönchengladbach up for its next two seasons, where they won the Bundesliga back to back to make it three in a row—and it was almost four. The end of the 1977–78 season was one of the most extraordinary in the Bundesliga, or any league for that matter. Entering the final day, Mönchengladbach and F.C. Köln were tied for first place, but Köln had a better goal difference (of ten goals). Somehow, Mönchengladbach won their final game 12–0 over the other Borussia, Dortmund—but Köln also scored a hatful, beating F.C. St. Pauli 5–0.

Mönchengladbach went to the European Cup on the back of their Bundesliga exploits, though they never quite managed to win it. In 1975–76 they were pipped on away goals by Real Madrid in the quarterfinals; Madrid were knocked out in turn by eventual winners Bayern Munich, who were in the competition because they'd won the previous one (and the one before that). The following season, Mönchengladbach made it two steps further, to the final, via a very late goal by Hans-Jürgen Wittkamp in the home second leg against Dynamo Kiev (the tie ended 2–1 on aggregate). In the final they faced English champions Liverpool in the Olympic Stadium in Rome.

And what a Liverpool team it was! Managed by avuncular Bob Paisley, the lineup included Ray Clemence in goal, Emlyn Hughes at center back, Ray Kennedy, Terry McDermott, and Jimmy Case in midfield, and curly-permed Kevin Keegan leading the line. This was also the peak of Borussia Mönchengladbach's team, captained as it was by Berti Vogts, with Rainer Bonhof, Uli Stielike and Horst Wohlers in midfield, and Simonsen and Heynckes up front. The game promised to be a classic, and so it turned out. In an era when so many European Cup finals were tight, single-goal affairs, this one sparkled.

Early on a bobbling, long-range shot from Bonhof skipped over Clemence and clanged against the post; a few minutes later, McDermott made a neat run into the box to score the first goal. Mönchengladbach plugged away, and a few minutes into the second half they scored a cracker of a goal from Simonsen, who spanked a shot across Clemence and into the top right-hand corner. For the next few minutes it was all Mönchengladbach, but they couldn't take their chances—including a one-on-one, Stielike vs. Clemence, in which the keeper made one of his best ever saves at the feet of the striker. Once Liverpool went in the lead from a Tommy Smith header, Mönchengladbach couldn't get themselves back into the game; it ended 3–1, and was Liverpool's first European Cup triumph. For Mönchengladbach it was more frustration, made worse the following season by coming up against Liverpool once again in the same tournament, only this time in the semifinals. Mönchengladbach won the first leg 2–1, but back in Liverpool, a team that now boasted Kenny Dalglish in place of Keegan scored three unanswered goals to head to the final (which they'd win once again).

Liverpool declined to enter the Intercontinental Cup in 1977, so Mönchengladbach took their place. In the first leg, in March, they got a creditable 2–2 draw in Buenos Aires against Boca Juniors, but the second leg was delayed until August and found Mönchengladbach in preseason mode: Boca won easily, 3–0.

After the final-day exploits in 1978 against Köln, Mönchengladbach had to settle for both second place and entry into the 1978–79 UEFA Cup—but no matter, as they won it. In the first leg, played against Red Star in front of 87,000 fans in Belgrade, Mönchengladbach earned a creditable 1–1 draw, and back in Germany, though only half as many fans showed up, an early Simonsen penalty won the tie and the trophy.

Since those heady 1970s, Borussia Mönchengladbach have become a solid, if unspectacular, Bundesliga side. In 1999 and 2007 they were relegated, though they bounced back to the Bundesliga quickly both times. They continue to breathe the fumes of the 1970s, though, and for many European football fans of a certain age, the words "Borussia Mönchengladbach" remain synonymous with thrilling nights of tense, dramatic soccer.

Location	Brugge, Belgium
Established	1891
Nicknames	*Blauw-Zwart* ("Blue-Black"), Club, FCB
Current stadium	Jan Breydelstadion (capacity 29,042)
Home colors	Blue and black
Leading goal-scorer	Raoul Lambert (1962–80), 213 goals
Most appearances	Franky Van der Elst (1984–99), 466 appearances

I f you ever find yourself in the town of Brugge, in northwest Belgium, a word of advice: probably best not to mention Liverpool Football Club.

Brugge is a pretty medieval port town, veined with canals like Venice or Amsterdam. It's also home to two soccer teams that play in the same stadium, the Jan Breydel; one, Cercle Brugge K.S.V., has won three league titles but has also spent plenty of time in the Belgian second division. The other, Club Brugge K.V., is an old, old team, established in either 1890, or—and here's a controversy—1891. Club Brugge has won a lot of league titles—13—but to fans of European football, Club Brugge represents the 1970s, and losing.

The mid-1970s was a time of dominance for Brugge; maybe it had something to do with their name change. For much of the century they had been R.F.C. Brugeois, but in 1972 they assumed the Flemish version of their name, Club Brugge Koninklijke Voetbalvereniging (the last two snappy words—"Royal Football Association"—refer to their "royal" status, conferred upon Belgian clubs only after an appropriately long history). That 1972–73 season, Brugge won the Belgian league for the first time since 1920, and by seven points, which is a lot when it's only two points for a win. On the back of that victory they entered the European Cup, where in the first round they thrashed Maltese side Floriana 8–0 at home, only to be knocked out by Swiss club Basel in the next round after an astonishing second-leg reversal, 6–4. The game stood at 4–4 on 68 minutes, until Ottmar Hitzfeld—who would go on to manage Borussia Dortmund to its Champions League victory in 1997—completed his hat-trick with two goals in the last 20 minutes.

There would be a three-year gap before Brugge won the league once again—in the meantime, in the 1974–75 season, they managed to squeak into UEFA Cup places, pipping Beerschot by one point to get the final spot. It proved to be a very lucky point, given that they made it all the way to the final. The campaign to reach it was filled with exciting moments. Brugge lost 4–3 in Lyon in the first round, first leg, only to win 3–0 at home to advance; in the second round, they lost 3–0 in Ipswich but won 4–0 at home, the final, winning goal coming with three minutes remaining. The third round featured two undramatic 1–0 victories over Roma, but in the quarterfinals Brugge overcame A.C. Milan. With the tie at 2–2 on aggregate, in Italy, Dirk Sanders scored for Brugge with 16 minutes to go to send the Belgian side through. And it would take an own goal by Hamburg's Manfred Kaltz, with five minutes to go in Belgium, for Brugge to make it to the final, where they faced Liverpool.

Being part of such a dramatic route to a final can sometimes mean one's "name is on the trophy," and surely Brugge fans must have felt this was the case when in the first leg they found themselves two up inside 12 minutes, and in Liverpool to boot. But soccer is a cruel game, and in the space of five second-half minutes, and despite the British commentator stating that it was "not Liverpool's night," the Merseyside team scored three times into the Kop end, the last a Kevin Keegan penalty after an Ashley Young-style swan dive outside the box by Liverpool's left winger Steve Heighway. A last-minute chance to equalize was spurned by Brugge, but by then all eyes had turned to the repeat game in Belgium.

That second leg was similarly dramatic. Brugge's Raoul Lambert, who'd scored the first goal in Liverpool, put the Belgian side ahead at home after just 11 minutes from the penalty spot after another poor refereeing decision. Four minutes later, Kevin Keegan once again delivered for Liverpool, this time striking home with great power after a pass from an indirect free kick.

It was hard on Brugge after their incredible run, but two years later they had the chance to exact revenge when once again they were paired with Liverpool in a European final, although this time it was the ultimate prize, the European Cup.

Brugge's route to the final was less dramatic in early rounds this time, but as the competition progressed, once again the Belgian side did everything they could to give their fans heart failure. Lambert delivered by scoring with 20 minutes to go against Atlético Madrid in Spain to get Brugge through to the semifinals on away goals, where they met Juventus. That semifinal tie required extra time in Belgium, with legendary Brugge winger René Vandereycken scoring with four minutes left to get Brugge to the final; a clear penalty for the Italian side was denied with seconds left to ensure the victory for Brugge, and heartburn for their fans.

Once again, Liverpool awaited, and Brugge would be without their key goal-scorer, Lambert. Played at Wembley Stadium in London, the final would be a terrible disappointment for Brugge fans. A one-way-traffic kind of match was graced by a fabulous finish by Kenny Dalglish just after the hour mark, followed by a celebration that included him hurdling an advertising hoarding, which was no mean feat given that he's barely 5 feet 8 inches tall. Brugge's lack of ambition leached the game of much of its drama; there would be only one winner, and one goal was all that was ever going to be needed.

In fact, those were the years of 1–0 European Cup finals— between 1972 and 1984, there were nine of them. In Belgrade and Glasgow and London and Munich and Madrid and Paris and Rotterdam and Athens and Brussels, this traveling show of what should have been the greatest games ever played tended to be a series of dull, undramatic affairs.

As for Brugge, well, they knew how to win with drama in qualifying rounds, but in the ultimate test—that second final against Liverpool in particular—they bored their fans, as so many other teams in the late seventies did. Since then, they have won eight Belgian championships, but in Europe they've done little. Until that changes they will be the 1970s' club of almost-glory, the team in all white watching the team in all red pass shiny trophies from hand to happy hand.

Location	Cardiff, Wales
Established	1899 (as Riverside A.F.C.)
Nicknames	The Bluebirds
Current stadium	Cardiff City Stadium (capacity 28,000)
Home colors	Red and black
Leading goal-scorer	Len Davies (1920–31), 181 goals
Most appearances	Phil Dwyer (1972–85), 573 appearances

Let us now compare two painters: Alisher Apsalyamov, a 23-year-old from Kazakhstan, and Walter Bartley Wilson, a Bristolian lithographer and artist who died in 1954. The first is said to have helped paint Cardiff City's stadium in the summer of 2013, all in order to gain "work experience." It's important to note, however, that Mr. Apsalyamov is good friends with U-Jiun Tan, one of the eleven children of Vincent Tan, Malaysia's ninth richest man and chief shareholder owner of Cardiff City Football Club.

Walter Bartley Wilson, on the other hand, knew no billionaires. He was born with a disability that left him having to walk with sticks, and yet his love of sport led him to establish what would become Cardiff City Football Club, way back in 1899. By 1910, a century before the Malaysian takeover, Wilson did entreat a local aristocrat, Lord Ninian Edward Crichton-Stuart, to underwrite the club's expenses, and as a thank-you, Cardiff City, newly professional, named their new stadium Ninian Park.

And so Cardiff City set out on the long road of their history as the Bluebirds, playing in blue and white. Sadly, within five years of turning pro, the club was left without its benefactor when Lieutenant-Colonel Lord Ninian Edward Crichton-Stuart of the 6th Welsh Territorials, as he now was, in attempting to save his close friend, one Major R. C. Browning, near La Bassée in northern France, took a German sniper's bullet to the head, dying instantly.

The club persevered, and by 1924 they had persevered enough to gain the dubious distinction of being the team who lost the league by the smallest margin possible. That year, the great mid-1920s' Huddersfield Town side started their stellar run of First Division championships (they would win three in a row). In 1923–24, they scored 60 goals and let in 33; Cardiff City, for their part, scored one goal more, but also let in one goal more. This equates to a goal average—goals scored divided by goals conceded, which is how the league was settled until 1976, rather than the goal difference used since—of 1.818 for Town, and 1.794 for City. No league before or since has been so close.

In 1925, Cardiff lost the FA Cup final to a single Sheffield United goal, but two years later they won their first major trophy, beating Arsenal 1–0 on April 23, 1927, at Wembley, to win the cup (they are still the only non-English side to win it). Cardiff had been in the Football League for a scant seven years, "Bluebirds" playing in blue and white.

Nothing much came to them after that, as they bounced between (usually lower) divisions, until a fine team was put together by coach Jimmy Scoular in the late 1960s. In 1968, Cardiff City found themselves in the semifinal of the European Cup Winners' Cup, having won the Welsh Cup year after year. They faced a second leg at home against Hamburg (the first leg, in Germany, had ended a very creditable 1–1). This was their greatest moment since 1927, and the second-tier team, led by 19-year-old boy-mountain John Toshack up front, trailed 2–1 with 12 minutes to go. The heaving Ninian Park thousands—some 43,180, to be precise—chorused "Cardiff! Cardiff!", a distinct Welsh lilt to their cries. Brian Harris, the Cardiff captain, did what captains should do and scored with a glancing header to tie the tie. Young Cardiff fans ran on to the field to celebrate.

It was to no avail. One and a half minutes into stoppage time, a speculative shot by Uwe Seeler—who two years earlier had been the subject of one of the most iconic soccer photographs ever taken, hanging his head as he walked off the field having seen his Germany side lose to England in the 1966 World Cup final—was horribly mangled by Robert Wilson in the Cardiff goal, and somehow the ball ended up in the back of the Ninian Park net. Cardiff were out, but what history had been created in that European night in the Welsh capital. (The next year, in the same competition, Cardiff City would beat Real Madrid 1–0 at Ninian Park, before losing 2–0 in Spain.)

But British football pays scant homage to history. Consider recent events. After 80 years as the team from Maine Road, since 2003 Manchester City have played at the Etihad Stadium, named after the Abu Dhabi airline. For even longer, 93 years, Arsenal graced Highbury in north London, but since 2006 they have played at the Emirates Stadium, named after Emirates Airlines of Dubai. Hull City A.F.C. (Association Football Club), so called since their founding in 1904, may become Hull Tigers, if a "rebranding" by owners Assem and Ehab Allam goes through; Assem said the word "City" was "common" and "lousy," hence the requested change.

And so to Cardiff City. New owner Vincent Tan changed their colors to red shirts and black shorts for the 2013 season, their first in the English Premiership, after more than a century in blue. Their new club crest, instituted on June 6, 2012, relegated the bluebird to a measly area at the bottom so that a large red dragon could dominate over the words "Fire & Passion." But fans are no respecters of history, either: when Ryan Giggs, a few days shy of his fortieth birthday, ran onto Cardiff's pitch for his first ever Premiership game in his home town, the Manchester United player was lustily booed.

In 2013, Alisher Apsalyamov was appointed Head of Recruitment for Cardiff City, replacing Iain Moody, manager Dave Malkay's right-hand man, and the guy who had attracted and signed a number of quality players as the Cardiff squad entered the top flight for the first time since 1962. (Vincent Tan subsequently fired Dave Malkay, too, replacing him with former Manchester United supersub Ole

Gunnar Solskjaer, though the Norwegian couldn't save City from relegation straight back to the Championship.) Apsalyamov, the young man who had painted the walls of a stadium to gain work experience, was, for a few months at least (he stepped down after it was revealed he didn't have working papers), in charge of buying and selling players for a Premiership team, a team that has played at Cardiff City Stadium—not Ninian Park—since 2009.

Location	Glasgow, Scotland
Established	1887
Nicknames	The Bhoys, The Hoops, The Celts
Current stadium	Celtic Park (capacity 60,355)
Home colors	Green and white
Leading goal-scorer	Jimmy McGrory (1922–37), 472 goals
Most appearances	Billy McNeill (1957–75), 790 appearances

Is there a team in world soccer with a more recognizable kit than Celtic F.C. of Scotland? Looking like a mint confection, those green and white hoops are known throughout football. But is there a team in world soccer more associated with sectarian differences than "Catholic" Celtic? Their archrivals in Glasgow, "Protestant" Rangers F.C., is the answer, but it's a close-run thing.

So it goes in Scottish football. The two top teams for most of Scottish football history, who between them have won 84 percent of championships contested since the league began in 1890, are also starkly divided along sectarian lines.

It's hard to get a grasp of the domination of Celtic and Rangers in Scotland until one looks at the history of the Scottish league. From 1890 to 2012, when Rangers were forced into the lowest division after bankruptcy, either Celtic or Rangers has finished in the top two spots every season except four. In three of those years, Rangers finished third (1897, 1903, and 1960). Only in 1964–65 did neither Celtic nor Rangers finish in the top three, and even so Celtic won the Scottish Cup and Rangers won the Scottish League Cup, beating—who else?—Celtic in the final. There is surely no other footballing nation where this kind of dominance exists, and this alone might account for the fierceness of the rivalry.

But since their inceptions, Celtic and Rangers have also defined themselves as much by their religious and cultural differences as by their efforts to garner footballing supremacy. So the story of the "Old Firm," as the rivalry is known, is necessarily one of great history and constant achievement marred by bigotry and exclusion, glory tarnished by smallness.

In *The Ball Is Round*, David Goldblatt describes the formation of Celtic by a Marist priest, in 1887, as not just "to alleviate poverty in Glasgow's East End parishes," as Celtic F.C.'s own website has it, but also as "an instrument for keeping Catholic football players in a Catholic institution," and that pretty much sums it up. Irish immigrants to the bustling city of Glasgow, and Scots of Irish descent, gravitated toward Brother Walfrid's new club, and the pronunciation of their name by Gaelic speakers (as "CELL-tik") overcame the original sound ("KELL-tik"). Taking players from another Irish-Scots team, Hibernian, and being able to draw upon the estimated quarter of a million Glasgow-area Irish-descended Scots, Celtic quickly won their first set of championships, four in all, in the last decade of the nineteenth century. The first, in 1893, came some months after their move to Celtic Park, which remains their stadium. None of these victories came in the green and white hoops, but by 1903 the shirt design was in place, and that decade also produced six championships in a row, from 1905 to 1910. 1909 also saw one of the worst examples of Celtic–Rangers violence, when a second Scottish Cup final replay, played on April 17, ended, at full-time, 1–1. Celtic players, expecting/agitating for extra time, stayed on the field while Rangers players trudged off. The resulting impasse led to an extraordinary riot at Rangers' Hampden Park stadium in which parts of the stadium were set ablaze. Neither team won the cup that year, but not because anyone else won it—this is Scottish football, after all.

Back and forth went the two teams, dominating this decade, dominating that. Celtic owned the teens, winning in 1910, 1914–17, and 1919; then, a barren spell: they only won the league five times before 1966, though in 1957 they won the Scottish League Cup, beating Rangers 7–1 in the final, leading to Celtic fans singing, to the tune of Harry Belafonte's 1957 hit "Islands in the Sun," "Oh, Hampden in the sun, Celtic 7, Rangers 1."

By the mid-1960s a great team had finally appeared, helmed by the legendary manager Jock Stein. Domination in Scotland be damned, this team was going to excel in European football, too, bringing Britain its first ever European Cup triumph. The team, almost all of whom were born within shouting distance of Celtic Park, were a skillful, attacking side—they have since been likened to the great Hungarian attack-minded sides of the 1950s, as well as to the later Total Football of early 1970s' Netherlands. In the 1967 European Cup final, they faced a dour Inter Milan side. Celtic's going a goal down early meant the *catenaccio*-loving Italians could basically put eleven men on their own goal line, but Celtic were not to be thwarted. The "Lisbon Lions," as they came to be known, finally broke through in the Portuguese capital after 63 minutes through their full back, Tommy Gemmell. Celtic subsequently laid siege to the Inter goal, and got their reward with just seven minutes to go when a shot by Bobby Murdoch was deflected by Steve Chalmers and finally got past Giuliano Sarti in the Italian goal.

Once again, crazy Celtic fans intervened, and though the post-whistle pitch invasion was without violence, captain Billy McNeill received the trophy after an armed escort out of the ground and back in again to the podium. Stein spoke for many soccer fans that night when he said, "Winning was important, aye, but it was the way that we won that has filled me with satisfaction. We did it by playing football; pure, beautiful, inventive football. Inter played right into our hands; it's so sad to see such gifted players shackled by a system that restricts their freedom to think and to act. Our fans would never accept that sort of sterile approach."

Celtic would reach the final of the tournament again in 1970, but lost to Feyenoord, ironically at Inter Milan's home ground, the San Siro. And though they dominated the Scottish league in the 1970s and 1980s (winning eleven titles in those two decades), crowd trouble was never far away—1909 wasn't the only year for a good old Celtic–Rangers riot at Hampden Park.

In 1980, as the Celtic players, who had just won the Scottish Cup 1–0, went up to receive the trophy, down on the field their jubilant fans celebrated, having breached lax security. By the time the defeated Rangers players were being handed their losers' trinkets, a full-scale war had broken out, sparked when one young Celtic fan kicked a ball into the Rangers' goal. Massed ranks of Rangers fans scaled the fences and charged retreating Celtic supporters, only for Celtic fans to regroup and charge back. Hand-to-hand combat ensued; bottles (empty, which didn't help) and cans (full, of either beer or something that was once beer) were thrown; a mere dozen police officers stood between the braying hordes until more on horseback came to help, wielding large white batons (all the rest were outside, where the trouble usually happened). One of the horses was called Ballantrae, was notably white, and was ridden by a 22-year-old policewoman called Elaine Mudie. A gray-haired man, at least 60 years old, was seen to fling a bottle toward the Celtic fans, though most of the fighters were no more than kids. Injured fans were laid out in the goals and goalmouth; one fan was trampled by a police horse. The Scottish commentator Archie McPherson likened the scene to *Apocalypse Now*, saying, "Let's not kid ourselves, these supporters hate each other."

Since then, things have calmed down a bit, thanks to a subsequent ban on all alcohol at Old Firm games, and a tempering of passions that has naturally come from the suburbification of soccer throughout Britain and elsewhere. There is still trouble—a game in May 1999, at Celtic Park, featured missiles and pitch invasions—and there is still tension. But the old bonds of sectarianism are less prevalent (Rangers finally signed Catholic players, for a start). All that's left is a kind of torpor in Scottish soccer, the back-and-forth of Celtic–Rangers, and sometimes it seems the best we can hope for is for Celtic to lose a game to Inverness Caledonian Thistle, as they did in 1998, leading to the now-immortal *Sun* newspaper headline, "Super Cali Go Ballistic, Celtic Are Atrocious."

CENTRAL COAST MARINERS

Location	Central Coast Region, Australia
Established	2004
Nicknames	The Mariners
Current stadium	Bluetongue Stadium (capacity 20,059)
Home colors	Yellow and navy
Leading goal-scorer	Matt Simon (2006–12, 2013–), 40 goals
Most appearances	John Hutchinson (2005–), 217 appearances

A good commentator can make or break a soccer game. Great moments in soccer commentary abound through the years: Ken Wolstenholme's magical line "There's people on the pitch, they think it's all over . . . it is now!" from the 1966 World Cup final; Barry Davies' "Interesting . . . very interesting. Oh, look at his face, just look at his face!," referring to Francis Lee's visage after he scored a goal for Derby County against Manchester City on April 1, 1975; even Andrés Cantor's ridiculous "*Goooooooolllll!*" call can still bring chills of excitement.

And then there are the "color men," sidekicks who revel in their own loquaciousness, even if what they say often makes scant sense. Currently, there are two high priests of such lofty language. The first among equals is Geordie Ray Hudson, of beIN Sport, who has been known to say things like "Lionel Messi, genius of geniuses—he's like Doctor Spock, he's out of his Vulcan mind . . . running like he's got a food mixer down his shorts and it's set to 'Beat.'" The other is a man heard less often on US TV, but his analysis and flights of fancy have elevated a sport in a country that has altogether too much else to think about besides football.

The sport of soccer in Australia lags well behind rugby league and union, cricket, and even that excuse for the shortest possible shorts, Australian Rules football. The team that has most personified the attempt to make soccer relevant is Central Coast Mariners, who were founded in 2004, a couple of years before the Australian A-League got off the ground.

Theirs is not a glamour franchise. For a start, that name. Though they represent an actual area of New South Wales, which starts about 50 miles north of Sydney, there were other—some might say, more poetic—options available to them from names of towns in the area. They could have been Woy Woy United (and managed by lisping England manager, Roy "Woy" Hodgson?); the Brooklyn Nets, after a town on the Hawkesbury River; or even, as homage to Sheffield Wednesday, Tumbi Umbi Tuesday (though the Mariners have inked a backroom deal with Wednesday's archrivals in England, Sheffield United). But their limited imagination when it comes to their name hasn't stopped this small club being the best overall team since the A-League began.

The Mariners reached the inaugural A-League final, where they were narrowly defeated by Sydney F.C., 1–0. Sydney, unlike the Mariners, have brought in a host of former superstar players, such as Dwight Yorke, Benito Carbone, Juninho Paulista, Kazuyoshi Miura, and Alessandro Del Piero, but it's the Mariners who've consistently built solid, winning teams (the Mariners did sign former Chelsea and Man United keeper Mark Bosnich, but he doesn't really count).

In 2008, the Mariners won their first major Australian trophy, taking the Premiership title, though they would again lose in the Finals Series, this time to local rivals the Newcastle Jets. Losing yet another final in 2011, this time to the Brisbane Roar on penalties, they would nevertheless win the Premiership again in 2012, and the following season the Mariners would finally win the biggest prize of all. In the A-League Finals Series, the Mariners beat the Western Sydney Wanderers with two goals either side of half-time.

The future of the Central Coast Mariners, and the A-League, seems bright, and that's saying something in a country that has not fully embraced soccer. Before the A-League, Australia had had only the National Soccer League, which never captured the imagination of a sport-saturated country. And that might be because the National Soccer League didn't have the other high priest of linguistic excess, Andy Harper.

Harper is one of the color commentators on A-League broadcasts, and his knowledge of the game is exemplary. Even better, he's been known to throw in Ray Hudson-like elocutions. In describing an overelaborate player, Harper was heard to describe his efforts as featuring "more flicks than an eighties hair salon," and when describing a weak attempted block, Harper said the defender was "tidy on the ball, but he tackles like a turnstile." Every league deserves some Ray Hudson, and some Andy Harper; and in the latter, Australia has a beacon of sense and nonsense who might just make soccer a spectacle out of a sport.

Location	London, England
Established	1905
Nicknames	The Blues, the Pensioners
Current stadium	Stamford Bridge (capacity 41,623)
Home colors	Blue and white
Leading goal-scorer	Frank Lampard (2001–), 210 goals
Most appearances	Ron Harris (1961–80), 795 appearances

From a man with a fat everything to a man with a fat wallet, the history of Chelsea Football Club has often been about excess.

The man with the fat everything was Willy "Fatty" Foulke, a 300-pound goalkeeper who played for Chelsea in its earliest years and who inspired the derisory chant heard all over British soccer grounds, "Who Ate All The Pies?"

The man with the fat wallet is Roman Abramovich, one of the richest men in Russia. Not only does he own the world's biggest yacht—the quarter-of-a-billion-dollar *Eclipse*—but in 2003 he took over Chelsea Football Club. He was not the first to splash the cash at Stamford Bridge. The club has always spent big money: witness the £10,000 they paid for Scottish center forward Hughie Gallacher in 1930 (the equivalent of about a million dollars now, and that was in extremely tough times). Abramovich has spent more than a billion dollars on players for Chelsea. And what has it bought them, all this money? Well, for about a century before Abramovich, it bought them just about zilch.

By the time the nineteenth century turned into the twentieth, the

Football League had been in existence for 12 years, but it still featured no teams from the capital, London. A businessman called Henry Augustus "Gus" Mears had bought a piece of land called Stamford Bridge in West London in 1896, in the heart of what was then, and still is, considered a cosmopolitan part of the city. By late 1904, Mears was ready to walk away from his grand plan for a London soccer team when his colleague, Fred Parker, was supposedly bitten by Mears's dog, and his refusal to make a fuss convinced Mears to have the courage of his convictions. If that story sounds a bit like management guru fodder, no matter—by May 1905 Chelsea had been elected to the Second Division, even though they had yet to play a game.

It was hardly the start of a shining history of regular trophies. Despite spending oodles of cash on players like Hughie Gallacher (a man so broken by allegations that he'd harmed his son, Matthew, during a family argument, that he threw himself in front of a train in June 1957), the best Chelsea could do was to draw massive crowds. During their first season 67,000 showed up to watch them play Manchester United; 30 years later, a staggering 82,905 attended a local derby with Arsenal, a number that is yet to be surpassed in English league football. But it would be 1955 before they won their first championship, and only then because they stopped buying difficult stars like Gallacher and opted instead for solid professionals. It paid off: a 3–0 home win against Sheffield Wednesday gave Chelsea its first taste of real success.

The following season, they finished 16th, just four points shy of relegation.

By the time the 1960s came around, Chelsea the place was outstripping Chelsea the team in terms of glamour. Free-scoring Chelsea product Jimmy Greaves had been sold to A.C. Milan in 1961—his 132 goals (100 of them before he was 21) in just 169 games for Chelsea wasn't enough to keep him in London when similarly swank Milan came calling. On the back of his departure, Chelsea were relegated in 1962, having won just nine of 42 games, though they would come back in 1963. Chelsea the place was the home of Mary Quant and the "Chelsea Look," the Kings Road fashion boutiques featuring colorful prints on dresses whose hemlines stopped somewhere above the knee. The players, in their turn, wore their sideburns long and their kipper ties short, and the swagger morphed into a kind of success on the field. Chelsea finished third in the league in 1970 and won the FA Cup that same year after a replay against Leeds United, then *the* team to beat in England.

On the back of that victory, the swinging Chelsea team of leather boots—for fashion, as well as for kicking a football—entered the Cup Winners' Cup. Breezing through the early rounds, they came up against reigning Cup Winners' Cup holders Manchester City in the semifinal, winning both legs 1–0. As a reward, they faced Real Madrid in the final in May 1971.

After a tense first half in the final, which was held in Greece, Chelsea took the lead via Peter Osgood 10 minutes into the second half, only for Ignacio Zoco to equalize with one of the last kicks of the game. Two days later Chelsea triumphed in the replay, 2–1, on goals by John Dempsey and that man Osgood. It was Chelsea's first European trophy.

The heady days didn't last. In 1974–75 they would, as in 1962, win just nine games and be relegated, this time for two seasons; and in 1978–79, they managed to win just five games and finish bottom once again. By this time, too, the Chelsea brand of swinging swagger had been replaced by the specter of the Chelsea Headhunters, a hooligan gang who terrorized England up and down. (They were not above leaving a calling card on victims, nor espousing racist views; legend has it that one unfortunate American bartender was almost killed in the mid-eighties because he was "taking British jobs.") With all that going on, it's probably no surprise that on May 5, 1982, just 6,009 fans attended a local derby at Stamford Bridge between Chelsea and Leyton Orient. The club was hemorrhaging money as well as cachet, and in 1982 they were bought by British businessman Ken Bates for the grand total of £1. Hardly beloved by the Chelsea faithful at any point in his reign, his Chelsea team struggled to an 18th-place finish in the

Second Division in his first year in charge, a late goal by Clive Walker in the penultimate game helping to keep them from the drop.

Chelsea returned to the First Division in the 1984–85 season, and then only for three seasons, suffering yet another relegation, this time in bizarre circumstances. The league had decided that the least bad team in the relegation zone of the First Division should play the champions of the Second Division in a two-leg playoff. Chelsea were that best of the worst; Middlesbrough the best of the lower division. The first game in the playoffs ended 2–0 to Middlesbrough, and back at a Stamford Bridge that still featured a running track wide enough to accommodate, bizarrely, parked cars behind one of the goals, Chelsea got a goal back in the first half. But they barely looked like getting a second, and they were relegated once again.

The following season Chelsea garnered 99 points in winning the Second Division and headed back to the top tier, where they have stayed ever since. The 1990s were, like all decades it seems, an up-and-down time for the club, and featured such abominations as Ken Bates banning legendary Peter Osgood from Stamford Bridge because he dared to criticize the club's drift. On the plus side, at least Bates had kept Stamford Bridge for the club, the rights to the stadium having somehow found their way to a bunch of property developers; it took Bates years to fight them off. And in 1996 he brought diminutive Italian genius Gianfranco Zola to Stamford Bridge.

It's hard to quantify the effect Zola had upon Chelsea and its fans. The tiny man played 229 times in seven years, but that figure does little justice to the love he inspired. Zola led Chelsea to FA Cup wins in 1997 (in which Roberto Di Matteo, who would go on to lead the club to Champions League glory in 2012, scored from 30 yards after 42 seconds) and in 2000; and to the Cup Winners' Cup in 1998, the final of which Zola didn't start due to injury. But here is how legends are made: just 20 seconds after coming on, in the second half, Zola chased a lobbed ball through the middle. Finding himself one on one with the Stuttgart keeper, he did the unthinkable—instead of slotting the ball past the goalie, or trying to go around him to score, Zola blasted the ball from just inside the box, high and hard and into the top right-hand corner. It was the kind of strike that makes fans go utterly crazy and love a player unconditionally for the rest of time. Zola hadn't been on the field a minute; it was the only goal of the game.

That Chelsea team of the late 1990s and early 2000s flickered and won in the odd cup competition, but it never quite took off. It wouldn't be until 2004, a year after Abramovich bought Bates out for a reported £140 million, that Chelsea finally won the championship once more and firmly established themselves as one of the top clubs in Europe. By then, the Premiership had been going for more than a decade and the cash had been rolling in. Chelsea joined Arsenal and Manchester United as the dominant teams when the big money hit—since its inception in 1992, the Premiership has been won by one of those three teams every year except two (Blackburn Rovers in 1995, and Manchester City in 2012).

Chelsea's mid-2000s' dominance came via a fast and muscular team coached by José Mourinho. Self-described as "the Special One," he had burst onto the English football scene not with Chelsea but via a 50-yard celebratory run down the Old Trafford touchline when his team, Porto, scored in the last minute to knock Manchester United out of the 2004 Champions League. (Porto would go on to win the tournament.) Brought to Stamford Bridge after that triumph, and despite former coach Claudio Ranieri having taken the team to second in the league and the semifinals of the Champions League, Mourinho immediately brought in a host of new players. Gone was Zola, but already in place were Joe Cole, Frank Lampard, John Terry, and Claude Makelele—Mourinho added Peter Cech in goal, Arjen Robben on either wing, and, most significantly, a mountain of a player from the Ivory Coast by the name of Didier Drogba up front.

That first season with all these pieces in place, 2004–05, was no contest—Chelsea won the league by 12 points over Arsenal. Drogba muscled his way to goal after goal, and Lampard chipped in with a bunch from midfield; Cech was pretty much unbeatable at the back, standing as he did behind the stingiest defense imaginable. They lost one game all season and amassed a staggering 95 points, to this day not bettered in the Premiership era. Opponents scored only 15 goals against Chelsea, also a record. In Europe, though, they lost in the Champions League semifinals to Liverpool, who went on to win the tournament. The following season, Chelsea won the Premiership once again, this time by a mere 12 points over Manchester United. They let in seven more goals than the previous season in losing a staggering five whole games, but once again failed in Europe, being knocked out of the Champions League early by Barcelona.

Mourinho, despite these triumphs at home, had only one season left. That one featured injuries and what he called "survival football," but losing the league to Manchester United, and going out once again to Liverpool in the semifinals of the Champions League, spelled the end for the Portuguese manager. Abramovich had unchosen the Special One.

So began a managerial merry-go-round as dizzying as any in the recent history of professional football. Treating the club like a man treats his choice of necktie, over the next six years Abramovich hired and fired Avram Grant, Luiz Felipe Scolari, Ray Wilkins (caretaker for one game), Guus Hiddink (caretaker for 22), Carlo Ancelotti, André Villas-Boas, Roberto Di Matteo, and Rafael Benitez, then finally rehiring José Mourinho in 2013. It's a ridiculous list—ridiculous in the level of talent he managed to attract, and ridiculous that such talent was summarily thrown out on a whim.

Perhaps the worst treatment of all was saved for Roberto Di Matteo. Ascending to the footstool below Abramovich's throne in March 2012, he steered Chelsea all the way to the Champions League final, but no good deed goes unpunished in the Roman world.

Chelsea had been to the final once before, when Avram Grant led them to Moscow in 2008, only to lose the final against Manchester United. Doing so in a town where Abramovich keeps a home, and in such comical circumstances, was clearly not going to keep Grant in a job. That final featured Didier Drogba getting sent off during extra time for slapping United's Nemanja Vidić, and then a penalty shootout in which Chelsea captain John Terry slipped as he took what should have been the winning kick. The ball skewed against the post and harmlessly away, Terry cried—much to the amusement of everyone not in Chelsea blue—and United went on to lift the trophy when Nicolas Anelka's kick was saved by van der Saar in the United goal.

The Champions League was becoming a bugbear, but former Chelsea player Di Matteo got them there in 2012. It was quite an achievement, given that the team was past its best. Terry was injured; in midfield, Lampard wasn't quite the engine he had been, though Juan Mata added a touch of class to an otherwise ordinary team. Up front, Drogba was now 34 years old, and wasn't helped by his striking partner, Fernando Torres, who had failed to do anything well since his massive move from Liverpool in 2011—not pass, not shoot, not head the ball, not control it, not score, and often not avoid red cards in crucial games. How could this team overcome a Bayern Munich side featuring former Chelsea star Robben, who was now reaching his peak, plus Franck Ribéry, Bastian Schweinsteiger, Philipp Lahm, et al.? Bayern were the best team in Europe by a mile that season, even though Chelsea had knocked out Barcelona in the semifinals, a victory sealed by—what? wait a minute!—that rarer-than-gold thing, a Fernando Torres goal, two minutes into injury time in Spain.

The 2012 Champions League final was a tight game, though as expected Bayern dominated. They saved their breakthrough till late, Thomas Müller scoring with a back-post header with barely seven minutes to go. It was surely going to be another one of those nights for Chelsea, but Didier Drogba was determined to make it as dramatic as possible. With two minutes to go he scored a thundering header from a corner to take the game into extra time, only to then foul Franck Ribéry in the box. Up stepped Arjen Robben to surely put Bayern ahead for good, but Cech made a superb save low to his left and the game wandered into penalty kicks. Mata missed the first for Chelsea, but it would be their only blemish—Bayern missed their last two penalties, and somehow this Chelsea team, who had just finished sixth in the Premiership, took the Champions League trophy.

Six months later, Roberto Di Matteo—hero of 1997 as a player and of 2012 as manager—was summarily fired. On returning to Chelsea in the summer of 2013, José Mourinho said, "The past is history, even my past." Few men would have used the word "even" in such a statement—but then, few men would work for Roman Abramovich twice.

Location	Mexico City, Mexico
Established	1916
Nicknames	Las Águilas ("The Eagles"), Los Azulcremas ("The Blue and Creams"), Los Millonetas ("The Millionaires")
Current stadium	Estadio Azteca (capacity 105,000)
Home colors	Yellow and navy
Leading goal-scorer	Luis Roberto Alves, known as Zague or Zaguinho (1985–96, 1997–98, 2003), 162 goals
Most appearances	Cristóbal Ortega (1974–91), 711 appearances

According to a survey conducted by Mitofsky Consulting in 2013, if you're a football fan in Mexico, there's an almost one-in-two chance that you hate the country's most successful side, Club América. This is akin to the New York Yankees Rule in American baseball, or the ABU (Anyone But [Man] United) Rule in British soccer: be successful, or rich, or both; you'll see how much we want you to fail.

"Las Águilas" ("the Eagles"), as they're commonly known, were founded in 1916 in Mexico City, and on Columbus Day, hence the American-themed name. A "fourpeat" of Primera División championships in the mid-1920s led to América's players forming the bulk of the Mexican side that played in the first World Cup, in 1930, but it wasn't much to write home about from Uruguay. Mexico lost all three of its games with a combined goal difference of minus nine (that was the World Cup in which the US team reached the semifinals, where they lost 6–1 to Argentina).

In the 1940s, the great rivalry with Guadalajara (Chivas) took shape, and continues to this day in what is known as the Mexican Superclasico. But it wasn't until 1966 that Club América won its first Primera División title as a professional team; they have won ten more since. More than anything, though, Club América has put Mexican football on the international map, not just via the 1930 World Cup, nor by being the first Mexican team to play outside of the country, when they toured Guatemala in 1923, but later in transAmerican competitions. Five-time winners of the CONCACAF Champions League/ Cup (the tournament for North American teams which has been consistently dominated by Mexican teams), they finally broke South America's stranglehold on the Copa Interamericana, that strange beast that pitted the champions of North and South America against each other. The tournament was held just 17 times in 30 years—the last one, in 1998, was won by D.C. United—but during its brief existence it found time to allow Club América to achieve its greatest moment in international play.

In 1977, América lost to Boca Juniors in the tournament, but found themselves facing them again the following year. This time, the game swung back and forth. Club América, in their all-yellow strip, had slightly shorter shorts than the all-blue shorts of Boca Juniors, and this seemed to give them extra pep. A disputed first goal for Club América looked for all the world like Geoff Hurst's non-goal goal for England in the 1966 World Cup final—only in this case, América's goal *did* indeed cross the line before bouncing away. Pretty much every player on the field surrounded first the referee, then the linesman, then the referee again, but despite the entreaties of the Boca players, the goal stood. Boca Juniors later tied the game after a swift break down the left wing, and the teams headed to extra time.

With barely any time left on the clock, Club América were awarded a free kick 25 yards out, just to the left of center. Up stepped Chilean midfielder Carlos Reinoso, a man still considered a legend in Mexico City. The wall in front of him featured fully seven Boca players, and by the time Reinoso nonchalantly clipped the ball with his sweet right foot, this wall was probably five yards from the ball, not the allowed ten. No matter. The ball curved and dipped so violently that it crossed the Boca goal line at knee height. It was the perfect free kick, causing the commentator to scream that it had been delivered by *"el gigante maestro!"*

And with that, Reinoso takes off running; no one is going to catch him, not his teammates, not the fans who have spilled onto the field, no one. He peels his yellow number five shirt off his back, twirling it high in the air, as fans who have remained in their seats scream at the goal and at the sight of Carlos Reinoso's expansive pelt of chest hair (it's the original "Ryan Giggs"). No one hated Club América that night: they were the champions of the Americas; they were, finally, what their name says.

But that wouldn't last. At least half of Mexico is now back to hating Club América.

CLUB OLIMPIA

Location	Asunción, Paraguay
Established	1902
Nicknames	*El Decano* ("The Dean"), *El Expreso Decano* ("The Dean Express"), *La "O"* ("The 'O'")
Current stadium	Estadio Manuel Ferreira (22,000 capacity)
Home colors	Black and white
Leading goal-scorer	—
Most appearances	—

Here's a fairy tale:

Rotterdam, in the late nineteenth century: one of the busiest ports on the planet; money flowing in and out like water; opportunities in every shipment, on every tide. The city was in the midst of its heyday, more so even than when it was one of the pillars of the Dutch East India Company's world domination, some 200 years earlier. So why would a smart young man, 18 years old and ready to make his way in the world, decide that this was the perfect time to leave his vibrant home town behind and sail west?

Weather—it came down to the weather. Eighteen-year-old William Paats of Rotterdam suffered from a respiratory ailment, and the harsh winters sweeping in off of the Vesterhavet, as the Dutch call the North Sea, made at least half of every year a painful challenge for a young man with limited lung capacity. But 6,500 miles southwest of the Netherlands lay a country where the humidity was usually high and the temperatures mostly balmy, a hot and droplet-filled place for a young man who couldn't breathe: Asunción, Paraguay.

So that's where Paats and his concerned family landed, right before the start of the twentieth century. And it turned out that Paats was really something: he settled quickly, got into business and joined the Masons, married, and sired a daughter. But his first wife soon died, and, having packed the kid off back to the Netherlands, he remarried a year after his bereavement. After that, his business boomed in the humid capital. As a physical education instructor on the side, Paats thought it might be fun to show the Paraguayans a soccer ball he had bought in Buenos Aires, Argentina.

That's how soccer came to landlocked, empty-of-people Paraguay. Even today, there are still only 6.5 million people living in a country about the size of California (by comparison, 38 million people live in California). Paats introduced football, established the biggest club, Olimpia, and invented the Football Association of Paraguay. Almost overnight, so the story goes, this country, which lies as a geographic buffer between the soccer heavyweights of Argentina and Brazil, discovered the beautiful game thanks to the Dutchman with the double vowels and the leaky lungs.

So much for the fairy tale. Though William Paats is often referred to as the father of Paraguayan football, can it really be true that one Dutchman could bring a sport to an entire country, and so quickly? More: when someone is described as "the father of" something, doesn't the skeptic wonder? In this case, it pays to be skeptical, as the truth might well be more mundane: a different fairy tale, something to do with British railroad workers, calling themselves "Everton" after the other team in Liverpool, and how they'd challenge Asuncionistas to a game . . .

Either way, even though Paraguay banished the Europeans (in the form of the Spanish) in the early nineteenth century, Europe got its own back by colonizing their sports via soccer less than a hundred years later. Soccer is the number one sport in Paraguay now, and Club Olimpia is its most storied and successful team—in fact, they are one of the most successful in all of South America.

But it didn't start out that way. Even though Paats named the team after Mount Olympus (and thereby the Olympics), it took them six years to win the nascent league, in 1912. Since then, they've won the Primera División a full 39 times, including "threepeats" in the 1920s and 1930s, and five in a row from 1956–60. But their greatest time of dominance came after the ascent of a man with the wonderful name of Osvaldo Domínguez Dibb.

Domínguez Dibb, a businessman, and politician rather too friendly with the Fascist dictator Alfredo Stroessner, became president of Club Olimpia in 1976, and quickly the team lived up to their billing as the biggest in Paraguay. From 1978 to 1983, only one team won the Primera División, but even more importantly, Olimpia also won in international competition.

In 1979, and for the first time in Paraguayan history, Club Olimpia won the coveted Copa Libertadores. Olimpia's run to the championship was a tour de force. The only game they lost was in an early group stage, and even then it was played in the ridiculous altitude of Bolivia's La Paz stadium, which sits at a very cool 12,000 feet, making a high-octane sport like soccer nigh-on impossible.

In Asunción, on Sunday, July 22, 1979, Club Olimpia won the first leg of the final against the legendary Boca Juniors of Argentina, 2–0. But the win was not without divine intervention. On a streamer-strewn field, and already one goal to the good, a speculative long-range free kick by Olimpia's Miguel Angel Piazza bobbled innocuously along the rutted pitch until the very moment it reached the kneeling Boca keeper, where it bounced up like a jack-in-the-box, up and over the poor soul's right shoulder and into the back of the net.

(Soccer fans and commentators often cite this kind of freak moment as a goalkeeping error—Blackburn Rovers keeper Tim Flowers is often excoriated for a similar incident in a 1996 game against Liverpool, when a scuffed shot by Stan Collymore hit a rut and bounced entirely over him and into the net. But it's little more than an act of God, and a comic one, for which one is always grateful.)

The second leg of the 1979 Copa Libertadores was a boring 0–0 draw, but it delivered Club Olimpia its biggest triumph—that is, until, as reigning Copa Libertadores champions, they beat Swedish team Malmö in the Intercontinental Cup. They repeated their Copa Libertadores win eleven seasons later, so bookending their most successful spell (though they lost the subsequent final of the Copa Interamérica in 1991 to Club América from Mexico). Though they again won a tranche of Primera División titles in the late nineties, since then Club Olimpia has been in decline. It wasn't until 2011 that an Olimpia side won the league in Paraguay, but in typical fashion, they repeated the following year. It remains to be seen if this will begin another era of one-party rule, another fairy-tale run in the looming footsteps and wheezy breaths of a distant Dutchman, William Paats of Rotterdam.

Location	Santiago, Chile
Established	1925
Nicknames	*El Eterno Campeón* ("The Eternal Champion"), *Los Albos* ("The Whites"), *El Cacique* ("The Chieftain"), *El Popular* ("The Popular")
Current stadium	Estadio Monumental (capacity 47,347)
Home colors	White and black
Leading goal-scorer	—
Most appearances	—

A cross town, in the stadium of your archrivals, the opponents of the dictator's regime sit huddled in the changing rooms and offices. They have been rounded up, arrested, and are awaiting their fate, which could be a mock murder or a real one. There are thousands of political prisoners there. So what do you do, Colo Colo of Santiago, Chile, when the Estadio Nacional of Universidad de Chile is being used as a holding station for those the dictator deems dangerous?

Why, you make the dictator the "Honorary President and Number One Fan" of your club!

Welcome to the Chile of General Pinochet. As honorary president, in the mid-1970s he made funds available to build Colo's current stadium, Estadio Monumental, though not enough funds to make it Estadio Funcional; after its first five games, Monumental was closed because the seats were uncomfortable and there were insufficient bathrooms.

The stadium, finally opened for good in 1989, is sometimes also called Estadio Monumental David Arellano, after an altogether different Chilean to Pinochet. Arellano was one of the men who, in 1925, established the Colo Colo club. It was named after a legendary sixteenth-century leader of the indigenous Mapuche people of Chile and Argentina. Barely two years after the club was founded, on May 2, 1927, Arellano, known for his flashy bicycle kick (later known as the *chilena* in certain footballing circles), led his team on the first ever tour of Europe by a Chilean soccer club. But during an exhibition game in Valladolid, in northwestern Spain, Arellano accidentally collided with another player; the blow was serious enough to lead to peritonitis and Arellano died the next day, at the tender age of 24. He was 6,500 miles from home.

To this day, Arellano's death is commemorated on Colo Colo's badge via a black line; below the line there is a cartoon, which is nothing more than an embarrassing depiction of what white people think a Mapuche chief looked like. Death is never far away for Colo Colo; in 1987, they kindly loaned players to Alianza Lima after members of the Peruvian team were killed in a plane crash. And though Arellano's own story is one of dreadful ill luck, his team's history is littered with trophies: 30 Chilean championships, ten Chilean cups, and, most notably, the 1991 Copa Libertadores.

Colo Colo reached the final of the Copa Libertadores in 1973 only to lose in a third-game playoff, and after extra time, to Independiente of Argentina. In 1991, Colo Colo successfully followed the standard procedure for teams in major tournaments during their group stages, which is to draw your away games and win your home games. Three wins and three draws—including a late penalty save against fellow Chilean team Concepción, to preserve the 0–0 tie—were enough to get Colo Colo, led by their much-traveled Croatian manager Mirko Jozić, through to the knockout rounds. After a 3–0 victory over LDU Quito of Ecuador, a result that should have been much bigger, Jozić commented, *"Hubo momentos para reír, y otros para llorar"*—basically, "There were moments to make you laugh, and others to make you cry."

In the knockout stages, Colo Colo were knockout. After a tense 0–0 draw on the road in Lima, Peru, against Universitario, the Colo Colo keeper, saddled with the sadly appropriate name of Daniel Morón, said, "God wants us to win and qualify for the next phase." Back in Santiago, Colo Colo were leading 2–1 when a header by Universitario's Andrés "Balán" González crossed Morón's goal line, but that Morón was clearly onto something vis-à-vis divine intervention. The ref said no goal, and Colo Colo marched on.

The first leg of the quarter finals was a 4–0 massacre of Nacional of Uruguay, though "massacre" seems an unfortunate word to use when your country, though no longer ruled by Pinochet, still employs him as its commander-in-chief. Despite dropping the second leg 2–0, Colo advanced to the semifinal, where they beat crack Argentine side Boca Juniors, led by center forward Gabriel Batistuta, 3–2 on aggregate. The second leg in Chile, which ended 3–1 to Colo Colo, is remembered mostly for the 17-minute mini-riot which featured numerous Boca Juniors players picking fights with police and photojournalists, one of whom was badly injured, and for a Chilean police dog, a German Shepherd called Ron, who bit Navarro Montoya, Boca's goalkeeper. (Colo Colo fans still visit Ron's grave to honor his service.)

After all that sturm und drang, the two-leg final against Olimpia of Paraguay, the reigning champions of the Copa Libertadores, was almost painfully free of drama. A 0–0 draw in Asunción was followed by a convincing 3–0 win in front of 66,000 fans at Estadio Monumental David Arellano. The highlight of the match was a beautiful passing move and goal by Luis Pérez (his second of the night), a center forward who had only just been drafted into the team. But the game was really no contest—the white and black of Colo Colo was indeed the best team in South America that year.

Since that Copa Libertadores victory, Colo Colo have nosedived and were declared bankrupt in January 2002. A new company, Blanco y Negro, bought out the debt, ensuring both the long-term survival of the club, and yet more presidential involvement in it—Sebastián Piñera, former president of Chile, had been a stakeholder in Blanco y

Negro. His stated aim was to bring the Copa Libertadores back to Chile; and though Piñera divested himself of involvement in Blanco y Negro when he became president, his country still awaits another generation like the one more than two decades ago that brought Colo Colo, and Chile, international footballing fame.

F.C. COPENHAGEN

Location	Copenhagen, Denmark
Established	1992
Nicknames	*Byens Hold* ("The City's Team"), *Løverne* ("The Lions")
Current stadium	Parken (capacity 38,076)
Home colors	White and blue
Leading goal-scorer	César Santin (2008–13), 84 goals
Most appearances	Hjalte Nørregaard (2000–05, 2006–10), 320 appearances

Football Club København, as it is written in Danish, are known by the abbreviation FCK.

It's therefore worth spending time at the website of FC København. You can browse FCK TV, OM FCK, which is presumably a Zen-like activity that Sting and Trudie Styler would enjoy, and have a MIT FCK. There are FCK highlights, KlubFCK, and FCK Away. There's something for everyone.

Also, they're not really one team; they're a mixture of two very old and established teams, who came together in 1992 to pool resources and overcome limited fan bases. The first of those two teams is the oldest football and sports club on mainland Europe, Kjøbenhavns Boldklub, which was established in 1876. There are only 15 British teams older than Kjøbenhavns Boldklub, and they have won 15 Danish championships. They also gave the world Michael Laudrup, the brilliant Danish forward who graced Barcelona and Real Madrid, among other teams, who once managed Swansea City, and for whom all soccer fans are grateful; and Nicklas Bendtner, the

Arsenal striker who once said, "If you ask me if I am one of the best strikers in the world, I say yes because I believe it." (Few soccer fans are thankful for Nicklas Bendtner.) By the time of the merger, Kjøbenhavns Boldklub had fallen on hard times, and when the Danish Superliga began in 1991, they were nowhere to be seen, having been relegated the year before.

The other team making up Football Club København is Boldklubben 1903, established exactly when you think they were, and seven times winner of the Danish league. Outside of Denmark, their finest year was their last, when despite averaging crowds sometimes as low as 2,000, they managed to make the quarterfinals of the 1991–92 UEFA Cup. Along the way they had probably their finest night.

On October 23, 1991, a Bayern Munich team featuring top players like Thomas Berthold, Christian Ziege, Stefan Effenberg, Thomas Strunz, and Olaf Thon, traveled to Copenhagen to face B 1903 in the second round of the UEFA Cup. Few gave B 1903 much of a chance, and sure enough, Brazilian center forward Mazinho gave Bayern the lead after half an hour. So sure were the German team of their superiority that Mazinho barely celebrated the goal, jogging back to his own half with a faint smile and the odd handshake.

An hour later, it was 6–1 to B 1903.

B 1903's equalizer came from a corner five minutes after Mazinho's goal. Ten minutes into the second half a penalty made it 2–1, and the crowd—swelled to six times its average size—sensed something was up. There then followed two goals in three minutes around the hour mark—the first after horrible Bayern defending, the second from another corner—causing the B 1903 coaching staff to stand up excitedly from the park benches upon which they were sitting (accommodations in the old Gentofte Stadion were a bit primitive). A fifth goal came on 77 minutes after yet more Keystone Kops defending. The Germans, standing in a neat line and playing for an offside that never came, watched as Brian Kaus, a substitute, slotted the ball home with nary a care in the world. Gasps turned to hysteria two minutes before the end when Iørn Uldbjerg waltzed through the shell-shocked Bayern back line to force home a sixth. At this, the Danish commentator trotted out a German phrase we can all understand: "Auf Wiedersehen."

A consolation goal that night, plus a late Mazinho penalty back in Munich, made the aggregate score a more respectable 6–3, but nothing took away from the achievement of B 1903, not even the quarterfinal loss to eventual runners-up Torino of Italy. As a last hurrah for B 1903 it would be hard to beat, and yet in the first season of the newly-formed Football Club København, the Danish Superliga was theirs, as it would be nine more times.

It was a banner time for Danish football generally. In 1992, on the back of Yugoslavia being thrown out of the European Championships as that country disintegrated, Denmark were picked as the replacement team and promptly won the tournament. Anchoring that side was Man United keeper Peter Schmeichel and Copenhagen defender Torben Piechnik, as well as a host of players from Brøndby I.F., including the other Laudrup, Brian.

Brøndby had dominated the early years of the Danish Superliga, but by the new century, Copenhagen had returned to the top of the pile. They even made it out of a Champions League group headed by Barcelona in 2010–11, after a creditable draw against the Spanish superclub in front of nearly 40,000 fans in Parken Stadium. In that game, Lionel Messi scored after half an hour, but Copenhagen equalized immediately, and after good home wins against Panathinaikos and Rubin Kazan they advanced. In the knockout round they faced a strong Chelsea side who despatched them easily, but for a brand-new club this was progress indeed.

Now if only someone had pointed out that to an English speaker, FCK might not have been the best acronym for a football club.

Location	São Paulo, Brazil
Established	1910
Nicknames	*Timão* ("Helm"), *Time do Povo* ("The People's Club"), *Todo Poderoso* ("Almighty") ("Joker")
Current stadium	Arena Corinthians (capacity 48,000)
Home colors	White and black
Leading goal-scorer	Cláudio Christovam de Pinho, known as Cláudio (1944–57), 306 goals
Most appearances	Wladimir Rodrigues dos Santos, known as Wladimir (1972–85), 805 appearances

They came to Brazil as merchants, and the Brazilians called them *mascates* or *turcos*—peddlers or Turks, slurs both. But really they were from Lebanon and Syria, and once they became established, the slurs turned to grudging respect. These immigrants from the Middle East stayed to establish stores, own factories, and buy real estate. Between 1895 and 1901, the number of Syrian–Lebanese businesses in São Paulo went from six to five hundred. This influx from lands 7,000 miles to the east helped transform a country, and this city in particular, in the space of a few decades.

But it was not all business. One spot in São Paulo—the biggest city in Brazil—is profoundly connected to this Syrian–Lebanese influx, and is also crucial to the establishment of one of the great Brazilian soccer teams, Corinthians. A Syrian immigrant, Assad Abdalla, went from peddler to owner–builder of a large neighborhood, the Parque San Jorge, on the southern banks of the Tiete River, which runs east to west through the center of the city. In the mid-1920s, the Abdalla family sold the portion of the Parque being used by the Esporte Clube Sírio (Syrian Sporting Club) to Corinthians so they would have somewhere for their fast-growing team. Established in 1910 by railwaymen, this was a team for working people (previously, the sport had been largely an upper-class hobby), and quickly started to do well in the São Paulo State Championship. By the time they purchased the Parque San Jorge site in 1926, they had already won five state championships (they have won 27 in total). There was no national Brazilian league until the late 1950s, due to the size of the country, so winning the São Paulo State Championship was no mean feat.

Corinthians soon outgrew San Jorge, often using Pacaembu or Morumbi stadiums in São Paulo. In fact, though it is one of the biggest teams in Brazil (and the world), Corinthians has often struggled to find a stadium commensurate with its importance. With that in mind, their 2014 move into the new arena in the eastern section of the city built for the World Cup is historic.

Though the construction of new stadiums in Brazil has been fraught with political controversy and unrest, the Arena Corinthians confirms one thing: that the team is now considered one of the top Brazilian sides. After years of dominating the São Paulo State Championship, later innovations in league play saw different state champions pitted against one another. Corinthians won those competitions five times, including three times in the 1950s. Since Brazil's Série A started, they have also won that competition five times.

Perhaps their most celebrated side came together in the early 1980s around one of the greatest ever Brazilian playmakers, Socrates. Known as "O Doutur" ("the Doctor"), the heavy-smoking, bearded genius was more than just a footballer (though just as a footballer, his size, strength, and ability to pick a pass were unequalled, and probably still are). A staunch proponent of democracy at a time when Brazil had been run by the military since 1964—and when his own team was too-too strictly run for a man who described himself as an "anti-athlete"—Socrates famously announced to a massive crowd in São Paulo in 1984 that he would leave Brazil if free elections were not allowed; they weren't, and Socrates moved for one season to Fiorentina in Italy. (In 2004, at age 50, he also played 12 minutes for a non-league team in Yorkshire, England, Garforth Town, late in a 2–2 draw against local rivals Tadcaster Albion. "The second I got out on the pitch I suffered a terrible headache," Socrates said. He would have played a second game, but Simon Clifford, owner of Garforth, demurred after "[Socrates'] warm-up, [which] had consisted of drinking two bottles of Budweiser and [smoking] three cigarettes.")

In 1998, Corinthians dominated Campeonato Brasileiro Série A, winning by ten points; but they had bigger fish to fry. In 2000, the first FIFA World Club Championships were held, and in Brazil to boot. Corinthians qualified on the basis of their 1998 victory (they would also win the 1999 championship, again by ten points). This was the Corinthians team of Freddy Rincón, the Colombian who would later be investigated for drug trafficking; Luizão, who played for each of the four major São Paulo teams at some point; Edu, who would be part of both of the Série A winning teams and this FIFA World Club side before moving to Arsenal (he is now Corinthians' director of football); and Edilson, the much-traveled "Capetinha" ("Little Devil") who won the World Cup with Brazil in 2002.

In the qualifying group stage of this inaugural FIFA tournament, Corinthians topped the group that included the Nicolas Anelka-led Real Madrid by a goal difference of just one, but it would be enough to propel them to the final, where they would face fellow Brazilian team Vasco da Gama, of Rio, in front of 73,000 fans in the Maracanã Stadium. Many felt the Rio team would win, especially as they had the great Romário up front. But after a 0–0 draw, played at typical Brazilian walking pace and featuring few clear chances thanks to Corinthians' stringent defense, the game went to penalties. Vasco's captain Edmundo had an opportunity to take the penalties to sudden death (both teams had missed one), but skewed his shot yards wide of the right post, giving Corinthians victory in the first ever FIFA Club World Championships—and in the home of their Rio rivals, no less.

Animal lovers also celebrated, as legend has it that Edmundo (nicknamed, ironically enough, "Animal") got a chimpanzee drunk in 1999 during a birthday party for his son.

Even better was to come for Corinthians in 2012. They had won their fifth Brazilian title in 2011—clinched the day Socrates died at the young age of 57, but playing an anti-football, dirty game that *O Doutur* would have hated. That sent them to the Copa Libertadores, where in the group stages they let in a total of two goals in six games. On the way to the final via the knockout stages they did even better, shifting just one goal (they once again pipped Vasco da Gama, winning their second leg 1–0 at the Pacaembu on a very late goal by Paulinho, who would subsequently move to Spurs in England).

In the final, the so-far-unbeaten-in-the-tournament Corinthians faced Boca Juniors of Buenos Aires, with their superstar Juan Riquelme playing his last two games for the club. Yet another tight first-leg game seemed to have gone the way of the Argentines after Facundo Roncaglia scored with less than 20 minutes to go, a goal which was madly celebrated by Boca old boy Maradona up in the stands, as well as by nearly 50,000 screaming fans. But Romarinho equalized a few minutes later, silencing the mostly Argentine crowd, and the tie swung toward Corinthians. Back in São Paulo for the second leg, Emerson scored twice in the second half to bring Corinthians its first ever Copa Libertadores. The goal-scorer dedicated the win to the "33 million fans" of Corinthians, which is a surprisingly exact and almost correct number, given that a recent study has them being followed by 16 percent of a country of 200 million people.

That year, Corinthians also won their second World Club Championship. This time the road to the final was relatively simple, consisting of a single game against Africa's best team, Al-Ahly of Egypt. An impressive 15,000 of those "33 million" Corinthians fans made the trip to Toyota, Japan, to watch the game, which despite the noise for Corinthians was dominated by the African team. Better finishing would have seen Al-Ahly in the final, but a first-half header by Paolo Guerrero was all Corinthians needed to advance.

Awaiting them in the final were 2012 Champions League winners Chelsea. Once again it was the head of Guerrero that won the game as he powered a nod past three separate Chelsea defenders standing on the line. (Take a bow, Joe Cole, David Luiz, and Ramires.)

It was a world away from São Paulo, and the land sold to Corinthians by Assad Abdalla—nearly 70,000 people in Yokohama watched as the Brazilian team raised the World Club trophy for the second time. Fireworks exploded, tinsel rained down, but everything has a habit of coming full circle: as the Corinthians players, few of whom probably knew about their Syrian–Lebanese origins, bounced up and down in delight, the gaggle of Middle Eastern air stewardesses who had helped present the medals turned away and wandered off into the freezing Japanese night.

CRUZ AZUL

Location	Mexico City, Mexico
Established	1927
Nicknames	*Los Cementeros* ("The Cement Men"), *La Máquina* ("The Machine"), *El Azul* ("The Blue"), *Las Liebres* ("The Hares")
Current stadium	Estadio Azul (capacity 35,161)
Home colors	Blue and white
Leading goal-scorer	Carlos Hermosillo (1991–98), 169 goals
Most appearances	—

C ement, that's how it started—though the history of Cruz Azul continues with a curse.

In 1927, workers at a Cemento Cruz Azul factory in Mexico decided they wanted to form a football team. Mexico had only recently come out of its revolution, and the factory, already the oldest such in Mexico, built itself back to full health in the decade after the end of the conflict. By the time soccer came around, Blue Cross (Cruz Azul) had unions and a collective bargaining agreement for its workers, though they still made a pittance compared to the owners. Nonetheless, sport was, as it so often is, an opiate, and for the next 30-odd years the fledgling Cruz Azul team played as amateurs, winning the state championship of Hidalgo and eventually joining the Mexican second division.

It was a modest beginning for the *cementeros*, but it drew enough attention that in 1960 the company built a stadium in Jasso, Hidalgo, the site of the cement works, 40 miles northwest of Mexico City. With the infrastructure in place, all that was needed was a good team. Fortunately, in the next two decades, a couple of coaches would turn the team into winners: Jorge Marik and Raúl Cárdenas.

Marik is a Hungarian, from Budapest, who in 1949 fled his Soviet-occupied country hidden in a truck, alongside the great László Kubala, a striker who would go on to be the third highest scorer ever for Barcelona. Marik bounced around South America as a player before landing some coaching gigs in Mexico. By the 1961–62 season, cigarette perennially in hand, he had taken over Cruz Azul—and after just a couple of seasons they had won the second division and were headed to the big dance.

The manager who truly transformed Cruz Azul for good, though, was Raúl Cárdenas. He had played for Mexico in three World Cups, and by the 1968–69 season he was leading Cruz Azul to their first national championship. A second-place finish the next season was followed by a "fourpeat" of championships. In the second of those four, Cruz Azul finally brought in non-Mexican players, and moved operations from Hidalgo to Mexico City's Azteca Stadium, which had been open for six years and had been graced by Brazil's extraordinary display in the 1970 World Cup final, a game watched by 107,412 fans. (In three games in the space of four June days in 1970—the Italy–West Germany semifinal, the third-place playoff between Uruguay and West Germany, and the Brazil–Italy final—a staggering 314, 259 people attended games in the Azteca.) There weren't quite that many to watch Cruz Azul lift its third trophy, but those who attended the semifinal between Atlas and Cruz Azul, in Atlas in 1973, would have been in for something memorable: 35 minutes into the game Atlas were down to six players, and the game was abandoned. In the final, Cruz would knock off León six minutes before the end of extra time in a third game, the first two having ended tied. That late, late goal for Cruz Azul was scored by León's George "Tarzan" Davinho, an Argentine who no doubt performed the jungle man's trademark yodel of despair when he put the ball into his own net.

Three more titles in the next few years would accrue, in 1973–74, 1978–79, and 1979–80. Cruz Azul had arrived, but it would be almost two decades before another title, and sometimes a win can be a loss. That championship was sealed after Carlos Hermosillo—known as *"El Grandote de Cerro Azul"* ("the Big One from Cerro Azul," his hometown)—scored a penalty against León with a few minutes left in extra time. So far so good, especially as Hermosillo was playing with broken ribs. But he'd gotten the penalty after León keeper Ángel Comizzo kicked him in the face, drawing blood. Refusing the referee's entreaty to wipe it off, Hermosillo buried the penalty, but since then, neither León nor Cruz Azul have won squat, leading to the fashioning of a theory that both teams are suffering from the Comizzo Curse. Neither team can break free until they face each other once again in a final, so the story goes, and no blood is spilled.

Cruz Azul have lost a number of close finals since 1997, including the Copa Libertadores final of 2001. That year they led a charmed life through the tournament, even knocking out Argentine heavyweights River Plate on their way to a showdown with the other great team from Buenos Aires, Boca Juniors. In the first leg, Boca went to Mexico and won 1–0 on a late, late goal from superstar Marcelo Delgado. The 115,000 fans in the Azteca Stadium that June night must have feared the worst, as no team had ever won a Copa Libertadores final in La Bombonera, Boca's famed stadium.

The scene for the second leg was as breathtaking as usual. All three tiers were packed, flares blazed, and streamers fell everywhere, including all over the field. The Cruz Azul players must have been quaking in their boots, but they didn't show it. Just before half-time their beloved striker, Juan Palencia—he of the gaudy ponytail running halfway down his back—put them one up from a corner, and though both teams missed a hatful of chances, it proved to be the only goal of the game. Boca Juniors had finally lost a finals game at home. Diego Maradona, watching high in the vertical stand on one side of the pitch, turned away in displeasure.

With the aggregate score tied, the match went to penalties. Palencia, his ponytail swaying extravagantly, buried Azul's first, but then it all went wrong. Their second attempt was saved, their third skied a mile over the bar, their fourth skied even higher—in fact, that last one might never have come down from outer space. It had been taken by Julio Pinheiro, a naturalized Mexican who was born in Brazil, and with it, he and his teammates had handed the title to Boca Juniors of Argentina.

The Comizzo Curse was cemented in place.

CRUZEIRO

Location	Belo Horizonte, Brazil
Established	1921
Nicknames	*A Raposa* ("The Fox")
Current stadium	Mineirão, officially Estádio Governador Magalhães Pinto (capacity 62,170)
Home colors	Blue and white
Leading goal-scorer	Eduardo Gonçalves de Andrade, known as Tostão (1963–72), 248 goals
Most appearances	José Carlos Bernardo, known as Zé Carlos (1965–77), 619 appearances

He was a right winger, but not political. He liked French fries, so everyone knew him by a nickname. He wore number seven—but Roberto Monteiro, a.k.a. Roberto Batata ("Potato"), made his final journey not along the right flank of a soccer field, but from Cruzeiro's Estádio do Barro Preto to the Cemitério do Bonfim in Belo Horizonte.

It is a beautiful place to rest. A city of avenues and lakes and parks 3,000 feet above sea level and surrounded by mountains, Belo Horizonte lies in the southeastern section of Brazil, about 300 miles north of Rio. Meaning "beautiful horizon," the city boomed at the start of the twentieth century on the back of industrialization and a wave of Italian immigration—a million Italians moved to Brazil in the last ten years of the nineteenth century, and fully 30 percent of Belo Horizontians still claim some sort of Italian heritage. Naturally, a football team followed—established in January 1921 as the Societá Sportiva

Palestra Itália: a team for Italians only. This closed shop lasted just a few years, though the team still wore a version of the Italian flag on their socks, and green shirts. The team quickly prospered, winning three state championships; its future looked bright. But war was on the beautiful horizon.

Brazil didn't enter World War II until 1942, but when it did so—on the side of the Allies—suddenly all things Italian were *non grata*. Societá Sportiva Palestra Itália, a.k.a. Belo Horizonte, became Cruzeiro ("Southern Cross"), and two decades later, wearing blue shirts, they dominated the regional Campeonato Mineiro, winning seven titles in ten years. In the middle of that local success, Cruzeiro also beat Santos—a team featuring Pelé up front—to win the national championship in 1966. The first leg of the final game featured one of the great Cruzeiro performances of all time: Santos were thrashed 6–2 in Belo and then beaten 3–2 at home, for a staggering aggregate score of 9–4 to Cruzeiro.

Cruzeiro had arrived, and were aided by bucketfuls of goals by midfielder Tostão ("Little Coin"), a Belo Horizonte native who is said to have once scored 47 times in a game as a six-year-old. (Clearly there was no mercy rule in 1950s' Brazilian soccer.) Graduating to Cruzeiro's full squad, Tostão bagged 249 goals between 1964 and 1971, while also gracing Brazil's national side wearing number nine, where he famously scored against Peru in 1970 from an angle so tight it doesn't have a degree associated with it.

But the success of Tostão's team was limited to the Mineiro league. It wasn't until 1976—with Tostão retired, due to the after-effects of a detached retina he received when a ball hit him in the face—that Cruzeiro finally won the biggest prize of all. It would be a victory horribly marred by tragedy.

Cruzeiro made the 1976 Copa Libertadores by finishing a distant second to Internacional in the 1975 Brazilian championship. In the group stages that all changed, as Cruzeiro won five of its six games, including a 5–4 victory at home to the champions. The only unbeaten team in those group games, Cruzeiro then faced LDU Quito and

Alianza Lima in the semifinals group stage. On their travels they dominated both teams, with a 4–0 win in Lima. Two days after their return from Peru, on May 13, 1976, Roberto "Batata" fatally crashed his Chevette on the Fernão Dias highway, en route to see his wife and child. He was two months shy of his 27th birthday.

When Alianza Lima visited Brazil for the return match, hearts were heavy, but the Cruzeiro players had a plan: their fallen teammate had worn number seven, so when the Brazilian team went 7–1 in the lead, they stopped scoring.

And so to the final, where they faced Argentine side River Plate, who had needed a one-game playoff to reach the showdown with Cruzeiro. The fierce and sad hearts of the semifinals followed the Brazilian team to the first leg of the final, where they hammered River Plate 4–1. But the Copa Libertadores was then decided by points (two for a win, one for a draw, zero for a loss), not average scores, so when Cruzeiro lost the away tie in Buenos Aires 2–1, a third game was needed.

The two teams traveled to Santiago, Chile, where Cruzeiro would go two up—the first from a Nelinho penalty in the first half, and the second from Eduardo on 55 minutes, a stunning strike from wide right that should have won any final anywhere. Surely this was their year . . . but not so fast. River Plate scored two quick goals right after Eduardo's belter, via a couple of extremely dodgy refereeing decisions (a penalty and a free kick, neither of which should have been awarded), and the Cruzeiro players went nuts, surrounding the official. The game wandered toward extra time, but fortunately the ref finally got something right, awarding an obvious free kick to Cruzeiro on the edge of the River Plate box. There were two minutes to go.

One can only imagine the feelings running through Joãozinho's heart as he stepped up to take the kick. His fellow striker was gone, borne on a fire truck from the Belo Horizonte stadium to a Belo Horizonte cemetery just two months before. Joãozinho was a hometown boy born and bred, but perhaps before all these thoughts could inhibit him, and with the wall still being marshaled and players milling around, Cruzeiro's number ten stepped up and dinked a perfect sand wedge free kick over the River Plate wall.

Almost before the ball hit the back of the net Joãozinho was off, running madly toward the Cruzeiro bench, bouncing up and down like a crazy man. Back at the edge of the box, the River Plate players, incensed at the alacrity with which Joãozinho had taken the kick, fought with anyone within reach, throwing punches. But it didn't matter: Cruzeiro had won the Copa Libertadores for themselves and for Roberto "Batata."

The following season they would lose in the final of the same tournament to the other team from Buenos Aires, Boca Juniors, when they missed their last penalty kick in a shootout; they would also lose the 1976 Intercontinental Cup to Bayern Munich.

The next two decades were a time of decline for Cruzeiro, and it was not until 1997 that they again made the final of the Copa Libertadores. That season they beat Sporting Cristal of Peru 1–0 over two legs to win their second title. Six years later they won the 2003 Campeonato Brasileiro Série A by a record amount—they scored an amazing 102 goals on the way to amassing 100 points from 46 games. They also won their regional competition and the Copa do Brasil, the only team to ever win all three in one year. Since then, they have once again regressed to simply winning their regional title over and over, though they did make the final of the Copa Libertadores in 2009, where a Juan Sebastián Verón-inspired Estudiantes of Argentina came back from one down in Belo Horizonte to beat Cruzeiro with two second-half goals. In 2013, they finally added their third league title, after dominating the season; they led the league by eleven points on the final day, scoring 35 more goals than second-place Gremio.

There is a tradition now that football teams add a star to their crest every time they win a major tournament. That is never an option for Cruzeiro, no matter how many Cope Libertadores or Brazilian championships or regional tournaments they win. Their crest already features five stars, and will always do so: they are Alpha, Beta, Gamma, Delta, and Epsilon, the five most visible stars in the Southern Cross.

CSKA MOSCOW

Location	Moscow, Russia
Established	1911
Nicknames	*Koni* ("Horses"), *Krasno-sinie* ("Red-Blues"), *Armeytsy* ("Militarians")
Current stadium	Arena Khimki (capacity 18,636)
Home colors	Red and blue
Leading goal-scorer	Grigory Fedotov (1938–49), 135 goals
Most appearances	Vladimir Fedotov (1960–75), 426 appearances

CSKA ("Central Sports Club of the Army") Moscow, and before that the Central Sports Club of the Ministry of Defense (CSKMO), and before that the Sports Club of the Central House of the Soviet Army (CDSA), and before that the Sports Club of the Central House of the Red Army (CDKA), and before that the Experimental and Demonstrational Playground of Military Administration (OPPV), and before that the Experimental and Demonstrational Playground of Military Education Association (OPPV), and before that the Amateur Society of Skiing Sports (OLLS). Surprisingly for a team backed by the might of the Soviets, in all those years they never got past the first round of the UEFA Cup or the second round of the European Cup. But like the Soviets themselves, they dominated Russia. Once CSKA were unshackled from Communism and all those names, they charged ahead, all the way to a European final.

You know that old cliché "It was harder to miss"? Never was it more true than in the second half of the 2005 UEFA Cup final in Lisbon. Playing that night were Sporting Lisbon—so it was basically a home game for them—and CSKA Moscow, who brought a paltry 2,000 fans to the party.

The first half was all Sporting, as befits a team being screamed at by 45,000 home fans. CSKA barely made it out of their own half, and the pressure told on the half-hour mark when Sporting's left back, the Brazilian Rogério, curled a fantastic shot from 25 yards past Igor Akinfeev in the Moscow goal (the poor man didn't move).

The second half started in much the same way, until the tide turned with one of the most extraordinary misses you'll ever see. After yet another save by Akinfeev, the ball broke to the right foot of the left-footed Chilean midfielder Rodrigo Tello. Taking a touch onto his left foot, Tello wellied a shot across goal, and there, standing on his own, was Rogério once again. He was maybe two feet from the goal line. True, Tello's cross–shot came at Rogério fast, but still, what happened next was utterly hilarious: instead of letting the ball hit him and thereby roll into the net (it couldn't have gone anywhere else, given that he was basically standing on the goal line), Rogério managed instead to calmly pass the ball back across goal and into the disbelieving hands of the still-prone Akinfeev, who clung on like he'd fallen overboard and someone had thrown him a float. Harder to miss? It was actually a brilliant piece of defending.

Worse was to come. Out of nowhere, CSKA scored from a free kick to level the game; then, after a breakaway, it was suddenly 2–1 to the Russian team. With two goals in nine minutes the Sporting Lisbon crowd went silent, and with 15 minutes to go, the ball found its way to the wonderfully-named Vágner Love, a dreadlocked Brazilian center forward who had somehow found *his* way to Moscow (and for whom he would score 85 goals in two spells). Rounding the keeper, Love was standing as far from the goal as Rogério had been just a few minutes earlier, but in this case, and with no one to beat, Love nevertheless drew back his right boot and cannoned the ball into the back of the net.

It was an appropriate way to win a first European trophy—CSKA was, for many years, intimately connected with cannons, being the Soviet army's house team. In 1951, CSKA won the Soviet league, losing only three games all season. The following year they won their first three games, and then disaster struck: that CSKA side formed the majority of the Soviet Olympic team that faced Yugoslavia in Helsinki. A first game, in which the CSKA/Soviets were 5–1 down, was saved by an astonishing four-goal comeback, but in the replay CSKA/Soviets lost 3–1. Even though they were top of the league, CSKA were forced to resign from the league as retribution for losing to Yugoslavia and its leader, Tito, who was much hated by Stalin. (Fortunately for CSKA and the world, Stalin died on March 5, 1953, and CSKA were allowed to re-form, showing up in third place in 1955. They wouldn't win another league title until 1970, and nothing else in the rest of the Soviet years.)

By late 1991 the Soviets were gone, replaced, especially in Moscow, with a rapacious capitalism that left many people lining up for hours merely to enter newly-sprouting electronics stores without any hope of buying anything (in the winter of 1992, such lines were everywhere; this writer knows, because he stood in one). For a few, the riches were untold, as Boris Yeltsin's regime split the Soviet empire into smaller countries and handed the control of Russia's goods and services to a small number of men who would become so wealthy that they had no idea what to do with all their cash. CSKA, for their part, faced financial ruin once the state stopped sponsoring them, and for a team that was established in 1911 and that had won seven Soviet championships since 1946, it was a hard fall. It would take until the new century, and an influx of money from none other than Roman Abramovich, via a company called Sibneft, an oil concern, for CSKA to be able to afford players like Love. Eventually, Gazprom (which took over Sibneft) ended their association by changing their financial allegiance to Zenit St. Petersburg, but not before CSKA had thrown off the shackles of state ownership and had actually won something worth winning, that 2005 UEFA Cup. Since then, their European exploits have taken a horrible turn, as the visit of Manchester City in the 2013 Champions League elicited racist chanting by a large number of CSKA fans, specifically against City's Ivorian midfielder Yaya Touré.

D.C. UNITED

Location	Washington D.C., USA
Established	1995
Nicknames	DCU, Black and Red
Current stadium	RFK Stadium (56,000 capacity)
Home colors	Black and red
Leading goal-scorer	Jaime Moreno (1996–2002, 2004–10), 131 goals
Most appearances	Jaime Moreno (1996–2002, 2004–10), 329 appearances

I f you want to know what people think of soccer in Washington D.C., you should really ask Joe Public.

Joe Public is a Trinidadian soccer team owned by Jack Warner, the former FIFA vice president who was thrown out of every soccer administration of which he was a member because of corruption allegations. Warner created Joe Public in 1996 so that Trinidad and Tobago could nurture some quality players to help them reach the World Cup one day. (It hasn't happened yet, even though Joe Public gave the world the silky skills of Cardiff City's Kenwyne Jones.)

It may be that, like much of Jack Warner's career, the Joe Public experiment will fail. As a harbinger of what was to come, two years into their existence they traveled to RFK Memorial Stadium in Washington D.C. to face United in the quarterfinals of the CONCACAF Champions Cup. They lost 8–0.

But it was no real disgrace—Joe Public had come up against a good D.C. United team. A founding member of Major League Soccer in 1996, United became the team to beat. It took a while for them to get going, though. Their first four games were all defeats, and by July they were 6–10, hardly championship material. But they turned it around through the summer and fall, and by October 20 they found themselves up against the Los Angeles Galaxy, who had convincingly won the Western Conference, in the MLS Cup final.

The day of the final was a brute. A nor'easter had blown through Boston, and the game at Foxboro was played on a waterlogged pitch in intensely cold temperatures. What transpired, however, was a mini-classic, even though two of the worst haircuts in the history of soccer were on display. On L.A.'s right wing, Cobi Jones wore a mullet of dreads with shaved sides, while Jeff Agoos, playing at the back for D.C., sported a ponytail long enough that he should have been called Jeff Ahorse.

While the scores were tied in haircuts, in the match that mattered, which was being played on what resembled a water polo field, L.A. were two up with 17:45 to go (those were still the days of the clock counting down in MLS). From somewhere, D.C. conjured two late goals against L.A.'s soaked defense and their tiny, lime-green-uniformed goalie, Jorge Campos, the second a "36 mph Pepsi Power Shot" from six yards out with eight minutes to play.

The game went into overtime, and four minutes in, the execrable golden goal rule came into play when Eddie Pope powered a magnificent header into the back of the net from a Marco Etcheverry corner. (The golden goal, where the first team to score in overtime wins, was used variously in world tournaments between 1993 and 2004, and led to teams standing around on the halfway line hoping they wouldn't concede and thereby end the game.) Cue D.C. players sliding across the wet field like kids—the first ever MLS champions.

D.C. United would beat the L.A. Galaxy again three years later, after having won the second MLS Cup in 1997 and been beaten finalists in 1998. With future USA manager Bruce Arena at the helm, D.C. played a brand of efficient, solid football, epitomized by the work-horse John Harkes, the US captain who returned from a sojourn in the UK to lead the team. The D.C. team looked light years ahead of the other, more ponderous, trying-to-find-their-feet MLS franchises, with players like Etcheverry and Bolivian Jaime Moreno setting the tone. And in Eddie Pope—he was just 22 years old when he scored that bullet header in 1996—they found an attacking defender who couldn't stop himself scoring crucial goals, and usually in championship games.

In 1998, having beaten Joe Public 8–0 in the first round of the CONCACAF Champions Cup, they won one more game against León of Mexico before reaching the final. Eddie Pope scored the only goal of the game to bring D.C. its first international trophy (though only 12,000 people showed up to see it), and even better was to come, when in November of the same year D.C. faced solid Brazilian outfit Vasco da Gama in the last ever final of the Copa Interamericana.

After a first leg in D.C., Vasco held a meager 1–0 advantage (and at least twice as many people showed up this time). The second leg was held, oddly, in Fort Lauderdale, and given that the town is 1,000 miles from the capital and 4,000 miles from Rio de Janeiro, it's amazing that 7,000 people showed up. What they got to see was yet another winning goal from that man Eddie Pope, wearing, like all the other D.C. players, a version of Manchester United's away kit from 1975–80, a white shirt with three black stripes down the left side of the front. Tony Sanneh had put D.C. in the lead before Pope sealed the win with 13 minutes to go. In the year when they'd been pipped to a third consecutive MLS title, they had won two international competitions, and they would go on to win one more MLS Cup, in 2004, beating the Kansas City Wizards 3–2. Managed now by Piotr Nowak, that game featured an appearance on 65 minutes by Freddy Adu, at the time the most famous player in the United States owing to his age: just 15.

Poor Freddy Adu—his fortunes have pretty much matched D.C. United's ever since he played for them. Probably too young, probably not as good as people hoped, the "new Pelé" wasn't even an old-enough Adu, and his career fizzled out.

As for D.C., they haven't won much in nearly a decade (the US Open Cup in 2008 barely counts as a trophy), and in 2013 they ended the MLS season with the worst record of all teams, winning just three games, tying seven, and losing 24. Where they go from here depends on whether or not they can force through the building of a soccer-dedicated stadium somewhere in the D.C./Baltimore area. Soccer simply doesn't work in American football stadiums anymore: the plastic pitches, scrubbed out 10-yard markers, and the distant fans adding up to a terrible supporter experience for American soccer fans, who know the difference. D.C. has always played at RFK Stadium where, in 2005, the grounds staff weren't even able to lay out a rectangular soccer field correctly, leading D.C. United and the New England Revolution to play on what was described as merely "a parallelogram."

Location	Kiev, Ukraine
Established	1927
Nicknames	*Bilo-Syni* ("White-Blues")
Current stadium	NSC Olimpiyskiy (capacity 70,050)
Home colors	White and blue
Leading goal-scorer	Oleh Blokhin (1969–87), 211 goals
Most appearances	Oleh Blokhin (1969–87), 432 appearances

Two innovators—one a scientist, one a football man—invented a kind of Moneyball for footballers, a full two decades before Billy Beane and the Oakland A's did it for baseball. That they did so in the heart of Soviet-controlled Ukraine makes it all the more remarkable. The result was a string of victories at home and two European Cup Winners' Cup victories. Along the way, the two geniuses ensured that the Ukraine would give the world one of the best center forwards European football has ever seen.

Valeri Lobanovski was the football man, and Anatoly Zelentsov the geek. Lobanovski took over as coach of Dinamo Kiev in 1973, and Professor Zelentsov joined him, both of them having honed their techniques for five years with F.C. Dnipro Dnipropetrovsk, a team based three hundred miles southeast of Kiev. Together, the soccer man and the professor tracked players' performances using computing and statistical analysis previously unheard of in the world of football. Lobanovski and Zelentsov would split a typical pitch into nine areas so that they could see what each player did with and without the ball in each area; players were also judged on a number of other attributes, including endurance, reflexes, and memory. As for actually playing the game, teams were taught a set of preconceived passing moves, so that each man barely had to look up. If this sounds like anti-*futbol*, the very opposite of skills honed on the beaches of Rio de Janeiro, well, it was.

Zelentsov was an especially fascinating man. Having left academia to follow Lobanovski to Kiev, he set about building a database tracing every Dinamo player; his key idea was that if a player had the ball, then the other nine outfield players should automatically, "unemotionally," move into the correct position to best receive a possible pass. His book about "modeling" such plays for players was banned by the Soviets because they saw in his emphasis on function over tactics an implicit criticism of their system. Both he and Lobanovski saw themselves as theater directors, "blocking" out scenes so that nothing was left to chance.

Appropriate then that the greatest beneficiary of these theories was the bull-like center forward Oleh Blokhin. Not the most silky of players, Blokhin nevertheless was able to learn where to be and when, so that midfielders were able to slant passes over defenses where he would appear, the right man at the right time, in one of those imaginary "nine squares." The result was a string of Soviet league victories in the 1970s and 1980s and, most significantly, two European triumphs, both featuring Blokhin—one early on in his Kiev career, and one at the very end.

But this was all to come. Long before European triumph, there was European tragedy. Kiev was hit hard by the German invasion in 1942, with thousands of Ukrainians sent to labor camps and worse. The two main soccer teams of the day, Dinamo and Locomotiv Kiev, joined forces to play as F.C. Start, the Kiev bakery team. As Start, they beat a German team 5–3 on August 9, 1942. That much everyone agrees on. The game, a rematch of an earlier one, has since become known as the Death Match, as it was claimed that the Germans shot the Soviet players to avenge the loss. The truth is probably more prosaic, if still horrible. Since the opening of Russia, historians have speculated that Soviet propaganda morphed some later arrests and deaths of Ukrainian players into the "Death Match" narrative, but at least they didn't bowdlerize the story altogether, as the Sylvester Stallone/Michael Caine/Pelé movie *Victory* did in 1981. (In that film, rather than brutal retribution, Allied POWs, standing in for the Start players, come back from 4–1 down to tie the game 4–4, and then escape from their POW camp.) Either way, it was a terrible time for Kiev and for its football teams, one of whom, Dinamo, had come into being in 1928, initially funded by the secret police.

As the postwar Soviet machine ossified and centralized, only Dinamo was able to challenge the power of the Moscow clubs, the Torpedo–Spartak–CSKA–Locomotiv (Moscow version)–Dynamo axis. Dinamo won five Soviet league titles in the late sixties and early seventies before the arrival of Valeri Lobanovski and Anatoly Zelentsov; after that, they won eight titles before the end of Communism, and five after.

It was in the mid-1970s that Lobanovski's and Zelentsov's theories bore real fruit. In 1975, Dinamo Kiev became the first Soviet team to win a European tournament, and then they won another the same season. Blokhin was at the height of his preprogrammed powers, scoring at will. In the final of the Cup Winners' Cup in May, Dinamo dominated Hungarian side Ferencváros by playing their usual brand of solid, tight, somewhat boring football. It's worth wondering, however, what Lobanovski and Zelentsov made of the second and third goals—the second, a left-foot screamer from Volodymyr Onishenko, was certainly not out of any preconceived playbook, and the third, a solo effort by Blokhin, involved a slaloming run, a feint, and a rounding of the keeper. Four months later, Dinamo bested the Karl-Heinz Rummenigge/Gerd Müller Bayern Munich in a two-leg Super Cup final—Blokhin scored all three goals, one in Munich and two back in Kiev. That same year he received the European Footballer of the Year award, the first Soviet player since Lev Yashin to do so.

Eleven years later, Lobanovski and Zelentsov and Blokhin were still at it. Blokhin scored five goals on the way to the 1986 Cup Winners' Cup final, including two at home to Czech side Dukla Prague in the first leg of the semi-final. (Dukla Prague would become well known in Britain three years later when the song "All I Want for Christmas is a Dukla Prague Away Kit" appeared on the debut record by cult indie band, and staunch Tranmere Rovers fans, Half Man, Half Biscuit.) In the final, Blokhin scored yet again, one of two late goals that added to one very early one to beat Atlético Madrid 3–0. Blokhin's goal came from a no-look pass over the defense, no-look being possible because, in the Dinamo way, Blokhin simply had to be there to receive it—in the theory of "modeling," he had no other choice except to show up in place and finish the chance, and the guy making the pass didn't even need to check.

Amidst all this preprogramming, it was gratifying to see a runaway chicken appear on the field in the first half—both Atlético and Dinamo players dove to get it, but all missed.

Since the Blokhin days (he scored 211 goals for Kiev, a record for the Soviet leagues), Dinamo has continued to do well in Russian competitions, mostly on the back of Andriy Shevchenko, their best goalscorer and biggest superstar since the great Oleh. The club has been tarnished, however, by racist fans—in 2013, they were ordered by UEFA to play some games behind closed doors. The official website of Dinamo Kiev commented, "The number of people of another race in Ukraine is close to [a] statistical error. That's not our fault! It has historically developed in such a way . . . the UEFA website and other sources stated that racist behavior was noticed at the NSC Olimpiyskiy [Dinamo's stadium] during Champions League games against PSG and F.C. des Girondins de Bordeaux . . . during both of these games some fans raised their hands and shouted something like 'sieg heil.' It just looked like that. Some also demonstrated pictures which looked like crosses and swastika[s]."

It is thought that between 8 and 10 million Ukrainians died in World War II. At Babi Yar, a ravine just outside Kiev, 33,000 Jews were

killed in late September 1941. These days, if you visit the Dinamo stadium, you can find a monument to four of the players said to have
been killed after the Death Match. Up in the stands, some fans are
thought to have raised a hand to the skies and shouted *"Sieg heil"*—or
at least, "it just looked like that."

DINAMO ZAGREB

Location	Zagreb, Croatia
Established	1911 (as Građanski)
Nicknames	*Modri* ("The Blues")
Current stadium	Stadion Maksimir (35,123 capacity)
Home colors	Royal blue
Leading goal-scorer	—
Most appearances	—

f you want to know how political turmoil is manifested in the fortunes of a soccer team, have a look at the official website of Dinamo Zagreb. In its history section, it happily reports that the name of the club is "*currently* GNK Dinamo" (emphasis added). Behind this seemingly innocuous statement lies a recent history of football being subsumed under the harsh weight of an ethnic war. No one side comes out of it with much credit, and not much of it is to do with the game as played on the pitch. Sadly, the story must still be told.

In all the turmoil of its years, Dinamo Zagreb has had many names, though before 1945 there was technically no such team. Originally, there were two dominant teams in Zagreb: one, HSK Građanski Zagreb, was a working-class team formed in 1911 by a Croatian hat salesman, when Croatia was still under Austro-Hungarian control. The other was HASK, established eight years earlier by a cadre of students from Zagreb University. Both teams won the fledgling Yugoslav league and cup at least once, though HSK Građanski Zagreb were the more storied team.

All this came to a halt with the end of World War II and the newly installed Communist regime of General Tito. The prewar, Croatian-based teams were disbanded in favor of clubs okayed by the central authority that now ran the country. Yugoslavia has always been a hodgepodge of nationalities and ethnicities, and many credit Tito for enabling it to thrive, especially in the 1960s and 1970s, especially as he often told first Stalin, and then the Soviets, where to go. His was an independent form of state socialism, and if nothing else it kept the country from spinning into destruction. In terms of soccer, in May 1945, players from both HSK Gradanski Zagreb and HASK were brought together by governmental order to form Dinamo Zagreb. As Dinamo, they won the Yugoslav top division four times, though after 1958 they would go dry until 1982.

In European competition, they made it to two Inter-City Fairs Cup finals. On the road to the 1963 final they notched one of their best ever results, traveling to Munich for a quarterfinal in which they went 4–0 up after just an hour. A late consolation goal by Bayern couldn't stop Zagreb advancing all the way to the final, where they lost both legs, home and away, to Spanish club Valencia.

In 1967, Dinamo went one better, but not without huge slices of luck—and it was actual luck, not metaphorical fortune. With scores tied after the first-round, two-leg affair against Spartak Brno of what was then Czechoslovakia, the winner was determined by the toss of a coin. Already, in the second round, the first use of the away goals rule ever in the tournament had helped Zagreb past Dunfermline Athletic of Scotland. By the time they faced Spartak Brno and that coin toss, it must have felt as though Dinamo's name was on the trophy, and so it proved.

In the final, Dinamo faced the Don Revie-managed Leeds, a solid outfit featuring Jack Charlton, Billy Bremner, Norman Hunter, and Peter Lorimer, a team which James Lawton in the *Daily Express* described as "not the foremost of pretty-pretty stylists," which just about summed them up. In Zagreb, Dinamo exposed Leeds's defensive reputation with two unanswered goals, the second of which caused Bobby Charlton's brother to fling his arms around in despair.

Back in Leeds, Don Revie's men made a bunch of chances, none better than the Rod Belfitt header and follow-up shot by Billy Bremner which was cleared off the line. Dinamo lived dangerously, but were worthy of their 0–0 draw and 2–0 aggregate win.

Tito died at the start of the 1980s, and fissures in the Communist regime he left behind grew wider each passing year. In particular, nationalist pride grew. Dinamo Zagreb, though created by Communist fiat, nevertheless had maintained a kind of Croatian subidentity, and by the mid-1980s a band of "ultras" had formed, the Bad Blue Boys, who were both staunch Dinamo fans and Croatian nationalists. After Tito, Dinamo–Red Star Belgrade games represented competing political claims for the country as much as they were soccer matches. By 1990, open conflict was inevitable.

The game on May 13, 1990, was no game at all—a ball wasn't kicked, though there was plenty of anger. *Delije*, the Red Star "ultras" closely connected with the Serbian regime, traveled the 245 miles northwest to Zagreb for the game, led by Arkan—real name Željko Ražnatović—a former gangster who became a Serbian paramilitary leader. Dinamo Zagreb's Bad Blue Boys had been fostered and encouraged by Franjo Tudjman, the Croatian nationalist leader. Inevitably, violence began in the city of Zagreb itself and continued in the Stadion Maksimir proper. Rocks were thrown, Red Star fans ripped hoardings off walls to use as weapons, Bad Blue Boys threw stones and seats, running battles ensued, fans charged at each other, knives were wielded. It was a horrible scene, made even more so when a police officer (turns out he was a Bosnian), Refik Ahmetović, claimed he had been urged by his fellow officers to shoot Dinamo's defender and captain, Zvonimir Boban (Ahmetović later said, "My colleagues who were near me were convincing me to shoot him in the back, to kill him. I didn't do it. They were talking me into it the whole time. I told them, 'If you want to shoot, you have your own guns. I won't shoot.'") All Boban knew at the time was that the officers were arresting Croats, and to come to their aid Boban aimed a running kick at Ahmetović, sending him to the floor.

It is upon such actions, and at such times, that national heroes are made. Immediately, Boban was surrounded by fans eager to keep him alive; the supporters not already on the field cried "Boban! Boban!"; and he instantly became a locus of pride for the Croatian people. Though he was banned by the Yugoslav league for six months and missed the 1990 World Cup in Italy for his actions that day, Boban was unrepentant. (He would later join A.C. Milan and have a stellar footballing career. Ahmetović, for his part, fled to Bosnia.)

To many, this riot signaled the real beginning of the war in Yugoslavia (a monument outside Stadion Maksimir claims as much, though this is hardly how history gets written). Bad Boys Blue were heavily recruited for the Croatian nationalist side, and *Delije* for the Serbian nationalist side. Dinamo Zagreb removed themselves from the rump Yugoslav league and helped create the Croatian football league—along the way, Tudjman insisted they be renamed HASK Gradanski, and then Croatia Zagreb, as he found the word Dinamo "too Communist" (compare Dinamo Tbilisi, Dynamo Moscow, et al). The war raged—after five years around 140,000 people lay dead, the phrase "ethnic cleansing" had become known to all, and the former Yugoslavia had split into Bosnia and Herzegovina, Croatia, Serbia, and Montenegro. In December 1999, Tudjman, since 17 days after the Dinamo–Red Star riot the president of Croatia, died of cancer; two months later, on February 15, 2000, Dinamo Zagreb reverted to their 1945 name. One month before that, on January 14, Arkan was assassinated before he could appear before a war crimes tribunal—apparently he knew too much about Slobodan Milošević's Serbian war machine.

By then, the horrors of the Croatian war of independence, the Bosnian war, the Kosovo war, were all thankfully in the past, though what a toll they had levied upon the people of the former Yugoslavia. To speak of mere soccer is to risk the trivial, but football itself continued throughout those dark days, as though 22 men on a field might assuage, for 90 minutes, the horrors of war. Dinamo continued to win Croatian league titles by the hatful (16 and counting) and provide the world, but mostly Tottenham Hotspur, with quality players: Luka Modrić, Niko Kranjčar, and Vedran Ćorluka all ended up at Spurs (the second via Hadjuk Split and Portsmouth, the latter via Manchester City), though Dinamo also sent Eduardo to Arsenal, a fact most Arsenal fans do their best to forget.

The past won't let anyone forget for long. In April 2011, Dinamo once again changed their name, this time to GNK Dinamo Zagreb in honor of their Gradanski roots. Dinamo Zagreb is *currently GNK Dinamo,*" and if it stays that way because the team and the country is stable and peaceful, surely no one is going to complain.

Location	Buenos Aires, Argentina
Established	1905
Nicknames	*Los Pincharratas* ("The Rat-Stabbers"), *El León* ("The Lion"), *El Orgullo de la Ciudad* ("The Pride of the City"), *Los Capos de La Plata* ("The Bosses of La Plata"), *El Único Campeón de la Ciudad* ("The Only Champion of the City")
Current stadium	Estadio Único (53,000 capacity)
Home colors	Red, white, and black
Leading goal-scorer	Manuel Gregorio Pelegrina (1938–52, 1954–56), 235 goals
Most appearances	—

F ew teams have a more appropriate nickname than the organization that hails from a suburb a few miles southeast of Argentine capital Buenos Aires: Club Estudiantes de La Plata. Known to many as *pincharattas*, or rat-stabbers, some fans of Estudiantes say the name refers to Felipe Montedónica, a local man who killed rats with a big stick in the marketplace and who loved the team; others think it refers to the medical students who have historically played for the club. For many fans of soccer outside of La Plata, the name hits upon one of the darker truths of their playing history: Estudiantes was once one of the most brutal teams to ever curse the beautiful game, and the team against which they earned that reputation didn't behave much better either.

It was 1968. Manchester United had, that summer, won their first ever European Cup and now faced Estudiantes in the inaugural World Club Championship (later known as the Intercontinental Cup). Estudiantes were in the final on the back of their Copa Libertadores victory over Palmeiras of Brazil, which was a triumph in itself for a team that wasn't then, and still isn't, considered one of the top teams in Argentina. In that series of Libertadores finals (three games were needed to separate the sides), Juan Ramón Verón, father of the future Estudiantes and Manchester United star Juan Sebastián Verón, had scored three times, one in each game. "*La Bruja*" ("the Witch"), as he was known, was the undoubted star of the final.

The first leg of the final would be held in Buenos Aires on September 25, 1968, with a second leg slated for Old Trafford in Manchester three weeks later.

There was ill feeling from the start, much of it surrounding the United midfielder Nobby Stiles, a short, pugnacious player who had upset the Argentine national team two years earlier by tackling hard against them for England in the World Cup. By the time the first game started, it was clear that Stiles was in for a beating: kicked, butted, and even told off by a Paraguayan linesman for standing too close to an Estudiantes player, Stiles held out until 10 minutes from the end, when he gesticulated about his unfair treatment and was red-carded. The football? One might hope that a match featuring Bobby Charlton, Denis Law, and George Best—three Manchester legends—would be a spectacle, and that it was, but one of repeated kickings and retaliations.

At the time, Estudiantes had perfected a style of football based on the theories of Osvaldo Juan Zubeldía, their coach, which centered around clever, "professional" fouls, the offside trap, and thinly veiled violence. Denis Law remembers the game in Argentina as "no better than a bloodbath," in which Estudiantes "kicked and scratched and bit, pulled every lowdown trick in the book." There was spitting, too, lots of it; Estudiantes also got away with a 1–0 win.

Back in Manchester, the second game, according to Law, was "considerably cleaner," though an early header by Verón pretty much sealed the tie, leaving United needing three goals they never looked like scoring. Sadly, the British team's frustrations ran high too, causing George Best to strike out at José Hugo Medina two minutes from the end—both were sent off. Best later said, "[Medina] was being booked for kicking me for the hundredth time so I decided I'd had enough. I didn't even wait—I just hit him and walked off. I'd already decided in Argentina if it was going to carry on there wasn't much point trying to play football because they weren't going to let ya." United fans did little to scale the moral heights by raining down coins upon Medina as the referee violently pushed the Estudiantes defender in the back, and off toward the changing rooms. Worse was to come—though United notched a late goal to make the score on the night 1–1, as the players ran off the field, Alex Stepney, United's keeper, took one last shot at an Estudiantes player, smashing him across the face with his left fist. It was a brutal end to what had been two of the ugliest games ever played at club level.

But those anti-football tactics worked—Estudiantes won three Copa Libertadores in a row, from 1968 to 1970, though they had to wait nearly three decades for their next. By then—2009—Manchester United star/failure Juan Sebastián Verón, *La Brujita* ("the Little Witch"), who had started his career with Estudiantes, was back plying his silky trade in their midfield. Verón junior led his team to a two-leg victory over Cruzeiro of Brazil, Estudiantes coming back from a goal behind in Brazil with two late strikes to clinch the title.

The win was some consolation for Estudiantes' narrowly losing the previous year's Copa Sudamericana to Cruzeiro's country-mates Internacional, the winning goal for the Brazilian outfit being scored four minutes before the end of extra time in the second leg. It was a second leg that featured three sendings off—two of which came for Estudiantes players a minute after letting in the winning goal.

EVERTON

Location	Liverpool, England
Established	1878 (as St Domingo's F.C.)
Nicknames	The Toffees, The Toffeemen, The Blues, The School of Science, The People's Club
Current stadium	Goodison Park (40,157 capacity)
Home colors	Royal blue and white
Leading goal-scorer	Dixie Dean (1925–37), 383 goals
Most appearances	Neville Southall (1981–98), 751 appearances

There should be a support group for fans of teams in cities where one club has all the silverware: in New York it would appeal to Mets fans, in L.A. the Clippers, in Madrid Atlético. Two World Series wins versus 27 for the Yankees; zero NBA titles against 16 for the Lakers; nine La Liga titles against Real's 32. And then there's Everton, the other team in Liverpool: so far behind Liverpool's domination that it must be hard . . .

Wait a minute. Though Liverpool have won 18 English titles, Everton have won nine; Liverpool have won the FA Cup seven times, but Everton have won it five. Of course, in European competition there's no comparison—Liverpool's five European Cup/Champions League titles, three UEFA Cups and the same number of UEFA Super Cups blasts Everton's measly 1985 Cup Winners' Cup out of the water. But domestically, at least, it's not quite the mismatch you might imagine.

The club was born out of Sunday school at the St. Domingo Methodist Church in Liverpool. By 1879 they had settled on the name Everton (a district of Liverpool) and were playing at Anfield, of all places. When the Football League began on September 8, 1888, Everton were one of the 12 founding members. It was in those distant days that Everton, known for obscure reasons then and now as the Toffees (no one knows for sure why that's their nickname, though the influence of a couple of Liverpool candy stores—Ye Ancient Everton Toffee House, and Mother Noblett's Toffee Shop—are often cited), wore black with a red sash, and won the third ever league title in those shirts, pipping Preston North End by two points, just as Preston had pipped Everton the previous year by the same amount. John Houlding, the club president, doubled Everton's rent after the 1891 win, so four years into their league life Everton moved to Goodison Park—considered the world's first purpose-built soccer stadium—leaving Houlding to found Everton F.C. and Athletic Ground Limited, a.k.a. Everton Athletic, and thereafter Liverpool F.C. (So Adam = Everton, and Eve = Adam's spare rib = Liverpool.)

By the start of the new century Everton were in their royal blue, the color they still wear, and ensconced in Goodison Park, which opened in August 1892. But it would be 1915 before they won another title, though they won the FA Cup in 1906 when it was still considered the better competition, beating Liverpool 2–0 in the semifinal before knocking off Newcastle United 1–0 in front of 75,000 fans at London's Crystal Palace.

Cue Dixie Dean. William Ralph Dean, known as Dixie, was born in Birkenhead, on the Wirral, the other side of the river Mersey from Liverpool proper. He was an Everton supporter from the get-go, and joined his beloved team in 1925. Dean was a man with a square head which seemed a tiny bit too small for his powerful body. He wore his slicked hair parted in the middle and a sly smile on his pockmarked face—and, eventually, he became one of the most prolific goal-scorers the world has ever seen. In 399 games in 12 years for Everton, Dixie Dean scored a ridiculous 349 goals. One of them, after 52 minutes of the 1933 FA Cup final—a game in which he both captained the team and picked it, Everton having no manager at the time—was part of a

3–0 victory over Manchester City. The Pathé News commentator said, "There's Dean scoring his goal, Langford lying flat on his face, a disappointed man in a disappointing team. Hard lines, Langford." After the game, Pathé would bring the two captains—Dean and Man City's Sam Cowan—into a room for an interview, in which Dean looks straight into the camera and toasts the victory, a glass of champagne in one hand, a cigarette in the other. "Here's to Lancashire," Dean says, "and may the cup stay in Lancashire. If Everton don't win it, may another Lancashire club win it. Hear hear!" Cowan joined him in the toast to Lancashire, smiling wanly and slugging at his bubbly.

Everton had also won the league in 1928 (though they were relegated in 1930 for a season) and again in 1932, both years with Dean scoring freely—60 (!) in 1927–28, and a mere 44 in 1931–32. A glimpse at some of the results Everton posted at Goodison those years reveals just how free-scoring Dean and his team could be: in the first season you can find a 7–0 and a 7–1; a 5–2; two 4–1s and a 4–0. Altogether, home and away, they scored 102 goals; contemporary commentators called their football "scientific," leading to another nickname for the skillful, precise soccer Everton has always tried to play, the "School of Science." In 1931–32, they went nuts: home games featured a 9–2 and a 9–3; an 8–1; a 7–2; a 6–1; and two 5–1s and a 5–0. They notched a staggering 116 goals, home and away, and yet still only won the league by two points over Arsenal—Aston Villa, ten points behind in fifth, scored 104 goals themselves.

Eventually even Dean dried up, scoring just one goal in five games in his last season (1937–38) for Everton. Even with Dean gone, Everton managed to win the 1938–39 title, the penultimate season before World War II intervened. Two titles and an FA Cup in the sixties made Everton one of the preeminent teams of that decade, too. The 1963 champions lost just six games all season behind the goal-scoring exploits of Roy Vernon and Alex Young, both of whom scored more than 20 goals, though even combined they were still well shy of the single season Dixie Dean notched in 1927–28. Three years later, Everton won the FA Cup in a game many believe to have been one of the best finals ever played—two down after an hour, Everton scored three times in the last half hour to steal the trophy from Sheffield Wednesday, and by the end of the decade, and on the back of stars like squeaky-voiced Alan Ball, World Cup-winning Geoff Hurst, and future Everton managers Colin Harvey, Joe Royal, and Howard Kendall, they won their seventh league title, running away with it by a cool nine points over a very fine Leeds United side.

But then nothing came of it; the team stopped performing; legendary coach Harry Catterick left, and the 1970s were a dark time. By 1981, Kendall had been appointed manager, and he created an Everton team as good as if not better than any before seen. In goal, Neville Southall always looked like he'd just rolled out of bed, but little got past him; up front, Graeme Sharp and future commentator Andy Gray latched onto the work of a fine midfield that included Peter Reid, Trevor Steven, and Kevin Sheedy, among others. Their first taste of success came in the 1984 FA Cup final, which they won 2–0, via Sharp and Gray, over Watford. This led them to the Cup Winners' Cup and their finest ever victory, a 3–1 splattering of Bayern Munich at Goodison in the semifinal. Bayern were one up at half-time, but three goals in a stirring second half took Everton to the final, where they beat Rapid Vienna by the same score.

More was to follow: this classic Everton team trounced Liverpool for the 1984–85 league title (they won by 13 points), along the way beating them 1–0, home and away—the Anfield game featured Graeme Sharp's best ever goal, a 30-yard volley into the top right-hand corner. The following season Liverpool regained the title, only for Everton to win it again in 1986–87. The two teams went back and forth all decade, it seemed—even when they weren't winning the league— in head-to-head games like the 1986 FA Cup final, which Liverpool won over Everton to do the double, and the same final three years later, just a few weeks after the Hillsborough disaster.

But it will never be known how good that mid-1980s Everton team really was. After the 1985 Heysel Stadium disaster, in which Liverpool fans rioted, causing the deaths of 39 Juventus fans at the European Cup final, all British teams were barred from European competition for five years (Liverpool got six). No team suffered more than Everton from the misdeeds of their neighbors, and by the time the ban was lifted, Everton were back to being a solid top-half-of-the-table team, which they have been ever since. There are still Merseyside derbies to remember—the 1991 FA Cup fifth-round replay at Goodison featured extra time, eight shared goals, and, a few days later, the resignation of Liverpool's heartsick manager Kenny Dalglish, a man who had been to many of the funerals of the 96 Hillsborough victims, including four in one day.

Everton has faced no such tragedy. Famously well run, often well managed, with a fierce support, the "other team in Liverpool" still finds itself looking across Stanley Park to Anfield, and to a team with an even more illustrious history and more glory, but with so much sorrow around it, too.

Location	Istanbul, Turkey
Established	1907
Nicknames	*Sari Kanaryalar* ("The Yellow Canaries")
Current stadium	Sükrü Saracoglu Stadium, Istanbul (50,509 capacity)
Home colors	Navy blue, yellow, and white
Leading goal-scorer	Zeki Riza Sporel (1915–34), 470 goals
Most appearances	Müjdat Yetkiner (1980–95), 763 appearances

t was the best of times, it was the worst of times, to be a young Turk in the Ottoman Empire. For six hundred years, the empire had swaggered around the Balkans and points east, but by 1900 the center could no longer hold. There were wars in the Balkans (two), the dreadful Armenian genocide, and Turkish nationalists were pressing for secession. So it was little wonder that when the young Turks of the Kadiköy section of Istanbul wanted to form a football team, they had to do so in secret.

It was not a time to be forming groups, teams, clubs, organizations of any kind, and especially not in football, which was loathed by the Istanbul elite. The three men of Kadiköy —Mr. Nurizade Ziya Songülen (president), Mr. Ayetullah (general secretary), and Mr. Necip Okaner (captain), all students at St. Joseph's College—kept their team under wraps for a year. They named it after the nearby Fenerbahçe peninsula, down in the southeastern corner of the city, on the Sea of Marmara. By 1908, however, the sultan was dead, and once he was cold in the ground Fenerbahçe and other teams went legit, openly joining the Istanbul League and playing football without fear of reprisal or religious controversy.

Then, nothing much for five decades, just a bunch of local games in the Istanbul League (which Fenerbahçe won 15 times) while the Ottoman Empire collapsed, Turkey proper prospered, and two devastating world wars came and went. Then, in 1959, a professional league was established, and lo and behold, Fenerbahçe won the first season's title, and the second. They would win four more in the sixties, three in each of the seventies and eighties, a single title in 1995–96, before dominating once again in the new century, when they won six of fourteen possible titles, and came second every other year except two (2003 and 2009). (Galatasaray won five titles in the same period.)

It is with the latter that Fenerbahçe shares one of the most, shall we say, *passionate* local derbies anywhere in the world. Known as the Kitalar Arasi Derbi (Intercontinental Derby, because Galatasaray play in Europe and Fenerbahçe play across the Bosphorus in Asia), its first recorded riot was in February 1934, and since then the matchup has always teetered on, and sometimes fallen into, a state of violent anarchy. As recently as May 2013, a Fenerbahçe fan, Burak Yildirim, was stabbed to death by two Galatasaray supporters after the final game of the season.

In recent years, Fenerbahçe's cachet has fallen hard, following a match-fixing–bribery–organized crime scandal that sent its chairman, Aziz Yildirim (no relation to Burak Yildirim), to jail. It was no isolated incident—the club is suspected in at least 13 separate games of bribes, threatening referees, you name it—and they were banned from playing European football for two years. For a club born in dangerous secrecy, this evidence of behind-the-scenes collusion to merely win a bunch of matches casts a shadow all the way back to a time when three young men were desperate to kick a ball all the way from Asia to Europe.

Location	Rotterdam, Netherlands
Established	1908 (as Wilhelmina)
Nicknames	*De club aan de Maas* ("The Club on the Meuse"), *De Stadionclub* ("The Stadiumclub"), *De Trots van Zuid* ("The Pride of South")
Stadium	*De Kuip* ("The Tub"), officially Stadion Feijenoord (51,117 capacity)
Home colors	Red, white, and black
Leading goal-scorer	—
Most appearances	—

Maybe the grounds staff were on strike, like the rest of Italy. How else to explain the San Siro pitch being more rutted than a farmer's field?

It was May 1970. Since late 1969, Italy had been embroiled in what came to be known as *il autunno caldo*, "the hot autumn" (which carried on through winter and spring), a time of massive industrial action in the northern part of the country. On May 6, the San Siro stadium in Milan was due to host the European Cup final, which that year was to be contested by the 1967 winners, Celtic, and a team new to European Cup finals, Feyenoord of the Netherlands.

The state of the pitch should have ruined the slick passing routines of two of the continent's more cultured teams. But what transpired was a fine game of football and, after 120 minutes, a new name on the big silver European Cup.

Feyenoord had been founded, in 1908, as Wilhelmina F.C., by a bunch of students, one of whom, Kees van Baaren, actually owned a football, which saved him and his pals from using newspapers wrapped in brown paper. It took four years and a few attempts to settle on a name everyone liked: Feijenoord, after the section of Rotterdam on the Nieuwe Maas river where so much of the city's port life happened. (They would, in 1973, change their name to the easier-to-pronounce-for-English-speakers Feyenoord, the spelling we'll use here because, well, we're English speakers.) It took just over a decade to record their first Eredivisie title and they've notched 13 since then, though nothing since 1999. But it is in Europe where Feyenoord, for a few years at least, prospered.

Before World War II, Feyenoord won three titles in five years, but once the Nazis razed the city during the Rotterdam Blitz of May 14, 1940—leaving little standing in its medieval center but the fifteenth-century St. Lawrence church—the prewar momentum was gone for the Dutch club. The Germans occupied their stadium, known as De Kuip ("the Tub"); and though football continued, few cared as to the outcome of games.

In the 1954–55 season professional soccer came to the Netherlands, and by the following decade Feyenoord, along with archrivals Ajax, was dominating the Eredivisie. In the years from 1960–70, Feyenoord finished first, first, fourth, fourth, first, second, second, second, first, second. Ajax too won the league four times that decade, but they also had a few years where they slipped, ending 13th one season. As much as any team ever had one, this was Feyenoord's golden time, and was capped by that visit to the bobbly pitch in Milan's San Siro Stadium in 1970.

The game started well enough for Feyenoord, with a few chances flying toward Evan Williams in the Celtic goal, but then after half an hour, a mixture of chutzpah and terrible refereeing gave Celtic a shock lead. A free kick to Celtic one yard outside the Feyenoord box was sneakily back-heeled by midfielder Bobby Murdoch another five yards away from the Dutch goal. Tommy Gemmell, Celtic's left back known for his powerful shot and fiery temper (he once ran 10 yards to kick West German player Helmut Haller, who had fouled him, while playing for Scotland), hammered a ball through the wall and past the referee, who was standing between the wall and the goalkeeper. It was a ridiculous position to take and clearly blocked the goalkeeper's view. The ball whistled past the unsighted Eddy Pieters Graafland, and Celtic were a goal to the good.

The lead didn't last long. Two minutes later, a game of head tennis in the Celtic box resulted in a goal for Feyenoord's captain, Rinus Israël. From then on it was chance after chance for Feyenoord, the poor state of the pitch hardly affecting their play. Eventually, the game went to extra time, where Feyenoord almost lost the match in the first seconds: a sloppy pass, direct from the kickoff, let Celtic's John Hughes run unimpeded toward the Feyenoord goal, only for Graafland to make a great save. (Israël did his best to score in the same incident, with a subsequent back pass to the keeper that only just stayed out.) With four minutes left, a ball over the top of the defense was clearly handled by the back-pedalling Celtic captain, Billy McNeill, but no matter. Ove Kindvall, Feyenoord's Swedish striker who scored 129 goals for the Dutch team in just five seasons, ignored the hand ball, toe-poked the ball over the Celtic keeper, and Feyenoord had won the cup.

On the back of the victory, Feyenoord faced Estudiantes of Argentina in the 1970 Intercontinental Cup. In La Bombonera stadium, in Buenos Aires, Feyenoord quickly went two down, both from goalkeeping errors by Eddy Treijtel. (The second recipient of Treijtel's gifts was Juan Ramón Verón, whose son Juan Sebastián Verón would grace world football two decades later.) But Feyenoord were a hardy team. They managed to escape the cauldron of La Bombonera with a fine 2–2 draw, Kindvall once again scoring (all four goals in the game were headers).

Back in the Netherlands, in front of 63,000 fans—the stadium had been fitted with extra bleachers for the game—Estudiantes played their usual brutal style of football. But Feyenoord kept their cool. Treijtel made up for his errors in Argentina with an astonishing save in the second half to keep the game tied, and eventually the European champions, via substitute Joop van Daele with a great strike from the edge of the box, scored the only goal of the game. They were European, and world, champions.

The following decade promised much for the Dutch side, and they managed to win two Dutch titles and a UEFA Cup, though the latter victory over Tottenham Hotspur was marred when Spurs fans rioted in the stadium, and through Rotterdam itself, during and after the second leg. At half-time of that game, the Spurs chairman even addressed his team's fans, saying they were "disgracing the British people," but to no effect. In 2002, Feyenoord once again won the UEFA Cup, the victory over Borussia Dortmund coming two days after the assassination of Pim Fortuyn, the right-wing, anti-Muslim politician. Some Feyenoord fans, a section of whom liked to bait the Ajax fans with anti-Semitic slogans (Ajax being associated with Jewishness), bemoaned his loss. Five years later, Feyenoord were thrown out of the same competition after their fans rioted in the French city of Nancy. Huge debts followed; managers came and went; their best players (such as Dirk Kuyt and Salomon Kalou) left. Their last Eredivisie title was at the end of the last century.

Nowadays, when Feyenoord score a goal, the fans sing their version of "I Will Survive" by Gloria Gaynor.

Location	Florence, Italy
Established	1926
Nicknames	*Viola* ("Purple"), *Gigliati* ("Lilies")
Current stadium	Stadio Artemio Franchi (47,282 capacity)
Home colors	Purple
Leading goal-scorer	Kurt Hamrin (1958–67), 208 goals
Most appearances	Giancarlo Antognoni (1972–87), 429 appearances

A team makes it to a major European final; they are pitted against another club from the same country—in fact, their archrivals. The first leg, played on the road, starts well enough: 1–1 after 10 minutes. But two second-half goals to the home team . . . well, the away goal helps, but at 3–1 down something special will need to happen to turn this around.

There's one thing that probably *won't* help: selling your best player to your archrivals *on the day of the second leg.*

Oh, Fiorentina, the *viola* (purple) team of Florence—what were you thinking?

It's bad enough that they were established by a member of the Italian aristocracy who would become a notable Florentine Fascist. The Marchese Luigi Ridolfi Vay da Verrazzano, a direct descendant of the fifteenth-century Lorenzo the Magnificent (an uber-Medici patron of the arts who helped support Leonardo da Vinci, Michelangelo, and Botticelli), brought together a cycling club and a gymnastics society into Associazione Fiorentina del Calcio on August 26, 1926. (Florentines love to allude to a sport played during Lorenzo the Magnificent's time that resembled football, as though the club was actually established in the late 1400s.) Five years later Fiorentina entered Serie A, and in 1956 won their first Scudetto, and by a massive 12 points, over A.C. Milan; they lost one game all season, 3–1 away to Genoa. This terrific Fiorentina team went all the way to the final of the European Cup the next season, where they faced Real Madrid. It seemed like a fix was in, however. The game was played in Madrid, and with 20 minutes to go, a foul a full two feet outside the box resulted in a penalty to Real. It was a horrendous decision (Enrique Mateos, the fouled man, was even offside when he received the ball). The great Madrid goal machine Di Stéfano stepped up and blasted the ball past Giuliano Sarti in the Fiorentina goal. That Sarti had edged forward as far as the six-yard box when Di Stéfano struck his kick was neither here nor there—Di Stéfano seldom missed from 12 yards. Another breakaway six minutes later, another Real goal, and it was all over for Fiorentina.

All over, but not for long. In 1960–61 they won their first European trophy, the Cup Winners' Cup. Their opponents in the final, Rangers, had had an adventurous time getting there. Against Ferencváros of Hungary in a preliminary round, Rangers had squeaked through 5–4 on aggregate thanks to two late goals in Scotland and a lateïsh one in Hungary. In the quarterfinals they made no mistake, however, beating Borussia Mönchengladbach 3–0 in Germany and an astonishing 8–0 in Glasgow (they were five up at halftime). Fiorentina weren't too shabby either, beating the Swiss outfit F.C. Lucerne 6–2 at home. Both teams aced their semifinals, and so headed to the two-leg final.

In that, the first season of the Cup Winners' Cup, fans got their money's worth. 80,000 of them showed up at Ibrox, Rangers' home ground, but an early and a late goal by the ironically-named Luigi Milan gave Fiorentina a strong lead to take back to Italy. Sure enough, in front of 50,000 fans at the Stadio Communale, Milan scored again for Fiorentina, and though Rangers replied on the hour mark, Fiorentina won 2–1 on the night and 4–1 on aggregate.

The following season Fiorentina made the final again, but a 1–1 draw against Atlético Madrid, in Glasgow of all places, led to a replay in Stuttgart in which Fiorentina were trounced 3–0.

In 1968, Fiorentina once again lost only one game on the way to their second Scudetto, and then . . . nothing of note, unless you count horrible luck and bad losses. They probably deserved to win a third Scudetto in the 1981–82 season—as a club they still claim it as rightfully theirs—only to be pipped by Juventus. Both teams were tied on the final weekend, but Fiorentina had a good goal disallowed at Cagliari, while Juventus scored a disputed penalty via the sweet left boot of Irishman Liam Brady. With calm hindsight, it might be pointed out that the penalty was perfectly legitimate—it was a clear hand ball on the line—but calmness disappeared from the Juventus–Fiorentina rivalry that day.

It was made worse by that transfer on the day of the second leg of the UEFA Cup final in 1990. Juventus had aced the first leg in Turin 3–1, but on May 16, the day of the second leg, it was announced that a young Fiorentina center forward by the name of Roberto Baggio would be joining Juventus. Cue riots; cue the fleeing of Flavio Pontello, who owned the club until he sold it to a movie director, Mario Gori; cue relegation. For what it's worth, that second leg was the perfect embodiment of Italian club soccer in the late 1980s: it finished 0–0, and Juventus had the trophy—and fledgling superstar Roberto Baggio. By 2002, Fiorentina's finances were in such disarray that they went into administration, and were gone.

Re-formed with a slightly different name to fool everyone (Associazione Calcio Fiorentina e Fiorentina Viola), Fiorentina joined the fourth level of Italian football, Serie C2. By 2004—and after a bizarre promotion from C2 to Serie B in 2003 for "sporting merit" reasons, whatever that means—they were back in Serie A, only to get thrown back into Serie B in 2006 for their part in betting on games (they were reinstated with a points penalty, the way of Italian soccer administration being long on intrigue and short on transparency). Since then they have been a solid, if sometimes relegation-threatened team.

They still have their moments. In May 2012, Fiorentina's manager, Delio Rossi, found himself being sarcastically applauded by Serbian international forward Adem Ljajić when Rossi substituted him during a game against Novara. Retribution was swift—Rossi, incensed by the blatant show of disrespect, walked up to Ljajić, sitting on the bench all sweaty and angry, and punched him. Rossi was subsequently fired; Ljajić was eventually sold to Roma, though he no longer plays for his national team, Serbia, as he refuses to sing their national anthem.

Location	Rio de Janeiro, Brazil
Established	1895
Nicknames	*Mengão* ("Big Mengo"), *Rubro-Negro* ("The Red-Blacks"), *O mais querido do Brasil* ("The most beloved of Brazil")
Current stadium	Estádio do Maracanã (76,804 capacity)
Home colors	Red, black, and white
Leading goal-scorer	Arthur Antunes Coimbra, known as Zico (1971–83, 1985–89), 508 goals
Most appearances	Leovegildo Lins da Gama Júnior (1974–84, 1989–93), 857 appearances

n the beginning, it was not *futbol* but rowing. It started not for the love of athletic pursuit but for the *"conquistando o coração das garotas do bairro"*—winning the hearts of the girls from the neighborhood. But the boat sank in the waters off Rio de Janeiro, though all eight rowers were saved. This was the Clube de Regatas do Flamengo—a well-to-do group of young men doing what young men have always done: try to appeal to young women.

It took many years for the rowing club to become a soccer team, and even then it was frowned upon—soccer was deemed déclassé and effeminate. It took the defection of nine Fluminense players from the state championship team in 1911 to create the soccer club that would become, one day, Fluminense's fiercest rivals: Flamengo.

Having shucked off the stuffy rowers, Flamengo set about creating a solid football team out of students and urbanites (though it took a while for black players to be accepted there, and even longer for that to happen at Fluminense). Flamengo are still considered the working-class team of Rio (former coach Júlio César Leal said they were supported by "30 million paupers," which seems a bit harsh—but then, he was also once Fluminense's manager).

Flamengo played their first game in 1912, and quickly set about winning the state championship, the Campeonato Carioca, over and over and over (their first win was in 1914, then 1915, then 1920, then 1921 . . . to date, it's 32 wins and 30 times runners-up in almost a century of play). They have won one more title than Fluminense so far, and games between them—the Fla-Flu, as legendary Brazilian journalist Mário Filho nicknamed it—feature massive crowds, a festival atmosphere, and all the passion one might expect from two teams separated by nothing at all (both teams play their biggest games at the Maracanã, a.k.a. the Estádio Journalist Mário Filho).

Eventually, Brazil created a national championship in 1959, no mean feat in a country the size of the United States. Flamengo wouldn't take part until the late sixties, but by 1980, the greatest ever Flamengo side dominated the national league—and in 1981, they also won the world.

It began with three Campeonato Cariocas in a row in the late 1970s, and then, in 1980, Flamengo lost just two games all season in winning their first national championship. Heading off to play in the Copa Libertadores the following year, the side sparkled with the talents of Leandro and Mozer at the back, Júnior and Zico in midfield, and Adílio, Nunes, and Tita up front. It was a team filled with stars, and it reached its peak in 1981 with both a Copa Libertadores victory and a world championship.

In the Copa Libertadores, Flamengo struggled in the group stage and might not have made it to the semifinals were it not for the indiscipline of their opponents, Atlético Mineiro, also of Brazil. Mineiro had lost the Brazilian championship in 1980 to Flamengo after a 3–2 defeat at the Maracanã—now, in a one-off playoff game, the two teams faced each other in the Estádio Serra Dourada in Goiania. There was bad blood from the start: referee José Robert Wright remembers "*uma atmosfera muito pesada*" (a very heavy atmosphere), though he undoubtedly contributed to the farce that was about to unfold.

The first Atlético player to get a red card, after just 20 minutes, was Reinaldo after a fairly innocuous tackle on Zico; a few minutes later, Éder followed him down the tunnel, having accidentally bumped the referee while rushing to take a free kick. (Perhaps all these histrionics were something to do with the crazy way that the grass was cut that day, dark squares next to light squares, and inside each, alternating light circles and dark circles—it was enough to send anyone out of his mind.) Éder quite understandably fell to his knees in horror at his red card; cue a pitch invasion by Atlético's bench, and in the melee two more players were sent off, Palhinha and Chicão. Police now ringed the nausea-inducing field. On 37 minutes, the fifth and last sending-off came for Atlético, this time defender Osmar Guarnelli. With only six players left on the Atlético team, Wright had no choice—the game was abandoned. The referee marched away, straight-backed and proud, and Flamengo were awarded the win.

The semifinals were more straightforward: Flamengo waltzed through them, winning their games with ease. The final, against Chile's Cobreloa, was a three-game affair—the first two were shared: 2–1 to Flamengo in front of 94,000 people at the Maracanã, and 1–0 back in Chile to the hosts. Without an away goals rule in place, a third game was needed, and both teams headed to Montevideo, Uruguay. Flamengo dominated the game, with Zico scoring both goals (he had also scored both in the first leg). Flamengo were finally Copa Libertadores champions. But an even greater night awaited.

The 1981 Intercontinental Cup featured a dream matchup: the Flamengo of Zico versus the European champions, Liverpool, featuring Kenny Dalglish, Graeme Souness, Alan Hansen, and nutter Bruce Grobbelaar in goal. The two teams headed for Tokyo, with neutrals praying for a classic game.

What they got instead was a masterclass by Zico. There were times he was surrounded by four or five Liverpool players, but with a drop of the shoulder and a foot on the ball, he caused his opponents to fall, fade, stop dead in their tracks—it was as if he was the only player on the field. He used the nutmeg like other players use a five-yard pass. His ball for the opening goal by Nunes was a 35-yard pitching wedge that stopped on a dime beyond the despairing head of a Liverpool defender; it had precision and backspin, like the greatest golf shot you ever saw. Nunes couldn't miss; nor could he again four minutes before half-time, latching on to a Zico pass made at such an innovative angle few players would ever have seen it. That goal added to an Adílio tap-in after a Zico free kick had been spilled by Grobbelaar to make it 3–0 at the break. A very fine Liverpool team had been crushed by the best player in the world.

That great Flamengo team would win the Brazilian national championship again in 1982 and 1983, but only three times since (1987 in a breakaway league, 1992, and 2009). But they will always have Arthur Antunes Coimbra, "Zico," once described in typically modest fashion by Pelé as "the one who came closest to me." It takes the greatest player in history to know he is.

Location	Istanbul, Turkey
Established	1905
Nicknames	*Cimbom, Aslan* ("The Lion"), *Sari-Kirmizililar* ("Yellow-Reds"), *Avrupa Fatihi* ("Conqueror of Europe"), Gala (mostly used outside of Turkey)
Current stadium	Turk Telekom Arena (52,652 capacity)
Home colors	Red, yellow, and white
Leading goal-scorer	Metin Oktay (1955–61, 1962–69), 538 goals
Most appearances	Turgay Seren (1947–67), 631 appearances

Years later, it's strange to watch video of the Manchester United team arriving in Istanbul in November 1993 for what became one of the most notorious Champions League games ever played. In the minds of many, what the superstars of United faced was a mob of Galatasaray fans hell-bent on murdering each and every one of them. The truth, however, is a bit different.

Stories abound, usually told by United players, of evil harassment in their brief stay in the Turkish capital, of life-threatening gestures, violence, brutality, near-death. Many of the stories coalesce around one of the most iconic images, a bloodcurdling sign waiting for the players as they arrived at the airport, which read "Wellcome to Hell" (sic).

But the actual sign? It's about three feet by two feet, on flimsy yellow paper, held up by a smiling fan. It reads "WELLCOME TO ALI SAMI YEN HELL" (Ali Sami Yen was, until 2011, the Galatasaray stadium), and all around the words the Galatasaray supporter has added little stars and circles—you know, to prettify it. The chanting fans all smile at the United players, who smile back from the comfort of the team bus. Gary Neville and David Beckham look a bit nervous, but they're both 18 years old.

There were some terrible scenes in Istanbul—after the 0–0 draw that eliminated United from the competition, striker Eric Cantona was assaulted by a police officer, while captain Bryan Robson, in trying to help Cantona, got eight stitches in an elbow wound. A brick that came through the bus window landed where defender Steve Bruce's head should have been but fortunately wasn't. Worst of all, a large number of United fans were arrested for no reason. But "hell?" Hardly.

What United had wandered into was the home of one of the most passionate clubs in all the world. Galatasaray was imagined in 1903 during a literature class at the Galatasaray High School, which is more than five centuries old and has produced countless statesmen, businessmen, artists, and scientists. It also produced a cadre of boys who wanted to play soccer, one of whom, Ali Sami Yen, had watched Brits in Istanbul play the game. He and his pals wanted in, and by 1905 they had established their club, with Ali Sami Yen becoming the first president (because, according to his autobiography, he was "good at greasing the ball and blowing it up. I used to treat that ball as if it were my child"), and his name would eventually adorn the stadium opened in December 1964. The initial plan for the team was a simple, if ironic one, given what happened 90 years later to Manchester United: "Our objective was to play in a team like the British, have our own colors and name and beat non-Turkish teams."

Quickly the team began to dominate the Istanbul league, winning three years in a row (1908–10), and then eight more times before World War II. By the end of the fifties, Turkey had a professional league, a competition Galatasaray has won 19 times, equal with Fenerbahçe. Their rivalry with Fenerbahçe, known as the Kitalar Arasi Derbi, has grown in that time to be one of the most violent in world football.

Sometimes, the football is beside the point. One of the most notorious moments occurred after the second leg of the final of the 1996 Turkish Cup. The first leg had ended 1–0 to Galatasaray, and the second leg, played across the water in Fenerbahçe, ended 1–1, giving the cup to the away team. According to Galatasaray's then manager, Scot Graeme Souness, "the Fenerbahçe vice president had made some smart-arse comments about me being a cripple earlier in the season," so at the end of the match at Fenerbahçe's Şükrü Saracoglu Stadium, Souness thought it would be a good idea to run halfway along the length of the pitch and plant a Galatasaray flag in the middle of the center circle. As a provocative gesture it comes close to shouting "Fire!" in a crowded theater, and it was only slightly ruined by the fact that the game was played in the middle of a cold spell that had left the ground hard, causing Souness, wrapped up in a bulky soccer-coach jacket, to have to prod three times before the huge flag would stand up. Nonetheless, from then on Souness was afforded the nickname "Ulubatli Souness" by Galatasaray fans, after Turkish hero Ulubatli Hasan, who, at age 25, was killed for raising the Ottoman flag on the top of the walls of Constantinople during its famous siege in 1453.

When a reporter from the UK's *Independent* newspaper asked Souness years later if anyone from his club was angry at him for the warlike gesture, he replied, "No way. I got the biggest kiss of my life, from the [Galatasaray] president," a statement that says more about Souness's romantic life than one might ever want to know.

Galatasaray's finest achievement on the field was a "fourpeat" at the end of the 1990s that led to European triumphs—they were the first and only Turkish team to win a major European trophy, the 2000 Europa League. But the victory was marred by violence along the way. Galatasaray entered the tournament through the back door, ending third in their Champions League group behind Chelsea, who went to the Ali Sami Yen and beat the Turkish champions 5–0. In the Europa League, Galatasaray had an easier time of it, not losing a game, though tragedy stalked the tournament. On Thursday, April 6, 2000, before the first leg of the semifinal, fights between Galatasaray and Leeds United fans in Istanbul's central area, Taksim Square, left two Leeds supporters, Christopher Lofthouse and Kevin Speight, dead; many more were injured. Peter Risdale, Leeds' chairman, had to help identify the body of Mr. Lofthouse in the hospital. For what it's worth, Galatasaray won that night and drew the return leg to reach the final.

The game itself, played in Copenhagen against Arsenal, was a goalless draw, and in extra time the great Gheorghe Hagi was sent off—but Arsenal couldn't snatch a goal. The final went to Galatasaray after they held their nerve on penalties (oddly, one of their penalty takers was the prolific Turkish striker Hakan Sükür—he scored; one of Arsenal's was the Croat Davor Šuker—he missed). But once again, trouble flared, in the form of a running riot in City Hall Square during which some 500 Arsenal fans ran at the assembled Galatasaray supporters. One report suggested the fighting lasted a full 20 minutes as police "panicked" and didn't intervene.

It was another sad night for Galatasaray. Their subsequent peaceful victory in Monaco at the European Super Cup in 2000 (they stunned Real Madrid, 2–1, in extra time) reminded football fans that here was a vintage team—Taffarel in goal, Popescu at the back, Hagi in midfield—with passionate fans who didn't always draw unwonted attention to their passion. Sometimes, their hell had pretty little stars drawn all around it.

Location	Gothenburg, Sweden
Established	1904
Nicknames	*Blåvitt* ("Blue-White"), *Änglarna* ("The Angels"), *Kamraterna* ("The Comrades")
Current stadium	Gamla Ullevi (18,416 capacity)
Home colors	Blue and white
Leading goal-scorer	Filip "Svarte-Filip" Johansson (1924–34), 333 goals
Most appearances	Mikael Nilsson (1987–2001), 609 appearances

In a recent *Daily Telegraph* portrait of the man Swedes call "Svennis," Sven-Goran Eriksson is described as coaching "at some of the biggest clubs in European football, including Benfica (twice), Fiorentina, Sampdoria and Lazio, whom he guided to the Cup Winners' Cup in 1999, before he accepted the lucrative England job in 2001."

Notably absent is the team with which he won his biggest trophy. Sure, he won Serie A and a Cup Winners' Cup with Lazio, and reached a European Cup final with Benfica, but an actual victory in a significant European tournament? That would be the 1989 UEFA Cup, with IFK Gothenburg of Svennis's homeland.

Sweden is a cold place to play soccer—so cold that their league runs March to November rather than the more usual August to May. Gothenburg have won the various incarnations of the Swedish league (too many to list here) 18 times since they were formed in October 1904, after an evening meeting between students and others at one Café Olivedal in Gothenburg. Once established, they almost instantly became archrivals with Örgryte Idrottssällskap, a.k.a. ÖIS, another

Gothenburg club. David Goldblatt, in *The Ball Is Round*, tells the story of matches between the clubs in 1912 and 1913 in which there were fights, pitch invasions, last-minute penalties not able to be taken—the full nine yards of fledgling soccer hooliganism. Sadly, the blue-collar (IFK)–middle-class (ÖIS) rivalry is now no longer as intense, especially after 12-time champions ÖIS went bankrupt in 2011 and were relegated to the Swedish third division. (Oh, and as for class conflict, well, Sweden now has the seventh highest per capita income on the planet, ahead of the US, Japan, and Germany.)

Given that Swedish football is off-schedule with much of the rest of the continent, it's impressive that IFK Gothenburg have managed to win not one but two UEFA Cups in their history.

The first came in 1981–82. Gothenburg had spent some time in the second division in the 1970s, but with the ascension of legendary striker Torbjörn Nilsson to the team, they turned their fortunes around. By 1982, and with Sven-Goran Eriksson as coach, they were by far the best team in Sweden (they won the league in a title playoff decider, and the Swedish Cup); and in their European campaign, they knocked out some solid clubs on the way to the final. It wasn't plain sailing: in the second round they needed a last-minute penalty from defender Stig Fredriksson to snatch a victory over Sturm Graz of Austria. Dispatching Dinamo Bucharest and Valencia in the next two rounds (the latter after Swedish fans had paid the team's expenses to travel to Spain, Gothenburg often being a team with severe financial constraints), they again needed late heroics from Stig Fredriksson to defeat F.C. Kaiserslautern in the semifinal, the second leg of which went to extra time.

In the final, Gothenburg faced another German team, Hamburger S.V. The first leg was a tight affair, played on what resembled a cow pasture. Though May can be sublime in certain parts of Europe, in Gothenburg, according to weatherspark.com, "the average probability that some form of precipitation will be observed in a given day is 52%." It had certainly rained that night, if the pitch was anything to go by, but a single goal for the Swedish team with three minutes to go sealed the victory. The then dark-haired Eriksson displayed his habitual sanguinity when faced with joy as Tord Holmgren knocked the ball past the keeper, through the mud and puddles, and into the back of the Hamburg net.

The second leg was a different story. In Germany, Dan Corneliusson opened the scoring for Gothenburg after 25 minutes with a bullet to the top right-hand corner, and from there on it was all Gothenburg. After an hour, the great Nilsson outran the entire Hamburg defense for 40 yards for the second goal, before Corneliusson was hauled down in the box five minutes later. That man Fredriksson scored again, burying another penalty once the single pitch-invading Swedish fan was caught by German police.

Three months after the victory Svennis was gone, off to Benfica. Five years later, Gothenburg—having lost a European Cup semifinal to Barcelona in 1986 on penalties—won the UEFA Cup again, this time beating Scottish side Dundee United 2–1 on aggregate. By 1987, Torbjörn Nilsson was gone too, replaced by two other Nilssons: Roland and Lennart. But that tournament was really all about Dundee United, a relatively tiny team who had knocked Barcelona out in the quarterfinals—a Barcelona with Mark Hughes and Gary Lineker up front, but which shifted two goals in the last five minutes at the Camp Nou to the orange-clad Scottish minnows. The final, needless to say, was a letdown if you're Scottish, but for the Swedes—all those Nilssons and Johanssons and Anderssons and Larssons and Fredrikssons (Stig was still at center back)—it was bliss.

In recent years European success has been scant for Gothenburg, except for the 1994–95 Champions League, in which they topped a group that featured both Manchester United and, you guessed it, Barcelona; in Sweden, six championships between 1990 and 1996 have been followed by only a single triumph since, in 2007. Svennis continues to manage soccer teams—since his high point at Gothenburg, he's coached and/or technically directed Benfica twice, Roma, Fiorentina, Sampdoria, Lazio, England, Manchester City, Mexico, Notts County, Leicester City, Thai club BEC Tero Sasana F.C., Al-Nasr of the UAE, and Guangzhou R & F in China.

GRÊMIO

Location	Porto Alegre, Brazil
Established	1903
Nicknames	*Tricolor, Imortal* ("Immortal")
Current stadium	Arena do Grêmio (60,540 capacity)
Home colors	Blue, white, and black
Leading goal-scorer	—
Most appearances	—

As a player he was known as *"Perna-de-Pau,"* or "Pegleg," a phrase reserved for the worst of Brazilian footballers. Fortunately, he became more known for his coaching, and by another nickname to English speakers: "Big Phil." Luiz Felipe Scolari won the 2002 World Cup with the Brazilian national team, but his coaching philosophy is about as beloved as his skills were on the field.

Scolari was born in the southern Brazilian state of Rio Grande do Sul, 180 miles northwest of its capital, Porto Alegre. Porto Alegre is so far south it might as well be in Uruguay. Sitting just 240 miles north of the border, the city of 1.5 million people was settled first in the nineteenth century by the Portuguese, then by the Germans—many, many Germans—and then the rest of Europe filled the place out, including Italians to whom the Scolari family traces its roots. To this day the people of Porto Alegre claim almost 80 percent European descent, and for many years one of its main football teams, Grêmio, established in 1903, remained a whites-only, German-descended team. Their main rivals in Porto Alegre, Internacional, went mixed early, but Grêmio stubbornly stuck to a different vision of Brazil, even though their first president, Carlos Luiz Bohrer, displayed a pleasing melange of nationalities in his mere name.

The first hero of those amateur days was Eurico Lara, a goalkeeper who played 16 seasons for Grêmio. In his last match, he was substituted at half-time with heart problems after having stopped a shot by his own brother; so the story goes, he either died two months later or directly after the game. Either way, the legend continues when Grêmio fans eulogize him in their anthem ("*Lara, o craque imortal*"— "Lara, the immortal ace").

Clinging first to being whites-only, then to its amateurism, held Grêmio back, though they did well in their region, winning the state championship of Rio Grande do Sul eleven times before joining the first national Brazilian championship in 1959. But their brand of football was utilitarian, rather than expansive in the more typically Brazilian style, and they didn't come close to winning a national championship until their decade arrived: the 1980s.

In 1981, Grêmio finally won the Brazilian league, which was perfect timing given that they'd just doubled the capacity of their old Estádio Olimpico Monumental to 85,000. Two years later they went a step further, winning the Copa Libertadores for the first time, but that win was not without its controversies.

The tournament went well for Grêmio early on—they waltzed through the group stages with five wins and a draw. The semifinal group was a different story. Up against a strong Colombian team, América, and Estudiantes of Argentina, each of the three teams won a game to begin the round robin. Then Grêmio traveled to La Plata in Argentina to face Estudiantes.

What transpired was little short of a boxing match, and a frozen one at that. The temperature that July night in 1983 was just 28 degrees, and before the game even started, an Estudiantes player got a yellow card for dissent. It went downhill from there: Estudiantes had a player sent off for retaliating after a tackle; a little while later, during a "let's-surround-the-ref-and-intimidate him" melee, one of the Estudiantes players pushed the hapless man in black in the back, who then brandished a straight red card at the wrong guy. It was at this point that it became clear the referee was in danger of being lynched, surrounded as he was by players, officials, cameramen, and police officers. The minutes-long argument finally dissipated, but even with the Argentine side down to nine men, somehow they took the lead from the restart of the game. Grêmio equalized, leading to a chest-bumping argument between a linesman and an Argentine player; comedy had turned into farce. In the second half, Grêmio went up 3–1, the third goal being a solo effort by Renato that would have graced a better game. Then a linesman got hit in the head with a missile; two more Estudiantes players were sent off, and yet they ended up tying the game 3–3 via a late scrambled goal. For a team with a history of violence-marred games, Estudiantes had reached rock bottom; for Grêmio, it mattered not—they went on to the final game where they beat Peñarol of Uruguay with a late goal in the second leg.

In the Intercontinental Cup that year, Grêmio beat Hamburg, in Tokyo, with another goal by Renato in extra time. They were the champions of the world, and yet hardly beloved. Scolari came to manage them for one season in the mid-1980s, and then returned in 1993 to lead them to their second Copa Libertadores, in 1995. His style—all pressure and defense and conservatism—was roundly loathed in Brazil (even Grêmio's official website notes it was a "team without stars"), but Grêmio's quarterfinal games against top Brazilian team Palmeiras might have dispelled some of the doubters. Featuring greats like Rivaldo, Roberto Carlos, and Cafu, Palmeiras lost the first leg in Porto Alegre 5–0, though they almost made up for it in the return leg, winning 5–1. It wasn't enough, and Grêmio went on to the final. Once again, after the drama of the earlier rounds, the final was something of an anticlimax, Grêmio getting by Atlético Nacional of Colombia with some ease, 4–2 on aggregate.

Scolari led Grêmio to their other Brazilian league title the next season, before leaving to wander from team to team until he brought his country a World Cup victory in 2002. Grêmio lost a Copa Libertadores final 5–0 on aggregate in 2007, and have also been rele-gated in the new century, though they are now back in the top tier. And they gave the world Anderson, Manchester United's center midfielder—the only Brazilian in the history of football to be one-footed, unable to pass to a teammate on a consistent basis, and over-weight. At least, unlike Big Phil, he doesn't have a "wooden leg," though some wonder.

Location	Guadalajara, Mexico
Established	1906
Nicknames	*Las Chivas* ("The Goats"), *Las Chivas Rayadas* ("The Striped Goats"), *El Rebaño Sagrado* ("The Sacred Flock"), *Los Rojiblancos* ("The Red-and-Whites")
Current stadium	Estadio Omnilife (capacity 49,850)
Home colors	Red, white, and blue
Leading goal-scorer	Salvador Reyes (1953–67, 2008), 122 goals
Most appearances	Ramón Morales (1999–2010), 373 appearances

They are the team of "Crazy Goats," swine flu, Mexicans only, and Little Peas.

The nickname "Crazy Goats" was, like many such monikers, at first an insult, but the best way to remove the sting from words is to appropriate them as your own. So it was with *"Chivas Locas,"* the name hurled at fans of the Mexican side Club Deportivo Guadalajara in 1949. By the strange morphing of language, Club Deportivo Guadalajara is now better known as Chivas, and gave their name to the decade-long offshoot, Chivas USA, before its rebranding. How many English-speaking American fans know that they were called goats is an open question.

Chivas was founded by a Belgian immigrant, Edgar Everaert, who moved to Mexico just after the start of the twentieth century—but it was not founded as Club Deportivo Guadalajara. To celebrate his coming together with a number of Mexican, French, and Belgian devotees of this new-to-Mexico game—some of whom sported terrific names, such as Calixto Gas and Max Woong—Everaert called the new organization the Union Football Club. But Everaert, a smart man, realized that adding the name of a town made fans more likely to be loyal (he himself was from the soccer-mad city of Brugge in Belgium, and to this day, Chivas's red and white stripes resemble the kit Brugge used to wear). So the Union Football Club quickly became Club Deportivo Guadalajara, and eventually Chivas.

Once they were crazy goats, Chivas began to excel as a team in the newly minted professional Mexican league. By the 1940s, Chivas had instigated a "Mexican citizens only" rule for its players. After their first professional title in 1957—won on a last-minute goal in the final match by Chava Reyes, after a season that saw them beat archrivals Club América 7–0—Chivas won an unprecedented four in a row from 1959 to 1962, and two more in 1964 and 1965, giving them an impressive seven in nine seasons.

That extraordinary team, known in Mexico as the Campeonísimo, was renowned enough around the world to embark, in spring 1964, on the first tour of Europe by a Mexican side. Featuring players with the nicknames Cuate, El Cura, Tigre, Jamaicón, Bigotón, and Chololo, Chivas dazzled early in the tour before the travel and the intense game schedule wore them out. In the first game, against Barcelona, they revived from 2–0 down to draw the game—this against a team who three days earlier had finished behind only Real Madrid in La Liga. A loss to Seville on May 6 somewhat soured the trip, as it had been a vicious game of football, Seville narrowly winning 3–2, but later swings through France, Belgium, Germany, and Czechoslovakia confirmed Chivas as a top world team.

Alas, their later history has been spotty—where other teams in Mexico have imported quality players from other countries, Chivas's all-Mexican roster has seemed to sometimes hold them back. A total of eleven Mexican championships has been offset by scant success in competitive international games, and financial troubles.

Their best finish to a season was in 2010, when they came second in the Copa Libertadores. The only reason they were in that competition was because, in the previous year, teams had refused to travel to Mexico to play them because of the 2009 flu outbreak, which is thought to have begun in the Mexican state of Veracruz, some 500 miles east of Guadalajara. During the pandemic more than 70,000 cases of H1N1 flu were confirmed in Mexico, with more than 1,300 deaths; schools, restaurants, cinemas, museums, all were closed. In 2010, and with the pandemic contained, Chivas were invited to play in the Copa Libertadores as a makeup for the previous year.

They almost won it. In the round of 16 they squeezed by Argentine side Vélez Sarsfield 3–2 on aggregate (3–0 at home, 0–2 away), and beat Libertad of Paraguay by the exact same scores in the quarterfinal. The semifinal saw their best performance, traveling to play Universidad de Chile in Santiago and winning 2–0, which set up a final against Brazilian powerhouse Internacional.

At their Estadio Omnilife (!) in the first leg, Chivas went ahead right on half-time, but couldn't stop Internacional scoring twice in the second half. Chivas tied the tie in Brazil, once again right before half-time, but three second-half goals (plus one late consolation to Chivas) gave Internacional the title.

Perhaps things would have been different if Chivas hadn't sold their superstar striker, Javier "Chicharito" ("Little Pea") Hernández, to Manchester United in the spring of 2010. On July 31, United traveled to Mexico to play an exhibition game against Chivas, to help celebrate the official opening of the Estadio Omnilife. Chivas won the game 3–2. Their first goal, a stunning left-footed strike from 25 yards after just eight minutes, was scored by Hernández, playing one last half in the red and white stripes of his Crazy Goats (he played for United in the second half). On August 8, Man United beat Chelsea in the Community Shield, their second goal scored by Hernández. Two day later, Chivas lost the first of their Copa Libertadores final games at the recently opened Estadio Omnilife.

GUANGZHOU EVERGRANDE

Location	Guangzhou, China
Established	1954 (semi-professional); 1993 (professional)
Nicknames	Southern China Tigers
Current stadium	Tianhe Stadium (capacity 50,000)
Home colors	Red and white
Leading goal-scorer	Luiz Guilherme da Conceição Silva, known as Muriqui (2010–), 73 goals
Most appearances	Feng Junyan (2003–), 243 games

When Guangzhou Evergrande won the Asian Football Confederation Champions League, in 2013, a small concussion ran around world football. For years, Chinese soccer had lagged behind the rest of the world, especially given the resources, and the sheer number of people, the country could bring to bear if it cared to. Soccer in China has been widely thought to be notoriously corrupt, and it was certainly terrible to watch. But with Guangzhou Evergrande winning a major tournament, perhaps things were changing?

Guangzhou Evergrande is not a new team, nor is soccer in China a new phenomenon. *Cuju*, a sort of pre-soccer runabout with a ball and a single goal, was played as early as 2 BC. Much later, Mao was said to be a goalkeeper, and Deng Xiaoping attended football games at the Paris Olympics in 1924.

Established in June 1954, Guangzhou Evergrande entered a then new Chinese football league, only to get immediately relegated—which is saying something, so lousy was the standard. It never much improved, and 50 years later, the game in China was almost comically pointless. The Chinese government apparatus chose which young men to train, but they weren't very good at it (their expertise was in gymnastics and ping pong). Players, officials, and referees routinely took bribes. By the end of the twentieth century, four Guangzhou Evergrande players had been revealed as taking bribes, and the team had been relegated again.

The country as a whole didn't fare much better. China qualified for the nearby Korea–Japan World Cup in 2002, and though they were unfortunate to be drawn in the same group as Brazil, they also drew Costa Rica and Turkey, hardly the most formidable opponents. In their first game in the 2002 World Cup, against Costa Rica, China held out until the 61st minute, but by the 65th they were two down, which is how the game ended. No one gave China a hope against Brazil, and sure enough they were three down at half-time, though Brazil took it easy on them in the second half and the final score was a mere 4–0. In the final game against Turkey, many millions of Chinese fans simply hoped for a goal, but the game ended 3–0. In China's first appearance at a World Cup, they not only failed to score a goal but had to bear the pain of South Korea almost making the final.

Back in the Chinese leagues, money kept changing hands and games kept getting fixed. In 2006, Evergrande got some private funding, finally, from a Guangzhou company, and the next year joined the shiny new Chinese Super League. Three years later, they were relegated again after—you guessed it—yet more match-fixing.

Guangzhou Evergrande cleaned house one more time and rejoined the Super League. In 2011, they won it, and would win it for the next two years. By May 2012, former Italy boss Marcello Lippi was Guangzhou Evergrande's manager, and in 2013 they went all the way to the AFC Champions League final, where they faced F.C. Seoul of South Korea.

The game began with Seoul taking an 11th-minute lead, but after an hour Guangzhou Evergrande were 2–1 up, thanks to Brazilian import Elkeson and Chinese superstar Gao Lin. Guangzhou Evergrande's South American imports proved crucial; in adddition to Elkeson, Evergrande boasted fellow Brazilian Muriqui and Argentine Darío Conca, who had helped take Fluminense all the way to the 2008 Copa Libertadores final. (Guangzhou Evergrande were paying Conca more than $12 million a year.) In that first leg, Seoul eventually equalized; but when Evergrande held the South Korean team to a 1–1 draw back in Guangzhou in the second leg, China finally had something to crow about in soccer.

Guangzhou Evergrande's win took them to the FIFA Club World Championship, where they were overwhelmed 3–0 by Bayern Munich (it could have been many more), but nearly beat Atlético Mineiro in the third-place playoff, making them, for one season at least, the fourth-best team in the world.

HAJDUK SPLIT

Location	Split, Croatia
Established	1911
Nicknames	*Bili* ("Whites"), *Majstori s mora* ("Masters from the Sea"), *Dalmatinski ponos* ("The Pride of Dalmatia")
Current stadium	Stadion Poljud (35,000 capacity)
Home colors	White and blue
Leading goal-scorer	Frane Matošić (1935–38, 1940–41, 1944–56), 729 goals
Most appearances	Frane Matošić (1935–38, 1940–41, 1944–56), 739 appearances

They were tired, ill, and hungry, and their country was under siege, yet still they wanted to play football.

When Italian Fascists took over the coastal city of Split in April 1941, Hajduk Split was expected to join the Italian soccer league as A.C. Spalato, the Italianized name of the city. But Croatian nationalism had been fermenting too long for the Hajduk players to go along with such a plan, and they reluctantly ceased playing. When, in 1944, the Nazis arrived, the Hajduk players fled to the tiny island of Vis, 40 miles south of Split, where Tito, his partisans, and British soldiers were helping to keep the island free from invasion.

Legend has it that Hajduk Split scored their first ever goal via a deflection off a knee, but Šime Raunig, the goal-scorer, claimed later that he had used his shin. Either way, they all count. It was June 1911; the club had been around for just four months, having been established by four Croatian students in a pub in Prague some 650 miles north of their hometown, Split. Knee or shin, Šime Raunig and his

Hajduk teammates scored nine unanswered goals that day, so beginning a proud history in Yugoslav football.

By the time they arrived on Vis, they were in bad shape, the war having taken a terrible toll on them and their compatriots. Still, football was a great lure and, forming a team, Hajduk traveled to Bari, Italy, to take on the British Army in front of 50,000 fans. Sadly, the game was no contest—the fitter Brits ran out 9–2 winners. But the end of the war was in sight, and football had returned to Hajduk Split.

Once the war was over, Hajduk won three championships in the 1950s, though they often faced points deductions from a capricious, Tito-dominated football federation. In total they won the old Yugoslav top division nine times, and came second on eleven occasions. Their best ever decade was the 1970s; in those years they won the league four times and the Yugoslav Cup five times, including the double in 1974.

In European competition they struggled, often against British opposition. In a 1972–73 Cup Winners' Cup semifinal, they lost a tight, two-leg affair, 1–0 on aggregate, to Leeds United. The *Guardian* report of the second goalless game noted that "Leeds United . . . spoiled the carnival atmosphere in Hajduk Split's compact stadium . . . with a performance which was calculated to depress anyone who still believes that football should have joy and feeling, and freedom of expression."

Just over a decade later, Hajduk tried again, this time against Tottenham Hotspur. In the semifinals of the 1984 UEFA Cup, Hajduk staged their home leg at their current Poljud ground, which was opened in 1979. Mark Falco, the Spurs center forward, missed a penalty early on and then missed the follow-up, only to score at the third attempt when Hajduk failed to clear. But Hajduk hit back with two goals in the second half, setting up a good chance to progress after the second leg in London. Alas, a hand ball on the edge of the box led to a Micky Hazard free kick and goal, and the Croatian team couldn't find a response, going out on the away goals rule.

Subsequent European adventures for Hajduk Split have sometimes been marred by the political situation, as the former Yugoslavia violently broke apart into its various states—games have been played outside of Croatia at times of conflict. At home, the formation of the Croatian League in 1992 has led to a fossilization of football in the "new" country. In more than 20 years, there have only been four times when Dynamo Zagreb and Hadjuk Split haven't both appeared in two of the top three positions. Hadjuk have won the league six times and finished second 12 times; Dynamo's record is 16 wins (including nine in a row up to 2014) and three seconds. The two teams share an "eternal derby," though it isn't quite as crazy as the eternal derby played between neighboring Serbian teams Red Star and Partizan Belgrade. What they lack in passion, however, Hajduk's fans make up for with offensive comedy. In 2013, after a clear penalty for their team in an eternal derby wasn't awarded, they mailed the poor referee a Dynamo Zagreb shirt, a Dynamo scarf, and a blind person's white stick.

In 2009, Hajduk finally got one over on British opposition. They staged a rematch of that 1944 game in Bari, Italy, against the British Army; this time, in their Croatian hometown, the professionals of Split hammered the plucky Tommies, 9–1.

Location	Hamburg, Germany
Established	1887
Nicknames	*Die Rothosen* ("The Red Shorts"), *Der Dinosaurier* ("The Dinosaur")
Current stadium	Imtech Arena (57,000 capacity)
Home colors	Blue, white, and red
Leading goal-scorer	Uwe Seeler (1953–72), 507 goals
Most appearances	Manfred Kaltz (1971–89, 1990–91), 744 appearances

Jan Åge Fjørtoft, a mild-mannered Norwegian striker, once called German coach Felix Magath "the last dictator in Europe." Other players hated him, too. Some called him "Saddam," though avowedly behind his back; others, "Qualix," a mixture of his name and the German verb "to torture" (*quälen*). Jefferson Farfán, a Peruvian winger playing for Schalke 04, once ran over to the bench where his former manager, Magath, sat coaching Wolfsburg, and called him "*hijo de puta*"—that is, one whose female parent plies her trade as a professional sex worker.

Yet in the German city of Hamburg, Felix Magath is a hero still.

Hamburg has had a soccer team for a very long time. Way back, a club called Sport 1887 Germania boasted a player by the name of Hans Nobiling. Nobiling would wander off to São Paulo in 1897 and help establish the sport in Brazil. Back in Germany, two other teams, Hamburger F.C. and F.C. Falke Eppendorf, joined with Germania in 1919 to create what Germans now know officially as Hamburger S.V., and the rest of us know in English as Hamburg. The team was north German champion ten times between 1921 and 1933, and "German champions," pre-Bundesliga, five times. Hamburg was also one of the 16 teams to make up the first Bundesliga season, in 1963–64.

It would take until the late 1970s for Hamburg to build a winning side. Their first European trophy arrived in 1977, when they overcame a fine Anderlecht team to win the Cup Winners' Cup, 2–0. Their first goal, a penalty after 78 minutes, came from the foot of striker Georg Volkert, and the second, from midfielder Felix Magath.

The following season, Hamburg would sign Liverpool star Kevin Keegan to join Magath up front. Keegan had just won the European Cup and been named European Footballer of the Year, but his first season with Hamburg was lowlighted by a midseason friendly on New Year's Day, 1978, when Keegan and his team traveled to the Loh-mühle Stadium to face VfB Lübeck. After five minutes, Keegan was fouled by Erhard Preuss, a defender, and again five minutes later. On 11 minutes, Keegan got his own back, knocking Preuss out with a sin-gle punch. Keegan was banned for two months, but once back he transformed himself, and Hamburg.

Hamburg would win their first title in almost 20 years in 1979 on the back of Keegan's 17 league goals, and went off to the European Cup the following season in buoyant mood. They made it all the way to the final, having knocked out Real Madrid in the semifinal (they lost the first leg 2–0 in Spain, but thrashed Madrid 5–1 in Germany, even though Keegan failed to score). In the final, Keegan failed to score again, and Hamburg lost to English minnows Nottingham For-est in one of the worst finals ever played.

Keegan went back to England the following season, but Ham-burg would recover, winning the Bundesliga in 1982 (though they lost the UEFA Cup that year to Gothenburg) and 1983. In between those two league wins, they also recorded their greatest ever triumph.

In the 1982–83 European Cup, Hamburg had a relatively easy road to the final, but once there, they faced the Trapattoni-managed Juventus of Dino Zoff, Claudio Gentile, Gaetano Scirea, Marco Tardelli, Paolo Rossi, and Michel Platini. On paper the game was a mis-match—but that's why it's played on grass, as the old joke goes. And thanks to Magath, Hamburg would win their first and (so far) only European Cup victory.

The game began at walking pace—so slow, in fact, that at one point Hamburg players Manfred Kaltz and Jürgen Groh managed to tackle each other in Juventus's half and still retain the ball. Right after that bizarre moment, the ball was worked out to Magath on the left. Magath shimmied, causing Italian midfielder Roberto Bettega to jump in the air like a ballerina, then Magath cut in, took a cultured swing with his left foot, and the ball screamed across Zoff and into the top right-hand corner. It was a goal worthy of winning any match, and it won this one—Juventus created little, and the cup belonged to Hamburg.

Since then: nothing. Hamburg have become a mid-table nonen-tity in German football; Felix Magath has turned into a manager most players and fans love to hate; and when a Hamburg side featuring for-mer top Dutch star Rafael van der Vaart lost 9–2 to Bayern Munich in March 2013, the best the team could offer as an apology was to invite their long-suffering supporters to a barbecue, where, presumably, hamburgers were served.

HAPOEL TEL AVIV

Location	Tel Aviv, Israel
Established	1927
Nicknames	Red Devils, The Workers
Current stadium	Bloomfield Stadium (14,413 capacity)
Home colors	Red and white
Leading goal-scorer	Yehoshua "Shiye" Feigenbaum (1964–79), 131 goals
Most appearances	Yaacov Ekhoiz (1974–92), 454 apperances

Though in this case he belied his nickname of "Super," at least Mario Melchiot was better than Marcel Desailly, Albert Ferrer, William Gallas, Eidur Gudjohnsen, Graeme Le Saux, or Emmanuel Petit. Getting sent off is one thing—kicking out at an opponent for pretty much no reason, as Melchiot did, suggests, at the very least, a lack of basic intelligence—but acting like a coward (see below), like those others named, is something else entirely.

On October 18, 2001, Chelsea faced the first of a two-leg UEFA Cup tie against the Israeli team Hapoel (pronounced "ha-POIL") Tel Aviv. Just five weeks after 9/11, the situation in the world was tense; on October 17, Israel's tourism minister had been assassinated at the Hyatt Hotel in Jerusalem, only adding to the sense of disquiet.

It can't be easy being a soccer team in Israel. For a start, on a sporting level the country is mostly obsessed with basketball, not soccer; add in an often precarious security situation and a geographical position that has confused football authorities (is it Europe? is it Asia?) for years, and you can see how just playing the game can prove harder than it should be.

Hapoel Tel Aviv has suffered—and overcome—plenty in its nearly 100-year history. Originally a "federation of Hebrew workers," they played in the Palestine League, winning it in 1934 and 1940. After the establishment of the state of Israel, they won the new Israeli League for the first time in 1957 and seven times since (13 league titles in total); they also won an oddly constituted, six-team Asian Club Championship in 1967 after receiving byes all the way to the final.

But it is in European competition that they have made the most news. This traditionally leftist club—their nickname is "the Workers" and their crest features a hammer and sickle—has managed to overcome their difficult situation to win a bunch of big games. None was bigger than the night Chelsea sauntered in. The Chelsea players had (shamefully) been given the option by the club to not travel to Israel if they were afraid: Desailly, Ferrer, Gallas, Gudjohnsen, Le Saux, and Petit opted to stay home. The Chelsea owner, Ken Bates, said he disapproved, and even the normally staid *Daily Telegraph* commented, "The Chelsea players who stayed away...and who could encourage others to follow suit will be about as popular in Israel as Osama bin Laden."

As for the game, it didn't go well. Melchiot kicked out at Tel Aviv's captain, Shimon Gershon, and was red carded in the 54th minute; with three minutes to go, Gershon scored from the penalty spot after John Terry comically dove and handled the ball in the area—the Hapoel fans, packing the Bloomfield Stadium, fell into hysterics. In the last seconds of the game, Serghei Cleşcenco rose to power a header home, sending the Israeli team to London with a 2–0 lead. There, Hapoel scored first, meaning they were three goals up; a second-half goal by Zola for Chelsea couldn't prevent the Israelis from advancing.

In that second leg, five of the six cowards had rejoined the team (one of them, William Gallas, made the mistake that led to Hapoel's goal). Future Chelsea and England captain John Terry, in typical form, commented, "No one's held anything against the lads who didn't go." In comparison, Shimon Gershon walked off the Stamford Bridge pitch in tears; he had previously excoriated the six professional footballers who had refused to do their jobs, saying that getting through to the third round had been his "personal mission."

Mission accomplished. Hapoel made it to the quarterfinals of the UEFA Cup that year, but were knocked out by A.C. Milan. The first leg wasn't played at the cauldron that is the Bloomfield Stadium in Tel Aviv, as UEFA moved the game to Cyprus due to "security concerns." Hapoel beat Milan 1–0, though only a few thousand Tel Aviv fans were there. No Milan fans showed up, and the game was conducted in "relative silence," according to the UK's *Daily Mirror*. Back in Italy, Hapoel were knocked out, losing 2–0.

There has never been a terrorist attack at a Hapoel game.

Location	Houston, Texas, USA
Established	2005
Nicknames	Orange Crush, *La Naranja* ("The Orange")
Current stadium	BBVA Compass Stadium (22,000 capacity)
Home colors	Orange and white
Leading goal-scorer	Brian Ching (2006–11, 2012–13), 69 goals
Most appearances	Brad Davis (2006–), 238 appearances

N o wonder they chose the name Dynamo: they've packed a lot into their brief history.

The Houston Dynamo started with a bang. In their very first season, 2006, they won the MLS Cup, and then won it again their second year. But it wasn't entirely a fairy tale: the Dynamo were actually a relocated San Jose Earthquakes team. The Earthquakes had been in MLS since its inception in 1996 and had already won two MLS Cups, in 2001 and 2003, as well as the Supporters Shield in 2005—meaning that this "new" Houston-based team had, in fact, already tasted plenty of success.

The Houston move came about because the owner of the Earthquakes, the Anschutz Entertainment Group, couldn't convince California it needed a soccer-only stadium—so clearly money was a factor. Still, it must have been a wrench for Dominic Kinnear and his players to move nearly 2,000 miles east to Texas. Kinnear had helped build the team along with Frank Yallop, before the latter's move to run the Canadian national team in 2004. Kinnear had played in MLS and came to his head coach's job with one self-professed mandate: to acquire players who fitted in. Kinnear opted to not bring in a designated player—the MLS-appointed stars who earn many times what regulars do. As a result, Kinnear was able to create a team based around a horribly old-fashioned idea: loyalty. No one had given them a chance in 2005 out west, and they had won the Supporters Shield. With their move to football-obsessed Texas (football, not soccer), once more no one gave them a prayer.

So the Houston Dynamo went and won the championship. The team, based around talented left winger Brad Davis, with Dwayne De Rosario rampant in midfield behind the goal-scoring exploits of Brian Ching, squeaked through the conference semifinals thanks to an injury-time goal from Ching against Chivas, then swept aside the Colorado Rapids to make the final. There they met the New England Revolution, featuring future commentator Taylor Twellman up front. Twellman opened the scoring with just seven minutes to go in extra time, only for Ching to immediately equalize, sending the game to a shootout. And though Brad Davis missed one of the Houston penalties, both De Rosario and Ching scored theirs, and when Pat Onstad saved Revolution's Jay Heaps's kick low to his right, the Dynamo had their first MLS Cup trophy.

The following season, Houston faced New England once again in the final; frustration from the previous year made it a chippy game. Twellman opened the scoring, as was his wont, and with half an hour to go it wasn't looking good for a Dynamo repeat. De Rosario, though, was having none of it. His neat cross to the far post found Zimbabwean Joseph Ngwenya, and his comical whiff at the first attempt was followed by a splendid finish at the second. A clear head butt by Revolution winger Khano Smith—a player whom the fans of English club Lincoln City would later vote their worst in 2010—garnered only a yellow card, but no matter: with quarter of an hour to go, De Rosario got a powerful header on the end of a typically beautiful Brad Davis cross. At 2–1, the Revolution had a golden opportunity to send the game to extra time once again, but Onstad made a brilliant save with his feet from a Jeff Larentowicz header, and Houston were on their way to a repeat.

Since then, the Houston Dynamo have become the team who sometimes show up in the regular season but tend to find themselves going far in the post-season anyway. The New York Red Bulls knocked them out of the post-season in 2008, before the L.A. Galaxy became their bogey team: In 2009, Houston lost a conference final to the West Coast outfit, missed the playoffs altogether for the first and only time in 2010, and then got beaten by the L.A. Galaxy in the MLS Cup final two years in a row (2011 and 2012). In 2013, Houston lost another conference final, this time to Sporting Kansas City.

In 2012, the Houston Dynamo finally got their "soccer-only" stadium, the BBVA, a place which also hosts rugby and the Texas Southern University (American) football team.

Location	Buenos Aires, Argentina
Established	1904
Nicknames	El Rojo ("The Red"), El Diablo ("The Devil"), Rey de Copas ("The King of Cups")
Current stadium	Estadio Libertadores de América (40,000 capacity)
Home colors	Red and navy
Leading goal-scorer	Arsenio Erico (1933–46), 293 goals
Most appearances	Ricardo Bochini (1972–91), 638 appearances

What is it with Argentine soccer and the hand of God?

Any English football fan can tell you where they were the exact moment Diego Maradona rose above England's keeper Peter Shilton in the 1986 World Cup and "headed" the ball into the net to give Argentina a 1–0 lead in the quarterfinals. Maradona didn't use his head at all—he merely punched the ball and made it look like it was his head. Later, he would declare it was the "hand of God" that had scored. Four years earlier, Britain had routed Argentina in a different kind of conflict, the Falklands War. And here was another Argentine not following international rules, went the cry . . .

Eight years before Maradona's crime against international law, another Argentine "hand of God" moment had almost caused a similar injustice, not to mention a riot, an abandoned game, and lord knows what else. It was January 25, 1978, and the second leg of a matchup between the team of the decade, Independiente, and Talleres de Córdoba. This second game would decide the national champions—the first leg had ended 1–1 at Independiente's stadium in

Buenos Aires, a fine result for the little team from 500 miles northwest of Argentina's capital. All Córdoba needed was a low-scoring draw or a win in the second leg, and they would be champions.

It would have been a famous victory if Córdoba had pulled it off. Independiente had destroyed all before them for much of the 1970s. They had been founded in 1904 as an offshoot of a team connected to a well-to-do store called La Ville de Londres on Avenida de Mayo, the superwide street that runs east-west through the center of Buenos Aires. The team, Maipú Banfield F.C., was run by the same Brits who ran the store—they were happy to take dues (50 cents per month) from the young Argentines who worked there, but wouldn't let them play. So the workers, desperate to play the game, formed their "independent" club—hence the name—and three years later they arrived at their permanent home in an industrial section of Buenos Aires, south of the center and close to the docks and the ocean: Avellaneda. In 1908, they adopted a red shirt, the color of the socialist working man and of Nottingham Forest—their president, Arístides Langone, had watched Forest play on a tour of Argentina. By 1912, Langone's team had reached the top division, where they have stayed (almost) ever since.

By 1931, Independiente were a professional team. They won their first two professional titles in 1938 and 1939, and another three years after the end of World War II. Three more followed in the 1960s—this was also the decade they won their first two Copa Libertadores—but nothing quite compares to Independiente in the 1970s.

That decade started with two more back-to-back championships. In 1972 they went to the final of the Copa Libertadores once again, beating Universitario of Peru 2–1 on aggregate (the first leg in Lima had ended 0–0). Though it was their third Copa Libertadores in eight years, few could have imagined that this 1972 triumph was to be the first of four in a row.

Part of the domination in the next three years came from the combined boots of Ricardo Bochini and Daniel Bertoni. Bertoni was a right winger, and would go on to score Argentina's final goal in the

1978 World Cup final victory over the Netherlands. His service from the flank set up goals for the finest player Independiente ever had, the great Bochini. He played a staggering 638 official games for the club across nearly 20 years (though with exhibition games and the like the number is closer to 1,000), and would have scored more than his 105 goals had he not found himself doing national service in the middle of his career. Nonetheless, Bochini won a World Cup medal in 1986, though he only got five minutes' playing time late in the Belgium–Argentina semifinal, playing behind Diego Maradona, who had already scored the two goals that would take Argentina to the final. Maradona has claimed Bochini as his footballing idol, and as he entered the field in the Azteca Stadium that June day in 1986, Maradona is said, by Jonathan Wilson in the *Guardian*, to have shouted to Bochini, "Maestro, we've been waiting for you."

But it was with Independiente that Bochini shone most brightly. In 1972, his first season, he was a mere 18 years old, but by the 1973 final he was becoming established in the attacking part of Independiente's midfield.

The 1973 Copa Libertadores victory was a protracted affair, and if the away goals rule had been in place, it wouldn't have happened. In the first leg on May 22, Colo Colo, Independiente's opponents, got a very fine 1–1 draw in Argentina; the second leg, a week later in Peru, was goalless. A third game was played in neutral Montevideo, and with 13 minutes to go in extra time, Miguel Giachello scored for Independiente, making it 2–1 on the night.

Bochini came into his own in the Intercontinental Cup that year, held in Rome, against Juventus. By now he was in the starting eleven, and with 10 minutes to go he scored a fabulous goal in front of a crowd of just 22,489. Juventus had missed a penalty and a bunch of chances already, but those who did show up saw a maestro—two, in fact—at work. On the 80th minute, Bochini and Bertoni worked a series of neat one-two passes from the halfway line all the way to the edge of the box. Once there, the ball finally fell to Bochini and he dinked a little chip over the legendary Dino Zoff in the Juventus goal. It was one of the great goals—the finish alone was sublime, but the work to get the ball to the box in the first place was of the highest order.

The "threepeat" of Copa Libertadores was completed in 1974 over the space of a week, once again over three games. An initial match in São Paolo ended 2–1 to the Brazilian side, though Independiente won the return leg 2–0, Bochini opening the scoring. A third game in Santiago settled it, a goal for Independiente in the first half bringing the Copa Libertadores to Argentina for the third time in three years, and the fifth time in nine seasons. In the 1975 final, Independiente faced Unión Española, only the fourth-best team in Chile that year, but they proved a tough nut to crack. It took Independiente three games yet again, but at the end they had captured the Copa Libertadores for a fourth time.

That would be it internationally in the 1970s for Independiente. At home, they faced stiff opposition, winning only two national titles that decade. The first, in 1977, had actually ended in 1978, against valiant Talleres de Córdoba.

Valiant, and also very lucky. In that notorious second leg, Independiente took the lead, only for two extraordinary incidents to threaten to spoil the game. The first was a penalty awarded to Córdoba that was extremely harsh—the Independiente defender jumped to staunch a cross and the ball hit his side/arm. With the score tied 1–1, worse was to come—a clear "hand of God" header gave Córdoba a 2–1 lead and all hell broke loose. Players swarmed around the referee, fans and officials invaded the field, and it looked like the game would be abandoned when three Independiente players, Enzo Trossero, Rubén Galván, and Omar Larrosa, were red-carded for protesting too much, and Bochini threatened to take the team off the field. But they stayed and the game continued, even though it was eleven players versus eight. Somehow, in a goal-mouth scramble in which the Córdoba keeper came off his line and took the legs from under his own defender, the ball fell to Bochini, and he made no mistake. The game ended 2–2, and this time away goals did count. Independiente were once again champions.

Independiente would go on to win a Copa Libertadores in 1984, and the Intercontinental Cup the same year over Liverpool, with Bochini still starting as Independiente's number 10. But after his retirement, a period of decline for the club set in. By the new century, Independiente were being forced to sell players like Sergio Agüero (he went to Atlético Madrid, then Manchester City) and a host of others to settle their massive debts. The low point came in 2013, when Independiente were relegated after a 1–0 loss at home to Pope Francis's favorite team, San Lorenzo. Not exactly the hand of God, but closer than most.

INTER MILAN

Location	Milan, Italy
Established	1908
Nicknames	*I Nerazzurri* ("The Black and Blues"), *La Beneamata* ("The Cherished One"), *Il Biscione* ("The Serpent"), *Baüscia* (Lombard for "Boasters")
Current stadium	San Siro; officially Stadio Giuseppe Meazza (capacity 80,018)
Home colors	Black and navy blue
Leading goal-scorer	Giuseppe Meazza (1927–40, 1946–47), 284 goals
Most appearances	Javier Zanetti (1995–), 845 appearances

They might be the "other team" in Milan, but what a record Internazionale possesses. They've won the Italian title 18 times, three European Cups, three UEFA Cups, and three Intercontinental/World Club cups. If A.C. Milan weren't also a huge part of the Milanese soccer scene, we'd all suck in a breath when Inter's name is mentioned. Alas, in Milan, Inter is like the just-as-handsome but younger brother; the just-as-smart but younger sister.

Inter came about when it became clear that, after almost a decade of playing the game, A.C. Milan would be a club for Italians only. Established in 1908 by a mixture of Italians and near-neighbor Swiss players, the new team, Internazionale, was dedicated to welcoming all comers, and happy to win its first title in 1910. Three more would follow between the two world wars, but for a brief while the Fascist dictatorship decreed that Inter would join with Unione Sportiva Milanese to become Ambrosiana. That team won the league in 1930, and fragrant though it sounds, it just wasn't Inter (though neither was the 1931 compromise, Associazione Sportiva Ambrosiana–Inter).

After World War II, and with five titles and a Coppa Italia already under their belt, Inter were finally allowed to settle on their true name, Internazionale. But it would be 1953 before another title came their way (they would repeat the following year). Then, in 1960, a coach came along who would bring Inter to its greatest successes, even if he did it on the back of defensive football that sometimes defines Italian soccer to this day.

Helenio Herrera was born in Argentina, but came with his family to Europe at age three. No one quite knows why the adult Herrera was so devoted to a defensive style of football—it may have been that while managing Barcelona in a 1960 European Cup semifinal, his team's efforts in trying to outplay Real Madrid were revealed for what they were, which was futile (Barça lost the first game, in Madrid, 3–1, and the second back in Barcelona by the same score—Puskás and Di Stéfano had run riot in both games). On the back of that 6–2 aggregate reversal Herrera had been fired, and had learned some kind of lesson, which was that one of the ways to win at football is to concede fewer goals than the other team. This is an entirely different philosophy to winning by scoring more goals, at least in emphasis, if not in logic.

So Herrera set about turning his new team, Inter Milan, into the world's most boring team . . . or so history would have us believe. The truth is a tad less cut and dried. Herrera did indeed popularize the concept of *catenaccio*, which favors a solid back five, replete with care-ful-to-not-go-rushing-forward-too-far sweeper, and a pressing game that aims to stifle the creativity of opponents. But that's not the entire story; Inter scored goals, too, lots of them, at least in European games.

In Italy, Inter were indeed stingy. In winning the 1963 Serie A title, Inter scored just 56 goals in 34 games, and let in only 20. The fol-lowing year, when Inter Milan won the league again, they at least aver-aged exactly two goals per game, though they let in nine more than the previous season; and, completing the "threepeat," they finally broke 70 goals, letting in 28. By contrast, in the European Cup, Inter Milan were relatively free-scoring.

The 1963–64 European Cup started in typical *catenaccio* fashion, with a goalless draw at Everton followed by a single goal by Jair in the Italian leg. Jair would score just 39 goals for Inter in his first five years with the club (he had a later spell of four years where he scored even fewer). Jair played alongside Luis Suárez—the non-bitey, non-Uruguayan version (he was from Galicia)—a player who had followed Herrera to Inter from Barcelona for a then unfathomably large fee of 250 million lire. Inter's front line also boasted Alessandro Mazzola, who would only ever play for Inter Milan in his 17-year career and whose father, Valentino, had been a member of the legendary Torino team that had perished in the Superga air crash in 1949.

For the rest of that 1963–64 tournament, Inter put the ball in the back of the net often: four times in each of their two-leg ties against Monaco, Partizan Belgrade, and Borussia Dortmund. In the final, Mazzola and Aurelio Milani shared the scoring as Inter overwhelmed Real Madrid, 3–1.

The baton had been passed—Di Stéfano and Puskás would never again lift the trophy for Madrid. The new style of tight, relatively inexpressive football had arrived.

Inter would win the European Cup the following year, 1965, too, and once again the facts belie the belief that they were only defensive. The first round saw them crush Dinamo Bucharest, 6–0, at the San Siro, behind two goals apiece from Mazzola and Jair, and one each from Luis Suárez and Milani. In the quarterfinals, Inter knocked out Rangers, a 3–1 win in Italy enough though they lost the second leg, 1–0, in Scotland.

The semifinals remain as controversial a set of games as Inter Milan has ever played. Facing a dominant Liverpool team led by Bill Shankly, at Anfield, Inter were well beaten, 3–1. Back in Italy on May 4, at a time when Italian soccer was riddled with fixed matches and paid-off officials, Shankly maintained that the referee, José Maria Ortiz de Mendibil, made enough dubious decisions to bring Inter's

3–0 win into question. Given that the referee's surname already contains the root word for "lying" (from the Latin *mendax*), suspicions remained for years, though a review of the questionable goals, the first and second, both scored in the first 10 minutes, suggest that only the first was a tad dodgy (an indirect free kick not taken as such). The second, in which Joaquín Peiró stole the ball from Liverpool keeper Tommy Lawrence during his pre-kickout routine, was a legal maneuver in 1965. Inter's third goal was one of the best that side ever scored, three passes up the middle of the field opening up Liverpool for Giacinto Facchetti to rifle home.

At the end of the game, Liverpool center back Tommy Smith chased after Mendibil and kicked him; the referee, oddly, took no action. The truth was that Inter Milan had been too good for Liverpool that night, even though it's also true that the Italians time-wasted and passed back as often as Liverpool themselves would do throughout their triumphant period in the late 1970s and 1980s.

In the subsequent 1965 final, Inter faced Benfica at their own ground, the San Siro. Eusébio, playing for Benfica, couldn't get a sniff, and a Jair goal two minutes before the half was all the defensively savvy Italian side needed.

Inter Milan won both the Intercontinental Cups their European trophies opened up, and both over Independiente of Argentina. In 1964, it took three attempts to overcome the Copa Libertadores winners, Mario Corso finally scoring the only goal of the third match for Inter after each team had won on their respective home soils. The following year, Inter defied their reputation as boring by slamming home three goals, two by Mazzola and one by the cunning Peiró, though Inter reverted to type in the second leg, killing the game stone dead (it ended 0–0, with both teams lucky to get zero).

Inter Milan reached a third European Cup final under Herrera, but in 1967 Jair was gone, and Luis Suárez was unfit. A slick and fluid Celtic side outplayed Inter, and more importantly, heralded a sea change in how winning football could be conceived. The stultifying Inter way was coming to an end, and Herrera was gone by 1968.

Another European Cup defeat, to Johan Cruyff's Ajax, in 1972, signaled the true end of Inter's heyday and the triumph of Total Football, though the writing had been on the wall ever since Herrera jumped ship to manage A.S. Roma.

The lights shone only for A.C. Milan at the San Siro, the stadium both Milan teams share, until the dawning of the new century. In 1994, Inter were almost relegated, and their three UEFA Cup victories in 1991, 1994, and 1998 are often considered an afterthought, given their 1960s' exploits. This is strange, though—that 1990s' team variously included Walter Zenga and Gianluca Pagliuca in goal, Lothar Matthäus, Diego Simeone, Youri Djorkaeff, and Nicola Berti in midfield, and Dennis Bergkamp, Jürgen Klinsmann, and the original, pudgy Ronaldo up front. Two of the victories, the first and last, were against Roman opposition (A.S. Roma, then Lazio), though the middle trophy, won in 1994, in which Inter beat Casino Salzburg (now F.C. Red Bull Salzburg) 1–0 twice, is probably best forgotten by lovers of attacking, or even mildly interesting, football.

The new century saw a resurgence for Inter Milan. They came within one game of winning the Scudetto in 2002, though a final-day defeat to Lazio handed Juventus the title; and they almost beat A.C. Milan in the 2003 Champions League semifinal. Amusingly, Inter lost on away goals, though both legs had been played at the shared San Siro.

When Roberto Mancini took over Inter in July 2004, things finally looked up for good. Though the 2006 Scudetto was handed to them by the Italian Federal Appeal Commission (Juventus and A.C. Milan had both finished higher, but they had also fixed games), Inter buried the strange taste of that victory by winning the next three Serie A titles. Between September 2006 and February 2007, Inter won 17 consecutive league games, an Italian record. Just before that record began, Zlatan Ibrahimović joined Inter and helped deliver two Scudettos; even so, Mancini was replaced by José Mourinho in June 2008. Mourinho brought the 2009 Scudetto to Inter and went one better in 2010, as Inter won its third European Cup/Champions League title.

Inter won that Champions League the hard way. In the group stages, they faced Barcelona, but advanced in second place. In the round of 16, Mourinho's old team Chelsea came calling, but Inter beat them 2–1 in both legs. A relatively easy quarterfinal against CSKA Moscow led to a rematch with group winners Barcelona, and the first leg, in the San Siro, saw Inter produce one its best ever performances. Though Pedro gave Barça the lead, Inter kept Messi quiet, and Wesley Sneijder, Maicon, and Diego Milito all scored for Inter. The second leg ended 1–0 to Barça, but their goal came way too late, in the 84th minute. Inter were headed to the Champions League final.

There, Inter faced Bayern Munich in Madrid, but it was to be Diego Milito's night, his two brilliant goals lighting up what proved to be an excellent final.

Mourinho had ants in his pants, however, and immediately moved on to Real Madrid. Inter had won the league, the Italian Cup, and the Champions League, but by the time the Italian Supercoppa and the FIFA World Club Championship came along in August and December respectively, 2010, Rafael Benitez was in charge.

Benitez delivered both trophies, though beating TP Mazembe of the Congo in the World Club Championship wasn't exactly Inter's most difficult task of that historic year. No one really loved Benitez at Inter, and five days after he helped Inter overcome mighty Mazembe, he was gone. (Benitez has been let go by Liverpool, Chelsea, and Inter Milan, having won trophies at all of them.) For Inter, the quest to best A.C. Milan, at least in the minds of soccer fans around the world, goes on.

Location	Porto Alegre, Brazil
Established	1909
Nicknames	*Colorado* ("The Red"), *Nação Vermelha* ("Red Nation"), *O Clube do Povo* ("The People's Club"), *Celeiro de Ases* ("Factory of Aces")
Current stadium	Gigante da Beira-Rio, officially Estádio José Pinheiro Borda (50,287 capacity)
Home colors	Red and white
Leading goal-scorer	Carlos Alberto Zolim Filho (1938–51), 485 goals
Most appearances	Valdomiro Vaz Franco (1968–79, 1982), 803 appearances

B e careful when you choose to praise Jesus: do not do so if you're already on a yellow card. For Paulo César Fonseca do Nascimento, a.k.a. Tinga, his love for the Son of God got him sent off in the biggest game of his, and his team's, history.

A long time before that night, there were actually two Sport Club Internacionals: one, from São Paulo, disappeared in 1933, subsumed into what would become Clube Atlético Paulista, which itself then became São Paulo F.C. The other was established in Porto Alegre, down in the deep south of Brazil, in 1909—and it was formed with a specific cultural remit: to reflect the "international" nature of Brazilian life. Their city-mates, Grêmio, adhered to a strict Germans-only policy, but not so Internacional. They were founded because three Milanese brothers (Henrique, José, and Luis Poppe) couldn't get a game with the established teams in Porto Alegre. Bent out of shape at the discrimination, they brought Internacional to life—the name is said to have been in honor of the club in São Paulo, whence they hailed, and Inter Milan, for their parents' hometown. Notably, the first chairman of the club, João Leopoldo Seferin, was just 17 years old—clearly, Internacional were determined to do it their own way every way.

The Colorados, as they're known because of their deep commitment to the color red (shirts, crest, etc.), won 18 state championships before 1970, including all but two in both the 1940s and the 1970s—clearly opening a club to all comers wasn't just the moral thing to do, but also smart in terms of results. When a Brazilian national league was formed in 1971, they joined and have never left (they were actually relegated in 1999, but the league fixed it so that they were awarded extra, and spurious, points to keep them up), and in the second half of that decade they won the title three times (1975, 1976—in which they won 19 of 23 games—and 1979, a season they completed undefeated). The next two decades, however, were barren, until the new century came around and, appropriately enough, this team dedicated to international play won two Copa Libertadores and a FIFA Club World Championship.

The first Copa, and the Club World Championship, came in 2006. Internacional had lost in the final of the Copa Libertadores in 1980, to Nacional of Uruguay. There had been one goal in the two games of the final that year, but 26 years later, goals flowed. Internacional's opponents in 2006 were the team the other Sporting Club Internacional had eventually become—São Paulo—meaning that the final was in some ways a clash of long-lost brothers.

The final started badly for São Paulo—their midfielder Josué was sent off in the first 10 minutes, and though Internacional also had a man dismissed in the first half, after an hour two goals from Rafael Sóbis had given Inter a valuable lead; the game ended 2–1.

The second leg didn't go much better for São Paulo. Inter took the lead after half an hour when São Paulo's keeper and captain, Rogério Ceni, made a hash of a simple cross and Fernandão stabbed in the loose ball. Though São Paulo equalized, the tie was put out of their reach in the 66th minute when Tinga nodded into an empty net. Already carrying a yellow card, the jubilant player figured it would be a good moment to raise his red Internacional shirt to reveal a T-shirt underneath that read "Obrigado Jesus." That was enough for Argentine referee Horacio Elizondo, who brandished a second yellow and a red at the unfortunately devout striker. (This is the same referee who sent off Wayne Rooney in a 2006 World Cup quarterfinal after he stamped on Portugal's Ricardo Carvalho; Elizondo also sent off Zinedine Zidane in the final of the same tournament for the infamous head butt to the chest of Italian Marco Materazzi. Can any referee have been involved in more famous dismissals?)

After Tinga's dismissal, the last half hour proved tense. São Paulo snatched a goal with five minutes to go, and had two chances to level the tie in the last minutes. Fans in the crowd were seen both praying and crying; Inter's coach, Abel Braga, wearing a Columbo-like raincoat with the collar up, was caught by cameras staring at the skies in supplication. Their prayers seemed to work; time ran out; Internacional held on to win 4–3 on aggregate. *Obrigado, Jesus!*

That same year Internacional faced Barcelona in the FIFA World Club Championships final in Tokyo. Internacional had had to overcome a stubborn Al-Ahly side to make the final, in a game that many thought could have been won by the Egyptian side (it would be the same story in 2012 for the unlucky Africans). By the Club World Cup championships, though, Tinga was gone, sold to Borussia Dortmund, and his close friend, Ronaldinho, was playing for the Spanish champions. No matter—a breakaway goal by Adriano Gabiru with eight minutes to go gave the Brazilian side the title, though the game had been poor. Internacional knew that the balance of power in the world game had long since shifted to European soccer, given that so many South American stars now plied their trade overseas. The only way for a team like Internacional to beat the likes of Barcelona was to bore them to submission. Mission accomplished.

Four years later, Tinga was back, his stay in Germany having failed to set the world alight, and once again he led his team to a Copa

Libertadores triumph, this time over Mexican side Guadalajara (a.k.a. Chivas). Two second-half goals in Mexico in the first leg of the final were canceled out by two first-half goals in each tie by Chivas, meaning that, as the second half of the second leg began, the scores were level. But Internacional's class showed as they scored three times—the third a lovely solo run and finish by Giuliano after Chivas had gone down to ten men—and a late consolation by the aptly-named Omar Bravo was not enough to get Chivas close enough to make a difference. Tinga was named man of the match, but not before Héctor Reynoso, Chivas's captain, had punched an Internacional assistant who had allegedly spat on Chivas's Marco Fabián after he'd scored their opening goal. A mini-riot ensued, ended only by the introduction of white-helmeted police and—once they'd stopped karate-kicking Chivas players—renewed celebrations by Internacional players.

It was, shall we say, an un-Christian end to the tournament. *Desculpe, Jesus!*

Location	Turin, Italy
Established	1897
Nicknames	*La Vecchia Signora* ("The Old Lady"), *La Fidanzata d'Italia* ("The Girlfriend of Italy"), *I Bianconeri* ("The White-Blacks"), *Le Zebre* ("The Zebras"), *La Goeba* (Gallo-Italic for "Hunchback")
Current stadium	Juventus Stadium (41,000 capacity)
Home colors	Black and white
Leading goal-scorer	Alessandro Del Piero (1993–2012), 289 goals
Most appearances	Alessandro Del Piero (1993–2012), 705 appearances

"They would keep their heads up . . . and be willing to start again if needed." So said Neal Bishop, the captain of Notts County F.C., after a visit with his team to Turin, Italy, in 2011. He was referring to the players on the Juventus side, whom Notts County faced in a historic friendly match to celebrate the opening of the Italian side's new stadium. But Bishop could have been talking about Juventus as an organization across its history. They've faced a lot in their more than 100 years.

They are called many things: the Grand Old Lady of Italian Soccer, Italy's Girlfriend, Lady-Killers, Hunchbacks, Zebras, *Bianconeri*: a team with so much history that along the way they've picked up a trophy cabinet filled with nicknames. They've won everything a number of times; they've seen great tragedies unfold; they've misbehaved and been sent to the naughty step; they've bounced back to greatness.

But around the world, to any true soccer fan, two syllables bring to mind one of the great football teams: "Ju-ve."

Pronounced "YOO-vay" in the Italian manner, these two syllables conjure Del Piero and Orsi and Vialli and Buffon and Zoff and Baggio and Capello and Charles and Brady and Platini and Pirlo and Zidane and Inzaghi and Rossi and Trezeguet and . . . the list of great players seems endless. But Juve also conjures the Heysel Stadium disaster and other deaths: those of 23-year-old left back Andrea Fortunato from leukemia, legendary sweeper Gaetano Scirea in a car wreck in Poland, and two trainees, Alessio Ferramosca and Riccardo Neri, who drowned after falling into a lake at the team's training center. It seems that for every trophy won, there is a price to pay for Juve.

They were founded three years before the twentieth century dawned, on a street bench on the Corso Re Umberto in Turin. Boys from the local high school, Massimo d'Azeglio, created the team from scratch, and being classical scholars, they came up with the name Juventus (the word means "youth"). Their first uniforms were pink and black, but pink is a color that easily wears out when washed over and over, and a man called John Savage, a Brit living in Turin, appealed to friends at home to send something the fledgling Juventus team could wear. When the parcel arrived in 1903, a set of Notts County kits tumbled out—black and white stripes that Juventus sport to this day.

Two years later the first Italian title, or Scudetto, arrived—the first of 30.

In 1906, a number of Juventus players and officials would quit to form Torino F.C., and by 1923 the Agnelli family, of Fiat fame, would be running the club. In 1925, a second Scudetto arrived for Juventus, and the first half of the 1930s saw five more—all in a row. Juve were already the dominant Italian team, lending many of their squad to the Italian national team which won the 1934 World Cup on Italian soil. The first goal of that final was scored by Raimundo Bibiani Orsi, who played 176 games for Juventus, as well as 13 games for Argentina—where he was born—and 35 for Italy (the rules about international allegiance have since changed).

By the start of the 1950s, Juventus were going for their tenth Scudetto, and the arrival of a huge Welshman ensured they would reach ten and more.

John Charles had already played nearly 300 games for Leeds United when he moved to Italy in 1957. "*Il Buon Gigante,*" as he became known (his vital statistics of 6 feet 2 inches and 200 pounds don't quite convey the mass of the man) was both a center back of renown and a free-scoring center forward. Umberto Agnelli, then president of Juventus, saw Charles play for Wales against Northern Ireland and contacted Ken Wolstenholme, Charles's agent. (Wolstenholme was the man who would go on to provide the most famous piece of commentary in the English language, his call of Geoff Hurst's final goal in the 1966 World Cup final: "There's people on the pitch, they think it's all over . . . it is now!") A deal was struck and Charles went to Turin, where his 93 goals in 155 *catenaccio*-affected games helped Juventus to three titles between 1957 and 1961.

After a so-so sixties, Juventus went trophy-crazy in the 1970s. They won five Italian championships and an Italian Cup, and finally broke through in Europe, reaching the final of the European Cup in 1973, only to come up against Johan Cruyff's legendary Ajax side. (They lost 1–0 to a very early goal.) As the decade progressed, the team got stronger and stronger, with the great Gaetano Scirea and Claudio Gentile at the back, in front of legend Dino Zoff in goal, and with Marco Tardelli up front, scoring for fun.

Led now by Giovanni Trapattoni, Juventus reached the final of the 1977 UEFA Cup, where they would play Athletic Bilbao. Juventus featured all Italian players; Bilbao, all Basques. In the first leg, the two teams were separated only by a fabulous looping header by Tardelli early in the first half. The second leg saw another early headed goal for Juve, this time from Roberto Bettega, and though Bilbao scored twice after that, Juventus would win on away goals.

The start of the 1980s brought four more championships in six seasons, as well as a Cup Winners' Cup triumph in 1984, but by then both Milan teams had won the much-more prestigious European Cup twice, and it was a conspicuous gap in Juve's trophy cabinet. They had lost another European Cup final in 1983, to Hamburg, and once again by a single goal scored in the first 10 minutes. In 1985 they found themselves back in the final—though this time, they probably wished they'd never made it at all.

The two teams that reached that 1985 European Cup final had dominated the tournament, both scoring 18 goals in eight games: Juventus and reigning European champions Liverpool. It was an eagerly awaited match: on one hand, a fluid and solid Trapattoni-led Juventus featuring Michel Platini, Paolo Rossi, Marco Tardelli, and Zbigniew Boniek, as ever marshaled by captain Scirea. On the other side, a free-scoring Liverpool side of Kenny Dalglish and Ian Rush, and coached by all-round good guy Joe Fagan, who had come up through the Liverpool organization starting in 1959 and had been a founder member of the famous "Boot Room" cabal created by legendary manager Bill Shankly.

In the end, it could be argued that the game should never have been played at all. An hour before it was to begin, Liverpool hooligans stormed a supposedly neutral area for fans in the rickety Heysel Stadium in Brussels. Filled with Juventus fans, the "neutral area" quickly cleared, but the resulting crush at a concrete retaining wall killed 39 Juve fans—ranging from a 58-year-old woman, Barbara Lusci, to an 11-year-old boy, Andrea Casula—and injured more than 600. The match was delayed an hour, until a decision was made to play the game to avoid further violence. For what it's worth, Juventus won the game 1–0 on a Platini penalty—a goal he bizarrely and very ardently celebrated with two fist pumps and a wide smile. To note that the trip on Boniek that gained the penalty was about 10 feet outside the box merely raises the specter that no one, not even the officials, really wanted a Liverpool victory. Juventus ran an ill-conceived lap of honor at the full-time whistle.

English teams had once again proven themselves to be followed by a minority of monsters; mainland Europe wouldn't have to endure such excesses for the next five European seasons (six for Liverpool), as British teams were banned from all competitions.

It was a terrible way to win a first European Cup, and no one has yet found agreement on how much the players knew before they played the game. Fans had ended up in the dressing rooms seeking treatment, and there is ample evidence that both sets of players knew plenty. The immorality of Liverpool captain Phil Neal's statement to the crowd before the game—that the players were "sick and tired of waiting"—is matched only by the massive celebrations in Turin that night after the "victory." The entire episode was dreadful and heartsickening from just about every angle.

Later that year, Juventus traveled to Tokyo to face Argentinos Juniors in the Intercontinental Cup final. It was a fabulous game, highlighted by a wonder goal by Platini that was wrongly disallowed for offside. After juggling the ball over a couple of defenders, he finished brilliantly with his weaker left foot—when the flag went up, Platini lay on his side on the Tokyo turf in disbelief, his hand behind his head like a supermodel doing "sexy." (He would get his revenge, once again celebrating after scoring the winning penalty at the end of a shootout.) Juventus would win another Scudetto in 1986, as well as another UEFA Cup in 1990 in an all-Italian affair in which the Fiorentina of a young Roberto Baggio were crushed 3–1 in Turin. By 1993, the Buddhist, ponytail-wearing Roberto Baggio was playing for Juventus, and they were winning their third UEFA Cup, a record 6–1 on aggregate over Borussia Dortmund. Another Baggio, Dino (no relation), scored three goals from midfield across those two legs, though four years later Dortmund would gain revenge by beating Juventus in the Champions League final.

The late 1990s were all Juventus—though they lost the 1995 UEFA Cup in another all-Italian final, to Parma, they still won the Scudetto three times, and finally won a Champions League without any hint of tragedy. Baggio (R.) had moved to Milan, and then Bologna, and then Inter in those years, but a new Juventus attack featuring Gianluca

Vialli, Fabrizio Ravanelli, and Alessandro Del Piero struck fear into European defenses. Del Piero, in particular, excelled. Be-ponytailed, deceptively quick, and a brilliant finisher, he was one of those rare players who could change a game in an instant.

The Champions League victory in 1996, over Ajax, came in the Olympic Stadium in Rome, which was appropriate given that Juventus draws its fans from across Italy, more so than any other Italian team. Shaven-headed Ravanelli scored early for Juve, nicking the ball off of Ajax keeper Edwin van der Saar and then rolling a shot along the goal line from a ridiculous angle way out right—somehow the ball went in, but underemployed physicists are still trying to understand how. Jari Litmanen equalized for Ajax just before half-time, and the game wandered into penalties. Vialli couldn't look as Vladimir Jugović stepped up to take the final kick, crying instead into Ciro Ferrara's shoulder—when Ferrara started to celebrate, Vialli and he collapsed into a loving heap. Vialli then raised the trophy, the last thing he'd do for Juventus before moving to Chelsea.

The rump of that European championship side bested another Argentine team, River Plate, in that year's Intercontinental Cup. This Juventus side featured a midfielder by the name of Zinedine Zidane, another in the long line of superstars who've wandered through Turin. Zidane would lead Juve to two more Scudettos, though he couldn't bring them a European Cup triumph as his team lost 1–0 to Real Madrid in the 1998 final.

In the new century, four more Scudettos came, though the oughts were tainted first by a Champions League final loss to archrivals A.C. Milan in 2003 (3–2 on penalties after a dull 0–0 draw), and by the 2006 *calciopoli* scandal, in which clear evidence of match-rigging meant that the club was sent to Serie B for the first time in its long history. The 2005 and 2006 titles, won under coach Fabio Capello, were scrubbed from Juve's list, and a number of players left. Other implicated teams were treated less harshly—Fiorentina and Lazio were initially sent to Serie B, but along with Milan and Regina ended up merely having points deducted for the following Serie A season. To his great credit, Del Piero stayed, helping Juventus win Serie B by six points—they lost just four games all season.

Back in the top flight in the 2007–08 season, it took Juventus until 2010–11—four seasons—to win another Scudetto, but they did it in style, remaining unbeaten all season and letting in just 20 goals in 38 games. It was yet more evidence that when it comes to defense, Italian teams are second to none. Another Scudetto followed in 2011–12, but in Europe Juventus have stalled, reaching just one final (the one they lost to Milan). Though they've won two European Cups, they've lost five finals, as many as any other team (Benfica and Bayern Munich have also lost five). But at home they are unparalleled, holding 30 Serie A trophies to the 18 each that the Milan clubs have won. They persevere: after Heysel, after relegation, after ignominy, after the loss of dear players, Juventus goes on, the youthful Old Lady of Italian soccer.

KAIZER CHIEFS

Location	Johannesburg, South Africa
Established	1970
Nicknames	*Amakhosi* ("Chiefs"), Glamour Boys
Current stadium	FNB Stadium, a.k.a. Soccer City, the Calabash (94,000 capacity)
Home colors	Yellow and black
Leading goal-scorer	Marks Maponyane (1981–91), 85 goals
Most appearances	Theophilus Doctorson "Doctor" Khumalo (1987–94, 1997–2002), 397 appearances

Benedict Vilakazi stands 5 feet 2 inches, and fans call him "Little Napoleon." A combative midfielder, he played 170 games between 1999 and 2007 for the Orlando Pirates in South Africa's Premier League. But there's one game he wishes he'd never played in, a goal he wished he'd never scored.

The Pirates are an old team by South African standards, around since 1937. Their archrivals across Johannesburg are the Kaizer Chiefs, a much newer team—they were established in 1970 when Kaizer Motaung, who used to play for the Atlanta Chiefs in the North American Soccer League, went back to South Africa to form a team.

It wasn't a good time in South Africa. Apartheid was as deeply in place as it had ever been. In February 1970, Winnie Mandela was placed under house arrest (her husband, Nelson, had been in jail on Robben Island since 1962); that same year, because it still insisted on whites-only sports, South Africa was banned from the forthcoming Munich Olympics, and its cricket team's projected hosting of a tour by England was canceled. To think of creating a soccer team at such a time was an act of great courage, and many thought Motaung mad—not just because of the political situation, but because he had once played for the Pirates. But he persevered, and soon the team was gaining fans across South Africa.

In the first match between the Chiefs and the Pirates, in April 1971, the Chiefs found themselves three down but staged a fine comeback, scoring their fourth and winning goal with three minutes to go. The following year, in the Champion of Champions Cup final, second leg, the Chiefs were two down to the Pirates at half-time, but the game ended 3–3 in regulation. Somehow the Chiefs then conjured four goals in extra time to win the trophy. Such games defined what was to become a famous rivalry, known as the Soweto Derby, but tragedy was always just a step away.

One player who joined Motaung in setting up the Kaizer Chiefs was Ewert "The Lip" Nene, also formerly of the Pirates, but in 1976 he was stabbed to death in the town of Springs, east of Johannesburg, amazingly during negotiations to sign a player to the Chiefs (one Nelson "Teenage" Dladla). Motaung later somewhat ironically commented that Ewert "[wasn't] a good administrator, but his human relations skills were superb." In that same year, Ariel "Pro" Kgongoane, the captain of the Kaizer Chiefs, died during the Soweto Uprising on June 16, when he was hit by a stray bullet.

Perhaps the greatest ever Chiefs player—and perhaps the finest African footballer to ever grace the game—was Patrick "Ace" Ntsoelengoe. An attacking midfielder, Ntsoelengoe had the perfect physique for the sport: low center of gravity, instinctual balance, and strength. In addition, he had what is commonly called "vision," perhaps the most important gift any player can possess. Splitting his time between the Chiefs and a number of North American Soccer League franchises—most notably, the Minnesota Kicks—Ntsoelengoe, a huge smile constantly on his face, played mostly off the halfway line, either waltzing past opponents with ease or placing passes, often with the outside of his foot, via angles rarely seen on a soccer field. He also scored goals—he was the fifth-highest scorer in the NASL—but in Africa he was legendary, helping to bring trophies to the Chiefs in nearly every season he played. Later, Ntsoelengoe would coach the Chiefs youth team, until he died of a heart attack in 2006 at just 50, and only a month before the World Cup came to South Africa.

But it was the events of 2001 that defined the sadness of the Kaizer Chiefs, and indeed also of the Orlando Pirates.

Apartheid finally ended in 1994 when a now free Nelson Mandela and his ANC won multiracial elections; two years later, the South African Premier League began. By 2001, the Pirates had won a title (and an African Champions Cup in 1995), and the Chiefs fans desperately wanted trophies, too. But on April 11, a Soweto Derby became the scene of the biggest tragedy in South African sports, when fans, forcing their way into the Ellis Park Stadium, overran security and a crush started to form. Poor Benedict Vilakazi, unaware of the tragedy unfolding, stepped up to score an equalizer for the Pirates, and all hell broke loose. Forty-three people died in the resulting crush; some of the bodies were laid on the field. One photograph shows a young boy crying as someone with a microphone tries to find his parents. Benedict Vilakazi later said, "I wish I didn't score that goal. Maybe those people would still be alive today." The game was abandoned, and though the Chiefs won three cup competitions—including an African Cup Winner Cup trophy in December, achieved with a last-minute penalty in Johannesburg against Interclube of Angola, and reached the final of the CAF Super Cup (where they lost 4–1 to Egyptian super club Al-Ahly), the deaths haunted both the Chiefs and the Pirates. It was especially poignant as something similar had happened in 1991, when the two teams had played a friendly at the Oppenheimer Stadium in Orkney, some 120 miles south west of Johannesburg: there, crowd trouble sparked a stampede that resulted in 42 deaths. History had repeated itself in the worst possible way.

Since those dark days, the Kaizer Chiefs have won three Premier League titles, and the Pirates three more, giving them one more in total than the Chiefs. In July 2006, the Chiefs beat Manchester United on penalties in an international friendly; they also beat both Spurs and Manchester City in later years. But the words of Benedict Vilakazi hang over every game they play, especially the Soweto Derby: "I pray that nothing like that happens ... again, because death isn't what football is about."

KASHIMA ANTLERS

Location	Kashima, Japan
Established	1947
Nicknames	None
Current stadium	Kashima Soccer Stadium (capacity 40,728)
Home colors	Red and navy blue
Leading goal-scorer	—
Most appearances	—

It might just be the greatest free kick ever taken, and that includes all the usual suspects, such as Ronaldo, Roberto Carlos, Didier Drogba, and David Beckham.

The player's name is Eddy Bosnar. Bosnar was playing for the Suwon Samsung Bluewings in the South Korean league. It was May 2012. Bosnar, an Australian of Croatian descent and a much-traveled player, lined up a free kick about 35 yards from the Ulsan Hyundai goal.

What happened next seems to defy some sort of physical law. Bosnar's run-up was quick, almost too quick, and when he struck the ball, his standing right leg was a step ahead of it. No matter—Bosnar's left boot connected with the football in an almost preternatural way and off it went, fast and hard. The ball rises from the turf, and before the goalkeeper has fully extended his hands, the white-hot orb has hit the back of the net. It's the kind of goal that makes a soccer fan giggle with awe.

Good for Bosnar, though he deserves his fame for something less flashy. A year earlier, in April 2011, Bosnar had stood in the train station of the Japanese town of Shimizu-ku, in Shizuoka Prefecture, holding a box. The city of Shimizu-ku, 100 miles south-east of Tokyo, had been spared significant damage from that spring's earthquake and tsunami, which killed an estimated 16,000 people. Nevertheless, players for the local team, Shimizu S-Pulse, had willingly waited for trains to arrive to collect money for victims. Bosnar, talking to the *New York Times*, said, "The boxes are soon full, not with coins but with notes."

Among the least of the victims of those terrible days in Japan was the professional soccer J-League. Established the same year, 1992, as the English Premiership, the J-League was the first concerted attempt to bring the pro game to a country that had been more obsessed with baseball than football. For the first 12 seasons, it followed a kind of South American model, splitting the year into two stages.

The first winners of the first ever stage, Kashima Antlers, have gone on to dominate the J-League. Before 2005, Antlers won five halves, and in 1996 they won both; from 2007–09, they won the league three times in a row. Partly this is due to the influx of Brazilian players and coaches who have traveled to the east coast of Japan to join Kashima Antlers. The most famous of these was one of the greatest Brazilians to ever play the game: Zico. The "White Pelé," as he was known, played for Antlers for three seasons before his retirement, and managed them briefly in 1999.

On March 11, 2011, as the earthquake struck, Kashima's stadium, situated a mile from the ocean, was badly damaged, even though the epicenter of the temblor was some 500 miles to the northeast, way out in the Pacific Ocean. Football stopped in Japan; the country had more important things to think about; it wouldn't be until April 23 that games began once again. The Kashima Antlers were well off the pace that season, as though it really mattered. Yet the image that remains, beyond the damaged stadium, Bosnar's astonishing free kick, and the Brazilians who have flocked to Kashima to coach and play in the championships, is that train station box, silent without coins, filled with paper.

L.A. GALAXY

Location	Los Angeles, California, USA
Established	1995
Nicknames	None
Current stadium	StubHub Center (capacity 27,000)
Home colors	White, navy blue, and gold
Leading goal-scorer	Landon Donovan (2005–), 106 goals
Most appearances	Cobi Jones (1996–2007), 306 appearances

"I would put our teams up against some Premiership teams in a second." So said Alexi Lalas in 2007, when he was still the general manager of the Los Angeles Galaxy. What he failed to mention was how his team would do for the rest of the 89 minutes and 59 seconds.

Lalas was so quoted the day the Galaxy signed David Beckham from Real Madrid for a reported $200 million, give or take. Beckham had done it all: six English Premiership medals with Manchester United, and single-handedly bringing them back from the brink of losing the 1999 Champions League final, a game notable, in the US at least, for color commentator Tommy Smyth's inane assessment that Beckham was having a bad game (Smyth has been called "possibly the most hated football commentator in history," by the *Guardian*). Beckham's performance for the last third of that final was exquisite, and American soccer fans had long since given up expecting Smyth to know the first thing about the sport, up to and including the fact that no one except him calls the goal an "onion bag." Beckham also last-minute free-kicked England into the World Cup in 2001, a 30-yard beauty into the Stretford End at Old Trafford, against Greece, that caused the British commentator to scream, "Give that man a knight-hood!" (He got the Order of the British Empire instead.) He would go on to win the La Liga trophy with Real Madrid in 2007, so the world raised at least one eyebrow when on January 11, 2007, it was announced he would join the L.A. Galaxy once the Madrid season was over.

Of course, about the relative strengths of MLS and the Premiership Lalas was patently wrong. MLS was streets behind the European game, though in renting Beckham, the Galaxy had done something very smart: they needed a player who could show the club, and the American soccer public, that despite the protestations of the likes of Lalas, there was still a lot to learn. It wasn't just about exposure, though it sure helped that Beckham was one of the most recognizable sports celebrity figures in the world. Beckham's ability as a football player would help the American game take a leap forward.

And so it proved. Witness his first performance in MLS, against the New York Red Bulls in August 2007. Beckham was still only half fit and didn't move much beyond the center circle, except to take corners. But the more than 60,000 fans who showed up to Giants Stadium (there were usually around 11,000) witnessed a masterclass in passing and crossing. After eight minutes Beckham had already made two goals for the Galaxy, and continued to whip in corners the like of which had never been seen in the league. The final score—5–4 to New York, including two by a very young Jozy Altidore—barely told the whole story. Beckham was here, and he was still one of the best players to ever strike a free kick, cross, or corner.

The Galaxy could have used him, or someone like him, in their first six seasons. A charter member of MLS, they reached the first, fourth, and sixth MLS Cup games, only to lose them all; in the third loss, in 2001, they were downed by Landon Donovan playing for the San Jose Earthquakes. They finally broke through with a win of their own the next year.

When Donovan joined the Galaxy in 2005, the team became truly formidable. They have reached four of the eight MLS finals between 2005 and 2013, winning three of them, and though it took

Beckham until 2012 to finally win an MLS Cup medal, a team made up of Donovan, Beckham, and Robbie Keane up front, Omar Gonzalez at the back, and managed by former USA boss Bruce Arena, would always have improved the overall quality of the league. And so it has proved. The MLS of Alexi Lalas's wild boasts has finally come of age since the influx of Beckham, Keane, Thierry Henry, and others who have brought a European sophistication to the game on the field. And the money has followed—Herbalife sponsored the Galaxy to the tune of $25 million over five years, and Time Warner Cable coughed up $55 million across ten years for the rights to televise their games. Some of this is undoubtedly the "Beckham effect," but soccer fans in the US are now smarter about the game itself than ever before. They knew, for example, that when Beckham was substituted with a few minutes to go in the 2012 MLS Cup final, with L.A. leading 3–1, that his subsequent announcement that he was done with the team could spell trouble—sure enough, a year later, L.A. were knocked out of the playoffs at the first hurdle by Real Salt Lake. The transfer value of that entire 2013 L.A. squad was said to be around $15 million, equivalent to a perfectly solid team propping up the English second tier (i.e., 26 places below the Premiership). But there's no doubt that the club has come a long way since losing three of the first six MLS Cup finals, a string of disappointments in big games only ended when Cobi Jones led the 2000 edition of the L.A. Galaxy to victory over Olimpia of Paraguay in the CONCACAF Champions Cup. It remains to be seen how they fare once Donovan and Keane move on; perhaps Alexi Lalas could return (he was fired in 2008 after a seven-game losing streak under then manager Ruud Gullit) to guide them to even greater heights.

Location	Rome, Italy
Established	1900
Nicknames	*I Biancocelesti* ("The White and Sky Blues"), *I Biancazzurri* ("The White and Blues"), *Le Aquile* ("The Eagles"), *I Aquilotti* ("The Young Eagles")
Current stadium	Stadio Olimpico (capacity 73,000)
Home colors	Sky blue and white
Leading goal-scorer	Silvio Piola (1934–43), 149 goals
Most appearances	Giuseppe Favalli (1992–2004), 401 appearances

I t is sad that we must pay him attention, but there is no alternative, so let's get it over with: Former Lazio legend Paolo Di Canio is a self-proclaimed Fascist. When he briefly ran Sunderland F.C. as their unhinged manager, he claims he was both a "top manager," and a "top man." Di Canio has "DUX" tattooed on his right arm—"DUX" as in "Il Duce," a.k.a. Mussolini, the totalitarian Italian leader Di Canio describes as "misunderstood." Di Canio quite happily delivered arm-in-the-air, three-fingers-in-a-shape salutes to Lazio fans during and after games. But heaven forefend anyone misunderstand him: as he points out for posterity, "I am a Fascist, not a racist."

No wonder Di Canio was right at home playing for Rome-based Lazio. Theirs is a history of military founders, Fascist owners and supporters, right-wing fans to this day, and "top men" like Di Canio running around making three-fingered salutes to "ultras."

Military officers established S.S. Lazio in 1900 as a running club, until a year later a guy called Brutus Seghettini, who had played soccer for Racing Club in Paris, explained the sport to these modern Roman athletes. By 1929, Lazio were in Serie A, and Mussolini had declared himself Il Duce. With legendary striker Silvio Piola well worth watching, the Fascist dictator declared himself a Lazio fan, showing up at games.

But Lazio were lucky to be a team at all. Two years earlier, a number of smaller Roman teams had been merged by the Fascist authorities to form A.S. Roma, but it took the intervention of another Fascist, General Giorgio Vaccaro, to stop Lazio being subsumed into this new club too. To this day, banners in the Stadio Olimpico, the stadium Mussolini built for the team and in which they still play, read, *"Generale Vaccaro, dal 1927 . . . GRAZIE!"*

On the field, for one of the two main teams that represent the capital of Italy, Lazio has massively underachieved. They have been relegated to Serie B a number of times for their poor football and also for match-fixing. In 1980, they were one of the key teams in the *totocalcio* scandal, in which two mostly incompetent match-fixing businessmen, Massimo Cruciani and Alvaro Trinca, did their best to get teams to throw games, often with unintended and hilarious results (the plot failed in one such game, a friendly between Palermo and Lazio, when the Roman team missed their flight to Sicily). When the investigation reached its zenith, players and officials were actually arrested at half-time of games being played on Sunday, March 2, 1980. The upshot of Cruciani and Trinca's handiwork was a forced relegation to Serie B for Lazio (and for A.C. Milan), and the ruination of the career of the one man who appeared at least partially moral in the whole thing, a Lazio midfielder by the name of Maurizio Montesi, who blew the whistle in an interview with *La Repubblica* newspaper, only to be banned for four months himself and then have his career crumble when other players and teams shunned him.

Lazio didn't seem to learn from *totocalcio*. In 1986, while in Serie B, they almost ended up in Serie C when they were docked nine points for the betting exploits of one of their players, midfielder and future right-wing political candidate Claudio Vinazzani—only a playoff kept them out of the *calcio cantina*.

Either side of the *totocalcio* relegation and the Vinazzani specta-cle, Lazio actually won a couple of things. Their first ever Scudetto came in 1974, on the back of the sterling play of future New York Cosmos superstar Giorgio Chinaglia; but by 1976 he was dazzling New Yorkers, and Lazio faded.

They would rise again in the 1990s on the back of the open-handed stewardship of club president Sergio Cragnotti and the acquisition of a number of top international players, including England's Paul Gascoigne (whose time in Italy was mostly a bust), and Juan Sebastián Verón and Hernán Crespo from Argentina. They became a solidly top-four team before winning their second title in 1999–2000 under the management of silver-haired future England manager and unlikely sex symbol Sven-Goran Eriksson, a man whose complicated love life would not be out of place in a daytime soap.

That Scudetto came a season after their only two major European trophies, the 1999 Cup Winners' Cup and the European Super Cup. The 1998–99 Cup Winners' Cup was hardly a vintage competition (this would be its last year, which was probably for the best). Lazio faced Lausanne-Sport, Partizan Belgrade, Greek minnows Panion-ios, and Lokomotiv Moscow before facing Mallorca—that's right, a team from an island the size of Rhode Island—in the final. Goals by Christian Vieri and Pavel Nedved were enough to overcome the Spanish team, but it was a good Lazio squad nevertheless, also featuring Marcelo Salas, Dejan Stanković, Alessandro Nesta, and future Manchester City coach Roberto Mancini. The core of the same team would win the European Super Cup that same year, beating a Manchester United team that had just won the Champions League, and would bring Lazio that second Scudetto, in 1990.

But Cragnotti would leave at the start of the new century—he and some of his family were accused of financial irregularities at their company—and Eriksson, Cragnotti's friend, left too. Almost unbe-lievably, in 2006 Lazio were yet again implicated in a match-fixing scandal—this one called *calciopoli*—in which referees were paid off to affect games; this wide-ranging scandal reeled in Juventus, A.C. Milan, Fiorentina, and other Italian clubs as well. Lazio's punishment was initially to be sent to Serie B, but further appeals brought it down to staying in Serie A with eleven points deducted, and finally with just three points deducted, though they were banned from entering the UEFA Cup for a season. Their president, Claudio Lotito, was banned from soccer for two and a half years.

The sorry Lazio tale continues. In 2012, Lazio fans were found guilty of racist behavior during games four separate times, and in late 2013, Paul Pogba, Angelo Ogbonna, and Kwadwo Asamoah, three black Juventus players, were targeted with racist abuse, leading to the north stand, where Lazio's "ultras" ply their ugly trade, being closed for a match. Of a previous UEFA sanction to close their entire stadium, Claudio Lotito said, "To suffer a punishment of one or two games behind closed doors, which will cause serious economic damage to the club and prevent fans from participating in an event like this, seems absurd to me." Absurd is right—after his abuse, Pogba noted, "They do that even though there are black players in their [own] team." Of course, it's also not above Lazio fans to boo their own black players (Aron Winter, a Dutch player, fled Lazio when he was called, among other things, a "black Jew"). Paolo Di Canio might claim the fans that still hold him in such high regard in Rome are not racists, just Fascists, but what is true is that the "ultras" of the north stand support a club that was founded by Fascists, was saved from extinction by a Fascist, play in a stadium built by Mussolini which is sometimes closed even to its own fans because of their racist abuse of players, has a history of match-fixing, and a couple of times in a century has managed to win a damned trophy. Who *wouldn't* want to be a Lazio fan?

LEEDS UNITED

Location	Leeds, England
Established	1919
Nicknames	The Whites, The Peacocks
Current stadium	Elland Road (capacity 39,460)
Home colors	White and blue
Leading goal-scorer	Peter Lorimer (1962–79), 238 goals
Most appearances	Jack Charlton (1952–73) and Billy Bremner (1959–76), 773 appearances each

There was a time, in the 20 or so years before the Premiership was established in 1992, that each of the largest urban areas in England had representative teams regularly playing in the old First Division. It seemed right: London, of course, had a few teams, usually Arsenal, Spurs, and Chelsea, as well as Crystal Palace and Fulham and West Ham and Charlton Athletic, and sometimes, sadly, the monsters of Millwall. The Midlands would send three or four teams (from Aston Villa, Birmingham City, West Bromwich Albion, Wolverhampton Wanderers, and even Coventry City); Manchester and Liverpool usually had two apiece, as did Tyneside (from Newcastle United, Sunderland, or Middlesborough); Nottingham Forest were winning both the league and the European Cup, and Notts County appeared in the final year of the First Division. Sheffield United and Sheffield Wednesday showed up, sometimes in the same season; Bristol City appeared before 1980—and even Brighton and Hove Albion were in the top division from 1979 to 1983.

And then there was Leeds United.

Leeds—or more precisely, the area around Leeds known as West Yorkshire—is considered the fourth largest urban settlement in England, boasting nearly 1.5 million residents. Given its size, it's not that hard to believe that Leeds United were once an English powerhouse team. In their most storied years, in the late sixties and early seventies, they won the League twice and came second five times, and fared well in European competition. Later, they won the last ever First Division championship in 1991–92, and between 1998 and 2002 they finished fifth, fourth, third, fourth, and fifth in the Premiership, while reaching the semifinals of both the UEFA Cup and, incredibly, the Champions League. They were a Big Club.

But by 2004, Leeds United were gone, relegated to the Championship and beyond, ending up in the Second Division, their lowest ever placing, in 2007–08. Now back in the higher reaches of the Championship, Leeds fans hope that the Premiership once again beckons, but how could it have gone so wrong for a team that once dominated the English leagues?

Leeds United came into being very late for a major club from a major city, only ascending to the Football League in 1920. (Compare that to a team like Doncaster Rovers, who, though geographically close to Leeds United, were formed some 41 years earlier and went on to win a number of trophies, including the Wharncliffe Charity Cup in 1923, before actually doing something worthwhile in beating Leeds in the 2008 League One playoff final.) Before that, as Leeds City, they had been disbanded by the Football Association after their brief tenure was marred by allegations of illegal payments to players during World War I.

And so was set the tenor of their history. Financial mismanagement would continue, on and off, for a century, reaching its nadir in the mid-2000s, when Leeds United were docked ten points for going into administration. Previous regimes had spent heavily on projected Champions League revenue without waiting for the team to actually qualify for the competition, and this profligacy would lead to them being relegated.

So, for the fourth largest city in England, Leeds has had a lousy time supporting a successful football team. Partly that is because Leeds is, by nature, a rugby town (and, to a lesser extent, a cricket town), with Leeds Rhinos being one of the most successful of all rugby franchises in British history. But beyond the financial misman-agement, Leeds has also been plagued by both bad luck and difficult characters, from the owners to the managers and on to the field. Taken together, these factors turned Leeds United into one of the least admired clubs in British football.

Even their most successful manager, Don Revie, brought with him baggage by the bagful. For a start, Revie was a man with a fear of ornamental elephants. He was, by all accounts, a very strange man; British journalist Andrew Mourant reports manifold stories of his oddness, including that odd factoid about fake pachyderms—pre-sumably he was unable to enter an Indian restaurant in Leeds, a city that boasts a large population of people from the subcontinent. Revie was also afraid of peacocks and held a strong belief that a gypsy curse hung over Elland Road, where Leeds have played for their entire history.

Originally a fine center forward, Revie took over the player-man-ager's role at then struggling Leeds United in 1961. With Revie at the helm, Leeds finally became a soccer town, coming second in the league in both 1965 and 1966, winning it in 1969 and 1974, and coming second again three years in a row, 1970–72. In Europe, too, Leeds saw success, making it to the final of the Inter City Fairs Cup in 1967 before losing 2–0 to Dinamo Zagreb, and winning the tournament in 1969 and again in 1971. At the heart of these Revie teams was a gang of players of whom it can be safely said that only their mothers, and die-hard Leeds fans, loved them: center backs Jack Charlton (brother of England and Man United legend Bobby), mercurial at best as a man and a player, and Norman Hunter, who was nicknamed "Bites Yer Legs" after a banner saying just that was displayed at the 1972 FA Cup final—a game Leeds lost to heavy underdogs Arsenal.

There was also midfielder Billy Bremner, a statue of whom now stands outside Elland Road. Bremner, who at 5 feet 5 inches was over-matched physically by many other players, nonetheless became noto-rious for his vicious tackling and love of a confrontation, none more memorable than the fight he had with Liverpool legend Kevin Keegan during the 1974 Charity Shield season opener. (Keegan had been incensed by a right hook landed by another Leeds charmer, Johnny Giles.) Perhaps the frustration of the Leeds players came from a nox-ious mixture of their unlovable natures and their careers as nearly-men, having come second so many times both domestically and in Europe. Revie's attempts to lift the gypsy curse never quite worked.

A kind of curse continued long after Revie was gone. For a start, Revie was followed at Leeds by Brian Clough, who lasted a mere 44 days—and then, on the night he was fired, sat for a painful TV inter-view with Revie, an interview that did little for the reputation of either man. Sample dialogue included a moment when Revie said, "Clough—[I'll call him that because] he calls me Revie—doesn't know [the play-ers]. He is a fool to himself." (The 44-day Clough fiasco later became a fine book by David Peace, *The Damned United*, which was turned into a terrific movie of the same title.) Revie left Leeds to manage England, but his reign was an uninspired one, with the team failing to reach either of the two major competitions into which he tried to lead them. At the end, Revie announced his resignation in a national news-paper rather than directly to the Football Association, and his reputa-tion never recovered.

The club Revie left behind has fared little better. Though many soccer teams have been plagued by hooligan fans in the last four decades, few inspire the fear that a visit from Leeds United still engen-ders. In a video of the aftermath of Giles's punch of Keegan in 1974, one can hear them singing that lilting classic of 1970s' soccer hooli-gans, "You're gonna get your fucking heads kicked in." A decade later, Leeds fans were involved in an ugly riot in Birmingham which led to the death of a 15-year-old Leeds fan, Ian Hambridge, when a wall gave way. The interim report by the government into this and other disas-trous scenes of soccer's *annus horribilis,* 1985—which included a terrible fire at Bradford City's ground on the same day as the Birmingham riot, killing 56, and the riot at the Heysel Stadium by Liverpool fans two weeks later which killed 39 Juventus fans—reads, in part, as though written by Cleese, Chapman, Palin, Jones, and Idle, of Monty Python fame. Even before the Birmingham–Leeds game started, "one coach, with Leeds supporters in, was directed to a coach park. It would have meant that supporters would have had to walk some 300 yards back to the stadium. Finding this to be an unacceptable imposition, and perhaps wanting to husband their energies for later violence, they just kicked out the side windows and left the coach that way." As the violence spilled into the stadium, Leeds manager Eddie Gray, a stalwart of the Revie era as a player, according to the report, "came on to the pitch to seek to placate the Leeds fans. All he got for his efforts was a stoning." Apparently, "some [Leeds] supporters managed to dislodge part of the concrete terracing. One used a pick axe." The riot, joined lustily by Birmingham fans, went on all afternoon and into the early evening. Summing up, Justice Oliver Popplewell, the author of the report, concurred with one police officer's assessment that the "frightening and terrifying scene ... more clearly resembled the Battle of Agincourt than a football match."

Leeds is a big enough city to warrant a major soccer team, and United continue to try to reach the Premiership. Quite how their unique approach to intra-club relations will go down in the more refined and heavily policed modern-day top flight remains to be seen.

LEVSKI SOFIA

Location	Sofia, Bulgaria
Established	1911
Nicknames	The Blues, The People's Team
Stadium	Georgi Asparuhov Stadium (capacity 29,200)
Home colors	Blue and white
Leading goal-scorer	Nasko Sirakov (1980, 1983–88, 1991–94), 206 goals
Most appearances	Stefan Aladzhov (1967–81), 473 appearances

The hoodlums—literally, they were wearing hoods—stood in a semicircle around the table, hovering, menacing, edging forward, waiting for their chance. Behind the table, poor Ivaylo Petev sat nervously, clad in the traditional blue shirt of Levski Sofia. It was October 2013, and Petev had just been revealed as the new manager of this, one of the most successful teams in Bulgaria. But at the press conference, a bunch of the team's "ultras" had turned up, angry young men who perceived Petev to be the worst thing of all: a fan of CSKA Sofia, Levski's archrivals.

Voices got louder; arguments broke out, and then it happened: two of the "ultras" stepped behind Ivaylo Petev and stripped off his Levski Sofia shirt, leaving him bare to the waist.

It was surely the low point for a team that has had its fair share of difficult times. Most likely founded as early as 1911 by a group of students in the Bulgarian capital, Sofia, it was initially called Sport Club Levski, after Vasil Levski, an Orthodox monk and anti-Ottoman revolutionary who was captured and hung in 1873. For students keen to create a soccer team for the ages, naming themselves after Bulgaria's favorite son was a smart move, yet throughout their history, Levski fans have had to put up with almost constant meddling from the descendants of the ruling Ottomans, the Bulgarian Communist Party.

As Sport Club Levski, they won six championships before the Soviet-backed regime changed their name to Dinamo Levski, in the Stalinist tradition. Not until four years after Stalin's death was the team allowed to revert to its original name. By then they were the dominant Bulgarian side.

But the Communists weren't done with Levski. In early 1969, the Bulgarian Interior Ministry took over the club and forced them to merge with Spartak Sofia, calling the new side Levski–Spartak. Under that name they played an extraordinary 1976 UEFA Cup quarterfinal, second leg, at home to the Cruyff–Neeskens edition of Barcelona. Levski had lost the first leg in Spain 4–0, but the game in Sofia, on March 17, was something else altogether. Levski scored twice in the first 10 minutes, though by half-time it was 2–2. Three minutes into the second period it was 3–2 to Sofia, but after an hour it was 4–3 to Barcelona. The last five minutes were worth the price of admission alone, as Levski scored twice to win the game 5–4, making them the only team to score five against Barcelona in European competition. Sadly, it wasn't enough to help them advance—they still lost the tie 8–5 on aggregate—but no one can ever take that result away from Levski Sofia.

What could be taken away, yet again, was their name.

In 1985, Levski faced their archrivals, CSKA, the Bulgarian army team, in the Bulgarian Cup final. CSKA had won more championships than Levski, had reached the semifinals of the European Cup twice, and had always had the support of the regime. There was no love lost, therefore, and the cup final got chippy early, no thanks to a referee, Asparuh Yasenov, being massively out of his depth.

CSKA scored first before the half-hour mark, via a clearly hand-balled goal—the CSKA front man, Georgi Slavkov, punched the ball past the last defender and scored. Slavkov is shown peeling away to shake a celebratory fist at the massed army officers sitting like bumps on a log in the stadium. Worse was to come: after 53 minutes, a perfectly good tackle by a Levski defender somehow resulted in a free kick to CSKA on the edge of the box, which they converted to make it 2–0. Levski players were starting to lose it, as many teams facing Hristo Stoichkov have been known to do (the 19-year-old Stoichkov, who could start a fight in an empty stadium, was playing for CSKA that day). Levski were reduced to ten men; then they had a terrible penalty awarded against them (CSKA missed it); then a Levski player tried to strangle a CSKA player (both were sent off). Stoichkov then put his pinkie finger on the shoulder of a Levski attacker in the box, who fell down as though he'd been shot, and another ridiculous penalty was awarded. Levski scored; the game ended 2–1 to CSKA; the referee was punched twice by Bobby Mihailov, the Levski keeper; a riot ensued on the field and in the stands. Five players, including Stoichkov, were banned for life (the bans were subsequently rescinded, especially when it became clear that Stoichkov was going to be a superstar player). Both teams were disbanded for a while, and Levski got yet another new name, Vitosha Sofia, which lasted until 1989.

1989 was the year the Berlin Wall fell, and with it came freedom for Levski Sofia—finally, they were allowed to be their own team. With that freedom came all the pitfalls of modern football, however. They reached the group stages of the Champions League in 2006, only to be drawn in a group featuring Barcelona and Chelsea. Sofia scored one goal in their six matches, and that in the 89th minute against Chelsea; they lost all six games. And despite winning a total of 26 Bulgarian championships, including five since the turn of the century, their "ultras" still think it's acceptable to strip a man of his shirt because of a perceived preference for an opposing team. The day after poor Ivaylo Petev was laid bare, he quit. Of the stripping, Petev was quoted as saying, "I didn't expect that such a thing could happen in the twenty-first century."

There is no evidence that Ivaylo Petev is a CSKA Sofia supporter.

Location	Liverpool, England
Established	1892
Nicknames	The Reds
Current stadium	Anfield (capacity 45,362)
Home colors	Red
Leading goal-scorer	Ian Rush (1980–87, 1988–96), 346 goals
Most appearances	Ian Callaghan (1960–78), 857 appearances

The club of Shankly, Paisley, and Fagan, but also of Don Welsh and Roy Hodgson; of Souness, Gerrard, Keegan, Dalglish, Owen, Torres, and Suárez, but also of Sean Dundee, El Hadji Diouf, Paul Konchesky, and Andy Carroll; of the Kop and "You'll Never Walk Alone," but also of Heysel and Hillsborough: Liverpool F.C., the greatest English side in the 1970s and 1980s, now working their way back to the highest level, and with enough history to fill ten books.

Liverpool was founded out of the embers of their city rivals, Everton F.C. A local brewer, businessman, and politician, John Houlding, had rented Everton a place to play at Anfield Road in the late 1880s. Houlding wanted to start making some money, and Everton, seeing the financial writing on the clubhouse wall, fled across Stanley Park, where they would build Goodison Park. Houlding, now with a ground but no team, established Liverpool F.C., and they played their first game in September 1892. The following season, 1893–94, Liverpool entered the Second Division and won it, but finished bottom of the First Division in their first season there. The next season, they again won the Second Division and headed back to the First.

In 1901, Liverpool won its first top-flight championship, and it would win three more before World War II, as well as the first played after the cessation of hostilities. But then, successive management failures by Don Welsh and Phil Taylor left Liverpool back in the Second Division and going nowhere. What was needed was a man to change Liverpool F.C. from top to bottom, and in December 14, 1959, a Scot by the name of Bill Shankly took over at a club that at the time couldn't even afford to water its own pitch.

Shankly had played 16 seasons at right half for Preston North End until 1949, after which he'd begun his managerial career. Moving to Anfield, Shankly found already in place a cadre of three brilliant coaches: Bob Paisley, Joe Fagan, and Reuben Bennett. Shankly, Paisley, Fagan, and Bennett went on to create the legendary "Boot Room," an inner cabal that would meet in the actual boot room of Anfield and plot training strategy, player acquisition, game-day tactics—everything to transform the club from a Second Division nonentity into a team worth watching.

And it worked. Shankly had a way with words, and Paisley knew tactics inside and out. In 1961–62, Liverpool were promoted after not losing a game all season at Anfield, with striker Roger Hunt scoring 41 goals. Hunt had been at Liverpool since he was 20, and at 24 he was reaching his peak. With Shankly in charge, Liverpool and Hunt became unstoppable. By 1964, Liverpool had won the First Division; they'd win the FA Cup the following year, and the league once again in 1966. In that 1965 FA Cup win, a Liverpool of Hunt, Ron Yeats, Ian Callaghan, Ian St. John, and Tommy Smith had, in extra time, overcome a brilliant Leeds side led by Don Revie (a team that featured Jack Charlton, Johnny Giles, Norman Hunter, and Billy Bremner—all those unlovable but excellent Leeds henchmen). It was an exciting final, with Hunt scoring three minutes into extra time only for Bremner to equalize, and future TV pundit St. John winning it with seven minutes to go. In Europe, however, Liverpool lost their first ever final, the 1966 Cup Winners' Cup, a killer loss in extra time to Borussia Dortmund after a shot cannoned off the post, out onto captain Ron Yeats, and back into the net. It would take until 1973 for Shankly to win a European trophy, the UEFA Cup, after a stirring two-leg final against another Borussia, this time Mönchengladbach (Liverpool won the first leg at Anfield, 3–0, and hung on, losing 2–0 in Germany). By then, Shankly had brought Emlyn Hughes and Tommy Smith into defense, in front of brilliant keeper Ray Clemence, and up front, Kevin Keegan and John Toshack got on the end of the excellent wing play of Steve Heighway. That team also won the First Division that year, taking their tally to eight league titles.

The following year, Liverpool made it to the FA Cup final, against Newcastle United. The game was a breeze, the Merseysiders trouncing Newcastle United 3–0 on goals by Keegan (two) and Heighway. The team—wearing an all-red strip to mimic Real Madrid's all white, a change first proposed by Shankly before their European Cup second-round tie against Anderlecht in 1965—was at its height. Shankly, however, was done.

Bill Shankly had transformed little Liverpool into a powerhouse team, on the cusp of something very special, but he was tired out. The man who had invented the "Boot Room," had hung the "THIS IS ANFIELD" sign in the tunnel, had been behind the adoption of the Gerry and the Pacemakers' version of "You'll Never Walk Alone" as a club anthem in the early 1960s, and had even once said, "Some people believe football is a matter of life and death. I am very disappointed with that attitude. I can assure you it is much, much more important than that," was gone. Taking over was his lieutenant, Bob Paisley. And it was under Paisley that Liverpool became the best team in England, and Europe, for nearly a decade.

In Paisley's first season as boss, Liverpool lost out to Derby County in the league, and were knocked out of the fourth round of the FA Cup by Ipswich Town, who would end third in the league behind the Merseyside team. Not the greatest start for Paisley, but once he was done, Paisley deserved to stand with the best managers of all time. Few fans on the Kop, the massive section of the Anfield Stadium which was then still all-standing, and where red scarves were held aloft and "You'll Never Walk Alone" was lustily sung before every game, could have imagined that these would be the years of their lives, but so it was—Liverpool's domestic and international domination would last a decade.

Between 1974 and 1983, when he retired, the smiling, peaceable Paisley brought six league titles, three European Cups, a UEFA Cup, and a host of lesser trophies back to Anfield. Once a solid, large defender, Paisley had played more than 250 games for Liverpool before and after World War II before joining the training staff. Though that first season as full manager ended in disappointment, in 1976 Liverpool won the league title and repeated the following year. Though Nottingham Forest would win in 1978, it was only a brief respite: Liverpool would be back on top in 1979, 1980, 1982, and 1983. And then there were the three European Cup titles.

The knock on Liverpool that those years of the European Cup only involved four ties before the final—first round, second round, quarterfinal and semifinal, home and away—omits that the tournament was for champions only, unlike now, where almost every team with a heartbeat enters the early stages of the Champions League.

Liverpool's first European Cup came in 1977, when they once again dispatched poor Borussia Mönchengladbach in a European final, this time 3–1. The following season, Liverpool repeated their European Cup win and this time they needed only three ties, receiving a bye in the first round. In the quarterfinals, they thrashed Benfica 4–1 at Anfield, and lo and behold, who would turn up in the semifinal but Borussia Mönchengladbach once again. A first-leg win for the German team suggested that an end to the jinx was at hand, but with the young attacker Kenny Dalglish replacing Keegan up front that season, back at Anfield Liverpool cruised to a 3–0 win.

In the 1978 final, played at Wembley, Liverpool outfought Brugge in a Liverpool-dominated game, Dalglish brilliantly finishing after 65 minutes. But the following season, Liverpool, who'd lost their league title to Nottingham Forest, were further humiliated when Forest knocked them out in the first round of the European Cup.

They would beat Real Madrid to win their third European Cup under Paisley, in 1981. A 1–0 victory, the game was hardly a classic, though Liverpool didn't care. Then, like Shankly before him, Paisley walked away, handing over the club to another "Boot Room" man, Joe Fagan. Like Shankly, Paisley had had his fair share of inane verbal moments, once quipping about future European Cup-winning Alan Kennedy's terrible debut against Queens Park Rangers in 1978 that "they shot the wrong Kennedy." But the club Paisley left to Fagan was in great health, and Liverpool would reach two more European Cup finals in the years right after Paisley quit. One, in 1984, they would win, as wobbly-legged Bruce Grobbelaar, in the Liverpool goal, put two A.S. Roma penalty takers off and won the cup for Liverpool; the other, a year later, would change Liverpool, and football, forever.

The Heysel Stadium disaster that May evening in 1985 was a low point in world soccer. Liverpool fans rioted and attacked Juventus fans, and 39 Italian fans died. Liverpool lost the match, which probably should never have been played, and were disgraced as a club. Fagan was shattered, and retired. English teams were banned from European competition for five years, Liverpool for six. Subsequent league titles under the managership of Kenny Dalglish, in 1986 (a year they pipped Everton to both the title and the FA Cup) and 1988, seemed hollow.

Hollow, but worse was to come.

On April 15, 1989, Liverpool were to face Nottingham Forest in the semifinal of the FA Cup. The game was to be played at a neutral stadium, as is the tradition for FA Cup semifinals, and Hillsborough, home of Sheffield Wednesday, was chosen. The start of the game was delayed because a large number of Liverpool fans were still outside the ground at kickoff time, and fatal errors by the South Yorkshire police led to the opening of gates and the non-control of a crucial tunnel. A crush at the front of the Leppings Lane stand quickly formed, and it became apparent that a great disaster was at hand. Ninety-six Liverpool fans died, and more than 700 were injured. To add insult to horror, for years police officials lied about the events and Liverpool fans took the blame for the Hillsborough disaster. It was only with the release of a report by the Hillsborough Independent Panel in 2012 that it became clear that most, if not all, of the blame should be laid at the door of the police. There is a special place in hell for two characters from that terrible time: Chief Superintendent David Duckenfield of the South Yorkshire police, who told damning and distracting lies to various investigators, and Kelvin Mackenzie, the editor of the *Sun* newspaper, who printed lies that Liverpool fans were so drunk that they'd urinated where they stood and attacked police (any such urination would have been from rank fear as the crush developed).

Football changed after Hillsborough. Standing sections in grounds were done away with, and a kind of corporatization of soccer fully kicked in. Fans in the Premiership now sit, and eat expensive food, and sometimes sing when they're told to; but no one dies watching the games, which is the main thing.

Kenny Dalglish, the Liverpool center forward who'd played at Heysel and managed at Hillsborough, went to many if not all of the funerals of the 96 victims. His team should have won the 1989 league season, but conspired to lose, 2–0, at home to Arsenal on the last evening. Dalglish was heartsick at the loss of life, and the subsequent stress led to his departure from the club.

Since 1992—when the Premiership began and the back-pass rule was abolished (meaning keepers could no longer pick up passes from defenders)—Liverpool have never won the league. Cynics suggest that much of the 1970s' and 1980s' Liverpool success was down to their stolid defensive efforts, which included thousands of back passes; either way, archrivals Manchester United now have more league titles than Liverpool, a cause for consternation on Merseyside.

One place Liverpool still outshine United, though, is in European Cup titles. In 2005, Liverpool found themselves 3–0 down at half-time of the Champions League final to A.C. Milan. No team had ever come back from three goals down in a European Cup final, but Liverpool managed to tie the game on a header by their new midfield genius, Steven Gerrard; a Vladimir Smicer beauty; and a Gerrard dive in the box that led to Xabi Alonso missing the penalty but slamming home the rebound. An extraordinary double save by Liverpool keeper Jerzy Dudek from Andriy Shevchenko led to penalties, and when Dudek "did a Grobbelaar," three Milan players, including Shevchenko at the end, missed. Liverpool were European champions once again.

That Rafael Benitez-led Liverpool side had hit well above its weight, and since then the club has struggled to get back to its previous glories. Liverpool almost went bankrupt in 2010 under the disastrous ownership of Tom Hicks and George Gillett, before being bought by Boston Red Sox owner John Henry. New hope arrived in the form of Uruguayan striker Luis Suárez, who in November 2013 set a new record for Premier League goals in a single calendar month, with ten. (The previous record, eight, was set in April 2003 by Aussie center forward Mark Viduka, with Leeds United.). Though Suárez has moments of madness—he called Patrice Evra "*negrito*" during a game, leading to an eight-match ban, and then refused to shake Evra's hand in the most public way possible before a Man United–Liverpool game; he also bit Chelsea's Branislav Ivanović during a game, leading to ten more games idle—he is Liverpool's best striker since Fernando Torres. Should Suárez stay at Anfield, and owner Henry retain his interest, a trophy will surely come their way sooner rather than later.

MANCHESTER CITY

Location	Manchester, England
Established	1880 (as St. Mark's); 1887 (St. Mark's evolves into Ardwick A.F.C.); 1894 (Ardwick evolves into Manchester City)
Nicknames	City, The Citizens, The Sky Blues
Stadium	City of Manchester Stadium, officially Etihad Stadium (capacity 48,000)
Home colors	Sky blue and white
Leading goal-scorer	Eric Brook (1928–39), 178 goals
Most appearances	Alan Oakes (1959–76), 676 appearances

Manchester United would be champions once again. Their closest rivals, Manchester City, having led the league for much of the season, had faltered, though on that last Sunday, City were top on goal difference. All City needed to do was match United's result on the last day and the league was theirs, for the first time in a couple of generations. But up in the blue half of Manchester, a relegation-threatened Queens Park Rangers had somehow conjured two goals against City's one. Time was pretty much up. In the other game, United were leading Sunderland, so Manchester City were about to lose the league.

Would it always be like this? United had dominated the Premiership since its formation in 1992, and Manchester City . . . well, this was their best chance to finally wrest the crown from the hated crosstown Reds. And they'd seemingly blown it. At 1–1, QPR's Joey Barton, an often violent and foolish player, formerly of Manchester City, had elbowed City's Carlos Tévez, formerly of Manchester United, and QPR had been reduced to ten men. By the 65th minute, QPR were somehow 2–1 up. The score held despite City's desperate attempts to make a comeback. The clock read 91 minutes and 14 seconds.

It had been 1968 since Manchester City had won the English championship, and even then that was only the second time they'd managed it. For a club of City's size, in soccer-mad Manchester, it was a disappointing history. They had been founded out of a church's good works. In the late nineteenth century, east Manchester was a tough place to live (parts of it still are), with unemployment and violence both rampant. St. Mark's Church in Gorton instigated sports for the "at-risk" men, as we would now call them, and West Gorton A.F.C. was formed, though an 11–1 defeat by Newton Heath in the FA Cup, in 1886, seemed to presage its difficult future (Newton Heath would eventually become Manchester United).

Revenge, in the form of a Manchester Cup victory over Heath in 1891 (Gorton were now Ardwick A.F.C.) led to Ardwick becoming one of the founding members of the Second Division, and by 1894, St. Marks/Gorton/Ardwick had morphed into Manchester City.

The new club won their first FA Cup in 1904, and 20 years later they began their long history at Maine Road in Moss Side, Manchester, just four miles from Old Trafford. Football would be entrenched on the south side of the city for the next 80 years (until City moved into the Etihad Stadium, back on the east side of town). But Maine Road hardly brought City success. A single FA Cup victory in 1934 was theirs, as was a league trophy in 1936–37, made sweeter by Manchester United's relegation the same season, but even then, the following season City themselves were relegated even though they scored 80 goals, more than any other team (they let in 77). That same year, United were promoted back to the First Division. And so it went.

Manchester City spent plenty of time out of the top tier, winning seven Second Division championships between 1899 and 1966 (and one in 2002). The late sixties, however, saw a fine City side come together, featuring the Mikes Summerbee and Doyle, wee Franny

Lee (as famous for British commentator Barry Davies's call after a particularly fine goal—"Oh, just look at his face!"—as for anything he did on the field), and Colin Bell. Coaching the team were two very different men: the regular-Joe Mercer and the utterly flash Malcolm Allison, a man who was described by the *Daily Mail* as "handsome, boastful, impulsive. A gambler, womanizer, drinker and smoker . . . remembered for his trademark cigar and fedora, and the zest for life which once saw him photographed in the players' bath at Crystal Palace with actress Fiona Richmond." The curse of United seemed lifted a little when the Mercer–Allison team won the 1967–68 championship on the last day, beating Newcastle United 4–3 in a thriller, consigning United to second spot. (Allison had paid a steeplejack to climb the Old Trafford stadium and lower their flag to half-staff before the local derby in March of that season.) United countered by winning the European Cup 18 days later.

City finally found themselves in a European final when they reached the 1970 Cup Winners' Cup Final, having won the FA Cup the previous season. Facing them was Polish side Górnik Zabrze, though fewer than 8,000 fans showed up that night in Vienna. City, wearing a change kit of Manchester United red and black, opened the scoring when Neil Young knocked a spilled shot past the "helpless, helpless, helpless" Polish keeper, Hubert Kostka. A few minutes later, Neil Young was knocked over "like a hurricane" by Kostka—it was more like an assault than an attempt to get the ball—and the ensuing penalty left City two up. A late consolation for Górnik was neither enough nor a consolation—City had won in Europe. It seemed as though good times had finally arrived in Moss Side.

They had not. It says perhaps too much about City that their finest moment in the ensuing 30 years came in 1974, when they nudged United toward relegation, but even then they didn't really. Denis Law, who had been one of United's greatest ever stars, at the end of his career found himself in the light blue of City and playing his old team at Old Trafford on the final day of City's season, April 27 (United had one more game on the following Monday). City themselves were only two points out of the relegation places, and with 10 minutes to go Law, receiving a clever pass from Lee, back-heeled the ball from the edge of the six-yard box past Alex Stepney in the United goal. In any other game it would have been cause for great celebration, but even though City's players hugged him (Bell even slapped him three times on the face as if to tell him to cheer up), Law looked shell-shocked. He was substituted, grief-stricken, a few minutes later; the game was abandoned when United fans stormed the field at the very end. Law had seemingly relegated his beloved former club, but he needn't have worried—other results that day conspired to send United down, win or lose. City ended four points off the drop themselves. Not much to celebrate for anyone, it seemed.

Thirty years passed; a single League Cup victory in 1976, and years of relegation and promotion, ensued. Malcolm Allison came back to serve as City's manager in 1979, but it didn't work out. United picked themselves up once Alex Ferguson took over in 1986 and started to dominate at home and in Europe; City wallowed, with chairman Peter Swales famous for, in the words of Allison, "the combover, the England blazer, and the suede shoes," and little else. Odd highlights occurred, such as the 5–1 mauling United received in 1989 after City finally made it back to the top flight after a three-year hiatus, but for United, at least, the Manchester derby had taken second fiddle to games against Liverpool and Arsenal and Chelsea.

Which brings us back to the 2011–12 season. Swales was gone, and City had been taken over by an Abu Dhabi-based investment firm. Money was flowing freely. Into the club came the likes of Robinho, and later Carlos Tévez, David Silva, Sergio Agüero, Mario Balotelli, and a host of other international stars. In December 2001, City once again traveled to United and spanked them, 6–1; the tide seemed to have turned. On May 13, 2012, they faced their final game of the season, tied with United at the top of the table. The clock read 91 minutes and 14 seconds; City were 2–1 down to ten-man QPR, and United were about to win in Sunderland.

A corner; a huge leap by another of City's expensive signings, the

Bosnian Edin Džeko, and suddenly it was 2–2. There were three minutes left of the five added on as extra. The QPR bench started to celebrate when they realized that other scores had gone in their favor, meaning they were safe from the drop. In Sunderland, the game ended 1–0 to Manchester United, and as the players learned that City were drawing, the title looked like it would be United's once more.

United were champions for 15 seconds. Man City's Sergio Agüero picked the ball up 30 yards from goal, played a one-two with Balotelli, and sprinted on. Agüero took a touch and blasted the ball at goal. The back of the net bulged, and Manchester City were champions.

The following season it was business as usual, as United, stung by the drama of their loss, won the league by eleven points over a faltering City. In Europe, City were ineffectual. Alex Ferguson, who had taken to calling City the "noisy neighbors," and who had delayed his retirement to get the championship back for United, finally called it quits. City changed managers once again, jettisoning the title-winning Roberto Mancini for Manuel Pellegrini. They spent another gazillion pounds on players, an outlay that left many soccer fans disgruntled when their dough helped pip Liverpool to the 2013–14 Premier League title, but at least they were back in the east of the city and still wore that light blue shirt. And they still hated United—that, it seems, would never change.

Location	Manchester, England
Established	1878, as Newton Heath L.Y.R.; name changed to Manchester United in 1902
Nicknames	The Red Devils
Stadium	Old Trafford (76,000 capacity)
Home colors	Red, white, and black
Leading goal-scorer	Bobby Charlton (1956–73), 249 goals
Most appearances	Ryan Giggs (1991–), 949 appearances

Manchester United, a team whose name is known wherever club soccer is followed, were, a half century ago, relatively *unknown* outside the UK. But all that would change in the air disaster now known by one word: "Munich."

Founded in 1878 as Newton Heath, the club was originally a railway depot's team and wore the Lancashire and Yorkshire Railway company's colors, green and yellow-gold. It wasn't until 1902 that they became known as Manchester United, but by 1908 they'd won their first English title, by nine points over Aston Villa and Manchester City. The following year they won their first of eleven FA Cups, beating Bristol City, 1–0. In 1911, United won their second league title.

Then Manchester United fell apart. John Henry Davies, who had invested in the club to keep it going in 1902, and continued to do so, died in 1927, and the money dried up. United spent a number of seasons in the Second Division, falling as far as twentieth in that league in 1934. They were far from a glamour club; they could barely pay their bills. In the final season before World War II, they were back in the top flight but finished 14th.

Who knows where United would have ended up without the man they appointed manager in October 1945: Matt Busby. A Scot whose miner father had been killed in World War I, Busby had almost emigrated to the United States, but instead got work as a collier himself before signing as a striker for . . . Manchester City. After playing 204 games, Busby signed for . . . Liverpool, where he played another 115 games, until 1941. Four years later, having played for United's two great rivals, he was given the manager's job at . . . United.

A Scottish former striker who assumed total control of Manchester United's recruitment, team management, and day-to-day running, leading them to unimaginable success after years in the wilderness? Alex Ferguson was not the first such man to corral Manchester United. After three second-place finishes in a row in the late 1940s plus an FA Cup win over Blackpool in 1948, in 1951 United finished second yet again, and in 1952 they won their third title. But that team was nearing its end, and Busby knew he'd have to build a new one.

Ignoring the idea that "you can't win anything with kids" long before the inane Alan Hansen said it in 1995 of Ferguson's young teams, Busby turned United into a club of young players, who became known as the Busby Babes—a wonderful if mercurial side. In the 1952–53 season, a new set of faces ran out onto the Old Trafford turf. There was David Pegg, an outside left; Tommy Taylor, a center forward; holdover Roger Byrne had matured into a superb left back and was captain, playing alongside center back Bill Foulkes; Dennis Viollet was another fine inside left; and, perhaps the jewel in the crown, there stood Duncan Edwards, a hard-tackling, surging midfielder who first played for United at the age of 16 and a half.

In 1955–56, the Babes went unbeaten at Old Trafford in the league, which they won by eleven points; the following season they won by just eight, though they lost the Cup final to Aston Villa, 2–1. On the back of those league wins, United had started to play in the European

Cup, and in 1958 they reached the quarterfinals, where another young player, Bobby Charlton, scored in the first leg at home to Red Star Belgrade, United coming back from 1–0 down to take a slender 2–1 lead to Yugoslavia.

The second leg was a typical Busby Babes performance; three up after half an hour on two goals from Charlton and one from Viollet, they leaked three goals in 12 second-half minutes and squeaked through. Manchester United teams never do it easy, never do it boring. Their results that 1957–58 season reveal just how it goes with young and/or United players (their average age when they won the league in 1956 was just 22). In November, Spurs had beaten United 4–2 at Old Trafford; the following week, United had drawn 3–3 at home to Birmingham City. In January they'd beaten Bolton 7–2, behind a Charlton hat-trick; the following week they'd just pipped Arsenal 5–4 at Highbury. They scored a lot of goals; they let a lot of goals in.

United were entertaining, at last, and after the Red Star game was done, they were through to the semifinals of the European Cup. But that night, United's world caved in. It was February 6, 1958; Munich, Germany. The team's plane was on its third attempt at a late-afternoon takeoff from Munich's ice-bound airport, after a layover from Belgrade, on its way back to Manchester. The weather was lousy, with snow general. The first two takeoff attempts had been aborted; the left engine kept surging, not a good sign. Fearing a needless overnight stay, the pilots of the British Airways Airspeed Ambassador attempted one last ascent, but the airplane overshot the runway, striking a house and then a hut. Those facing backward were mostly safe; those facing forward, not so fortunate.

On board was a football team filled with youth, and the potential of youth. Roger Byrne, the left back and captain; David Pegg, an outside left; Eddie Colman, a right half; Tommy Taylor, a center forward; Mark Jones, a center half; Bill Whelan, an inside right; Geoffrey Bent, a full back; and Duncan Edwards, a left half, who succumbed to his injuries 15 days after the crash—all were gone.

Matt Busby was gravely injured; he received the sacrament of Extreme Unction, commonly known as the last rites, on two separate occasions, though nine weeks later he left hospital and returned to Manchester. Bobby Charlton walked away from the crash with a slight concussion. He'd been facing backward. Three Man United staff members and eight journalists died, along with a travel agent, an airline steward, and the pilot. And a fan. A three-year-old survived.

The core of the Busby Babes had been decimated. Though the team made the FA Cup final that year, six of the previous year's players were now absent, and they lost to Bolton, 2–0. Busby himself wasn't told for weeks the full extent of what had happened; when he finally found out, he was guilt-ridden.

Busby rebuilt United around survivors Foulkes, Harry Gregg, and Charlton. He added signings such as Denis Law and David Herd, and brought a young George Best to the club. The new team won the FA Cup in 1963 and two more league titles (in 1965 and 1967), and headed off to the European Cup once again. Charlton, Best, and Law morphed into a divine-ish trinity who played dazzling football and scored for fun. Best, in particular, was probably the most skillful British player who ever got a game. A slight Northern Irish sprite, Best had ball skills to rival any Messi or Ronaldo—he once scored so many goals in an early round of the FA Cup that United manager Wilf M. Guinness made him play at full back for some of the game to avoid embarrassing United's opponents. Best dribbled, feinted, crossed, and scored, though his later alcoholic years were a sad reflection on how some famous footballers handle the stress (see under Paul Gascoigne, Diego Maradona).

Ten years after Munich, and having beaten Real Madrid 4–3 on aggregate after two late goals at the Bernabéu in the second leg of the semifinal, United reached the final of the European Cup, to be played at Wembley. Facing them was Eusébio's Benfica. The great Portuguese striker hit the bar in the first half after a mazy run; he was to be much feared. Though Denis Law was injured, Best was on fine form, and Charlton scored with a glancing header after 53 minutes. Jaime Graça equalized (and then hugged a cameraman) for Benfica, before Eusébio drilled a late shot straight at Alex Stepney in the United goal, pausing to applaud the keeper's save. In extra time, Best did what he did best, rounding the keeper to give United the lead; Brian Kidd, who would go on to be an assistant at both Manchester clubs, here on his 18th birthday added a third, before Charlton scored a fourth to seal the win. One can only imagine the feelings filling Charlton and Busby, survivors and now champions, the faces they must have seen in their mind's eye as they lifted the European Cup.

In 1968, Manchester City had beaten United to the league title by two points, and the following year United lost in the European Cup semifinals to A.C. Milan. Few knew then that United were headed to a new oblivion on the field.

The team of kids was now a team of older, less effective players, and Busby's time was drawing to a close. He retired a year after the European Cup win, though he did manage on a caretaker basis in 1970. But the club was in a deep decline, dogged by poor managers, poor teams, and hooligans in the stands. In 1974, United were relegated to the Second Division, just six years after being European champions.

United would come straight back, but the 1970s and 1980s were a time of massive underachievement for a club their size. They had become one of the most famous clubs in the world, attracting huge crowds wherever they played, but they failed to put out a consistently good team. Liverpool dominated in England and Europe, while United won the odd FA Cup and lost others, such as a heartbreaker in 1979 against Arsenal. A new chapter was needed, and it came in the form of another former striker from Scotland who was determined to do it his way.

Alex Ferguson had been a Rangers fan growing up, a team he eventually played for, though his mistake in the 1969 Scottish Cup final led to a Celtic goal, and the club never forgave him. In 1974, Ferguson took up management, and in 1983 he led northern Scottish minnows Aberdeen to the Cup Winners' Cup final, where they beat Real Madrid 2–1. English teams took notice, and in November 1986 Ferguson moved south to become manager of Manchester United.

What Ferguson found at the club was a hard-drinking bunch of players, little or no youth policy, and a club too big for its britches. He set about changing the culture, but results didn't immediately follow; he was probably on the verge of being let go after four trophy-less years, when a diminutive center forward called Mark Robins scored a late winner in an FA Cup game against Nottingham Forest, in January 1980, to save Ferguson's job. The history of Manchester United turned once again.

United would win the FA Cup that season, and the Cup Winners' Cup the following, beating Barcelona in the final on two goals by Mark Hughes. But the big trophy still awaited, as it had since 1967. In 1992, the first year of the Premiership, they would win the league for the first time in 26 years, and much of the credit went to one man: Eric Cantona.

Cantona, a French striker, had had a checkered career before he moved to Old Trafford. Among numerous offenses, he had been banned by the French F.A. for two months for having thrown a ball at a referee during a game and then compounded the offense by calling each of the members of the committee that heard his appeal "*un idiot*," one by one, to their faces. Cantona fled France and moved to Leeds United, where he helped them win the last ever First Division title. In December 1992, Cantona moved to United, and was the catalyst that turned the team into the dominant side of the last years of the twentieth century. Cantona's mere bearing was something to behold—he strutted around the field, making passes that were perfectly weighted, and when opportunity arose he would do something spectacular like chipping a goalkeeper from 25 yards, and follow it with a sneer as if to suggest everyone else on the field was beneath him (they often were).

In addition, two late headers by center back Steve Bruce against Sheffield Wednesday late in that season helped create the legend of "Fergie time," which suggests referees were unduly influenced by the fire and brimstone emanating from Alex Ferguson to play too many added minutes, though there is no hard evidence to suggest the legend is actually true. Instead, Ferguson opted for never-say-die players like Bryan Robson, Steve Bruce, Paul Ince, and Mark Hughes. But with their careers winding down, Ferguson, like Busby before him, brought on a cadre of young players to join Cantona, a group who would go on to dominate English football for a decade.

The 1992 FA Youth Cup was won by Manchester United, and featured David Beckham, Nicky Butt, Ryan Giggs, and Gary Neville. These four, plus Paul Scholes and Gary's brother, Phil, would go on to anchor a team that would win numerous league titles. Beckham, in particular, became a world superstar for his ability to cross a ball perfectly, hit extraordinary free kicks, and marry a Spice Girl. Cantona was inspirational, too, though his kung-fu kick on a Crystal Palace supporter in January 1995 led to an eight-month ban. Cleared to play for United once again in October 1995, Cantona set about winning the league single-handedly: between January 22 and April 8, 1996, United played 11 league games, and Cantona scored the only goal for United in six of them (he would also score the only goal of the 1996 FA Cup final against Liverpool, four minutes from time). Old Trafford, United's stadium, grew to be the biggest in club football. United's success had created a global brand, though with it came all the down-sides of when sports is dominated by cash—many United fans, though happy to turn up every week to watch their team win over and over again, still wondered where the soul of the club was being stashed amidst what midfielder Roy Keane called "the prawn sandwich brigade" filling the stadium.

The one place Cantona did not excel was in European football: he was often isolated by Ferguson's defensive away tactics, and was sometimes not even in the team due to European "foreign players" restrictions. By May 1997, Cantona had retired; two years later, in the 1999 Champions League, United scored twice in stoppage time to steal the trophy from Bayern Munich. Later iterations of the dominant United team of the 1990s and 2000s included prolific goal-scorers Andy Cole,

Dwight Yorke, Teddy Sheringham, and Ruud van Nistelrooy, unbeatable Peter Schmeichel in goal, hard tackling and always-on-the-edge Roy Keane in midfield, Jaap Stam, Denis Irwin, Nemanja Vidić, and Rio Ferdinand at the back, and three of the world's best strikers in Cristiano Ronaldo, Carlos Tévez, and Wayne Rooney. Rooney had been brought from Everton; a solid chunk of Liverpudlian talent, he quickly became, like Beckham before him, both the talisman of the team and a lightning rod for controversy. Nevertheless, in the first ten years of the Premiership, United won eight titles; they would win three more, in a row, between 2007 and 2009, and add a 19th, and a 20th, in 2011 and 2013.

United would also reach three more Champions League finals in four years under Ferguson (not including the Bayern classic of 1999). In the first of them, in 2008, they beat fellow English side Chelsea in Moscow, in front of Chelsea's Russian owner, Roman Abramovich. An early Cristiano Ronaldo header for United was canceled out by a Frank Lampard strike for Chelsea and Didier Drogba was sent off in extra time for slapping Nemanja Vidić, before penalty misses by Ronaldo and John Terry, slipping as he took the kick, set up Nicolas Anelka to keep the tie going in sudden death. But Edwin van der Saar in the United goal made an easy save, and United had their third European crown.

In two subsequent attempts, they would fail to get a fourth. In 2009 and again in 2011, United were utterly outclassed in the final by the best team in the world, Barcelona, losing 2–0 and 3–1.

In 2013, Ferguson retired. In his time with United, he'd won two Champions League titles, 13 Premierships, five FA Cups, four League Cups, the Cup Winners' Cup, and the opprobrium of all soccer fans who were ABU's (Anyone But United's). Handing over the reins to yet another Scot, David Moyes, Ferguson moved up into a director's seat opposite the stand named after him at Old Trafford, from where he watched the first season without him at the helm turn into a disaster on the field for his beloved United—it was their worst performance since the Premier League began in 1992. In April 2013, Moyes was fired and replaced for the final four games by the seemingly age-less winger Ryan Giggs, before Dutch legend Louis van Gaal took over in the summer of 2014.

Every year on February 6, fans of Manchester United remember the players and staff and journalists who died in the Munich air disaster. From its ashes, a club known around the world was born, one that, though now owned by the little-loved American Glazer family, is still one of the teams whose name inspires envy, hatred, and grudging respect.

But few modern-day fans know the name Willie Satinoff, the fan who happened to be traveling with his beloved Reds that fateful February night. Satinoff had made his money in cotton, had become good friends with Matt Busby, and often traveled with the team across Europe on their adventures. There was even talk he'd become a United director. He's buried in the Southern Cemetery in Manchester. On his gravestone an inscription reads, "To live in hearts we leave behind is not to die."

MONACO

Location	Fontvieille, Monaco
Established	1919
Nicknames	*Les Rouge et Blanc* ("The Red and Whites")
Current stadium	Stade Louis II (18,523 capacity)
Home colors	Red and white
Leading goal-scorer	Delio Onnis (1973–80), 223 goals
Most appearances	Jean-Luc Ettori (1975–94), 754 appearances

Whatare the odds that a tiny place like Monaco could produce a consistently successful soccer team? If anyone was ever tempted to argue that money doesn't equal success in football, they might look no further than the tiny principality of Rainier, Grace Kelly, and the lifestyles of the rich and famous.

At less than one square mile, Monaco is the second smallest country in the world by area—only Vatican City is smaller. Just over 35,000 people live crammed into its tiny confines, and just about all of them are wealthy. The *CIA World Factbook* lists Monaco, with its absence of income tax, zero unemployment, and its casino at Monte Carlo, in sixth place for Gross Domestic Product per head, behind only Qatar, Lichtenstein, Bermuda, Macau, and Luxembourg.

As a result, there's a lot of money in Monaco, and where there's a lot of money, there's a lot of successful football. A.S. Monaco are an old sporting club, the football side of it established on August 1, 1919, when a bunch of smaller teams (smaller, in Monaco?) banded together. (Uniquely in this book, Monaco has no local derby rival to speak of, being the only team in the country, and has always played in the neighboring French league, though that status is in question as its players don't currently pay income tax.) After some time playing as an amateur side, and then a few years as pros in France, Monaco almost made it to the top division in 1933, only to lose to St. Etienne and subsequently find themselves once again an amateur team. It took until 1953 for Monaco to reach the top league, and it was a time of reemergence for the country, too. Prince Rainier III, determined that gambling money alone wouldn't float the tiny country, turned the place into a tax haven, as well as a tourist haven and a banking center. Along the way, in 1956, he managed to snag one of the world's most beautiful actresses, Grace Kelly, making her Princess of Monaco and the country a symbol of the sophisticated, resurgent, and dashing postwar south of France.

Rainier was also a huge A.S. Monaco fan, as was his elegant wife—the new Princess even suggested changing their traditional uniforms to feature a diagonal split of red and white. The team repaid the Grimaldis' loyalty and interest with its first French title in 1961, on the back of the coaching of legendary Lucien Leduc and the seemingly preternatural force of that Grace Kelly design. Leduc—a balding man with a huge smile lighting up a perfectly spheroid head—looked like a football, and clearly knew how to coach a team to use one well. That first title was followed by another two years later, a season that also featured a French Cup win, but then disaster struck: Leduc quit to embark upon an odyssey of management positions (Servette, Algeria, Marseille, Stade de Reims, Standard Liège, to name a few), and a number of players left, too. By 1969 no amount of Rainier gold dust could save Monaco from slipping back into the second division.

It would be another ten seasons before Monaco again won the French Ligue 1, and again, Lucien Leduc was in charge. The team had faced another relegation in 1976, but had bounced back under the input of Gérard Banide, a coach who had created a training center for young players. Banide would lead the once again Leduc-less Monaco to a fourth title in 1982, and five years later a young coach by the name of Arsène Wenger moved to the land of casinos and Grimaldis.

It didn't take Wenger long to win over the fans—his first season ended in a championship trophy. With a cerebral and perfectly balanced Glenn Hoddle and a young Emmanuel Petit in midfield, and the bulky bulldozer Georgie Weah up front, the season after their league victory they lost a heartbreaking French Cup final to Marseille, 4–3. (They would gain revenge two years later with a last-minute goal against Marseille in the final of the same tournament.)

The 1990s saw Monaco finally reach a European final, after a stellar run through the Cup Winners' Cup in 1991–92. Along the way they beat Welsh side Swansea City 8–0 at home, and were confident going into the final against an adequate but not exactly exciting Werder Bremen side. Sadly, Monaco froze, committing two horrendous defensive errors either side of half-time to hand Bremen a 2–0 victory. At least there weren't many people there to see it: when you're a tiny country, you don't travel with a lot of fans, and only 16,000 people attended the final in Lisbon's Estádio da Luz, a stadium which could hold as many as 127,000 (the attendance for a game the year before the Bremen–Monaco final).

Wenger stayed until 1995 and built a team that, in addition to Petit, featured elegant French attacker Youri Djorkaeff, German striker-diver Jürgen Klinsmann, and the diminutive and super-skillful Belgian Enzo Scifo, but he couldn't deliver more trophies, a personnel-to-success ratio Arsenal fans recognize all too well. A new team was built by incoming coach Jean Tigana, featuring crazy keeper Fabien Barthez as well as a fledgling Thierry Henry, and that side won the French Ligue in 1997, the same year the principality celebrated 700 years of Grimaldi rule. Another title came in 2000, and another European final beckoned, this time the ultimate goal of all: the Champions League.

By 2003–04, Didier Deschamps—the former French midfielder once described by Eric Cantona in an acidic aside as a mere "water carrier"—was leading Monaco. In the Champions League, Monaco had navigated a fairly easy group and then knocked out Real Madrid and Chelsea in back-to-back ties to reach the final. With Patrice Evra at right back, Fernando Morientes up front, and Emmanuel Adebayor on the bench, it was a solid side, but in the final they once again froze. Facing them were a team led by a young José Mourinho. Porto had already knocked out Manchester United in the last minute of the first round at Old Trafford, and in the final the Monaco defending was once again abject. That Porto team of Costa, Carvalho, Costinha, Deco, and Carlos Alberto had too much for Monaco, easily winning 3–0.

Since then, Monaco has stalled. Two more seasons in Ligue 2 came and went, but in 2013–2014, with Claudio Ranieri at the helm, they finished second in Ligue 1. And once again the money was flowing: the 14th richest man in Russia, Dmitry Rybolovlev, had always wanted to live in Monaco, but his wife, Elena, didn't. After they split in 2009 (a split that would lead to the most expensive divorce in history—Elena got a cool $4.8 billion), the fertilizer magnate finally got his wish, and in 2011 he bought a 66 percent stake in the soccer club. On the back of his investment, before the 2013 season Monaco paid around $226 million in transfer fees to build a new team, including around $100 million for Radamel Falcão alone, even though the team attracts crowds of less than 10,000. Not to worry—Rybolovlev spent more than that on one penthouse apartment: La Belle Epoque, the Monaco domicile in which banker Edmond Safra mysteriously died in a fire in 1999.

Location	Montevideo, Uruguay
Established	1899
Nicknames	*Bolsos* ("Sacks"), *Tricolores* ("Tricolors"), *Bolsilludo*, *Albos* ("Whites")
Stadium	Estadio Gran Parque Central (26,500 capacity)
Home colors	Red, white, and blue
Leading goal-scorer	Atilio García (1938–51), 486 goals
Most appearances	Óscar Morales (1999–2010), 379 appearances

Uruguayan national hero José Gervasio Artigas drove the British out of Buenos Aires in 1806; he was subsequently captured at the Battle of Montevideo, but escaped. Later, he would lead 16,000 people across Uruguay in what is known as the "Oriental exodus." He is considered the father of Uruguayan independence.

No wonder, then, that when in 1899 students at Montevideo University wanted to form a football team—and one that wasn't dominated by British expats—they chose the colors of Artigas for their team, Nacional. (That those colors—red, white, and blue—are also the colors of the Union Jack flag seems to have escaped their attention.) Quickly the team came to be associated with Uruguay as a nation. Nacional represented the country in a game against Argentina in Buenos Aires in September 1903, winning 3–2, and when Uruguay won the soccer tournament at the 1924 and 1928 Olympics, the Montevideo side provided many of the players (six and eight respectively). They did the same in 1930 when Uruguay beat Argentina in the first World Cup final, 4–2; that team featured nine Nacional players. In between, in 1925 Nacional toured Europe for six months, only losing five of the 38 games they played. At home Nacional dominated, too, winning 11 amateur championships, and once Uruguayan football went professional in 1931, another 33.

Though they were known to European football fans, in the Americas Nacional had to wait to secure their first continental title, winning their first Copa Libertadores in 1971. They had already lost in the final three times previously, in 1964, 1967 (to Independiente and Racing, both of Argentina) and 1969, the last in a game against the execrable Estudiantes, also of Argentina, a team famous for its violent and underhanded tactics. Estudiantes would win again in 1970, beating the other major Montevideo team, Peñarol, and go for the "fourpeat" in 1971, but this time Nacional were ready for them. Each of the two legs finished 1–0, leading to a playoff in Lima, Peru, which Nacional won 2–0 on goals by Victor Espárrago and Argentine striker Luis Artime. The long dark night of Estudiantes was finally over; Artime's time was just beginning.

In the subsequent Intercontinental Cup final, Nacional faced Greek club Panathinaikos (they had been runners-up in the European Cup—Ajax, the winners, refused to play). Artime scored all three goals across the two legs for Nacional; Totis Filakouris scored Panathinaikos' two goals. Nacional were crowned world champions.

It would be almost a decade before they won the Copa Libertadores and the Intercontinental Cup once more, and again Nacional had one man to thank, in this case Waldemar Victorino. He scored the only goal of the final of the 1980 Copa, as Nacional beat Brazil's Internacional 1–0 on aggregate; he also netted the only goal of the 1980 Intercontinental Cup final, this time against Nottingham Forest, the European champions. Eight years later Nacional would once again do the double of Copa and Intercontinental, but this time there was much more drama. And once again, Nacional's fortunes would turn on the goal-scoring of one man.

In the 1988 Copa Libertadores, Nacional overcame yet another Argentine opponent, Newell's Old Boys. The first leg was a tight game, Newell's winning by a single goal, but back in Uruguay Nacional spanked their neighbors 3–0, the second scored by Santiago Ostolaza, who would go on—much later—to manage Nacional.

But it was in the Intercontinental Cup final that Ostolaza came into his own. His header at the far post from a corner opened the scoring against European Cup champions PSV Eindhoven of the Netherlands. That PSV team was a beaut, featuring Ronald Koeman and Romário, and coached by Guus Hiddink. With 15 minutes left, Romário leveled the game in almost exactly the same fashion as the Ostolaza goal (far post header after the keeper missed a corner), and the game went to extra time after Nacional missed a number of chances. Up stepped Koeman to smash in a penalty with 10 minutes left—it had been such a terrible dive and bad decision by the ref that the Uruguayan commentator had screamed the word "no" a full ten times with no breath. Nacional faced losing a game they had dominated. The game reached its final seconds with PSV hoofing the ball as long as they could, but Nacional snatched a corner, and there, once again at the far post, Santiago Ostolaza headed home after the Dutch keeper yet again missed the cross. This time, the Uruguayan commentators screamed "Gol!" over and over, and the game went to penalties.

Koeman smashed the first home; Yubert Lemos scored for Nacional; then Jorge Seré in the Nacional goal made a fine save, causing the commentators to scream "Superman!" But Nacional would miss their next two and eventually Eindhoven, in the form of Søren Lerby, stepped up to win the trophy, but he hit the bar; the penalties continued into sudden death. Each team scored and missed, missed and scored—there were screams of "Gol!" and "Superman!" and quiet moments when PSV scored or Nacional missed—until PSV's Berry van Aerle found himself facing "Superman!" Seré made a fantastic diving save to his right, leaving Tony Gómez with a kick to win it for Nacional. The commentators held their breaths, just in case they needed a lot of them.

And then it happened. "*Gol, gol, gol, gol, gol!*" on and on, until the voices of the commentators gave way to incoherence. Gómez had scored, and the Uruguayans of Nacional, playing in the colors of José Artigas, had finally vanquished the Dutch, as once they had the British.

NAPOLI

Location	Naples, Italy
Established	1904
Nicknames	*Partenopei* ("Neopolitans"), *I Azzurri* ("The Blues"), *I Ciucciarelli* ("The Little Donkeys")
Current stadium	Stadio San Paolo (60,240 capacity)
Home colors	Sky blue and white
Leading goal-scorer	Diego Maradona (1984–91), 115 goals
Most appearances	Giuseppe Bruscolotti (1972–88), 511 appearances

"He was like Christ on earth, like the Pope," said Gennaro Montuori, when asked by the *New York Times* in 2003 how he felt about Diego Maradona's time at Napoli F.C. By then, Maradona had been gone a decade, but during the Little Genius's seven seasons in southern Italy, Montuori had been the head of Napoli's "ultras," and had seen firsthand what the greatest player since Pelé had wrought in that poor city. Given that Maradona took a team from nowhere all the way to the Italian championship, twice, and to the UEFA Cup final, we can perhaps forgive Montuori his blasphemy. And anyway, Maradona really was that good.

Napoli F.C. was formed in 1904 as Naples Foot-Ball & Cricket Club by William Poths, a British worker for Cunard Lines. British sailors had been playing soccer with Neapolitans for a few years before the club was formed, and they continued to provide opposition once Poths' team was established. When a second Napoli side was formed, US Internazionale Napoli, a rivalry began which was ended when they merged in 1922. More name changes came and went, as did the team, from Serie A to B and back again, until a kind of stability arrived in 1964 when they lit upon their current full name, Società Sportiva Calcio Napoli. That year, they were also promoted to Serie A once again, where they stayed for more than 30 years. But it would be the 1980s before Napoli finally gave their fans something to savor.

It came in the form of the best player in the world at the time. Diego Maradona had spent the initial six years of his career in his homeland, playing first for Argentinos Juniors (his debut came just before he turned 16) and then Boca Juniors. A move across the Atlantic Ocean was inevitable, given that South American football seldom competed with European, at least in terms of wages. Barcelona came calling, though Maradona's two years there were underwhelming (he was sick with hepatitis, and was almost maimed by a horror tackle by Andoni Goikoetxea). Corrado Ferlaino, president of Napoli, pounced, bringing Maradona to southern Italy in 1984, but it took a while for the magic to appear. First, Maradona had to charm and horrify in equal measure at the 1986 World Cup in Mexico.

He would do so in the course of four second-half minutes in a quarterfinal against England. In the deficit column, Maradona horrified all—except the officials—by punching the ball into the net in the so-called (by Maradona himself) "hand of God" goal. Maradona has since added, "It was like pickpocketing the English and stealing a win." Four minutes later, Maradona sealed his position in the pantheon of greats with one of the finest goals ever seen at a World Cup, a slaloming 60-yard run from inside his own half that ended with him rounding the keeper to score. Argentina won the semifinal, beating Belgium on two goals by Maradona, then won a fantastic final over Germany, 3–2.

Returning to Italy after the tournament, Maradona was the most famous sportsman on earth, and almost a year later helped bring Napoli its first ever Scudetto, and the Italian Cup for good measure. For a team from the south to break the northern stranglehold over the league was one thing—for it to come via some of the most skillful and audacious soccer ever played was another. Maradona scored ten goals, but each seemed more beautiful than the last; and he was the perfect character for Naples: headstrong, passionate, a rebel. He seemed to stand for the city in its difficult relationship with the rest of the country.

Napoli would slip to second the following season, but in 1988–89 they went all the way to the final of the UEFA Cup. They had beaten Juventus in the quarterfinals and Bayern Munich in the semis, the triple threat of Maradona, Andrea Carnevale, and the Brazilian Careca being too much for most teams. In the final, Napoli faced, in the first leg, a Stuttgart side without its best player, a young Jürgen Klinsmann. Nevertheless, it took two late goals from Maradona and Careca to win the game after Maurizio Gaudino gave Stuttgart an early lead. In the second leg, Klinsmann was back from injury, and he equalized Alemão's opener to make the aggregate score 3–2. But two goals from Ferrara and Careca seemed to guarantee the trophy would head to southern Italy, until the appropriately-named Fernando De Napoli scored an own goal for Stuttgart, and Olaf Schmaler scored with a minute to go to make it 5–4 on aggregate. Somehow Napoli clung on to win; they would follow up with another Scudetto in 1990.

But then it all went wrong for Napoli and Maradona, as it did so often for the city, and for him.

The 1990 World Cup was to be played in Italy, and Maradona, misjudging Neapolitan opprobrium for the rest of the more prosperous country, begged Napoli fans to support Argentina when they faced Italy in the semifinal. It was a foolhardy thing to hope for, and Maradona paid the full price. Though Argentina won, with Maradona scoring the winning penalty in a shootout, in the final they lost a terrible game, 1–0, to Germany, and Italy's love affair with Maradona was over. The Italian Football Federation drug-tested him, announced they had found cocaine in his system, and banned him for 15 months. Though Maradona and his supporters claimed a conspiracy, it hardly mattered—he would never play for Napoli again.

For years Maradona couldn't even go back to the city, or anywhere else in Italy, as he still owed multimillions of dollars in taxes. His former team has never regained momentum, and in 1998 they were relegated. Though they made it back to Serie A in 2000, they went straight back down; they were bankrupt by the summer of 2004, and were thrown down into Serie C. The new, post-bankrupt club, owned by movie mogul Dino De Laurentiis's nephew, Aurelio De Laurentiis, was renamed Napoli Soccer for a couple of years, but is now back to both its S.C.C. Napoli name and Serie A. On match day, banners with Maradona's face on them still fly in Napoli's San Paolo stadium.

NEWCASTLE UNITED

Location	Newcastle, England
Established	1892
Nicknames	The Magpies, The Toon, Geordies
Current stadium	St. James' Park (52,404 capacity)
Home colors	Black and white
Leading goal-scorer	Alan Shearer (1996–2006), 206 goals
Most appearances	Jimmy Lawrence (1904–22), 496 appearances

The famous man in the black Homburg looks awed, like a fan—the player with whom he shakes hands bends forward a bit, modest with his sleeves rolled. On his feet, the player's boots are comically bulky, with great toecaps reinforced in order to be able to kick the dull leather rock—otherwise known as a mid-century football—which sits on the grass nearby, heavy and waiting.

It is May 3, 1952. World War II has been over for just seven years, and the man who led the Allies to victory, Winston Churchill, has been back in power as British prime minister for six months. Here he is, being presented to the teams prior to the FA Cup final between Newcastle United and Arsenal. As he meets Jackie Milburn, perhaps the most famous player to ever don the black-and-white stripes of the Geordie team, it's not too fanciful to see a hint of awe even in the great Churchill's eyes. "Wor" (Geordie slang for "our") Jackie had risen from the tough, coal-mining town of Ashington, just north of Newcastle, to become the most feared of striking predators—and a man who, when Churchill was leading Britain to victory during the war, remained a working miner even as he played for Newcastle United on weekends. As Joe DiMaggio was to mid-century baseball in the United States, so Jackie was to mid-century soccer in England, but even as he worked at the Woodhorn Colliery near Ashington, the pit manager sometimes refused to let Milburn train (it took threats of a strike by the other miners to change the manager's mind).

The city of Newcastle is the most northerly major conurbation in England, lying, at its closest point, about 45 miles south of the Scottish border—and this isolated situation, straddling the river Tyne and nestled against a raging and colorless North Sea, sets the city apart. It was once a place of coal mining, an endeavor that employed hundreds of thousands of Geordies (the nickname for locals) in the toughest job of all. Visitors who don't sport a Geordie accent are often treated with suspicion, until the legendary welcome of the place inevitably burns through—it is the most insular yet friendly town in England. It got a soccer team late compared to other parts of the country; a number of clubs existed in the area, but it wasn't until December 1892 that Newcastle East End, who had themselves subsumed Newcastle West End, became Newcastle United.

Despite the footballing detente, Newcastle remained a tough place to live. The Woodhorn Colliery had only 655 miners by the time it finally closed in February 1981—the northeast of England saw its mining industry decimated by 1980s' Thatcherism and its capitalism-trumps-all economics—and Jackie Milburn had long since hung up his boots, dying in 1988 from lung cancer. Cigarettes were said to have been part of his "bonus package" when he played for Newcastle, but then he'd also been a pit worker, so who knows?

A year after Milburn's death, his beloved Newcastle United were relegated to the second tier of British football, just as they had been in 1961, four years after he left the club. Before he left, though, Milburn had scored 200 goals for Newcastle United. The history of the team has ever been about two things: one, its legendary center forwards—like Milburn, and Malcolm Macdonald in the 1970s (95 goals in 187 games), and a couple of others we're about to meet—and two, false dawns of success followed by years and years of damaging lows.

Newcastle won that "Churchill Cup" final in 1952, just as they had won the competition the year before and would again in 1955. Relegation would happen again in 1978 (they would stay down for six seasons), and then, after five years back in the top league, Newcastle United was again relegated, in 1989. By 1992, they were facing a further relegation to the third tier of British soccer. Something had to be done: cue the intervention of another legendary center forward, this time sitting on the coach's bench.

Kevin Keegan had managed to wow Newcastle United fans in a brief stint on the field in the mid-1980s (his goal-per-game ratio for the northeast club—he scored 48 in 78 games—is far better than his 68 in 238 games for Liverpool, the place where he became a superstar). Back to manage Newcastle in 1992, Keegan was able to stave off relegation to the third tier and then built an attractive side which flirted with the greatest prize of all—the Premiership title—in 1995–96. But in typical Newcastle-is-cursed fashion, Keegan seemed to doom his team when on April 27, 1996, he delivered his now infamous rant against the Manchester United manager, Alex Ferguson. At one point in the season Newcastle United had been 12 points clear of the Manchester club at the top of the league, but a defeat at the hands of Man United in early March brought the gap to a single point. In April, Newcastle were further damaged by a last-minute winner by Stan Collymore, playing for Keegan's old team, Liverpool (the game ended 4–3), a stunning result that led Keegan to put his head against the inside of the Anfield advertising hoardings in sorrow, the same hoardings he'd so often approached with goal-scoring joy from the other side. It was no consolation for Keegan and his team that it had been part of one of the greatest Premiership games ever played, and a few weeks later, after Ferguson had suggested that teams don't play as hard when they're not playing United, Keegan snapped in a live TV interview, shouting, "I tell you honestly, I will love it if we beat them—*love* it." The rant was shocking in its stark revelation of the pressures of trying to outwit mind-games maven Ferguson. Alas, Manchester United won their final game to clinch the title, and Newcastle United's season ended in disappointment once again.

That much-heralded 1995–96 team was led by the other great center forward of Newcastle United's history, Alan Shearer, a man who scored more than 200 goals in just over 300 games for the club. A brutish player with a clinical right- or left-foot shot, a magnificent leap leading to a record number of headed goals in the Premiership (46), and the odd moment of mindless violence off the ball, local lad Shearer bullied his way through and above defenses just as Milburn had once done, though he couldn't lead his hometown team to silverware. Football fans never let him forget it—impish Manchester United supporters still sing a "Jesus Christ Superstar"-inspired chant about their hyper-limited center back of the day, which goes, "David May / superstar / he's got more medals than Alan Shearer." Even as manager of the team for a month at the end of the 2008–09 season, Shearer was unable to prevent their relegation once again to the second tier of English football.

But go back a century, and things looked so different for this proud club. If you followed the newly-minted Newcastle United at the start of the 1900s, you must have felt they would forever dominate the British game. They won the First Division three times—1904–05, 1906–07, and 1908–09, and once again in 1926–27—and appeared as losers in four FA Cup finals—in 1905 (played at Crystal Palace in front of 101,117 fans), 1906, 1908, and 1911. They won the cup in 1910, 1924, 1932, and three times in Milburn's day, as well as losing three finals much later—in 1974, 1998 and 1999. But apart from these shiny moments, few supporters think a solitary victory in the now-defunct Inter Fairs Cup of 1969 (a competition blighted by crowd violence during Newcastle's semifinal victory over Rangers of nearby Scotland), and a win in the long-forgotten Intertoto Cup in 2006, matches the passion and verve of the 50,000-plus Geordie fans who pack St. James's Park every weekend to roar on their black-and-white "Toon Army" ("Toon" is Geordie slang for "town"). Seasons often seem to be dedicated to the twin desires to merely beat their hated archrivals,

Sunderland, and survive in the Premiership. Newcastle's head-to-head stats against Sunderland—51 wins to 43, with 26 draws—barely tells the full story: Sunderland once beat Newcastle 9–1, in the 1908–09 season, and bested them in the 1990 Premiership playoffs, a victory that still stings. The Premiership effort, too, often teeters on the edge of relegation, which seems scant reward for fans whose intensity and commitment saw an average of 43,388 fans show up as Newcastle won the Championship, the country's second-tier division, in 2009–10. A club that has seen world-class greats like Paul Gascoigne, Peter Beardsley, David Ginola, Chris Waddle, Alan Shearer, Kevin Keegan and Malcolm Macdonald play for it in recent times, as well as legends like Hughie Gallacher, Jackie Milburn, and Bobby Mitchell in its more distant history, now awaits new saviors who understand the parochial, passionate nature of this distant corner of England and its urgent need for sustained success—for a day when a man with the stature of Winston Churchill might stand in awe of a man like Jackie Millburn, and a team like Newcastle United.

Location	Rosario, Argentina
Established	1903
Nicknames	*Los Leprosos* ("The Lepers")
Current stadium	Estadio Marcelo Bielsa (42,000 capacity)
Home colors	Black and red
Leading goal-scorer	—
Most appearances	Gerardo Martino (1980–90), 505 appearances

Newell's Old Boys are the definition of a nearly team, one that *nearly* but never quite wins the trophies and championships. But when you own arguably the best name in all of club soccer, who cares if you've never really won anything and once drove away the greatest player in the world?

Whatever else you might want to say about Isaac Newell, one thing is for certain: he liked to live near a river. Newell left his home town of Strood, in Kent, next to the river Medway, southeast of London, in 1869—he was 16 years old—and sailed 7,000 miles southwest, to the distant shores of Argentina. Awaiting Newell was the river Parana, 200 miles northeast of Buenos Aires. On its western bank stands the town of Rosario—birthplace of both Che Guevara and Lionel Messi—which was in thrall, when Newell arrived, to an infrastructure boom led by the British. Even though he was just a boy, Newell quickly found work as a telegraph operator for the railroads, but his heart was set on teaching, and within 15 years of arriving in Rosario, Newell had established the Colegio Comercial Anglo Argentino, a business school. By 1903, Newell's son,

Claudio, along with other students and alumni (the "Old Boys" of the name), had created Club Atlético Newell's Old Boys (not to be confused with the Buenos Aires team Club Atlético All Boys). What to wear? They looked to flags for inspiration, and so donned red for Newell's beloved England, and black for the Germany of Anna Jockinsen, Newell senior's wife. Then the Old Boys set about not winning very much.

Argentine club soccer has often had a complicated organizational structure, but it's hard to imagine it being more confusing than it was in the 1970s. Take 1974, for example, when Newell's Old Boys won their first major tournament. It had taken them 71 years to break through, but once they did, it was a mixed blessing thanks to the hoops through which they were made to jump.

To begin with, Old Boys pipped Boca Juniors by one point to win Group B of the 1974 Metropolitano Championship, the first half of the national championship before the Nacional took over for the second half. (By 1982, the two were reversed, and then in 1985 Argentina woke from its long Nacional—and Metropolitan—nightmare, and went to one league. Sort of.) The winners of the Metropolitano Championship Group A in 1974 were Newell's arch-, local rivals, Rosario Central, and the two led the next stage of the competition, the Final Tournament, played between the top two teams from each of the two Metropolitano Championships. Don't worry if you can't keep up—all that matters is that Newell's Old Boys won that final tournament by two points over Rosario Central, though the whole thing was marred by an extraordinary game played between the two clubs on June 2. The score was 2–2 with a minute to go when Newell's got a dubious penalty decision; all hell broke loose and the referee, who was badly injured by a rock thrown from the irate and rioting Rosario Central crowd, was subsequently jailed for pointing to the penalty spot.

The second half of the season ended with both Rosario-based clubs coming second in their respective groups (there were now four leagues instead of two, for some reason), but in the Final Tournament,

Old Boys fell apart, finishing bottom, winning just a single game and losing one match 6–1 to Vélez Sarsfield.

Since then, Newell's Old Boys have won five other Primera División titles, including 2013, and two titles at the end of the 1980s/ start of the 1990s. That Newell's team was probably the best ever, as it also reached two Copa Libertadores finals, only to lose both.

The first final, in 1988, almost didn't happen at all for the Old Boys, Newell's having to overcome fellow Argentine team San Lorenzo, 1–0, in a one-game playoff in order to make it to the knock-out stages. In the final, Newell's faced Uruguayan side Nacional, and though they won the first leg in Rosario, 1–0, back in Montevideo they were trounced 3–0, in a game yet again marred by pre-match rioting.

Four seasons later, Newell's made it to another Copa final, and the 1992 Libertadores features an even stranger set of results. In their first game, on February 26, Newell's conspired to lose 6–0 at home to San Lorenzo de Almagro, Pope Francis's favorite team—some kind of deity was clearly leading San Lorenzo that night, as a long-range free kick to make the score 1–0 was followed by a brilliant volley, a diving header, a goal that somehow slipped under the keeper and along the goal line, an empty-netter, and a deflection. Nevertheless, Newell's recovered to top their qualifying group, and sauntered through the knockout stages until they reached São Paulo, of Brazil, in the final. Both legs ended 1–0, leading to a penalty shootout. Surely Newell's could pull it off . . . but only if they knew how to take penalties, which they didn't. They scored only two, and two is usually not enough.

Newell's Old Boys are probably most famous now, apart from their wonderful name, for being the team that wouldn't pay for Lionel Messi's growth hormones. Messi was a tiny kid, and a member of a Newell's Old Boys youth team that lost one game in four years. Messi wasn't getting any bigger, though, and only a regimen of seven days of injections in one leg, seven in the other, could help him grow enough to become a top footballer. But it's not true that Newell's wouldn't pay—the club often ponied up about 300 pesos. (The actual cost of the treatments was 15,000 pesos per month.) Messi's father, Jorge, a factory worker, was quoted as saying, "If they had paid, naturally he would have stayed at Newell's." Messi and his family had no choice but to move to Spain, and to Barcelona, to the team that helped that little Old Boy grow into the best soccer player since Pelé.

Location	Harrison, New Jersey, USA
Established	1995 (as New York/New Jersey MetroStars)
Nicknames	Red Bulls, Metros
Stadium	Red Bull Arena (25,000 capacity)
Home colors	White and red
Leading goal-scorer	Juan Pablo Ángel (2007–10), 62 goals
Most appearances	Mike Petke (1998–2002, 2008–10), 169 appearances

When one is witness to a notable sporting moment, it does something strange to time. It's not that it slows it, or speeds it up—more like it warps it, so that time bends around what you want to happen: the pass hitting the receiver square in the chest, the deep fly turning into a home run, the three-pointer swishing through the net. For thousands of New York Red Bulls fans in October 2013, their time-warping moment came with a few minutes of extra time left against the Houston Dynamo, in a playoff game at their bespoke New Jersey stadium. But this time, there was a crucial difference: time warped around what they *didn't* want.

The game was tense. New York had just won their first ever "trophy," the Supporters Shield. In other parts of the footballing world, proving oneself the best team across an entire season would be the acme, but in the United States, the historical love of the pennant has given way to cursed playoffs, in which the achievement of a season is reduced to anyone-can-have-a-bad-day, one-off games, to produce a "champion."

The Red Bulls—originally, the New York/New Jersey Metro-

Stars, easily the worst name for a major sporting franchise ever concocted—had given the New York tristate area little to celebrate in their 18 years. Played in the not-fit-for-soccer Giants Stadium, their first game in 1996 attracted a crowd of over 46,000 fans, starved as they had been by a lack of top-flight soccer since the demise of the old North American Soccer League in the 1980s. The New York Cosmos had first dazzled (thanks to a host of stars including Pelé, Beckenbauer, and Giorgio Chinaglia), and then imploded when Pelé left. In 1994, the World Cup came to the States, and the time seemed ripe to try again.

Sadly, New York put a poor product out on the plastic grass of East Rutherford. Transient foreign stars like Roberto Donadoni, Juan Pablo Ángel, Lothar Matthäus, and Youri Djorkaeff joined American stalwarts like Tim Howard, Alexi Lalas, Claudio Reyna, Clint Mathis, and Jozy Altidore, but no great team was ever put together. In that first game in 1996, against New England, which this writer had the ill luck to attend, one of the dreariest matches imaginable had 15 seconds to go when Metro"Star" Nicola Caricola (once of Juventus, amazingly) inexplicably dinked the ball over his own keeper, the ponytailed Tony Meola, from six yards out—it actually would have been a brilliant finish if it hadn't also been a hilarious own goal. New York fans trace their ill luck to that moment—the Curse of Caricola, they call it—which is, of course, ridiculous. Like the Curse of the Bambino in baseball, and all such sporting curses, it amounts to little more than an excuse for a franchise's inability to create a team that can win. Once the Boston Red Sox built a good team and a good back office they started to win World Series titles; once the Chicago Cubs decide to do the same, they'll win too. Curses are, by definition, for losers.

In the case of New York, a single visit to the MLS Cup final in 2008, which they lost to Columbus 3–1, was all they had to show for their nearly two decades of play. It took the introduction of two top players from European leagues to turn their fortunes around.

The first, Thierry Henry, had scored freely and with great panache in the English Premiership, in Spain, and in World Cups for France.

His loping, insouciant play for New York sometimes made one wonder if he was bothered (Henry often seemed more concerned that goalkeepers took too long to kick the ball back into play than about the game itself, overtly counting down the seconds with raised fingers), but he offset such foolishness with highlight-reel moments. One of his best came in the final game of the 2013 regular season, a dipping volley from 25 yards that calmed nerves and led the team to a 5–1 rout of visiting Chicago, and thence to the Supporters Shield.

But it was the acquisition of Australian Tim Cahill that turned the Red Bulls into a fine team. The former Everton star's ability to head a ball effectively is unmatched in world football, and his combative nature and calmness on the ball meant the New York team finally looked like a club that could win everything.

And then came the Houston Dynamo. In the first leg of the playoffs in Texas, New York raced to a 2–0 lead on a—what else?—header by Cahill and a goal by Eric Alexander. But a rash challenge by Jámison Olave, their otherwise solid center back, in the second half brought a ridiculous red card from an overmatched referee, and by the end of the game the score stood at 2–2. Were this a different league, those two away goals would be a solid basis for victory over two legs, but this is Major League Soccer. Back in New York, the game ended 1–1 in regulation, and because away goals don't count double, the game went to extra time.

Cue the warping of that extra time. A clearly out-of-gas Houston team (they had played three games in seven days) slung a hopeful ball into the box, where a simple attacking header back across goal seemed to confuse the Red Bulls defense like a difficult equation in algebra. Houston's Omar Cummings, who had scored with seconds to go in the first leg, stuck out a foot, and it was then that time warped around the hopes of New York fans, amassed as their "ultras" were behind the goal. Those "South Warders," as they're known, gasped and screamed as Cummings's effort, a weak dribbler of a shot, somehow crossed the line—this writer and his daughter were sitting directly along the goal line and the ball was clearly over, horribly over.

As was another New York season. Though the Curse of Caricola might have been broken with the Supporters Shield, manager Mike Petke, who had played for the New York team more than any other player, noted afterward that it might take longer for *all* the curses to be broken (Petke said, "I guess you can't exorcise every demon"). A daft if understandable reaction: but Petke probably knows as well as everyone that teams win when they're good enough, not when God is finally watching.

Location	Norwich, England
Established	1902
Nicknames	The Canaries, Yellows
Current stadium	Carrow Road (27,244 capacity)
Home colors	Green and yellow
Leading goal-scorer	Johnny Gavin (1948–54, 1955–58), 132 goals
Most appearances	Kevin Keelan (1963–80), 681 appearances

Hailing from a sleepy and distant corner of England called East Anglia—a place, to borrow a phrase from an early review of *Waiting for Godot*, in which "nothing happens, twice"—Norwich City is hardly the most illustrious team to have ever played the Beautiful Game. In fact, the club is more known for its gaudy kit (canary yellow shirts, green shorts) than for what happens on the green grass.

When Flemish weavers, returning from the Caribbean, introduced canaries to East Anglia, the practice somehow led to a sporting nickname: Norwich City (established in 1902) were, and still are, the Canaries. It's hardly the fiercest moniker, and it was made further ridiculous by an early Norwich City decision which seems to have been: "Our nickname is the Canaries, so we may as well dress like them."

Garish though they appear on the field, their playing history is somewhat less bright: two English League Cup victories in more than 100 years are matched by two English League Cup final defeats in the same time, and that's about it. The closest Norwich City has ever come to gold was in the 1992–93 campaign, when they led for much of the first season of the newly-minted English Premiership, only to falter like a bird with a broken wing and finish third behind thoroughbreds Manchester United and Aston Villa. On the back of that third-place finish, however, they entered the UEFA Cup in 1993, so setting them up for their one true moment of sporting fame . . . not that anyone expected them to get further than the first round, in which they were to face German superteam Bayern Munich, captained by their midfielder-turned-defender Lothar Matthäus.

No British team had ever won in Munich's Olympic Stadium, and in the buildup to the game, few expected that to change. Some wondered if it would end 10–0; others hoped it wouldn't be more than 3–0 or 4–0. Either way, there was a sense that the German powerhouse team didn't expect much of a game.

With barely 12 minutes gone in that first leg on October 20, 1993, everything changed. There didn't seem to be any real danger as yet another hopeful Norwich City ball was lumped into the box, in the English fashion. For years, this had been the main knock on the game as it was played in Britain: to cultured German tacticians, or to the sanguine eyes of a Spanish crowd used to the passing game, the Anglo-Saxon affection for hitting passes long and high toward a towering center forward and hoping to feed off the scraps of his knockdowns was such low-percentage football as to be tantamount to a betrayal of it. But low-percentage does not equal zero-percentage, and that night in Germany, back-pedaling Lothar Matthäus, under scant pressure from diminutive Norwich attacker Mark Robins, lamely headed the ball away from danger in a tantalizing arc. It was the header of a midfielder playing out of position, and it fell to a man dressed as a canary.

Welshman Jeremy Goss is one of those players who, had he been a rock band, would have been described as a one-hit wonder. A perfectly adequate midfielder, he was known in soccer parlance for having a good "engine," meaning he had limited skills but could run and run and run. That night in Munich, his engine brought him to the edge of the box just as Matthäus's weak header came to earth; before the ball quite landed on German soil, Goss swung his boot at it.

In retrospect, Goss remembers the ball hitting "the top left-hand corner of the net," but memory is a fickle master: Raimond Aumann, Munich's keeper, never moved; the ball passed him at shoulder height and nestled halfway up the netting of the goal behind him. It was an excellent strike, and its importance remains undiminished even though it has been subsequently burnished into "the greatest goal ever scored" (it was no such thing). Norwich City followed it up with another goal before half-time (Bayern scored one too, but to no avail) to become the first (and, so far, the only) English team to win in the Olympic Stadium. Goss became a hero for a while, and back in East Anglia Norwich held Bayern 1–1 in the second leg, Goss again scoring, thereby winning the tie 3–2 on aggregate. It was a result no one imagined could happen; it was German arrogance in the face of plucky little Brits dressed like birds; it was as if World War II had never ended.

Alas, in Norwich's next game in the tournament they fell to two goals by Inter Milan's Dennis Bergkamp, one home, one away, both scored with less than 10 minutes to go in the game. City's European adventure was over, and though they didn't know it at the time, so was their brief moment in the sun. A year later they were relegated from the Premiership. Since then they've been up and down between the Premiership and the leagues below—their relatively empty corner of England will probably never boast a fan base big enough to propel a powerhouse club to challenge the big boys, even with the affluent current ownership of the UK's version of Rachael Ray, Delia Smith, and celebrity fans like Stephen Fry. But the fearsome-for-one-night Canaries will always have Jeremy Goss's golden volley and that win in Germany. And they will always wear yellow and green: a team of non-aggressive but pleasant enough birds, abandoned as they are in a far-away land.

Location	Nottingham, England
Established	1865
Nicknames	The Reds, The Tricky Trees, Forest
Stadium	The City Ground (30,576 capacity)
Home colors	Red and white
Leading goal-scorer	Grenville Morris (1898–1913), 217 goals
Most appearances	Bob McKinlay (1951–70), 692 appearances

Nottingham Forest, beloved of trivia quiz masters everywhere, for this oft-repeated question: Which is the only soccer team to have won more European Cups than domestic championships?

Forest's is a bizarre, and very old, story. Only their cross-city neighbors, Notts County, and Stoke City, from a town one hour to the west of Nottingham, are older. Forest were established in 1865, and immediately they decided to wear "Garibaldi red," after the Italian political–military giant then idolized worldwide for his exploits, and famous in the UK after a visit to Tynemouth in mid-century. (There's even a Garibaldi cookie in England, in which dried currants are squashed between what looks like desiccated cardboard. It tastes worse than it sounds.)

Forest's first game was against Notts County on March 22, 1866, and they were admitted to the Football League in 1892. It was the start of a long slog to success. A single FA Cup win in 1898 was followed by another 61 years later, but in between they spent a lot of time in the Second Division. In 1972, a daring and cocky young manager called

Brian Clough led Forest's local rivals Derby County to the English First Division title, an amazing feat for a relatively small club. More amazing still, Clough led Derby to the semifinals of the European Cup the following season, where they were knocked out by losing finalists Juventus.

Clough, by this point, was recognized as a genius man-manager, if a difficult and complicated man himself. A portrait of Clough by the *Guardian*, in 1983, was typical of the view of many; it described him as "a man of extraordinary contradictions." It went on, "[Clough] can be famously polite or infamously rude, minutely attentive or witheringly dismissive, mean or generous. Waiting in [an] airport, a certain journalist saw his Scotch grabbed off the table by Clough and dispatched with little ado . . ." An image of how difficult Clough could be was his post-Derby life. As chronicled in David Peace's *The Damned United*, he went to manage Leeds United in July 1974, but, unable to corral the players onto his side after their beloved former coach, Don Revie, had quit to manage England, Clough left after 44 days.

In January 1975, Clough took over at Nottingham Forest. At the time, Forest were languishing in the Second Division and had just been beaten by local rivals Notts County. Clough turned things around quickly, leading Forest to the First Division in his second season, 1977, and, in their first season back, didn't they go ahead and win the damned thing? Clough had brought his sidekick, Peter Taylor, to Forest, and had stocked the team with hardworking players like future Celtic, Villa, and Ireland manager Martin O'Neill, Frank Clark and Viv Anderson in defense, Ian Bowyer and John Robertson in midfield, and in goal, the great Peter Shilton. With the arrival of center forward Trevor Francis from Birmingham City for a first ever, £1 million transfer fee, Forest finally had a focus for their workmanlike attack. And though Francis wasn't eligible to play in the 1978–79 European Cup until the semifinal, against Malmö in the final he would prove the difference.

Forest had knocked out defending European champions Liverpool in the first round (in those days, teams from the same country were not kept apart in the early stages, as they are now), and then had scored freely on the way to the final. Facing them that May night in 1979 were Malmö, Swedish champions who were then only four games into their domestic season. It showed: with one team at the end of a grueling season and the other rusty from a layoff, the match was a drab affair. One side, Forest, was renowned for their sweet passing moves; the other, Malmö, was happy just to ruin and block (the *Guardian* later called it a "terrible game"). Trevor Francis provided the one moment worth remembering, a far-post diving header from a Robertson cross. Clough would say of Robertson, "A very unattractive young man, but give him the ball and a yard of grass, and he was an artist." Forest held on for the most unlikely of European Cup triumphs.

Forest finished sixth in the English First Division in 1980, a cool 12 points from first place (it was still two points for a win, so they were well off the pace). But they found themselves in the European Cup in any case, being holders . . . and didn't Nottingham Forest go ahead and win the damned thing all over again?

This, like the previous year, was hardly a vintage European season. Real Madrid were beaten 5–1 in the second leg of the semifinal, yet the team that eliminated them, Hamburg, led by British superstar Kevin Keegan, still came to the final as underdogs. And though they faced a Forest side shorn of an injured Francis, once again the Midlands side did enough. And it was all down to that artist, Robertson—cutting in from the left wing, he received a one-two from center forward Garry Birtles before curving a shot away from the German keeper and into the far corner. Once again, Forest had won a European final, once again 1–0.

And that was about it for the club from West Bridgford, Nottingham. Clough managed Forest through the 1980s and into the early 1990s, but by the end he was a shell of the fiery figure he had once been. Taylor had left Forest in 1982, and his friendship with Clough had subsequently ended. That whiskey on the airport lounge table became bottles anywhere, and Clough's alcoholism grew to affect his work. By 1993 Clough was gone, and Forest slipped down the leagues, at one point reaching the lower reaches of League One, the third level of the Football League (no European champion has ever fallen so low in domestic competition). An endless carousel of managers continues to this day—since Clough's demise, Forest have had 19 coaches in 20 years, one of whom, Alex McLeish, lasted at Forest four days fewer than Clough managed at Leeds United.

Since July 2012, Forest have been owned by the Al-Hasawi family, from Kuwait, who have expressed a desire to fulfill a three-to-five-year plan to get the club back to the Premiership. Six months after taking over, they fired popular manager Sean O'Driscoll to bring in McLeish. When that decision went south, Garry Birtles, the man who laid on the goal for Robertson in the 1980 European Cup final, commented, "It's so sad for the fans. There was so much optimism there. Now it's all gone."

NOTTS COUNTY

Location	Nottingham, England
Established	1862
Nicknames	The Magpies
Current stadium	Meadow Lane (20,229 capacity)
Home colors	Black and white
Leading goal-scorer	Les Bradd (1967–78), 137 goals
Most appearances	Albert Iremonger (1904–26), 601 appearances

A football club can have altogether too much history for its own good. Notts County, of the British East Midlands, is the oldest surviving soccer team in the world, but that longevity seems to weigh on it more like a burden than a joy, because when you're the oldest club in the world, the world expects something in return—a trophy or two, a team worth watching?—and Notts County has defiantly bucked those expectations pretty much from its inception.

Nottingham: the town of Robin Hood and Sherwood Forest, of lacemaking, and of one of England's oldest pubs (Ye Olde Trip to Jerusalem, circa 1189, nestled in a cave below the castle). It sits in the very middle of England astride the river Trent, which wanders through the southern side of town. The river, so long the engine of Nottingham's industrial growth, also separates the two football teams, County and Nottingham Forest (though only "Nottingham Forest Football Club" appears on Google Maps—Meadow Lane, where County plays, remains unnamed).

One landmark that does appear, just north of the river and alongside the Meadow Lane stadium, is Iremonger Road, named after a man who had hands "like the claws of a JCB" (the British company that is famous for its backhoes). Legend has it that Albert Iremonger, County's goalkeeper for 20 years (1905–25), was seven feet tall, but he was actually half a foot shorter than that. Iremonger was a darkly handsome man who sported both a glowering unibrow and a mustache the shape of the Lady Bay Bridge, which spans the Trent between the Forest and County stadiums. By the time he joined County from the wonderfully-named Nottingham Jardines, the club had been around for more than 40 years, having been established way back on November 28, 1862. (To put that date in historical context, in 1862 Queen Victoria had been on the British throne for just 25 of her 63 years, and on that exact date in American history, Union forces were repelling Confederates at the Battle of Cane Hill in Arkansas.) County would have to wait a quarter century for meaningful games, joining ten other teams to create the first Football League season in 1888. That first year featured a league made up of northern teams— though there were no Manchester teams, no Liverpool, no Newcastle or Sunderland, and, of course, no Arsenal, Spurs, or Chelsea: merely Accrington, Aston Villa, Blackburn, Burnley, Derby, Everton, Preston North End, Stoke, West Bromwich Albion, Wolverhampton Wanderers, and Notts County.

Notts County finished bottom.

Though County avoided being thrown out that first season (Stoke were jettisoned instead), since then their history has been merely that: based on history rather than achievement. Though they won the FA Cup in 1894 (their sole major trophy), they have otherwise bummed around in the middle reaches of the league system, sometimes (almost accidentally?) making it to the First Division, but mostly toiling away in the Second Division, sometimes the Third, and Fourth. In 1947, they somehow secured the services of Tommy Lawton, then one of the premier British strikers (and flatfooted, to boot— he wore inserts in his cleats), signing him from Chelsea even though County then languished in the Third Division. The £20,000 County paid for Lawton was a world record at the time, and in the next five years Lawton partially repaid his lowly owners by leading them to the Second Division in 1950.

But even this half-success was short-lived, and it took the intervention of manager Jimmy Sirrel in the early 1970s (Sirrel was renowned for his single massive tooth, hanging like a proboscis from his upper lip) to bring the team into the First Division for a while, though successive relegations once again took them down to the lower reaches of professional football. By 2003, they faced being thrown out of the Football League because of a quarter-million-pound debt (they just about survived); two years later, they finished 89th in the league system, just four shy of the very bottom place. It was the worst season in their long history . . . and yet, six years later, they found themselves in Turin, playing Juventus.

This, then, is the other reason Notts County remains a key team in the history of world soccer: they inspired the great Italian team Juventus with nothing more than their stripes.

The *Turinistas* originally played in a pink kit, but eventually, after too much washing (!), the shirts faded, and Juve were in search of a new uniform. John Savage, a Brit who played for Juventus in 1903, asked a friend back home to ship a new strip to Italy, and the friend, being a County fan, sent over the black-and-white stripes in which County still play (though the 2013 vintage looks like a bar code rather than the "aggressive and powerful" stripes which so appealed to Juventus). The connection was solidified in September 2011, when Juventus invited County to play an exhibition match to celebrate the opening of the new Juventus stadium. Amazingly, County, then of League One (third tier), held Juventus to a 1–1 draw—it was probably their greatest ever result, their long history once again providing them with just about the only thing worth mentioning.

Location	Piraeus, Greece
Established	1925
Nicknames	*Thrylos* ("Legend"), *Erythrolefkoi* ("The Red-Whites")
Current stadium	G. Karaiskakis Stadium (33,334 capacity)
Home colors	Red and white
Leading goal-scorer	Giorgos Sideris (1959–70, 1971–72), 239 goals
Most appearances	Kyriakos Karataidis (1988–2001), 363 appearances

Imagine this: five brothers on the same team, all forwards: the attacking quintet of Yiannis, Dinos, Giorgos, Vassilis, and Leonidas Andrianopoulos running at you. This was the beginning of Greek side Olympiakos, one of the two teams in Athens who between them win everything (Panathinaikos is the other). Outside of Greece, however, it's a different story.

Founded in March 1925, the team was partially funded by Andrianopoulos *père*, so it was natural that his sons got to play up front. Olympiakos started winning almost immediately. Their first championship, with the five Andrianopoulos boys in attack, came in 1931, and there were five more that decade; two more came in 1947 and 1948, once World War II was over. Seven more came in the 1950s, a paltry two in the 1960s, and three in the 1970s, before the 1980s began with four in a row. Olympiakos would win another in 1987, three in the 1990s, and since the turn of the century, they have won the league 12 times, only losing out in 2004 and 2010. Their 41 titles since 1927 makes them by far the most successful team in Greece (Panathinaikos have half as many). Olympiakos have also won 16 league and cup doubles. But in European competition, Olympiakos have been bedeviled by an Italian team who can't help but beat them. The bête noire of Olympiakos in Europe? Juventus.

In the Champions League of 1998–99, Olympiakos headed qualifying group A and faced Juventus in the quarterfinals. In Italy, Olympiakos did well to nick a last-minute penalty, having been outplayed, and the final score of 2–1 to a Zinedine Zidane-blessed Juventus meant that Olympiakos went back to Greece with an important away goal. Having already missed two golden chances, after 12 minutes of the second leg things looked promising when Siniša Gogić—known to the Greek chorus as "*Pappous*," or Grandpa, for the fact that he joined them in his thirties (!)—bravely headed home to tie the score. Olympiakos could dream, finally, that they might advance to the latter stages of a big competition, especially as they had that away goal in their back pockets. More chances came and went; then disaster struck. With the Greek chorus whistling for the end of the game, with five minutes to go a hopeless high cross into the area was flapped at by Olympiakos's goalie Dimitrios Eleftheropoulos, and the ball broke kindly off what looked like the right arm of Juventus center forward Antonio Conte. Hand ball or not—it wasn't given—Conte slammed the ball home. Olympiakos were out.

Five seasons later, Juventus poured acid on the hurt by beating Olympiakos 7–0 in a Champions League qualifying game. The following season, the perennial Greek champions would finish level on points with Liverpool in a Champions League qualifying group, but Liverpool were three goals better and advanced (all the way to the final, which they would win). They beat a very poor Manchester United side 2–0 at home in the Champions League knockout stages in 2014, but lost 3–0 in the return leg and were eliminated.

Olympiakos might want to stick to winning the Greek league over and over again. In Europe, unless they put five brothers up front, and they're all called Ronaldo, or Pelé, or Messi, it's not looking good.

Location	Marseille, France
Established	1899
Nicknames	*Les Phocéens, L'OM*
Current stadium	Stade Vélodrome (67,000 capacity)
Home colors	White and sky blue
Leading goal-scorer	Gunnar Andersson (1950–58), 192 goals
Most appearances	Roger Scotti (1942–58), 453 appearances

L et's say your team have a big European game coming up, but before that, you face a domestic match that doesn't matter that much. The best bet is to rest some players during that first match, or, if you play your full team, hope no one gets hurt, right? But a squad is only so big, and football is highly physical and filled with contact, so short of wrapping players in cotton wool or fielding no players at all, injuries are a real concern. You're probably going to have to hope for the best.

Or, if hoping for the best feels like too much of a risk, and if your owner is a multimillionaire with suspect morals, you could always hand over hundreds of thousands of dollars to your opponents to make sure that annoying little domestic game goes off without a hitch.

Welcome to the wonderful world of Olympique de Marseille and their former owner, Bernard Tapie. The French mogul initially made his fortune by buying up bankrupt companies, and by the early 1990s he had made enough cash to own Adidas for a few years. He also bought the venerable southern soccer institution Olympique de

Marseille—and nothing was going to get in Tapie's way of winning the biggest prize of all.

Tapie's behavior feels like the opposite of the ethos around which the club was established. Founded in 1892 as a general sporting club, a decade later the soccer team came into being. They chose "Olympique" because the Greeks had founded Marseille, a seaport on the Mediterranean; naturally, the club went with white with blue trappings, for the Greek flag, as their uniform. It took a while for Marseille to properly break the stranglehold of Parisian domination, but by end of the 1920s they'd won three French Cups, and in the thirties they'd add two more, as well as a first French league title. Once World War II ended, in the forties there would be a single cup and a single league title, then nothing much until a solid run from 1968 to 1972, during which time Marseille again won two of each on the back of the extraordinary goal-scoring exploits of Josip Skoblar, who bagged 44 goals in 1971 alone. By then, Marseille was a solid club, once in a while slipping out of Ligue 1 but mostly knocking about in the top flight. They were competitive, sometimes victorious and, apart from a lull in the mid-1960s (when no one cared about them), usually backed by huge southern crowds brimming with a heady mixture of French insouciance and Mediterranean passion.

Then came Tapie, who poured millions into Olympique de Marseille from 1986 on. Players such as Chris Waddle from England, German Rudi Völler, and the pick of a crop of fine French players including Jean-Pierre Papin, Basile Boli, Marcel Desailly, Didier Deschamps, and Eric Cantona, headed south to sparkle on the seafront. Five Ligue 1 titles in a row (1989–93) were the result, along with a place in two Champions League finals. It should have been Marseille's finest hour; instead, it turned into their darkest. And those five French titles would turn into four.

Tapie was determined that nothing would stop his team from winning the European Cup, especially as they'd reached the final in 1991, only to lose on penalties to Red Star Belgrade. By 1993, the latter stages of the competition had been split into two groups, the winners of which would head to the final in Munich.

In their first game, Marseille faced a rugged Rangers side featuring a bull-like center forward, Mark Hateley, who scored to make the final score 2–2. Marseille then won their first home game in the group stage, 6–0, over CSKA Moscow; at home to Rangers, they squeaked out a 1–1 draw, Hateley suspended after being sent off in Rangers' game against Brugge. Marseille faced a crucial final game against Brugge, which they won, 1–0. They were off to the final, where they would face A.C. Milan. But in between stood a Ligue 1 game against Valenciennes, a team that was trying to avoid relegation.

Corruption was rampant in every game of that previous paragraph, however. Drinks were said to have been spiked before the drubbing of the Russian side; Hateley's sending off against Bruges was a puzzler (he later claimed he'd been offered money to miss the Marseille rematch, but the sending off saw to it instead); it is claimed that there were payments made before that Bruges game; Valenciennes were certainly paid to take it easy against the team that would soon face a European Cup final. According to one source, Tapie said of the Valenciennes players, "We don't want them acting like idiots and breaking us before the final with Milan."

But these accusations were all to come. In the final itself, a flicked header by center back Basile Boli was enough to give Marseille the victory over Milan—many tears were shed, backs slapped, hands clasped, cheeks kissed in the French way. And then it all came tumbling down.

Once the allegations came to light, trials began. Tapie was thrown out of football; Marseille were stripped of their 1992–93 title, sent to Ligue 2, and thrown out of European competition for a year. They probably should have had their European crown taken away, too, but according to UEFA they remain the European champions of 1992–93. Tapie subsequently went to jail for a different set of financial misdeeds, and declared bankruptcy; in 1998, sorely in need of a boost, he appeared on French rapper Doc Gynéco's ironically-named disastrous flop track, "C'est beau, la vie."

Olympique de Marseille have never quite crawled out from under the stench of L'affaire O'M, as it's now known. They've lost two UEFA

Cup finals since their disgrace, though they did win the league in 2009–10. They remain a byword for all that's wrong with money and the beautiful game. In 2007, Bernard Tapie received more than $500 million in compensation from the French government for their under-valuing of Adidas (he had previously sold the sportswear company to Crédit Lyonnais, which was partly owned by the French government). But *"ce n'est pas beau, la vie"*—in 2013, Tapie was once again detained, as prosecutors built a case that the payoff from the government may have been fraudulent.

Location	São Paulo, Brazil
Established	1914
Nicknames	*Alviverde* ("Green and White"), *Verdão* ("Big Green"), *Porco* ("Pig"), *Academia de Futbol* ("The Academy of Football")
Stadium	Allianz Parque (45,000 capacity)
Home colors	Green and white
Leading goal-scorer	Ettore Marcelino Dominguez (1916–31), 327 goals
Most appearances	Ademir da Guia (1962–77), 901 appearances

I f you love Palmeiras, a Brazilian team from São Paulo, chances are you are of Italian heritage and/or you like penalties.

Palmeiras was founded in 1914 by four members of the large Italian emigrant community of São Paulo. In the last quarter of the nineteenth century, around 2 million immigrants arrived in Brazil; a large number of them were from Italy. São Paulo was attractive because land was available, as long as prospectors tendered help with the all-important coffee crop. Soccer followed the immigrants, and one day a notice went out in a newspaper, inviting Italians to join a new club. They would call it Palestra Italia ("the Italian Gymnasium").

By 1920, the Italian team had won its first São Paulo State championship, and would win it seven more times before 1940. It would also win the São Paulo–Rio interstate championship in 1933, establishing itself as a force beyond the confines of São Paulo and its region. But then war came, and everything changed.

After 1942, Brazil supported the Allied powers in World War II, and in that year all references to Italian (and Japanese and German) heritage were outlawed. Palestra Italia first changed their name to Palestra São Paulo but that was deemed inadequate, and so later that year Palmeiras—"the Palms"—was born. Nine years later, Palmeiras were the first "world champions."

In 1951, FIFA agreed to a Brazilian football-inspired competition called the Copa Rio, in which leading clubs from around the world would compete in Rio. Attendees were split into two groups: one featured the Brazilian side Vasco da Gama plus Austria Wien, Nacional, of Uruguay, and Sporting Lisbon; in the other group were Palmeiras, Juventus, Nice, of France, and Red Star Belgrade. Palmeiras came second in their group, having lost 4–0 to Juventus, but in the semifinals they dispatched Vasco da Gama to face Juventus once again in the two-legged final. A tight, 1–0 win in their hometown on July 18 was followed four days later by an entertaining 2–2 draw in Rio, and Palmeiras were champions.

Sadly, the tournament never quite got off the ground; teams declined to enter, and it would remain dormant for much of the rest of the century, until FIFA inaugurated their Club World Cup in 2000. But no one can ever take that win away from Palmeiras, and others would follow.

Palmeiras won the Rio–São Paulo competition once again the same year they won the Copa Rio (1951), and by the end of the 1950s, a truly Brazilian national league had begun. Palmeiras won the second title in 1961, but perhaps their finest domestic achievement came in the Rio–São Paulo tournament in 1965, which they won by battering many of their opponents. They scored seven against Pelé's Santos, and a bunch of goals against all their chief rivals, including three unanswered against Botafogo, which gave them the title.

Dramatic games featuring penalties then became Palmeiras's calling card. The first real sign of it was in 1988, when they faced Flamengo in a Série A game. Palmeiras went down to ten men after a dodgy red card, but still managed to score first. With the clock winding down, the Palmeiras goalkeeper, Zetti, was stretchered off after breaking his leg in a one-on-one with a Flamengo attacker. Up stepped center forward Gaucho to don the keeper's jersey, Palmeiras having no sub keeper on the bench. Though Gaucho let in a headed goal to square the game at 1–1, in the penalty shootout he not only nonchalantly buried his kick while wearing the borrowed goalkeeper's jersey (with barely a run-up, either), but also threw himself to his right twice to deny both Aldair and Zinho and give the victory to his team.

Further penalty magic came Palmeiras's way a decade later. Their coach, Luiz Felipe Scolari, had put together what is surely the best side Palmeiras has ever seen. Featuring a squad filled with superstars like Rivaldo, Edmundo, Alex, Zinho, Roque Júnior, and César Sampaio, the team made it to the final of Copa Libertadores in 1999. Penalties were crucial all the way. In the quarterfinals, Palmeiras saw off fellow Brazilian side Corinthians, 4–2 on penalties, and in the final itself, they faced Deportivo Cali of Colombia.

The first leg of the final, played in Colombia's second largest city, ended 1–0 to Deportivo via a header by Victor Bonilla, leaving Palmeiras with it all to do in the second leg back in São Paulo. That second leg was a nail-biter. With 65 minutes on the clock, the eagle-eyed Paraguayan referee noticed a hand ball in the box, and Palmeiras's midfielder Evair, who'd only been on the field a few minutes, duly dispatched the resulting penalty, to make the tie 1–1. Then disaster struck—the referee's eyes were so well attuned that he saw a foul in the Palmeiras box where there had only been a dive, and Martín Zapata, Cali's captain, scored from the spot, though with the strangest of techniques: he ran straight at the ball and used the outside of his boot to add tremendous spin to the shot, sending the keeper the wrong way. Palmeiras faced losing the game at home, until center forward Oseas scored with 15 minutes to go. A couple of minutes later, Andrés Mosquera kicked Oseas on his backside, and was red-carded; Palmeiras couldn't make the advantage pay, though, and at the very end of the game, the referee outdid himself, imagining an assault by Evair upon a Cali defender and red-carding the unlucky Brazilian.

Ten players each, then, but no matter—the game was headed to penalties in any case. Scolari could barely watch from the touchline as Zinho stepped up to take Palmeiras's first, which he duly smacked against the crossbar. Once again, Palmeiras faced ruin: Cali scored their first three, but Palmeiras kept their cool, too, and after Rogério scored for Palmeiras to even the score at 3–3, Gerardo Bedoya hit the base of the post for Cali. Euller then scored for Palmeiras, meaning that Zapata had to score his second penalty of the night to send the game into more penalties.

Would Zapata once again strike the ball oddly, hoping it would curve past the keeper? He certainly was approaching the ball directly, without a curved run-up. At the last second, Zapata struck the ball normally, with his instep, and it sailed five feet wide of the left upright. Palmeiras were Copa Libertadores champions.

Scolari quit in 2000, and since then has managed Cruzeiro, the Brazilian national side (to the World Cup title in 2002), Portugal, Chelsea, F.C. Bunyodkor in Uzbekistan (they paid him 13 million euros), and Palmeiras once again. In the meantime, Palmeiras spent time going back and forth from Série A to Série B, but as of the 2014 season, they would again be back in the top flight. Scolari, whose family are Venetian, left Palmeiras to once again run the Brazilian national team: an Italian-Brazilian, formerly the manager of a Brazilian club team that was once all-Italian, would be managing Brazil against Italy (and others) during the World Cup in Brazil. Perfect.

Location	Athens, Greece
Established	1908
Nicknames	*To Trifylli* ("The Shamrock"), *Oi Prasinoi* ("The Greens")
Stadium	Apostolos Nikolaidis Stadium (16,003 capacity)
Home colors	Green and white
Leading goal-scorer	Krzysztof Warzycha (1989–2004), 244 goals
Most appearances	Mimis Domazos (1959–80), 504 appearances

The shot came in from 30 yards, drilled along the ground and through a pod of players. When the ball emerged, it spun past the goalkeeper and into the corner of the net: 1–0 to Panathinaikos, and what's more, the goal had been scored at the legendary Kop end of Liverpool's Anfield Stadium.

It was the first leg of the semifinal of the 1985 European Cup. Barely 15 minutes had passed, but this was a wonderful start for the Greek side. As representatives of a country whose teams had abjectly failed to do well in major European competitions, to go one up over mighty Liverpool, in Liverpool, was an achievement.

Two seconds later, the score was once again 0–0.

Memories are long, and sore, in Athens. The authors of Panathinaikos's website history use the word "butchery" about that night at Anfield—an unfortunate word, given what happened seven weeks later in Heysel Stadium, Belgium. No one knew, of course, that this was the last time Liverpool would play in European competition for six years; all that mattered to Panathinaikos fans was that the referee had blown for offside and the goal wouldn't count.

It had taken a long time to get there. Established in February 1908, Panathinaikos went through a series of names in their early years, each of which resembled nothing more than options for health care in the United States: POA (Podosferikos Omilos Athinon— "Football Club of Athens"), PPO (Panellinios Podosferikos Omilos—"Panhellenic Football Club"—the team which adopted the green kits and shamrock emblem still worn), and finally, in 1922, PAO (Panathinaikos Athlitikos Omilos—"Panathinaikos Athletic Club").

By 1930, Panathinaikos were "butchering" their cross-Athens rivals, Olympiakos, 8–2 in a game, and winning championships. Their first came that same year, and they've won 19 more, including six in the 1960s and four in the 1990s, though Olympiakos have won twice as many. Since 1930, either Panathinaikos or Olympiakos have appeared in one of the top two positions every year, save eight seasons, and in 26 of those seasons, they've been one and two. Rumors of a fix being in, especially in favor of Olympiakos, continue. But at least Panathinaikos have made some inroads into European competition.

Their first brush with a big trophy came in 1971, when they faced Ajax in the European Cup final. That Panathinaikos team was managed by legendary Hungarian goal-scorer Ferenc Puskás, and they managed to knock out some top sides on the way to the final. In the quarterfinals Panathinaikos dispatched a strong Everton side, and in the semifinals they faced Red Star Belgrade, who whupped Panathinaikos 4–1 in the first leg in front of 100,000 fans, a fifth of whom had traveled from Greece. In the return, Panathinaikos upset the odds by winning 3–0, causing 30 Greeks to suffer heart attacks, according to a local newspaper. They were off to Wembley Stadium in London to face Ajax.

There was a lot at stake. For a start, Greek starlet Zeta Apostolou promised to take goalkeeper Takis Ikonomopoulos to a "hippy cave" in Crete for a weekend of dirty sheets as long as he kept a clean one in London. Bonuses were dangled; Puskás was said to be able to double his salary with a win. Alas, it was an Ajax side featuring Johan Cruyff, and the rest of that Total Football team weren't too shabby. Unfortunately for Panathinaikos, and for the hopes of Ikonomopoulos in particular, the game wasn't much of a contest. Just five minutes were on the clock when Ikonomopoulos's Cretan weekend disappeared, Dick van Dijk (sic) heading home. Though Panathinaikos would hold out until the 87th minute, a deflected goal made the final score 2–0. The scoreline doesn't quite reflect the dominance of that extraordinary Ajax team, however. (Later that year, Ajax declined to play the Intercontinental Cup and Panathinaikos took their place; Nacional of Uruguay beat them 3–2 on aggregate.)

And so to 1985, and that disallowed goal. Panathinaikos were led by the wonderfully-named Jacek Gmoch, and featured the Argentine star Juan Ramón Rocha in midfield. In that game in Liverpool, it was Rocha's brilliant strike from 30 yards that should have given Panathinaikos the lead, only for the referee to wrongly disallow the goal for offside. After that, things went downhill; Liverpool scored four unanswered goals, including one whose move began with a hand ball by Sammy Lee and ended with an Ian Rush shot that was probably from a (truly) offside position. There was no way back for Panathinaikos, and Liverpool went on to the final.

How different the football world might be had Panathinaikos made it to Belgium. Instead, Liverpool went, and their fans attacked the Juventus supporters, and the Heysel Stadium disaster happened, and everything changed.

PARIS SAINT-GERMAIN

Location	Paris, France
Established	1970
Nicknames	*Les Rouge-et-Bleu* ("The Red and Blue"), *Les Parisiens* ("The Parisians")
Stadium	Parc des Princes (48,712 capacity)
Home colors	White, red, and navy blue
Leading goal-scorer	Pedro Miguel Carreiro Resendes, known as Pauleta (2003–08), 109 goals
Most appearances	Jean-Marc Pilorget (1975–89), 435 appearances

magine London without a major soccer team (no Arsenal, Chelsea, or Tottenham), or Rome (no Roma or Lazio), or Madrid (no Real Madrid or Atlético Madrid), or even Moscow (no CSKA Moscow, Dynamo Moscow, Lokomotiv Moscow, or Spartak Moscow). Until the early 1970s, there was one major European capital where Saturdays came and went without access to top-class football: Paris.

How could this be? The French may not have displayed quite the same passion for soccer as for other sports—rugby and cycling have long gotten more rapt attention—but there was still a long history of the game being played there. Racing Club de Paris was the most recent professional club to attempt to charm the picky denizens of the French capital, but they had been relegated in 1964, dropping to 17th in Ligue 2 by 1966 and going out of business; fewer than 2,000 people had been showing up to watch Racing play. Unlike the residents of other European capital cities, Parisians felt no deep connection to this, or any, club. Parisians tended to consider football an entertainment, not an opportunity to indulge in tribal conflict, and if it wasn't entertaining . . . The French national team didn't make the Mexico World Cup in 1970, and even this was not the disaster it would have been for England, say, or Italy, or Germany.

In 1970, a consortium of businesses announced on a radio show that they were looking for people to commit to a team. Many subscribed, and so in August of that year, Paris Saint-Germain was born, a merger of Paris F.C.—a first, and short-lived, attempt to bring top-class football to the city—and Stade Saint-Germain. (The former would reform later, and still plays in the lower reaches of French football.) Initially in Ligue 3, PSG moved up quickly on the back of an infusion of both subscription money and business investment by Daniel Hechter, the renowned fashion designer. Hechter is also said to have designed the kits, which are based on Ajax's signature broad center stripe, but here morphed into a version of the French national flag. PSG would take over Paris's Parc des Princes stadium, and though there were lean times in the 1970s, by the mid-1980s they'd won the French Cup twice (the first time thanks to Argentine Osvaldo Ardiles's sterling work in midfield), and had snagged their first Ligue 1 title behind the goal-scoring prowess of Dominique Rocheteau.

It had been just 15 years since PSG was formed, but no good deed goes unpunished: By the mid-1980s, the "Boulogne Boys"—who stood in Parc des Princes' Kop of Boulogne section, and were just the kind of ardent fans a team needs to survive—had become known for their racist, violent behavior. The club did what it could to deter such problems, even setting up rival cheering sections, but all that really happened was that different factions of PSG fans ended up fighting one another as much as fans of other teams. Violence continued well into the 1990s and the new century. A riot after a UEFA Cup game against Israeli side Happoel Tel Aviv, in 2006, resulted in the death of Julien Quemener, a Kop denizen shot and killed by the police (Quemener had been part of a group chasing a Jewish fan and screaming racist slogans).

PSG won their only European title in 1996, when they beat Rapid

Vienna in the final of the Cup Winners' Cup. That PSG side's only superstar was Youri Djorkaeff, and the game was hardly a classic, though the goal that won it—a long-range, daisy-cutter strike by defender Bruno N'Gotty—was worthy of any game. The following year, PSG made it to the final again—wearing a change strip which was an almost exact replica of Ajax's kit—only to lose by a single penalty scored by Barcelona's Brazilian phenom, the original, fatter Ronaldo. He had been fouled in the box by none other than the previous year's hero, Bruno N'Gotty, and Ronaldo wasn't just fouled—it was the clearest penalty since God threw Adam and Eve out of Paradise for gumming a Granny Smith.

On the domestic field, three more Ligue 1 titles have accrued. The first, in 1994, came via the beautiful promptings of David Ginola; the other two, in 2013 and 2014, owed much to the less-beautiful-more-nutso promptings of Zlatan Ibrahimović. Ibrahimović is one of the greatest footballers to have ever played, and in semi-Cantona fashion he backs up his genius with enough outlandish statements to fill a chapbook. On the field, Ibrahimović towers over defenders (he's 6 feet 5 inches tall), and chases them down with both speed and intensity; and he makes the outrageous goal look ordinary. Off the field, his quotes are legend: as but one example, the Swede once described squaring up against Liverpool defender Stéphane Henchoz by saying, "First I went left, he did too; then I went right—he did too; then I went left again, and he went to buy a hot dog." Ibrahimović scored 30 goals in the title-winning season and continued scoring into the new season alongside PSG's new acquisition, Uruguayan goal-scoring machine Edinson Cavani, who cost the now Qatari-owned Paris club a cool 63 million euros. Ibrahimović reckons he's the best player in the world, and he may have a point some days; one of his goals from 2013 stands out as almost unfeasibly brilliant. In a game against Bastia, a deflected cross spun up in the air and Ibrahimović back-heeled it over his own left shoulder, scorpion-like, into the far corner. The gasp from the Parc des Princes fans said it all. (The same year, he also scored an overhead, bicycle kick, with his back to goal and from a full 30 yards, playing for

Sweden against England; FIFA adjudged it Goal of the Year.) Finally, Paris has a superstar to both support and be entertained by; if nothing else, his insouciance is Parisian in its way. For example, when asked what he'd bought his wife for her birthday, Ibrahimović replied, "Nothing, she already has Zlatan." Paris Saint-Germain has become the dominant French team of our time, and one of the most beautiful, culturally replete, and sophisticated capitals in the world now has everything, just like Ibrahimović's wife.

PEÑAROL

Location	Montevideo, Uruguay
Established	1891
Nicknames	*Manyas, Aurinegros* ("Gold and Blacks"), *Carboneros* ("Coalmen"), *Mirasoles* ("Sunflowers"), *Campeón del Siglo* ("Champion of the Century")
Current stadium	Estadio Centenario (capacity 60,235)
Home colors	Yellow and black
Leading goal-scorer	Fernando Morena (1973–79, 1981–83, 1985), 203 goals
Most appearances	Néstor Gonçalves (1956–70), 571 appearances

Stephenson's Rocket, the first steam train to capture the imagination of a world desperate to move at speed, made its inaugural run on September 15, 1830. Sadly, it killed a British MP by the name of Huskisson on its first journey between Liverpool and Manchester, but overcame this dreadful PR disaster by becoming the model by which all trains were designed for the next century and a half.

By the end of the nineteenth century, Rockets and their railways were being exported around the world, and to nowhere with more alacrity than resource-rich South America. Legions of British railwaymen, from navvies who laid the lines to the magnates who enjoyed the riches, swarmed into Brazil and Argentina, where timber and ore and people waited to be transported. But these stolid railwaymen, in high collars and severe suits, missed home, so they imported something else: their games (most often, in the beginning, cricket).

To Uruguay, too, they came. Once a Brazilian province, Uruguay became a sovereign nation a few months before the Rocket made its first, fatal trip. By the late 1800s, a cadre of railwaymen with names like Hudson and Henderson and Davenport and Hopkins—officials of the Central Uruguay Railway Company—had established the Central Uruguay Railway Cricket Club in Montevideo, the nation's capital. Eventually, it would morph into perhaps the greatest South American soccer team of all time, taking its name from the city's Peñarol neighborhood.

"*Serás eterno como el tiempo y florecerás en cada primavera*"—"You will be as eternal as time and flower each spring"—they wrote on the original club charter. Quickly, the arrival of soccer balls put paid to the emphasis on cricket. On May 3, 1892, Peñarol played a bunch of British expat schoolchildren at football, and won 2–0.

Since then, Peñarol have kept winning; they are arguably the most successful South American club side in history. There, in the second smallest country in South America, a place as flat as a pancake (highest point, just under 1,700 feet), where the twin joys of same-sex marriage and cannabis are legal, and where the country's motto, "*Libertad o Muerte*," recalls that of New Hampshire, Peñarol of Montevideo have won 47 national championships, five Copa Libertadores (including the first two ever played), and the Intercontinental Cup three times.

The first half of the twentieth century saw Peñarol win 17 national championships—including four in a row in the mid-1930s (they also "fivepeated" between 1958 and 1962)—but their greatest ever triumph came in 1949, when their legendary side, nicknamed *La Máquina del 49*, averaged more than four goals per game, better than almost any team in any major league in the world, ever. "The Machine" featured legends like center forward Alcides Ghiggia, holding midfielder "*El Negro Jefe*" Obdulio Varela, and Juan Alberto "Pepe" Schiaffino Villano, to many the best ever Uruguayan player (he was also a center forward). This trinity of geniuses formed the nucleus of the Uruguayan national side in the 1950 World Cup, a tournament they won "next door" in Brazil. That victory—in a country that had built a stadium (the Maracanã) simply in order to watch their team win the championship—remains a focus for Brazilian sorrow to this day, and Ghiggia, who scored the winning goal to silence the crowd (which is thought to have been 156 souls shy of 200,000, probably the biggest attendance for any soccer game in history), still hangs as a specter over Brazilian hearts.

But if Brazilian soccer heartache ever seems overdone, Uruguayan football has its "live free or die" moments too, none more so than in the Uruguayan Clasico between Peñarol and Nacional. It has become one of the most vibrant—and sometimes violent—local derbies in world soccer. One game in the mid-1990s featured 22 red cards, and in November 2000, six Peñarol players and a coach—as well as two players from Nacional—went to jail for a month after a fistfight at the end of their 1–1 game. They were arrested after a law was passed in 1995 making fighting at a sporting event—fighting by players, that is—a crime punishable by jail time. The judge who passed sentence, Paul Eguren, did so because the fight had created *"alarma social"*— and he should know, having been at the game, which was "played" at the Estadio Centenario in Montevideo, with his son. It is said that the six Peñarol players and the two from Nacional who cooled their heels in the Cárcel Central de Montevideo eventually reconciled in the slammer. (So that's nice.)

(There was a rematch in January 2014, during a "friendly" fixture. This time, a mass brawl saw nine players jailed overnight. The game ended Peñarol 4, Nacional 5—we're talking those arrested, not goals).

Lord knows what Hudson and Henderson and the rest of those Brits would make of such a show of violent passion. They were merely happy to have Peñarol play in yellow and black, the colors of Stephenson's Rocket. They could little imagine that the team that had begun as a cricket club for expats would, a few decades later, win the first two Copa Libertadores, in 1960 and 1961. In the latter victory, Peñarol of Uruguay once again broke Brazilian hearts, in the form of São Paulo club Palmeiras.

In the first leg, played in Montevideo, free-scoring Alberto Spencer, the "*Cabeza Magica*" ("Magic Head") Ecuadoran who still holds the record for the most goals in the tournament, nicked a winner a minute from time (he had scored in 1960's final, too). In the return in São Paulo, José Sasía scored for Peñarol after just two minutes; a late Palmeiras equalizer failed to prevent Peñarol winning its second of five Copa Libertadores, and cementing its reputation as a soccer powerhouse.

It's not just a South American phenomenon. Peñarol have beaten Benfica, Real Madrid, and Aston Villa in their three Intercontinental Cup finals. Manya, as Peñarol is nicknamed, may no longer dominate South American football (their last appearance in a Copa Libertadores, in 2011, ended in defeat by Brazil's Santos) as they once did, but the legend of Ghiggia and Schiaffino, Alberto Spencer and the incarcerated Clasico Six, echoes across the flat plains of this small country, squashed but unbowed as it is, between Brazil and Argentina.

POHANG STEELERS

Location	Pohang, South Korea
Established	1973 (as POSCO FC)
Nicknames	—
Current stadium	Pohang Steel Yard (25,000 capacity)
Home colors	Red and black
Leading goal-scorer	—
Most appearances	—

I f you're a fan of obscure joys, nothing quite comes close to the names of clubs that play in the Asian Club Championship, the premier competition of the Asian Football Confederation, which features teams spanning from the Middle East to Australia. Let us pause, then, to appreciate the (sadly now defunct) Thai Farmers Bank Football Club, who once played the Pohang Steelers of South Korea (both of whom have won the tournament). Or let us imagine the possible religious tensions involved in a game between Mohammaden SC of Bangladesh and Old Benedictans of Sri Lanka. They played each other on July 21, 1989; no word on who won the theological debate, but the followers of Allah bested the Christians by a score of 3–1.

On November 3, 1987, Federal Territory, of Kuala Lumpur, played China's August 1st; this utterly unromantic matchup ended 1–1. Fans of geopolitically significant games might have enjoyed Yamaha Motors, of Japan, versus April 25, the North Korean army's team. The North Koreans were too strong for the Japanese, running out 3–1 winners; sadly for everyone, the game was played in July. There is a team from India called Churchill Brothers; a team from Burma called Finance and Revenue, which was once the most successful clubs in Burmese history until a new league was formed which barred government ministries from fielding teams. A team from the Maldives called Victory SC won one game on a forfeit before withdrawing from the quarterfinals in 1993, thereby miserably failing to test the truth of their own name on the actual field of play. Compare Victory SC to Home United, of Singapore, whose name didn't stop them losing 6–0 when the Macau police department came to visit in 2000, and 5–0 in the return fixture, or "Home lost by six at home and by five away," if you prefer. But perhaps the team with the best name of all, at least to a poet's ear, is that of the other Maldives powerhouse, New Radiant Soccer Club.

In the second round of the East Asian section of the 1996–97 Asian Club Championship, New Radiant took on Jagatjit Cotton and Textile Mills, or JCT as they were known, of the Indian Punjab. JCT once inked a back-end deal with Wolverhampton Wanderers of the British Midlands, but they are now defunct, victim of India's long-held lack of interest in all things soccer. But even before they disappeared, JCT's two-leg tie against New Radiant hardly garnered world attention. New Radiant had only made it to the second round because their game against Pettah United F.C., of neighboring Sri Lanka, had been canceled due to the ongoing violence between the government of Sri Lanka and the Tamil Tiger separatist movement. In that second round home and away match, New Radiant beat JCT 2–1 on aggregate, and headed off to South Korea, 4,000 miles to the east, to play three games at the quarterfinal group stage against strong teams: Yokohama Marinos of Japan and two of the top South Korean sides: Seongnam Ilhwa Chunma and the Pohang Steelers, who have had some cool names of their own.

Established in 1973 and owned by POSCO, one of the world's top five steel makers, the Steelers' initial bland POSCO F.C. morphed into the POSCO Dolphins, then the POSCO Atoms, before eventually settling on the Steelers in 1997. Pohang itself used to be a sleepy seaside town on the east coast of South Korea until POSCO showed up; now it's a kind of Pittsburgh by the sea, with a soccer team.

Let's just say it didn't go too well in the 1996–97 Asian Club Championship for the tiny team from the beautiful Maldives. Between November 24 and November 28, New Radiant managed to lose all three games by a staggering 25–0 (combined). In the first game they were only 3–0 down to Seongnam Ilhwa Chunma at half-time, but let in six second-half goals; two days later, against the Steelers, they were just two down at the break, but lost 6–0 after 90 minutes. They saved their worst performance for last. Against Yokohama Marinos they were three down in 13 minutes, and seven down by half-time. Alberto Acosta, the 30-year-old Argentinian international getting a payday in Japan, managed to score five goals for the Marinos as they thrashed poor New Radiant 10–0. New Radiant would gain a modicum of redemption a decade later when they reached the semifinals of the Asian Football Confederation Cup—admittedly an inferior competition, but you can only beat what's in front of you. Along the way to their historic semifinal, New Radiant bested Happy Valley of Hong Kong 4–0 on aggregate, in what might be the most blissful two-leg cup match ever played.

With New Radiant out of the way in 1996, Pohang Steelers went from strength to strength in the Asian Club Championship, beating their arch Korean rivals Seongnam Ilhwa Chunma in the final with a penalty three minutes from the end of extra time. The win began a period of dominance for Pohang, who also won the tournament the following year. Having recorded victories by the staggering scores of 13–0 and 15–0 in earlier rounds, they won 6–5 on penalties in the final against China's Dalian Shide. (In 2009, Pohang won it for a third time, beating Al-Ittihad of Saudi Arabia.)

At home, the Steelers have won the K-League five times since they were founded in 1973, but it is internationally that Pohang has proved itself one of the top Asian teams for the last four decades. In 2009, on the back of their AFC win, Pohang, featuring bull-like Brazilian striker Denilson, reached the semifinals of the FIFA Club World Cup, the world's premier club tournament, where they were unlucky to lose 2–1 to Estudiantes of Argentina. Estudiantes, in turn, only lost in the final in extra time to a Barcelona team featuring both Lionel Messi (he scored the winner) and Thierry Henry. In the usually meaningless third-place playoff, Pohang beat Atlante of Mexico in a penalty shootout, making them nominally, and for one year at least, the third best club team in the world.

PORTO

Location	Porto, Portugal
Established	1893
Nicknames	*Portistas*, *Dragões* ("Dragons"), *Azuis e Brancos* ("Blues and Whites")
Current stadium	Estádio do Dragão (50,431 capacity)
Home colors	Blue and white
Leading goal-scorer	Fernando Gomes (1974–80, 1982–89), 289 goals
Most appearances	João Pinto (1981–97), 587 appearances

Who else but a wine merchant would establish a soccer club in Porto, the city on the Atlantic Ocean in northwest Portugal which lends its name to the fortified vino?

His name was António Nicolau d'Almeida, and in 1893, when he was just 20 years old, he founded Foot-Ball Club do Porto. It was lucky d'Almeida was young, as he was able to live to see both the establishment of the Portuguese football league in 1938 and Porto's early domination of it, winning the first two seasons (they had also won a fledgling league in 1935). It was a false dawn, however—from the end of World War II to the mid-1980s, Porto lagged behind Benfica, as all Portuguese teams did, and managed only four more titles.

Valencia lost the 1984 Cup Winners' Cup final to Juventus, 2–1, under coach José Maria Pedroto. Pedroto, known as *"Zé do Boné"* for his trademark flat cap, was already sick with cancer and asked the club to appoint one of his protégés, Artur Jorge. Jorge took Pedroto's team and molded it into a superb side—Jorge is still known to Porto fans as *"Rei Artur."* Jorge had been a fine goal-scorer for Benfica in his day, but was also serious about managing a soccer team, studying the theory of it both under Pedroto (who died in January 1985) and in then-Communist East Germany. Jorge was also serious about his mustache, a bushy statement that resembled the tail of a breaching blue whale.

The team Jorge led in the mid-eighties was a formidable one, featuring legendary right back João Pinto, who would play his entire career, more than 400 club games, for Porto. Pinto corralled a stingy defense, and up front, Fernando Gomes scored close to a goal per game in two separate spells with the club. Porto won four Portuguese titles (Artur was coach for the first two), but their greatest moment under King Arthur was in the 1987 European Cup final.

Porto reached the final with some ease (they won their first game of the tournament 9–0), but Gomes was injured for the ultimate game with German powerhouse Bayern Munich, a team that boasted Lothar Matthäus, Andreas Brehme, and Dieter Hoeness. Bayern scored first, and many must have thought they'd go on to win the trophy. But this was Bayern without its traditional luck, or *dusel*. Come the second half, Porto's Algerian striker Rabah Madjer decided to single-handedly win the game for his team.

Madjer is still a hero in Algeria for his play for the national team, and in Porto his name is whispered in hushed tones, too, all because of what he did in the 77th minute of that 1987 final. A Porto attack down the right ended with the ball breaking free in the six-yard box. Madjer had his back to goal, but some brains are quicker than others, and with a back-heel he flicked the ball past Hans-Dieter Flick (!) on the Bayern line. It's the kind of thing one might try in a pickup game in the park; but 1–0 down in a European final? Hardly.

Madjer still wasn't done. A few minutes later, a sparkling run down the left and a brilliant cross by the Algerian left Brazilian Juary with a simple finish, and Porto had come from behind to win the European Cup.

Later that year, Madjer scored an extra-time winner to give Porto a 2–1 victory over Peñarol in the Intercontinental Cup final. By then King Arthur had moved on, and would manage a slew of other teams, including Porto again, Benfica, and Portugal, but it would take the introduction of a new coach to bring Porto back to European greatness.

In the 1990s, Porto once again dominated the Portuguese league, winning every year except 1991 and 1994, but in Europe they failed, reaching just one semifinal (of the Champions League, in 1994). That year, Porto's assistant manager was a 31-year-old former journeyman midfielder named José Mourinho; he would continue his apprenticeship, first with Bobby Robson, and then with Louis van Gaal, at Barcelona, before brief spells back in Portugal, at Benfica (for just nine games) and União de Leiria. But all roads were leading back to the coast, and in January 2002 he took the job that would lead him to label himself "the Special One": manager of Porto.

Mourinho only led Porto for two seasons, but he packed a lot in. In his first year, Mourinho brought in Deco, Ricardo Carvalho, Dmitri Alenichev, Paulo Ferreira, and Hélder Postiga, and turned the team into a fabulous, hardworking, pressing unit. Porto won the league (over Benfica), the Portuguese Cup (against União de Leiria), and in May Mourinho took his team across the Iberian peninsula to Seville, where they would face Celtic in the 2003 UEFA Cup final.

It was a great game. After an hour the score was 2–2, Porto's goals by Deriel and Alenichev snuffed out by two fine headers by Celtic's Henrik Larsson. The game went to extra time, but after just six minutes a silly tackle by Celtic center back Bobo Baldé saw him sent off, and his team wilted without him. With five minutes to go, Deriel slipped past a bunch of Celtic defenders and smacked in the winner. Porto, and Mourinho, had won. But better was to come the following season.

In 2004, Porto once again walked the league, winning it five weeks early. This time in Europe, however, they went one better, reaching the final of the Champions League. They got there having dispatched Manchester United at Old Trafford in the round of 16, a game famous for both the last-minute goal by Costinha and the subsequent wild celebration of Mourinho down the Old Trafford touchline. In the final, Porto's pressing, muscular, high-tempo football was too much for A.S. Monaco, a team featuring a young Emmanuel Adebayor on the bench. The final score of 3–0 barely flattered Mourinho's men.

And then Mourinho was gone. By the time Porto won their second Intercontinental Cup, in December 2004, beating Colombian side Once Caldas after a nine-round penalty shootout, Mourinho was in his first spell at Chelsea. Mourinho not only quit, he also plundered his former team for players, and though Porto kept winning Primeira Liga titles—they've now won 27, including every year but one from 2005 to 2013—in Europe, a single Europa League victory over fellow Portuguese side Braga is all they have to show.

That victory over Braga would come under the leadership of André Villas-Boas, a Mourinho protégé and former assistant coach. Villas-Boas, too, would leave Porto for Chelsea, in 2011, right after Porto had gone an entire season without losing a game. At Chelsea, Villas-Boas presided over seven defeats in the Premiership in just over eight months, and he was gone by early March. That same year, the team Villas-Boas left behind, Porto, lost one game all season and won the Portuguese league by 16 points.

PSV EINDHOVEN

Location	Eindhoven, Netherlands
Established	1913
Nicknames	*Boeren* ("Peasants/Farmers"), *Rood-witten* ("Red-Whites"), *Philips*
Stadium	Philips Stadion (35,000 capacity)
Home colors	Red and white
Leading goal-scorer	Willy van der Kuijlen (1964–80), 308 goals
Most appearances	Willy van der Kuijlen (1964–80), 528 appearances

This is the history of Willy and René van der Kerkofs, of Ronaldo and Ronald Koeman, of the Ruuds Gullit and van Nistelrooy, of winning the European and the UEFA cups, and a family called Philips.

Koninklijke Philips N.V., the multinational electronics company, was established in the late nineteenth century, and by 1910, vestiges of Victorian patronage remained in the Phillips boardroom as they created a sporting club for their factory workers. The original soccer team, Philips Elftal, became Philips Sport Vereniging by 1916, and a decade later they reached the highest level of Dutch soccer, where they have remained ever since. PSV's first title arrived in 1928–29, but only three more would arrive before the 1970s. The second half of that decade, however, saw the first great Eindhoven team come together.

The names of that side still trip off the 1970s' soccer fan's tongue: Willy van der Kuijlen—still PSV's and the Eredivisie's highest ever goal-scorer—and the van der Kerkhof twins, Willy and René. Crumpled, perennially unimpressed-looking coach Kees Rijvers built a superb team around these fine players, and they swept all before them, winning the Dutch league three times in four years and the UEFA Cup in 1978. In that latter tournament, PSV entertained almost too much—their aggregate scores were 11–2, 6–3, 4–1, 4–3, and 4–3 again (over Barcelona). The 0–0 draw against SEC Bastia of France in the first leg of the final was an anomaly, but PSV made up for it at Philips Stadion in Eindhoven with a thumping 3–0 win, including two goals in two second-half minutes. (The core of the team also played for Holland in the final of the 1978 World Cup against hosts Argentina.) All good things come to an end in soccer, though, and a couple of years later Rijvers was fired as the team disintegrated.

Eindhoven fans didn't have to wait long—the next great team came in the mid-1980s and featured Ruud Gullit. In wonderfully Dutch fashion, the dreadlocked Gullit, a notoriously difficult to manage midfield powerhouse, did what so many of his compatriots had done before, which was spend more time criticizing the club and the coaches—anyone he could lay his hands on—than actually playing football. It is part of the reason soccer fans around the world love the Dutch; nary a World Cup goes by without one of their stars throwing his toys around, and PSV in the mid-eighties were no exception. Once Gullit went to Milan in 1987, the Ronald Koeman-led squad, benefitting from the absence of British clubs after the Heysel disaster and subsequent ban, went all the way to the European Cup final in 1988, even knocking out Real Madrid in the semifinals.

The final, against Benfica, who had the great Eusébio watching on their sideline, was hardly a classic, one in a long line of European Cup finals that were too tense to be any good. At 0–0, the game went to penalties, and, uniquely in a major final, both teams scored five each to start the shootout. Thus it moved to sudden death, watched dispassionately by PSV coach Guus Hiddink, hidden as he mostly was behind a mustache so burly it must have made breathing difficult. Anton Janssen, an extra-time sub for PSV, slotted home the first of the sudden-death pens, leaving Benfica's right back, António Veloso, having to score to keep the competition alive. But Veloso's little stutter steps did nothing to put off Hans van Breukelen in the PSV goal, and merely betrayed a player for whom the moment was too much. Van Breukelen wasn't fooled, and dived to his right to make an easy save. Eusébio looked away; Hiddink looked unmoved, and PSV's players looked delighted to have won the biggest trophy (metaphorically and literally) in European club football.

In the subsequent Intercontinental Cup final, PSV would lose on penalties to Nacional of Uruguay.

Guus Hiddink would move on, to Fenerbahçe in Turkey and then to the Dutch national side, Real Madrid, South Korea, Australia, Russia, Chelsea . . . you name it. Hiddink's management of South Korea led them to the semifinal of the Japan–South Korea World Cup (they knocked out Italy and Spain), and led to a stadium in South Korea being named after him—he already has a Dutch museum in his hometown of Varsseveld dedicated to his exploits, the excellently-named Guuseum. His subsequent management of Australia wasn't quite as successful, though he came within a dodgy penalty of forcing Italy into extra time in the knockout stages of the 2006 World Cup in Germany. In between his international exploits, Hiddink led PSV to three Dutch titles in a row; they would add two after he left to make a "fivepeat." Too often a selling club—van Nistelrooy, Arjen Robben, Park Ji-Sung, Alex, Jaap Stam, and Boudewijn Zenden are just a few of its recent former players—PSV continue to churn out stars whose sell-on prices fill Philips' coffers even higher, as if shifting a gazillion lightbulbs, headphones, Christmas lights, and electric toothbrushes wasn't already enough.

Location	Glasgow, Scotland
Established	1872
Nicknames	The Gers, The Teddy Bears, The Light Blues
Stadium	Ibrox Stadium (51,082 capacity)
Home colors	Royal blue, white, and red
Leading goal-scorer	Ally McCoist (1983–98), 355 goals
Most appearances	John Greig (1960–79), 755 appearances

I f only the stories were all about the football—the dash of a winger, the thunderous tackling of a midfield general, the fingertip saves of a lithesome keeper, the bullet header of a burly center forward. Instead, now and then we must sing of riots, and disasters, and sectarianism, and financial mismanagement. For the story of Glasgow Rangers F.C. is salutary, sometimes triumphant, too often sad, and since 2012, a full-blown debacle.

Rangers began in 1872 with Peter and Moses McNeil, Peter Campbell, and William McBeath, desperate to play a pickup game on Glasgow Green. A year later they went official, and on board came Hugh McNeil, another brother, as well as a couple more Campbells. Others soon joined, and the first league game came in 1890. That season ended with Rangers sharing the trophy with Dumbarton, a play-off game having finished 2–2. Come the next century, come more trophies, and by the beginning of World War II Rangers had won the Scottish league 24 times.

All well and good; but there had been terrible times, too. In 1899 Rangers moved into their new stadium, Ibrox; three years later, a part of the stand collapsed during an England–Scotland game and 25 people died. Though trouble between Celtic and Rangers dates back to the end of the nineteenth century, a Scottish Cup final replay between the two on April 17, 1909, revealed the mutual loathing in all its horror, as a massive, on-pitch riot, replete with fisticuffs, and fires in the stands, ended the game early (neither team was awarded the trophy).

Behind all the violence and ill feeling was a growing identification of Rangers with Scottish Protestantism, and Celtic with Irish Catholicism. By the start of World War I, these forces were firmly in place, and deepened as the century progressed. As a result, no openly Catholic player was brought in to play for Rangers until Graeme Souness signed Maurice "Mo" Johnston in 1989, more than a century after Rangers was founded. (As a result, Johnston's house was firebombed by Celtic supporters, and his father assaulted.)

After World War II, yet more championships came the way of Glasgow Rangers, though sometimes it seemed that all that mattered each season was how they fared against their Old Firm rivals, Celtic. The 1960s were a cruel time to be a Rangers fan; though they won the league three times, they also lost two European finals: the Cup Winners' Cup in 1961, 4–1 on aggregate to Fiorentina, and six years later the same tournament, 1–0 after extra time to Bayern Munich (it was Bayern's first European crown). Worst of all, that year, 1967, saw Celtic become the first British side to raise the European Cup trophy, the pinnacle of club achievement in Europe. And after 1964, Rangers wouldn't win the Scottish league until 1975.

In the meantime, there came a great high, matched by a great low, and a great low all on its own. The single great low came on the second day of January 1971, when yet another disaster at Ibrox, this time during an Old Firm game, cost 66 lives. Celtic had scored with almost the last kick of the game, and Rangers had equalized immediately; in the crush of fans first leaving in despair, then returning in joy, someone fell and a crush developed. Ibrox was subsequently revamped, but too late—the deaths had come after three other incidents in the 1960s alone.

The following year, Rangers made it to the final of the Cup Win-ners' Cup once again, where they would face Dynamo Moscow in what turned out to be a thriller, and a disaster, in Barcelona.

The tournament had already thrown up some amazing moments. In the first round, Chelsea defeated Luxembourg side Jeunesse Hautcharage by an aggregate score of 21–0, which is still a European record (Peter Osgood scored eight of the 21 goals across the two legs). The second round featured a ridiculous tie between Rangers and Sporting Lisbon, in which the second leg went to penalties when the Dutch referee, Laurens van Ravens, failed to understand the away goals rule. The tie was tied at 6–6, but Rangers had scored three away goals to Lisbon's two, meaning they had won. Van Ravens forced the teams to take penalties, which Lisbon won, 3–0. It took the interven-tion of Rangers manager Willie Waddell to point out the referee's error and for Rangers to advance. Rangers would then knock out Torino, gain a modicum of revenge over Bayern Munich, and then head to the final in Franco's Spain.

Twenty-three minutes into the game, Rangers' center forward, Colin Stein, latched onto a long lob over the Dynamo Moscow defense and whammed the ball into the back of the net. Cue pitch invasion by the Rangers fans, who had clearly misunderstood the legendary bru-tality of Franco's police force (and never before or since have so many kilts, sporrans, Union flags, and, oddly, sombreros, been seen on the Camp Nou grass). José María Ortiz de Mendíbil, the referee, was seen throwing his arms out in resigned confusion as he wondered what to do. The Scottish commentator said, "One shudders to think what's going to happen if Rangers win this game now . . . Pandemonium, bed-lam rolled up together, let loose." Once the fans had returned to the stands, with five minutes to go in the first half Rangers scored again, on a header by Willie Johnston (who would be thrown out of the 1978 World Cup for taking what he claimed was hay fever medication). Four minutes into the second half, a moon-brushing kick by keeper Peter McCloy evaded the Moscow defenders, and Johnston once again scored. It was 3–0, and Rangers had one hand on the trophy.

They almost didn't get the other hand on it. A terrible piece of defending by Tommy McLean handed Dynamo a goal with half an hour to go, and good saves by McCloy and a goal-line clearance ensued; with three minutes left Dynamo scored again, to make it 3–2. With Dynamo pressing, a free kick to the Russian team was seemingly misinterpreted by Rangers fans as the end of the game, and another massive pitch invasion ensued. Three minutes went by before the field was cleared; the Russian momentum had stalled; Rangers hung on; but the fans had ruined the night, drunkenly rioting with the Barcelona police at the true end of the game. The trophy had to be awarded in a back room of Camp Nou. Rangers captain John Greig reported that as he was handed the cup, a UEFA delegate said words to the effect of, "Here, take the cup, Glasgow Rangers, and go away." Go away they did—Rangers were subsequently banned from European competition for two years (later reduced to one).

Trouble and sectarianism continued. Simon Kuper, in *Soccer Against the Enemy*, reports that an Old Firm game in 1975 "inspired two attempted murders, two cleaver attacks, one axe attack, nine stabbings, and 35 common assaults." But football sometimes broke out, too—Rangers won nine championships in a row from 1989–97. Top players happily trod the road north to Scotland, including both Brian Laudrup and Paul Gascoigne. In 1998, Rangers named Lorenzo Amoruso as their captain; he was a Catholic. A year later, Amoruso admitted he'd made racist comments to Borussia Dortmund's Nigerian player Victor Ikpeba. (Even when Rangers win, they lose.)

Trouble continued to plague Rangers. In 2008, they reached the final of the UEFA Cup, which was to be held in Manchester. Facing them were an Andrei Arshavin-led Zenit St. Petersburg, and the little Russian winger would prove too much for Rangers, inspiring his side to a 2–0 win. Sadly, the whole event was marred by a massive riot by Rangers fans in Manchester city center. According to the BBC, some 130,000 of them had traveled down to watch the game, and when a large screen in the city broke, a small minority of the supporters, frustrated at being unable to watch the game, ran amok.

There was still further to fall for Rangers. On Valentine's Day 2012, and less than four years after appearing in a major European final, the club went insolvent and was placed in administration, and then, in June, liquidated by creditors. They were thrown out of the top tier of Scottish football—a league they had won a record 54 times (Celtic have won 44)—and ended up in the fourth level of Scottish football.

Their first game in the lowest possible Scottish division saw nearly 50,000 fans turn up, a world record for such a division. Rangers would win that league by 24 points in 2012–13, and be promoted. The following season, the team representing the newly constituted Rangers Football Club Ltd. won every game bar three draws in Scottish League One (which, despite its name, is actually the third tier of Scottish football), scoring 102 goals. Rangers are climbing back, which is wonderful news to at least half of the soccer fans in soccer-mad Glasgow.

RAPID VIENNA

Location	Vienna, Austria
Established	1899
Nicknames	*Die Grün-Weissen* ("The Green-Whites"), Hütteldorfer
Current stadium	Gerhard Hanappi Stadium (17,500 capacity)
Home colors	Green and white
Leading goal-scorer	Franz "Bimbo" Binder (1930–49), 267 goals
Most appearances	Peter Schöttel (1986–2002), 524 appearances

He still claims he was hit by something thrown from the crowd, but no one really believes him. In the film of the event, the bottle lands harmlessly, half a soccer field beyond him, but still the player goes down, clutching his head. These days, he's a snoop for the Austrian health service, doing his best to catch out cheats who need more help from the government than they're entitled to. Meet Rudi Weinhofer, the Rapid Vienna defender who single-handedly denied European glory to Scotland's Celtic, and who now spends his days exposing swindlers.

Celtic had been cruising to a famous victory in the 1984 Cup Winners' Cup second round. Though they'd lost in Vienna in the first leg, 3–1, back in Glasgow they had turned the tie around, and by the 68th minute were 3–0 up and heading for the quarterfinals. Sadly, some idiot in the crowd threw a bottle on to the field, and it was all the excuse Weinhofer needed. He claimed then, and still claims, that he was hit "by an object . . . I don't know what it was. I was bleeding from a wound and it was only once I was back in the dressing room I felt my normal self again." His normal self would see action in the replayed second leg after UEFA decided that the result should not stand. Rapid Wien won 1–0, in neutral Manchester, to reach the quarters.

From there, the traditional *Rapidviertelstunde* took over. This fast clapping by Vienna fans during the last 15 minutes of games is said to date back to before World War I. Rapid was originally the team of the working man, embodied by their striker Josef Uridil, a huge lunk of a man—he was nicknamed "the Tank"—who was so famous in the 1920s that there was a popular song written about him and he shilled for a number of products. Side by side with this "working-class" theology was a sense of obstinate commitment to the game, noted by David Goldblatt in *The Ball Is Round* when he recounts that one contemporary observer of the postwar Rapid Vienna said that "they never give up and fight to the final whistle." This was much in evidence years later in the "stolen" quarterfinal, when a late goal by Hans Krankl solidified their place in the semifinals. A goal by Antonín Panenka— he of the disguised penalty chip shot that now bears his name— against Dynamo Moscow in the second leg of the semis added to a fine 3–1 victory in the first leg to take Vienna to the final, where they lost to Everton, Krankl again scoring very late, only this time too little. (Everton's 3–1 victory in that 1985 Cup Winners' Cup final was a poignant one. Exactly two weeks later, fans of Everton's city-mates Liverpool were involved in the horrific Heysel Stadium riot which left 39 Juventus fans dead and more than 600 injured, and led to British teams being barred from European competition for years.)

This was the pinnacle of Vienna's international achievement (they also lost the 1996 final of the same competition, 1–0, to Paris Saint-Germain). Established as Rapid Vienna by 1899, they are unrivaled in Austria, having won 32 national championships, including the very first; their arch local rivals, S.K. Austria Wien, have won 24. Perhaps their greatest triumph came against the backdrop of their greatest adversity: in 1941, after Austria's annexation by Germany (in 1938), Rapid were forced to play in the German league. They went and won it, and in a style that revealed the true extent of *Rapidgeist*, the nickname for Vienna's sense of team spirit.

In a game they had to win to become champions, Vienna traveled to the Olympic Stadium in Berlin to face the best German side of those years, Schalke 04. In the newsreels of the game, men wear origami newspaper hats to ward off the late June sun, and Nazi officers applaud vigorously, sitting in their own section like a bunch of "ultras." It all seems so cheery, as though monstrosities like Sachsenhausen concentration camp were not a half-hour drive north of where the game was being played, as though that very day—Sunday, June 22, 1941—Germany wasn't beginning its foray into Russia, still the largest invasion in the history of war. That morning, Joseph Goebbels had announced Operation Barbarossa to the German nation, saying, "At this moment a march is taking place that, for its extent, compares with the greatest the world has ever seen."

By the afternoon, the Olympic Stadium was bursting with 90,000 soccer fans. By the 62nd minute Schalke were three goals to the good (they had scored twice in the first eight minutes), but that 62nd minute saw the game turn around. Schalke notched their third via the wonderfully named Heinz Hinz, only for Rapid Vienna to immediately reply via Georg Schors, and then a hulking, 6-foot-3-inch center forward called Franz "Bimbo" Binder took over, scoring a hat-trick in the following eight minutes to steal the championship for Wien. (Binder would also manage Wien three separate times after the war.)

So much for soccer. By the end of that sunny Sunday, some 2,000 Soviet planes had been destroyed, as the German Luftwaffe pushed eastward. In the camp at Sachsenhausen, few of the 6,000 Jews sent there after Kristallnacht remained—they'd long since been sent to Auschwitz, and Dachau, and Bergen–Belsen, hells unimaginable. Meanwhile, soccer fans witnessed a stirring win for Vienna, and *Les Préludes*, Liszt's third symphonic poem, blared out of radios (the Nazis often employed music to stir up enthusiasm for their efforts). Sublunary life continued, on streets, in towns, on football fields, but it did not continue for everyone.

Location	Madrid, Spain
Established	1902
Nicknames	*Los Blancos* ("The Whites"), *Los Merengues* ("The Meringues")
Current stadium	Estadio Santiago Bernabéu (85,454 capacity)
Home colors	White
Leading goal-scorer	Raúl González Blanco, known as Raúl (1994–2010), 323 goals
Most appearances	Raúl González Blanco, known as Raúl (1994–2010), 741 appearances

Real Madrid has been called "the greatest club side the world has ever known"—they are the richest club in the world and perhaps its most successful, and in 2000 they were voted FIFA's Club of the Century—and yet they remain widely unloved, except by their own fans. Their history is a troubling one, especially in the terrible Franco years, and that legacy hasn't been entirely expunged. As one small but telling example, their own history of the club, published on their official website, features a callout in the years 1931–40 heralding an "historical [*sic*] victory. On 13 June, 1943, Real Madrid destroyed Barcelona in the Cup." Madrid did indeed "destroy" Barcelona, by a score we won't legitimize here, but it is now generally agreed that the result came after a visit to the Barcelona changing rooms by the excessively-named José María de la Blanca Finat y Escrivá de Romaní, the Falangist Director of State Security, who is said to have reminded the Barça players that they played in Spain only at the pleasure of the regime. On the back of the ridiculously lopsided result, the administrators of the two clubs were jettisoned and fines levied—even Franco couldn't countenance such a travesty.

It is too bad, as Real's real history is one of extraordinary soccer achievements, such that it barely needs such blandishments. Founded just after the start of the twentieth century, Real were initially Football Club Sky, put together by teachers and students of Madrid's Institución Libre de Enseñanza, the Free Teaching Institution. By March 1906 they were simply Madrid F.C. In 1920 they got the royal ("*Real*") seal of approval from soon-to-be-ousted King Alfonso XIII, though they briefly lost it when Alfonso fled to Rome in 1931.

They won the Spanish Cup early and often—four times in a row from 1905 on—but it took until 1931 for their first Spanish league victory (they repeated the next year). In the aftermath of the debacle of the 1943 Copa del Generalísimo game against Barcelona, Real Madrid found itself without a president and turned to the man who would transform them into the Real Madrid that has swept all before it: Santiago Bernabéu Yeste.

Bernabéu had played for Madrid for 15 years, until 1927; he only managed 78 appearances, though some of them were as captain. As president, Bernabéu marshaled the Madrid members, a.k.a. the *socios*, whose financial clout helped build the Real Madrid stadium that is now named the Bernabéu in his honor. He also helped invent the European Cup, and then watched his club dominate it for its first decade.

The first European Cup final was played in 1956, in Paris, as Real Madrid faced Stade de Reims. The incomparable Argentine Alfredo Di Stéfano had joined Madrid from River Plate in 1953 and had already helped them win two La Liga titles, their first in 20 years. In the 1956 final, though, the Spanish powerhouse found themselves two down in 10 minutes. It would be up to Real's best players to turn the game around. Could they afford to lose the first ever European Cup final?

Besides the stadium he got built, Bernabéu's legacy also included a commitment to bringing the best players in the world to Madrid. It is a legacy that continues to this day. The men who run Real Madrid have never been afraid to hire the best and the brightest of world footballers to further their cause. Di Stéfano had initially signed with Barcelona, but an intrigue worthy of a medieval court ended when Bernabéu convinced him to join Real. (An initial ruling by the Spanish Football Federation that Di Stéfano had to play two seasons for Barça and two for Real was quickly realized to be foolish at best, and he joined Real full time.) Fellow Argentine Héctor Rial had also been brought to Spain by Bernabéu, in his case from Nacional in Uruguay. Rial and Di Stéfano were two of the first *galacticos*.

Their true worth came through that day in Paris. After half an hour Stade de Reims had been pegged back to 2–2, via goals by Di Stéfano and then Rial. But Stade were a gutsy team, and they made it 3–2 after an hour. Real equalized through a scrambled goal five minutes later. Cue Rial, popping up at the far post to win the game for Real. Madrid were the first champions of Europe, and they would go on to win the next four tournaments, too—defeating Fiorentina, A.C. Milan, Stade de Reims again, and Eintracht Frankfurt. That last game, in 1960, featured another *galactico*, Hungarian great Ferenc Puskás. He had been a member of his country's "Golden Team," which had gone unbeaten for an astonishing 32 games in a row and and in 1953 had beaten a strong English team at Wembley Stadium, 6–3. The following year, in Budapest, they beat England 7–1. But when the Hungarian Revolution of 1956 arrived, many of the team's players fled, and Puskás ended up in Madrid.

At home, Real Madrid also dominated La Liga. Between 1954 and 1969 they won 12 championships, including five in a row from 1961 to 1965. Puskás's presence in the Real Madrid side from 1958 to 1966 delivered a second wave of success to this team for the ages. Against Eintracht Frankfurt, at 3–1 at half-time, one might have imagined the game to be over, but Puskás was determined to make it so in spades. In the space of 15 second-half minutes he added a hat-trick to his goal on half-time, and even after a late two-goal flurry from Eintracht Frankfurt, Real won 7–3. This was a European Cup final; Real was playing against some of the best players in the world at the time. That same year, Real won the first ever Intercontinental Cup, thrashing Peñarol of Uruguay 5–1 in the second leg at the Bernabéu, the first leg having ended 0–0. Real were three goals up inside eight minutes that night in September—two from Puskás and one from Di Stéfano. (Gento would score the fifth after just 54 minutes.) It seemed as if Real might never lose another game.

The soccer gods had other ideas. Real faced Barcelona in the first round of the next European Cup, and lost. It would be six seasons before Real won again in Europe. Losing two European Cup finals, in 1962 and 1964, seemed only to deepen the mystique around the club, especially as the games were thrilling, if disappointing to Madrid fans. The 1962 final, against Benfica, was graced by a Puskás hat-trick, but also a winning goal by Eusébio (Benfica won 5–3). In 1964, Inter Milan beat Madrid to win the first of their two back-to-back titles. In fact, the early years of the European Cup were dominated by a small cadre of teams: between 1956 and 1973, the final featured at least one, and often two, of only seven teams: Real Madrid, A.C. Milan, Benfica, Barcelona, Inter Milan, Celtic, and Ajax.

By 1966, when Madrid won their last European Cup until 1998, the team, like the world, had long been bitten by the Beatles bug. Four of the players appeared in a sports daily, *Diario MARCA*, wearing Beatles wigs, and the team became known as the "Ye-yé," from "she loves you / yeah, yeah, yeah." In the 1966 final, Madrid would beat Partizan on two late goals, but only Gento remained from that classic team. More La Liga titles came—by 1980 they had won their twentieth—but in Europe, Real Madrid would have to wait.

When success returned, it did so without Bernabéu—and it came in the UEFA Cup, not the European Cup Bernabéu had created. Bernabéu died during the 1978 World Cup in Argentina; six years later, his beloved team won back-to-back UEFA Cups. The first win came against Videoton of Puskás's Hungary. Hailing from Hungary's ninth largest city, Székesfehérvár, Videoton were the original "team just happy to be here" in that final, and they duly lost 3–1 on aggregate, though in the second leg, at the Bernabéu, they managed to score with four minutes to go to beat Real Madrid 1–0 in front of nearly 100,000 fans. But the real drama in the tournament was in the semifinal, when Real overcame a 2–0 deficit to a Liam Brady-led Inter Milan, winning 3–0 in the second leg in Spain, even though Giuseppe Bergomi had been hit by a hard object apparently thrown from the stands after half an hour. The Italians formally protested, but the score stood.

The second UEFA Cup win came against F.C. Köln, but once again semifinal games versus Inter Milan were the real story. At the San Siro in the first leg, Inter beat Real 3–1, but in the second leg, three penalties out of five goals scored on the night left the tie tied after 90 minutes, 4–4. Up stepped Santillana, the Spanish forward with a Brazilian-style name, who in a sparkling career of nearly 20 years' duration scored nearly 200 goals for Real Madrid. Santillana's two in extra time that night took Madrid to the final, where they went one down in the first half hour to F.C. Köln, then scored five unanswered goals (the second leg ended 2–0 to the Germans, but no one really cared). That team of Hugo Sanchez, Michel, Jorge Valdano, Martín Vázquez, and Emilio Butragueño should probably have won more than two UEFA Cups and five La Liga titles in a row. That's how crazy it is to assess a team like Real Madrid—all that silverware, and yet they didn't quite hit their full potential.

Another European Cup came in 1998, as Predrag Mijatović scored the only goal of a tense and dull game against Juventus. That Juve team boasted Deschamps, Davids, Zidane, Inzaghi, and Del Piero, some of whom had won the Cup in 1996, and lost it in 1997. Of the three great late-nineties' Juventus teams, the one that lost to Real should never have done so. But that Real team of Mijatović, Raúl, and Seedorf wasn't too shabby either—they won the Intercontinental Cup over a very strong Vasco da Gama that year.

In 2000, another fine Real team, featuring Steve McManaman, Raúl, Morientes, and others, walked over Valencia in the rechristened Champions League final. By the new century, Real had also won 27 La Liga titles to add to their eight European crowns.

And so to the time of the *galacticos*. Since the beginning of the new century, Real Madrid had doubled down on its commitment to bringing the latest, greatest superstars to play at the Bernabéu. It seems now that all any player ever wants to do, once he reaches his peak performance, is head to Madrid and don the all-white strip. It doesn't always make for winning teams, however. The roll call is jaw-dropping: David Beckham, Zinedine Zidane, Roberto Carlos, Luis Figo, Ronaldo (the fatter, Brazilian one), Ronaldo (the hotter, Portuguese one), Kaká, van Nistelrooy, Gareth Bale . . . Trophies included the 2002 Champions League, via a 2–1 win over Bayer Leverkusen that was graced by probably the greatest goal ever scored in the final of that tournament, a left-foot volley by Zidane on half-time that owed as much to genius as it did to perfect technique; and the Intercontinental Cup that same year, over Olimpia of Paraguay.

For a while after that, Barcelona overtook Real Madrid at home, in Europe, and on the world stage. The "vintage Real Madrid" is sometimes stifled by teams created by massive spending, with no great thought about how to make the side jell, though in 2014 they won their record tenth European crown behind the steallar play of Cristiano Ronaldo and Gareth Bale. Watching these two go running off down the wings against city rivals Atlético in the final, their teammates happy to watch, was to realize that despite the extra-time victory, the only way *galacticos* dominate for a generation is by remembering, like Di Stéfano, Rial, Puskás, and other early greats did, that soccer games are won by eleven players, not one or two.

Location	Belgrade, Serbia
Established	1945
Nicknames	*Crveno-beli* ("The Red-Whites"), *Zvezda* ("The Star")
Current stadium	Red Star Stadium, a.k.a. Marakana (53,000 capacity)
Home colors	Red and white
Leading goal-scorer	Dragan Džajić (1963–75, 1977–78), 287 goals
Most appearances	Dragan Džajić (1963–75, 1977–78), 590 appearances

Major General Josip Jović, a 21-year old Croatian police officer, was riding a bus in the Plitvice Lakes park near the Serbian border. It was the last day of March 1991. He hadn't made the rank of major general at the age of 21, of course. Josip Jović was shot and killed by Serbian forces as he rode that bus, becoming the first mortal casualty of what would become the Croatian war of independence; for whatever it's worth, Jović was posthumously promoted.

It was the start of a terrible time in what would become "the former Yugoslavia." The amalgam of competing ethnic and national forces that General Tito had somehow kept together would fly apart in the worst conflict Europe had seen since 1945.

A couple of weeks after Jović's death, the top club side in the region faced a two-leg European Cup semifinal. But how could football fans concentrate on such a thing with Yugoslavia at boiling point? It would take an extraordinary couple of games to take people's minds away from the looming war, if only for 180 minutes. And that's exactly what happened when Red Star Belgrade faced Bayern Munich that "bloody Easter" in 1991.

Red Star Belgrade were founded after World War II, as Serbian Communists took over what was left of S.K. Jugoslavija, a team that had been disbanded by Tito for playing games during the war. In 1951 Red Star won their first championship, and by the late fifties they had joined Real Madrid and Manchester United as one of the dominant European teams. In 1957, Red Star narrowly lost to Fiorentina in a semifinal of the European Cup, while Real Madrid knocked out United in the other; the following year, United faced Red Star in the quarterfinals of the same competition. In the first leg, United came back from one down to win 2–1, their "Busby Babes" team of youthful stars showing that they were going to be something very special. In the second leg in Belgrade, United ran to a 3–0 lead in half an hour, but Red Star were a fine team, too, and three second-half goals squared the match, though United went through 5–4 on aggregate. It had been a brilliant game, lit up by both Matt Busby's stirring young team and Red Star's quality side, who had already won four championships in five years. On the flight home from Belgrade, United stopped over in Munich, and on a third attempt to take off in bad weather, their plane crashed through a fence and disintegrated, killing 23 on board, including many of Busby's Babes. The Red Devils of Manchester would forever be mournfully linked with the Red Stars of Belgrade.

Red Star came close to the European Cup final once again in 1971. A 4–1 home win against Greek side Panathinaikos seemed to secure their spot, only for their nerve to fail in Greece, where Red Star lost 3–0 and went out on away goals. More domestic success eased some of the pain, however, and by the end of the 1980s Red Star had won a cool 16 Yugoslav titles. They would win the last three, too, from 1990 to 1992, before the country went all to hell.

But before the war fully kicked into bloody gear, Red Star fans, led by the war criminal and all-round psycho known as Arkan, had traveled to Zagreb in 1990 to pitch a riot against Dinamo fans. Almost a year later, they found themselves in that classic, two-leg European Cup semifinal against Bayern Munich.

In the first leg, in Munich's Olympic Stadium, Red Star scored one of the greatest team goals ever seen. An attack by Munich floundered in Red Star's right back position when the great Michael Laudrup couldn't quite reach a pass two feet beyond him. Red Star's tough defender, Slobodan Marović, cleared to Duško Radinović who nonchalantly tapped a sweet left-footed sideways pass to Miodrag Belodedici, who in turn cleared to one of the greatest ever Belgrade players, Croat Robert Prosinečki. Prosinečki curled a brilliant pass down the right side where super-fast Dragiša Binić left the Bayern defense behind. A smart low cross to the far post, and Darko Pančev slammed the ball over the despairing dive of Raimond Aumann in the Bayern goal. From the time Marovic passed to Radinovic to start the move, to the moment Pancev took his shot, ten brief seconds had elapsed. The ball had traveled about 120 yards (about 100 meters). Red Star had just scored a goal in Olympic 100 meters qualifying time, in Munich's Olympic Stadium.

The game would end 2–1; in the second leg, Red Star got cocky and went down 2–1 themselves. Bayern hit the post late on, which would have almost certainly put the Belgrade team out. But with regular time up, a cross from Siniša Mihajlović was miskicked high into the Belgrade night by Klaus Augenthaler, who had scored Bayern's first goal that night. The ball seemed to hang, then swerve, then shoot to earth, where Aumann, the keeper, appeared nonplussed to find a leather orb hurtling toward him at such a strange angle. The German did his best to slap the ball over the bar, but he got it horribly wrong and merely punched the ball into the back of the net. That was that—4–3 on aggregate to Red Star, and they were on their way to the European Cup final. The two games against Bayern had produced some of the most dramatic football ever seen in the tournament, but now minds turned to other matters.

The final, against Marseille, was played on May 29, 1991, in Bari, Italy. Earlier that month, one of the first major clashes between Croats and Serbs had occurred in Borovo Selo, in the east of Croatia. There had been reports of atrocities committed against Croatian police, and Yugoslavia was spiraling out of control. The cup final hardly mattered against this backdrop; Red Star, so vibrant and fast and brilliant in the Bayern games, had clearly decided to blockade all thoughts of finesse, defending resolutely and seemingly hoping they'd make it to penalties. The terrible game, played at a terrible time, ended 0–0, and Red Star won 5–3 on penalties when Darko Pančev buried the fifth, Manuel Amoros having missed for Marseille.

It was to be the last great moment for Red Star. Subsequently, Serbian and Montenegrin, and then just Serbian, teams went off to play in their own league. And when they did, Partizan Belgrade, with whom Red Star share one of the most vibrant and often violent local derbies in the world, gained ascendancy. Red Star has won seven titles since 1992–93, when the breakup of the country and its leagues occurred, whereas Partizan has won 14.

Perhaps postwar Serbia has been too good to many of Red Star's stars. In July 2013, the *Daily Mail* reported that manager Slaviša Stojanović warned his players that "if you keep eating meat pies before practice and drinking two or three beers after it . . . you will amount to nothing."

Location	Buenos Aires, Argentina
Established	1901
Nicknames	*Los Millonarios* ("The Millionaires"), La Maquira ("The Machine")
Stadium	El Monumental, officially Estadio Monumental Antonio Vespucio Liberti (68,000 capacity)
Home colors	Black, white, and red
Leading goal-scorer	Ángel Labruna (1939–59), 293 goals
Most appearances	Amadeo Carrizo (1945–68), 520 matches

There were 20 minutes to go—20 minutes in which River Plate had to score two goals to avoid relegation. In their more than a century of playing soccer, they had never before dropped to the second division. This was a club that had won the Argentine title 35 times. By 2011, they were on the edge of an abyss.

The relegation playoff started well. Their opponents, Belgrano, had already had a goal disallowed when, after just five minutes, River Plate snatched the lead, on a fine right-footed drive by Mariano Pavone. One more unanswered goal, and River Plate would save their souls.

Rich souls they've been, too. Established, like their closest rivals Boca Juniors, in the docks section of Buenos Aires, River Plate soon fled the hardscrabble waterfront to more distant suburbs, and a spending spree in the early 1930s brought them the nickname they still wear, *Los Millonarios*. As a result of their love of a deal, they dominated for two decades either side of World War II, from the mid-1930s until 1957, when they simply stopped winning. In the 1940s, especially, they played a brand of keep-ball that prefigured the possession dominance of modern-day Barcelona. Along the way they picked up a new nickname, *La Maquina*, for their machine-like attacking verve, based around the free-drinking Juan Carlos Muñoz, and others, including José Moreno, Felix Loustau, and Ángel Labruna. Labruna still holds the Argentine record for goals scored—293—and he would later manage the club, bringing along the great Daniel Passarella, among others.

In 1943, at age 17, Buenos Aires boy and future superstar Alfredo Di Stéfano arrived at River Plate, and once he made it to the first team, in just 66 games he scored 49 goals, before leaving in 1949 for a club actually called Millonarios, in Colombia. There, Di Stéfano kept up his goal-scoring exploits with 90 in 102 games. By 1953 Di Stéfano was in Madrid, where he starred for a Real team that dominated European football for a decade; once again, his goal-per-game ratio was incredible: 216 goals in 284 games.

For Di Stéfano's hometown club, however, the run of victories ended as the sixties bled into the first half of the seventies. Back in 1966, River Plate had faced their first true heartache, losing a third playoff game, in Santiago, in the Copa Libertadores final against Uruguayan side Peñarol. Two up at half-time, and cruising, River Plate somehow conspired to let in two goals in six second-half minutes, and two more in six extra-time minutes. A third and perjorative nickname accrued: *Gallinas*, or, chickens. And it would start a strange run of appearing in a Copa final every ten years, on the sixes, from 1966 to 1996.

So a decade had to pass. With "the Kaiser," Passarella, anchoring a fine team coached by legend Labruna, River Plate finally won a raft of championships in the seventies, though once again in the Copa Libertadores they failed at the final hurdle: once again in a third playoff game, once again in Santiago, and once again very late on (Brazilian side Cruzeiro beat them with an 88th-minute winner). But they were still rich, having one team for domestic games and an equally good one for Copa Libertadores matches.

The curse was lifted in 1986 when River Plate finally won the Copa Libertadores. Behind legends Norberto Alonso and Juan *"El Búfalo"* Funes, they bested América de Cali, of Colombia. That same year, a dull Intercontinental Cup final saw River Plate dispatch Steaua Bucharest, 1–0, to become nominal world champions.

That River Plate team featured a young Hernán Crespo, in his last season before his record-breaking move to Italy, where he wouldn't score for the first six months, and then could do nothing but score.

In their long history, River Plate have amassed 35 national titles, and an alumni list from the modern era to rival any team, including Mario Kempes, Alberto Tarantini, Gabriel Batistuta, Martín Demichelis, Javier Mascherano, Marcelo Salas, Radamel Falcão, and many others. But they were, like many South American teams facing financial constraints, a selling club, and still huge debts accrued—which is why, in 2013, they faced a two-game playoff against Belgrano to avoid a first trip to the second level of Argentine football.

After Mariano Pavone had given River Plate the lead, they had held till half-time. But in the second half, Belgrano, a small club from the second division who would be promoted if they beat River Plate, equalized after hilariously bad River Plate defending. Then fortune seemed to smile on the Buenos Aires club—a clear dive in the box fooled the referee into awarding a penalty. Up stepped Pavone to strike a strong shot to the right of the keeper. But it wasn't strong enough; Belgrano's keeper smothered the ball, and the air seemed to hiss out of the Estadio Monumental.

The game never ended. Rioting fans forced an early finish, and with the River Plate players in tears in the center of the field, seats rained down, fires were lit, police officers injured—all the usual efforts of heartsick fans. River Plate went down, but they won the lower division and came back up to win a 36th national title in 2014. They were *Millonarios* once again.

Location	Rome, Italy
Established	1927
Nicknames	*I Giallorossi* ("The Yellow-Reds"), *La Maggica* ("The Magic One"), *I Lupi* ("The Wolves")
Current stadium	Stadio Olimpico, Rome (capacity 70,634)
Home colors	Red and yellow
Leading goal-scorer	Francesco Totti (1992–), 285 goals
Most appearances	Francesco Totti (1992–), 685 appearances

For a team hailing from one of the great capital cities in one of the great soccer nations of the world, A.S. Roma really haven't lived up to their billing. In their 87-year-history they've managed to win only three Serie A championships—compare that to Juventus of Turin's 29, or the 18 each won by the two Milanese teams, A.C. and Inter, or even lowly Genoa's nine. A.S. Roma seems to get by on trying to win two games a year, both against arch Rome rivals Lazio. But their history is not without highlights, and none is more notable than the story of Adriana and Antonietta Amadei, whose sacrifice brought Roma its first taste of the big time.

A.S. Roma was originally three different Rome-based teams—Fortitudo-Proroma, Roma Football Club, and Alba-Audace—amalgamated in 1927 by Mussolini and the Fascists into Associazione Sportiva Roma for one express purpose: to break the stranglehold of northern-based clubs. (Lazio refused to join.) Between 1929, when the real Italian championship was established, and 1941, the winners had all been northern teams: Juventus five times, Bologna four times, and Inter Milan three. Then along came Amedeo Amadei, brother to Adriana and Antonietta.

The Amadei family was avowedly blue-collar. The patriarch was a baker in the town of Frascati, a handsome town in the Alban hills 12 miles southeast of the capital. Amedeo was born in 1927, and by the time he could work he was made to do so, as a *"casherino,"* selling bread to local stores. In his spare time it was football, and by his early teens Amedeo had decided to try out for the newly formed Roma club. There were two problems: getting time off to attend a tryout, and convincing his father he should be allowed to play if selected.

In stepped Amedeo's sisters. Having lied that he'd spent a day cycling around the Alban hills and had suffered a punctured tire, Amedeo had to eventually admit that he'd attended an open tryout for A.S. Roma and had been picked. Mr. Amadei the baker was having none of it, until Adriana and Antonietta promised they'd make up the slack.

And so, on the back of their backs, Amedeo Amadei ran out to play for A.S. Roma on May 2, 1937, at the ridiculously young age of 15. He is still the youngest ever player in the top Italian league (and the one who most resembled, physically at least, French superstar Eric Cantona—the likeness is remarkable), as well as the youngest ever to score. Just a week after his debut, on May 9, he notched Roma's only goal in a 5–1 thrashing by the Tuscan team Lucchese Libertas (now of Serie D). After a brief stint on loan to Atalanta, Amadei returned to Roma right as World War II was starting. The Italian league, uniquely in Europe, plowed ahead despite the devastation all around, and in 1942 the first non-northern team was crowned champions: A.S. Roma, who lost only four games all season and were led by 18-goal stalwart Amedeo Amadei, playing at the head of a now fashionable diamond formation.

But that was about it; northern Italy's dominance reasserted itself in the form of one of its greatest ever teams, the mid-century Torino team that would be so cruelly wiped out in a plane crash in 1949. Even with the loss of that legendary side, the north continued to dominate the top league in Italy. It would be 1969 before a southern team, in the form of Cagliari, would win the league again, and since then southern teams have won Serie A only six times, A.S. Roma accounting for two, in 1983 and 2001. That 2001 team featured Francesco Totti, whom many consider to be Roma's greatest ever player—as one banner read, "No Totti, No Party"—but also Cafu, Zanetti, de Rossi, Montella, Samuel, Emerson, 20 goals from Argentinian superstar Gabriel Batistuta, and coaching from Fabio Capello.

In European competition, A.S. Roma have flattered to deceive. In 1999, as just one example, they knocked a Bobby Robson-managed, Alan Shearer-led Newcastle United out of the UEFA Cup, only to lose in the next round to a poor Leeds United side. They have also lost two Champions League quarterfinals in successive seasons to Manchester United—the second leg in Manchester in 2007 ended 7–1 to United.

Roma's finest moment was making it to the final of the 1984 European Cup, once more against British opposition—Liverpool—but it proved to be a game littered with ill luck for the Italian team. After 15 minutes the Roma keeper, Franco Tancredi, fumbled a cross, and the subsequent clearance cannoned off Tancredi's head (he was lying on the ground) and into the path of Phil Neal, Liverpool's right back, who buried the comical chance. Though Roma equalized just before half-time, a second-half onslaught brought no more goals for the Italian side, and the final went to the first penalty shootout in European Cup history. That shootout is now famous for Liverpool goalkeeper Bruce Grobbelaar standing on the goal line of Rome's Olympic Stadium—yes, Roma lost the final *at home*—and "[indulging] in some spaghetti-legs, circus antics," as British commentator Des Lynam later described it. Roma's center forward Francesco Graziani, clearly confused by Grobbelaar's wobble, contrived to blast the ball against the bar and over; Liverpool then scored to win the trophy.

And so from debacle to spectacle: the Rome derby, which is one of the most vibrant in world soccer. Fascist politics aside—Lazio fans delight in horrifying the world, and especially Roma fans, with their racist chanting and banners, such as *"Auschwitz La Vostra Patria, I Forni Le Vostre Case"* ("Auschwitz is Your Homeland, Ovens Your Homes")—winning the Derby della Capitale amounts to almost everything for A.S. Roma. Meanwhile, northern teams continue to dominate Serie A and to look to a wider world.

SAN JOSE EARTHQUAKES

Location	San Jose, California, USA
Established	1974
Nicknames	Quakes, The Goonies
Stadium	Buck Shaw Stadium (10,525 capacity)
Home colors	Blue, black, white, and silver
Leading goal-scorer	Ronald Cerritos (1997–2001, 2005), 61 goals
Most appearances	John Doyle (1987, 1996–2000), 132 appearances

They became the preeminent Major League Soccer franchise, and then they went away, taking their best player with them. The San Jose Earthquakes, playing as the Clash, were a charter member of the post-US World Cup MLS, joining nine other teams in 1996; they even played in the first ever MLS game, a 1–0 win over D.C. United. Their history stretches back before the shiny new league, however. For 14 years, they had been the Earthquakes in the North American Soccer League, though even with former Manchester United legend George Best on their roster they'd never managed to win anything. After a brief spell as the Blackhawks, the franchise folded, until it was revived as the Clash, in 1994, in readiness for MLS.

And then, for five years, nothing much happened. The Clash may have boasted Eric Wynalda in its ranks, then probably the best American player, but five managers in the first five years showed that the scrabble for success in San Jose was unsuccessful. Average attendances hovered in the 14,000 range, until one young man changed everything: Landon Donovan.

The future face of American soccer showed up in San Jose in

March 2001, after two years as an underutilized forward at Bayer Leverkusen in Germany. Just 19 years old, Donovan joined the newly renamed Earthquakes and its newly strong roster, which included Dwayne De Rosario, Ronald Cerritos, Manny Lagos, and Jeff Agoos. Coached by Frank Yallop, the Earthquake would go all the way to the MLS Cup final.

Played against the backdrop of 9/11, which had occurred just a month previously, the all-Californian final was an emotional, and excellent, game. Twenty minutes in, L.A., which had lost two previous MLS finals, in 1996 and 1999, took the lead on a strike by Luis Hernández. But Donovan and his blond-frosted hairstyle shimmered with attacking intent, and two minutes before half-time, having been left unmarked by the L.A. defense, he thundered a first-time shot into the top right-hand corner of the net.

The second half saw no more scoring, and so to golden goals, that brief, unloved rule in which a goal scored in extra time immediately ended the game. It took just six minutes. Dwayne De Rosario picked up the ball wide left, took on the retreating defender, and drilled a ball beyond the despairing dive of the keeper. San Jose had won its first MLS Cup.

Two years later, San Jose made it to the final once again, and along the way managed to play in a game for the ages. Once again, the opponents were the L.A. Galaxy. It was November 9, 2003; the second leg of the Western Conference semifinal. The first leg had seen L.A. win with two unanswered second-half goals. In San Jose for the second leg, L.A. scored two more after just 13 minutes, meaning San Jose had to score five to advance. Few of the 14,000 fans in attendance would have given the home team a chance. But by half-time, Agoos, after a fine free-kick routine, and Donovan, from a seemingly impossible angle, had at least tied the game on the night, though they still needed three more goals to win the tie.

Five minutes into the second half, it was 3–2 to San Jose, on a header by Jamil Walker, but for all their pressure, the Earthquakes couldn't get the vital fourth goal to send the game to extra time. With

89:01 on the clock, a searching cross from Richard Mulrooney on the right found the head of handsome Chris "Thor" Roner at the back post. Thor made no mistake and ran away handsomely, where he was happily mobbed by a bunch of Earthquake players less handsome than he. Golden goals beckoned, and once again it took just six minutes, as Rodrigo Faria ran clear of the L.A. defense and slammed the ball home. From 4–0 down, San Jose had won 5–4.

The final that year was an anticlimax by comparison, though it was still a terrific game. Two up at half-time against the Chicago Fire, the second half was a back-and-forth affair, with San Jose finally winning 4–2, Donovan scoring his second and the decisive goal of the night in the 70th minute. San Jose had its second MLS Cup.

By the start of the following year, things started to go south for the Earthquakes. A mooted rebranding as San Jose America led to then general manager Johnny Moore's resignation. Moore was replaced by Alexi Lalas, who not only let Donovan be traded to the L.A. Galaxy, but also oversaw the beginnings of a proposed move of the franchise to Houston. When a much-needed soccer-only stadium in the San Jose area never materialized, the Earthquakes packed up and left; by the 2006 MLS season, the San Jose Earthquakes were the Houston Dynamo.

It took until 2008 for the San Jose franchise to be re-established in California. For four of the six seasons since, they have failed to reach the playoffs.

SANTOS

Location	Santos, Brazil
Established	1912
Nicknames	*Peixe* ("Fish"), *Santástico* ("Santastic"), *Alvinegro praiano* ("Black and white of the beach")
Stadium	Vila Belmiro (16,798 capacity)
Home colors	Black and white
Leading goal-scorer	Edson Arantes do Nascimento, known as Pelé (1956–74), 1,091 goals
Most appearances	Edson Arantes do Nascimento, known as Pelé (1956–74), 1,116 appearances

ânio da Silva Quadros was president of Brazil for just seven months at the start of 1961, but in that brief time he tried to ban bikinis (in Brazil!). On the positive side, he did one thing for which he'll always be remembered: Quadros declared the 20-year-old Edson Arantes do Nascimento, a.k.a. Pelé, a "national treasure."

Fans of Santos F.C. can be forever grateful to the short-lived President Quadros, because in addition to his exploits for the Brazilian national team—which are legendary—at the club level Santos was Pelé, and Pelé was Santos. Quadros's quixotic order meant that no foreign team would be allowed to lure the "Black Pearl" away, and the effect was to help Santos become, alongside Real Madrid, probably the greatest club side of the 1960s.

They were formed in 1912, in the port town of Santos, which lies 50 miles south of São Paulo. Santos boomed at the turn of the last century thanks to—you guessed it—coffee exports, and today it's the busiest seaport in Latin America. In 1913, the club won their first trophy, the Santos City Soccer Championship, but it wasn't until 1935 that they won the Campeonato Paulista, the regional championship of São Paulo state. It would be another 20 years before they won another, but by then the young man nicknamed Pelé (no one knows why he was called that, by the way, and at first he hated it) was dominating the São Paulo state youth championships, leading his team, Bauru Athletic, to three straight titles from 1954 to 1956.

In that last year Pelé, at the age of just 15, joined Santos, and so began a love affair that lasted for nearly 20 years. In 1958, Pelé dominated the World Cup, scoring at will and leading Brazil to their first title; three years later, he did the same for Santos as they won their first Brazilian title. There followed a period of utter domination for Pelé and Santos—they would win the Campeonato Brasileiro every year from 1961 through 1965, and once again in 1968. On the international stage, Santos would win both the Copa Libertadores and the Intercontinental Cup, in both 1962 and 1963.

In 1962, in the final of the Copa Libertadores, Santos faced Peñarol of Uruguay, a team that had won the first two Copa Libertadores tournaments. A relatively undramatic first leg for this third ever tournament in Montevideo ended 2–1 to Santos; with Pelé out injured, their two goals were scored by his striking partner and fellow legend, Coutinho. The second leg was another thing altogether.

The game was chippy from the start, and often seemed to have more cameramen, police, fans, and staff on the field than players. As for the football, well, after 51 minutes the score was 3–2 to visiting Peñarol—Pelé was still missing through injury, and Santos faced losing the trophy in front of their home fans (though there were only 18,000 of them, Santos being a small place with a small stadium). As Santos prepared to take a corner, referee Carlos Robles was hit by a bottle—he woke up a long while later in the dressing room. There, he claimed, he was threatened by Santos officials who said that they could not vouch for his safety if the game was abandoned. Back on the field against his will, he told the players that the rest of the game wouldn't count but that they should play it so that he wasn't lynched; the message didn't seem to get through to the Santos players, who scored late on via Pagão and thought they'd won the game. But another missile hit a linesman after the goal, Robles canceled the game for good, and though the newspapers the next day featured headlines like *"O Santos empatou: e campeao de America"* ("Santos drew, are champions of the Americas"), the truth was that a third game would be needed to decide the title.

For that game, played in Buenos Aires, Pelé was back, and his two second-half goals added to an own goal from the first half to give Santos their first Copa Libertadores. The subsequent Intercontinental Cup cemented Pelé's worldwide reputation after his exploits in the 1962 World Cup had been hampered by injury (the same injury that kept him out of the first two Copa Libertadores final games). In the two legs of the Intercontinental final against fellow Portuguese-speaking Benfica, he scored five times—twice in the first game, and then a hat-trick in Lisbon, a game Pelé himself described as the best he ever played. Eusébio's Benfica had no answer, and Santos won 7–4 on aggregate.

The following year Santos repeated both titles. Coutinho scored three goals in the two legs against Argentina's Boca Juniors in the Copa final, and Pelé iced the cake in Buenos Aires, scoring the second of Santos's two goals with eight minutes to go—they won 5–3 on aggregate. This led to the Intercontinental Cup final, against A.C. Milan. Both ties, home and away, finished 4–2 to the home team. In the first game, in Milan, Pelé scored both of Santos's goals after Giovanni Trapattoni, who would go on to manaage numerous European club sides as well as the Republic of Ireland, had opened the scoring with just three minutes on the clock. The second game saw a crowd of more than 130,000 show up, but no Pelé, and still no result; a third game would again be needed. This one was less goal-packed than the first two—Pelé was again missing—and was decided on a penalty by Santos defender Dalmo.

And then, the amazing run of success was over. Santos, faced with financial strains caused by the tiny size of their fanbase and the onerous requirements of traveling around the Americas, stopped taking part in the Copa Libertadores. Instead, they traveled the world, parlaying Pelé and his teammates into huge crowds and big income in exhibition games around the globe. It was a sad end to the competitive nature of the club, and after that solitary Brazilian title in 1968, it would be the new century before they got back to the highest level.

And it would take the emergence of a new precocious talent to bring Santos back into winning ways. The Copa Libertadores of 2011 saw the explosion of Neymar onto the world stage. At just 19, and unburdened by any thoughts of being made a national treasure, Neymar played in 13 games in the tournament and scored six goals, but it was the nature of his play that had fans wondering if Pelé's ghost had finally been laid to rest. In the Copa final, Santos once again found themselves up against Peñarol, and no doubt hoping that no one threw objects at the officiating crew. The first leg in Montevideo ended in a goalless draw, but back in São Paulo Neymar opened the scoring just after half-time, and Santos went on to win 2–1 and clinch the title. A month later, Neymar scored a goal in a Brazilian league game against Flamengo that probably sealed his eventual move to Barcelona: cutting in from the left wing, he took a return pass and headed for the penalty box. Surrounded by four defenders, he rolled the ball under his right foot and then knocked it past a defender with his left—the poor guy probably needed a hip replacement after the game, so pretzeled was he. Neymar still had the keeper to beat, which he did with a fancy flick with the outside of his right foot.

It was an astonishing goal and deservedly won the FIFA Puskás Award, given to the "most beautiful goal of the year." But Neymar failed to score in the FIFA Club World Cup that year, as Barcelona trounced Santos 4–0. Perhaps the young Brazilian watched in awe, or jealousy—either way, though he won South American Footballer of the Year in 2011 and 2012, clouds were clearly rolling in. By May 26, 2013, he was crying as the national anthem played before his final game for Santos, and by month's end he was a Barcelona player. There was no law against it as there had been for Pelé—just as bikinis are still legal all over the beaches of Brazil.

SÃO PAULO

Location	São Paulo, Brazil
Established	1930
Nicknames	*Tricolor, Soberano* ("Sovereign"), *O Mais Rico* ("The Richest")
Stadium	Morumbi (66,795 capacity)
Home colors	Red, white, and black
Leading goal-scorer	Serginho Chulapa (1973–83), 240 goals
Most appearances	Rogério Ceni (1992–), 800 appearances

Armelino Donizetti Quagliato is smiling, an avuncular, calm man, happy to tell a simple story. For the interview, he is sitting in front of a soccer goal, a ball just over the line by the left-hand post. As imagery goes, it's neither subtle nor historically accurate.

Because Zetti, as Quagliato was better known, made his greatest save down by just such a left post, on the night of June 17, 1992. Zetti was playing for Brazilian side São Paulo against Argentina's Newell's Old Boys in the final of the Copa Libertadores, and the game had come down to a penalty shootout. So far, Zetti hadn't had to make a save, yet Newell's had missed two penalties—the first, when Eduardo Barizzo pushed his shot wide right, and the fourth, when Alfredo Mendoza skied his penalty about 20 feet over the bar. São Paulo had scored three of their four, so as Fernando Gamboa, a Newell's defender, stepped up, Zetti knew that a save would give São Paulo their first Copa Libertadores title.

It had been a long time coming. São Paulo were finally established as São Paulo in 1930, but their roots go back to the start of that century.

Charles Miller, who was half English but grew up in Brazil, spent time back in Britain at school in the latter part of the nineteenth century, where he played football. Eventually, Miller got some games for Southampton, which had been founded in 1885. Bringing footballs back to São Paulo, Miller created a team for his fellow British and German immigrants, but it was only for them. Football remained an amateur, society-obsessed sport well into the new century. By 1930, professionalism was coming to Brazilian soccer, and when Paulistano, another team from São Paulo, resisted, some of their players and members joined with some of Palmeiras's players to form what we now know as São Paulo F.C.

São Paulo quickly set about winning the Campeonato Paulista— five times in the 1940s (they had also won it in 1931). They would win a couple more in the fifties, and then nothing until 1970 and 1971, when they won the prestigious local title back to back. It took until 1977 for São Paulo to win their first national championship, a title they've won five times since (they've won 21 Campeonato Paulistas). But São Paulo are best known for being a formidable team in the Copa Libertadores.

Their first appearance in a Libertadores final came in 1974, a tie they lost to Independiente of Argentina after a third playoff game (the first two matches had been shared). But nearly 20 years later, São Paulo created a team that would feature in three finals in a row, all thanks to a genius coach called Telê Santana.

Santana helped put together two of the best Brazilian national teams ever assembled, neither of which managed to win the World Cup. Featuring legends such as Socrates, Zico, Serginho, Eder, Falcão, and Junior, the 1982 Brazil team famously lost 3–2 to Italy in one of the great World Cup games. Santana was criticized for being too enamored of *joga bonita*, the beautiful game, when he might have played more defensively (Brazil only had to draw to advance). Four years later, Santana failed again, this time with a team still featuring Socrates plus Alemão, Júlio César, and Falcão and Zico on the bench. *Joga bonita* couldn't really be blamed this time—Socrates missed the first penalty of a shootout against France, and though Platini missed his, too, Brazil went out 4–3.

It took Santana until 1990 to reach São Paulo (he managed five other Brazilian club teams after the 1986 World Cup), and immediately he built another wonderful team, and one that would dominate the first half of the decade. Players like Cafu, Leonardo, and Rai would go on to anchor the 1990 and 1994 Brazilian World Cup teams (the latter side would win it in the United States), but it was for São Paulo that these stars originally shone. Having won the Paulista and the national championship in 1991, and the Paulista again in 1992, São Paulo finally reached that Copa Libertadores final in 1992, where Zetti faced Gamboa. The penalty was a good one, but Zetti threw himself to his left and turned the ball around his left post. São Paulo were champions.

Six months later, São Paulo beat a wonderful Barcelona team in Tokyo to win the Intercontinental Cup. It was some victory. Rai scored twice, once in each half, against a Barça side made up of Zubizaretta in goal, Ronald Koeman at the back, Pep Guardiola, José Mari Bakero, Hristo Stoichkov, and Txiki Begiristain in midfield, Michael Laudrup up front, and Johan Cruyff on the coach's bench. The first goal came as Müller burned the very fine right back, Albert Ferrer, for pace, then decided to twist his blood a bit more before squaring for Rai, who beat Koeman to the ball to score. The second was even better, Rai curling a tapped indirect free kick the wrong way over the wall and into the top left-hand corner. Zubizaretta simply watched and admired; it was the perfect free kick, and a wonderful way to assert that you are a) the captain of Brazil, b) the captain of the Copa Libertadores champions, São Paulo, c) now the captain of the best team in the world, and d) out of the shadow of your elder brother, Socrates.

The following year, São Paulo repeated as Copa Libertadores champions. The two-legged final, against Universidad Católica of Chile, was effectively over after an hour, when Rai scored São Paulo's fourth goal. The game ended 5–1; the 100,000 fans packed into São Paulo's Estádio do Morumbi knew their team had one hand and about four fingers of the other on the trophy. Some hearts must have been aflutter in the second leg back in Santiago, however, when Universidad Católica scored twice in the first 15 minutes—but that was the end of the goals, and São Paulo had a deserved second Copa in a row.

They would repeat in the Intercontinental Cup, too. São Paulo should have been facing the winners of the 1993 Champions League, Marseille, but they had been banned after fixing matches, so A.C. Milan, the losing finalists, traveled to the National Stadium in Tokyo to face the South American champions.

It was a wonderful game. The Milan side was, like the Barça team the year before, one for the ages: Panucci, Baresi, Maldini, Costacurta at the back—you could begin and end right there. Add in Desailly, Albertini, Donadoni, and Papin, and São Paulo were up against it. But their team was no slouch: Rai had left for Paris St. Germain, but Cerezo now graced midfield, alongside Leonardo, and Müller and Palhinha were up front, all ahead of Cafu and keeper Zetti at the back.

What the 52,000 mostly Japanese fans got was a five-goal thriller. After just 19 minutes, a sweeping three-pass, left-to-right move ended when Palhinha slammed a cross home past Rossi in the Milan goal. That was how it stayed until the second half, when, three minutes in, Milan equalized via Daniele Massaro's brilliantly difficult finish from a huge, lobbed pass by Desailly. The ball must have gone 50 feet in the air but Massaro never flinched, ran on to it, and half-volleyed the probably ice-covered pill through Zetti's legs.

Eleven minutes later it was 2–1 to São Paulo, after Leonardo surged past Panucci at right back and crossed for Cerezo to tap in. Milan weren't done, however; their second goal was another brilliant effort. A lobbed pass by Donadoni was back-headed—who does that?—by striker Florin Răducioiu into the path of Papin, who buried his own header past Zetti. Răducioiu's vision defines "eyes in the back of the head," as well as "genius."

How would these two teams be separated after four brilliant goals? By the inside of a right ankle, of course. With just two minutes left, a lovely curved ball over the top of the Milan defense by Cerezo bounced between an onrushing keeper (Rossi) and Müller, but the Brazilian turned his back on the challenge. Somehow, the keeper's clearance struck Müller hard on his trailing right foot and ballooned into the net. It was a farcical way to end a wonderful game of football.

So for two years, São Paulo had been South American and world champions, led by Rai and coached by Santana. But in 1994, a Chila-vert-led Vélez Sarsfield beat São Paulo on penalties in the Copa Libertadores. At the World Cup, former star Rai was deposed from the Brazilian World Cup captaincy and warmed the bench. By 1996, Santana had suffered a stroke and retired; two years later, Rai returned for a swan song in São Paulo, though the team would have to wait seven more years before winning another major trophy.

When they did so, it was with an entirely new team, singularly lacking in superstars. But they made it to a couple of Copa Libertadores finals, in 2005 and 2006.

In the first, two teams from the same country squared off. Facing São Paulo were Atlético Paranaense, a team hailing from Curitiba, some 250 miles southwest of São Paulo. The first game, held even further south in Porto Alegre, ended 1–1, but the return leg was no contest, São Paulo waltzing past Paranaense, 4–0. Their last goal that night, in the 89th minute, was scored by Diego Tardelli. Tardelli's father gave him the surname in honor of Marco Tardelli, the Italian midfielder who scored a fabulous goal against Germany in the 1982 World Cup, a goal now more famous for the greatest goal celebration ever caught on camera, in which Tardelli runs away, fists shaking out to his sides, his face a rictus of extreme joy and disbelief. Diego Tardelli's goal celebration that night, in Estádio do Morumbi, had a vague resemblance to that of his namesake: the same look of disbelief, the same arms outstretched, and the run, arcing away from the goal into the joyous night.

Once again, São Paulo followed up their Libertadores triumph with a victory in the intercontinental tournament, now called the FIFA Club World Championship. In the final, they beat Liverpool 1–0 on a fine run and finish by Mineiro, Liverpool missing numerous chances to equalize (Luis Garcia had three headers either miss or hit the woodwork; Steven Gerrard also went close a couple of times).

The following year, another all-Brazilian final saw São Paulo lose 4–3 on aggregate to Internacional, a 2–1 defeat in the first leg at home being too difficult to overcome. The 2000s also saw São Paulo win the league title three years in a row, 2006–08. Charles Miller could surely never have imagined that a bunch of well-to-do Europeans at the turn of the last century could set in motion a club that has been world champions three times since.

SEATTLE SOUNDERS

Location	Seattle, Washington, USA
Established	1974
Nicknames	Rave Green
Stadium	CenturyLink Field (67,000 capacity)
Home colors	Green and blue
Leading goal-scorer	Fredy Montero (2009–), 60 goals
Most appearances	Osvaldo Alonso (2009–), 139 appearances

I f you own one of the more popular MLS franchises—say, in New York or Los Angeles—chances are your team will attract around 20,000 fans to each of their home games. Given that the league is still relatively new and still settling into the American sporting brain, this is a fairly healthy number. Some places are not so lucky: in 2013, the MLS Cup champions, Sporting Kansas City, during the regular season attracted an average of only 11,745 fans, the fewest of the 19 teams.

And then there's the Seattle Sounders.

The Sounders franchise was approved in 2007, after years of maneuvering that included a long fight to build a dedicated soccer stadium. "The Sounders" has always been the name of the main soccer team in Seattle, and once they began playing in MLS, fans started to take notice, even though they would have to watch games at CenturyLink Field, which they share with the Seattle Seahawks American football franchise.

In their first season as an expansion team, 2009, the Seattle Sounders attracted an average of just over 31,000 fans per game, an astonishing figure (they reached the playoffs that year, and all years since). In a game in August 2009 against Barcelona, featuring future New York Red Bulls star Thierry Henry, the crowd numbered almost 67,000. Clearly the folks backing Seattle, who included Hollywood mogul Joe Roth, Microsoft's Paul Allen, and *Wheel of Fortune*'s Drew Carey, were onto something. Five years down the line, the average attendance at CenturyLink Field hovers around 40,000. To put that in perspective, only seven of 20 teams in the English Premier League average more—Arsenal, Chelsea, Liverpool, the two Manchester clubs, Newcastle, and Sunderland. And when Seattle plays Portland, in games known as the Cascadia Cup, the numbers swell even further—in 2012, 66,452 saw Seattle beat Portland, 3–0, and the following year, nearly a thousand more showed up for a 1–0 Seattle win (though Portland subsequently knocked Seattle out of the playoffs). All this, and Seattle still doesn't have a dedicated soccer stadium; the boom in interest in MLS in the northwest has continued despite the fact that playing soccer on semi-grass is like playing ice hockey on a basketball court. The growth, fed by a better standard of play, more interested international stars, the maturation of all those kids running around local leagues, and wider coverage of the sport generally (see under: NBC's massive commitment to the English Premier League), looks like it will only get stronger.

So what happens on the plastic pitch in Seattle? The franchise has been dominated by one man since it began: German-born Sigi Schmid, the Seattle coach. Never a top player himself, Schmid had a distinguished career in college soccer, coaching the UCLA Bruins to three national championships. After winning a championship with the L.A. Galaxy (he also lost two), Schmid spent two undistinguished years in Columbus before moving to Seattle. A notoriously defense-minded coach, he's hardly adored, but Schmid's teams consistently perform. And while the administration of Seattle faces regular votes of confidence or no confidence from the fans (Drew Carey instigated this "management by fan approval" when he came on board), Schmid merely has to convince his betters that he's the man for the job, which he did again in 2013, despite that loss to archrivals Portland one step from the MLS Cup game. That Seattle team featured Clint Dempsey, though the American star looked both tired and a bit uninterested in playing in MLS (that said, Dempsey always looks uninterested until he scores; then he just looks annoyed). But it seems whatever happens on the semi-grass of CenturyLink Field, fans will continue to flock to see this new MLS franchise. Sounders fans deserve a trophy.

SHAKHTAR DONETSK

Location	Donetsk, Ukraine
Established	1936
Nicknames	*Hirnyky* ("Miners"), *Kroty* ("Moles")
Stadium	Donbass Arena (52,667 capacity)
Home colors	Orange and black
Leading goal-scorer	Andriy Vorobey (1998–2007), 114 goals
Most appearances	Mykhaylo Sokolovsky (1974–87), 400 appearances

There are many famous people called John Hughes—authors, politicians, scientists, a movie director—but few could have lived a life as notable as that of Welshman John *James* Hughes. Hughes was a functionally illiterate but highly successful businessman who in 1869, at age 55, sailed eight ships to the Ukraine filled with stuff and people, all in order to found an ironworks and mines. (The tsars needed a new naval fortress on the Baltic, and Hughes had gotten the gig.)

The settlement grew until after a few years it bore his John James's name—Hughesovka—and featured all the accoutrements of a parochial Welsh town, including a church, a hospital, and a tea shop. Later, after the tsar and his family had been shot and bayoneted in the cellar at Yekaterinburg, the town's name was changed to the barely believable Stalino; in World War II, the growing town harbored a concentration camp. Eventually, in 1961, the city of more than 700,000 people was renamed Donetsk. Around a million people live there now, and it remains an important, if somewhat unattractive, industrial center.

It is also the home of the first Ukrainian team to win the UEFA Cup, Shakhtar Donetsk.

Shakhtar, like the town, have gone through a number of monikers in their history. Founded in 1936, they were initially the Stakhanovets, after Soviet productivity expert/progaganda guru Alexey Stakhanov. In Soviet Russia, workers who exceeded their targets were called Stakhanovites, but successive sets of Stakhanovets players might not have qualified, as the team bummed around lower divisions without winning very much. But like their town they grew; their first Soviet title came in 1954 and their first cups seven and eight years later, though by then they were F.C. Shakhtar Stalino.

Eventually, F.C. Shakhtar Stalino morphed into Shakhtar Donetsk, though still great victories were out of reach. But as the twentieth century became the twenty-first, an influx of players arrived from a place as different from the Ukraine as one can imagine, and it changed everything.

It all started with Matuzalém Francelino da Silva, who was brought to Donetsk in 2002. Known, like so many Brazilians, by a single name, Matuzalém preceded Romanian coach Mircea Lucescu by a couple of years, but once Lucescu—former captain of a Romanian national team that nearly knocked Brazil out of the 1970 World Cup—was in place, the trickle of Brazilian transplants became a torrent. One of them, Fernandinho—who, like many Brazilians plying their trade in Donetsk, would eventually move to a bigger club (in his case, Manchester City)—has been quoted frankly about the lure of that gritty mining town in eastern Ukraine: "Of course money is the main thing," Fernandinho said. The money, provided by owner Rinat Akhmetov, the richest man in the Ukraine, has brought the likes of Willian (later with Chelsea), Luiz Adriano, Ilsinho, and Jádson (he'd go back to Brazil) to the club. Along with Fernandinho, this quintet helped bring Shakthar its first and only major European crown: the 2009 UEFA Cup.

The real drama of that tournament came in the semifinal, when Shakhtar faced the other main team from Ukraine, Dinamo Kiev.

Shakhtar had started the season in the Champions League, in a group featuring Barcelona in all their pomp. Nevertheless, only two late Lionel Messi goals in Donetsk had saved Barcelona in their first game against Shakhtar, and in the return leg, an already qualified Barcelona lost 3–2 to the Ukrainians. But Shakhtar still finished third in the group and thereby entered the UEFA Cup, where they knocked out Tottenham Hotspur, CSKA Moscow, and Marseille, before facing Kiev in the semi.

In the first leg, Fernandinho scored a crucial equalizer to enable Shakhtar to head back to Donetsk with a 1–1 draw. In the second leg, a scorcher by Jádson was canceled out by Guinean Ismaël Bangoura for Kiev, proving that players flocked to Ukraine from all over the globe. So the all-Ukraine semifinal was tied at 2–2 on aggregate; extra time and penalties loomed. With barely a minute to go, Willian raked a 40-yard pass right to the wing, where Ilsinho nipped in front of the left back, cut inside, beat another defender, and buried the shot in the back of the net. Shakhtar had beaten Dinamo in their biggest ever game, and in the very last minute, and were off to the UEFA Cup final.

It was bound to be an anticlimax after all that. A 2–1 win over German club Werder Bremen came thanks to two more "Brazilian" goals, from Luiz Adriano and Jádson, though extra time was needed. Shakhtar were UEFA Cup champions.

At home, Shakhtar have won nine of the 14 championships contested this century, including the last five. And a new crop of Brazilians has come to play (a recent Champions League game saw Fred, Douglas Costa, Alex Teixeira, Taison, Luiz Adriano, Bernard, Eduardo, and Fernando named among the 18 match-day players). Clearly, if Ukraine was good enough for a middle-aged man from Newport, Wales, in 1869, it's good enough for talented young twenty-first-century men who grew up near the beaches of Brazil.

SPARTAK MOSCOW

Location	Moscow, Russia
Established	1922
Nicknames	*Narodnaya Komanda* ("The People's Team"), *Spartachi Krasno-Belye* ("The Red-Whites"), *Myaso* ("The Meat")
Stadium	Lokomotiv Stadium (until 2014) (28,800 capacity), Otkrytie Arena (after 2014) (44,000 capacity)
Home colors	Red and white
Leading goal-scorer	Nikita Simonyan (1949–59), 153 goals
Most appearances	Fyodor Cherenkov (1977–90, 1991–93), 494 appearances

"An incident occurred yesterday in Luzhniki [Stadium]. After the football match, some spectators were injured." And that was all Moscow's evening newspaper wrote.

It was October 20, 1982, exactly three weeks before the death of Soviet leader Leonid Brezhnev. Visiting Moscow that ice-cold night were a Dutch side called Haarlem F.C. They were in the Russian capital to face Spartak Moscow, both teams hoping to advance to the last 16 of the UEFA Cup. The temperature was barely 14 degrees, and the officials at the Luzhniki Stadium decided to cram the 16,000 fans into two sections, leaving the rest of the vast ground snow-covered.

The game itself was hampered by the terrible cold. Spartak scored early, and late, but that last goal, a header from a corner by defender Sergei Shvetsov with 45:11 on the clock, was one Shvetsov surely wished he'd never scored.

As the game wound to a close, fans were leaving via a spectator tunnel to get to the metro station; no one wanted to stand around in more cold waiting for a train. There are conflicting reports on what happened next: a woman lost a shoe, the police pushed people down the icy stairs, fans rushed back from taking their leave in order to celebrate Shvetsov's goal. Whatever triggered it, the result was catastrophic: anywhere from 66 (official Soviet version) to 340 fans died in the resulting crush. The number is still hotly debated, but at least the news of the terrible disaster has finally come to light.

Soviet football was never far from the politics and industry of that vast country. In Moscow, for example, Dinamo came out of the secret police, Torpedo from vehicle factories, Locomotiv from the trains, CSKA from the massive army. But Spartak was the "people's team." This was easier said than done in a country where all forms of association were staunchly controlled by an unwieldy and often brutal state apparatus. But even within such strictures, a man like Nikolai Starostin could find a way to bring organized football to regular Muscovites.

The team Starostin created, Krasnaya Presnya, was founded just a few years after the Russian Revolution. In 1934, with state support, Nikolai and his three brothers transformed the team into Spartak Moscow—named for Spartacus, the legendary gladiator, military strategist, and Kirk Douglas character. Two years later, at Nikolai Starostin's prompting, a national league began in Russia, and quickly it became clear that Spartak's main rivals, Dinamo, stood for state control whereas Spartak stood for something else entirely. This "people's team" would win that new league in 1936, 1938, and 1939, but nothing was straightforward in Soviet Russia.

Stalin's henchman, arch-proponent of the gulags—and, according to Stalin, when introducing him to Roosevelt at Yalta, "our Himmler"—Lavrenti Beria was also a staunch Dinamo Moscow fan. When Spartak beat Dinamo in the 1939 cup final, Beria insisted the semifinal be replayed *after* the final (hard to believe, but true). When Spartak *still* won, the odious Beria set to work on getting rid of the Starostin brothers. An accusation of a plot to kill Stalin sent the brothers, in 1944, to Siberia for a decade; Nikolai was brought back to Moscow in 1948 by Stalin's son, Vasily, who was a friend. Again Starostin was apprehended and sent this time to Kazakhstan; once Stalin died in 1953, and Beria was subsequently executed, the Starostins were finally set free. Nikolai took over the Soviet national team for a couple of years, and then became president of Spartak for nearly 40, until 1992.

In that time, Nikolai Starostin watched Spartak add eight league titles to the five before he became president in 1955; in all, they've won 21. Since 1980 they have been on a formidable run: runners-up that year and again in 1981, 1983, 1984, and 1985, they won the Russian league in 1987 and 1989, were runners-up in 1991, won the league in 1992, 1993, 1994, 1996, 1997, 1998, 1999, 2000, 2001, and were runners-up once again in 2005, 2006, 2007, 2009, and 2012. Few teams anywhere in the world can match such a record over a 30-year span. (But then, few teams had access to the billions of rubles provided by sponsor Gazprom, Russia's sort-of-private, sort-of-state-run energy company.)

In Europe, though, Spartak have won nothing. They have reached the semifinals of the Cup Winners' Cup, the UEFA Cup, and the European Cup, but have never made it to the final. Perhaps their best result was on the way to their semifinal appearance in the European Cup. On March 20, 1991, Spartak beat an Alfredo Di Stéfano-managed Real Madrid 3–1 in the Bernabéu; after being a goal down, two by Dmitri Radchenko in the first half, and one by Valeri Shmarov in the second gave them a famous victory (the great Madrid hero Di Stéfano resigned a few days later). But Marseille beat Spartak in the semis, and that was that. In 1995, they won every game of their Champions League group stage, scoring 15 goals and letting in just four (though it was a terrible group, featuring Blackburn Rovers, Legia Warsaw, and the Norwegian side Rosenborg). Before the knockout stages began Nikolai Starostin died, and Spartak sold their best players; they were knocked out by Nantes with some ease. Since that time, LUKoil has taken over the funding of the team, and a string of eight managers in nine seasons has seen them ossify.

It took seven years for Russians to hear some of the details of the Luzhniki disaster; to this day, the full story has not been revealed. And the memory of those lost Spartak fans, be it 66, be it many more—not to mention the example of Nikolai Starostin's extraordinary life—has been tarnished by the morphing of the "people's team" into one whose fans sometimes spout racist views. In Robert Edelman's *Spartak Moscow: A History of the People's Team in the Workers' State*, the author quotes Gennadi Larchikov, a venerable sports journalist, calling Spartak "the team of intellectuals and hooligans." On October, 30, 2013—almost 31 years to the day of the Luzhniki disaster—just the hooligans showed up: a Russian Cup game between Spartak and Shinnik Yaroslavl, a lower division side, was ruined when the Spartak fans rioted. One of them displayed a Nazi flag. Thirty-one years after that taciturn report of the Luzhniki disaster in the Moscow evening paper, a Russian newspaper, *Sport Express Daily*, wrote of the 2013 riots, "If this mayhem created by the fans is not ended, then it is going to be the end of football in our country." Football continues in Russia, but then, so does the racism.

SPORTING LISBON

Location	Lisbon, Portugal
Established	1906
Nicknames	*Sportinguistas, Leões* ("Lions"), *Verde-e-Brancos* ("Green and White")
Stadium	Estádio José Alvalade (50,095 capacity)
Home colors	Green, white, and black
Leading goal-scorer	Fernando Peyroteo (1937–49), 694 goals
Most appearances	Vítor Damas (1966–76, 1984–89), 743 appearances

I magine building a stadium and, in the exhibition game to formally open it, showing off a young player your club thinks might be something special. Then imagine the opponents in that friendly being so impressed they snatch away the player, and he goes on to be one of the best who has ever laced up a pair of boots. Then, later, imagine hosting a major international cup final in that still-new stadium, and the home team makes it all the way! Then, they lose.

This is the story of Sporting Club of Portugal.

It was the first day of July 1906 when the Sporting Clube de Portugal was founded, and a year later they played their first soccer match. In the first few years of the century the club had been about socializing, but under the guidance of José de Alvalade, who wanted them to be "the greatest [club] in Europe," Sporting quickly focused on serious sports (they would eventually name their stadium after Alvalade). By 1923, Sporting had won their first Championship of Portugal (they would win three more during the 1930s), and once the Primeira Liga was founded in 1938, Sporting would dominate it, winning five titles in both the 1940s and the 1950s. Domestically, the 1960s were less productive, as Sporting won just three titles (they have won 18 in total), but the sixties also saw the club's finest performances in European competition.

In the 1963-64 Cup Winners' Cup, Sporting "welcomed" Apoel F.C. of Nicosia, in Cyprus, to the Estádio José Alvalade on November 13 for a first-leg, second-round tie. It would be a historic night. After 20 minutes Sporting were three up, though Apoel would score after 24 minutes to make it 3–1. Apoel seemed like a dangerous side, having won the first leg of their first-round game against S.K. Gjovik-Lyn, the now-defunct Norwegian side, 6–0.

But it was not to be; Sporting went crazy. At half-time, Sporting were 6–1 to the good, and by the end of the game they had added another ten unanswered goals. Domingos Mascarenhas scored six, a record, and Tobias Figueiredo a second-half, nine-minute hat-trick (the slacker). The second leg was a bit of an anticlimax, ending just 2–0 to the Portuguese side. The aggregate score was 18–1, which pretty much defines walkover.

Waiting for Sporting in the quarterfinals were the Manchester United of Bobby Charlton, George Best, and Denis Law. With the final score in the first leg 4–1 to the English side, on a Law hat-trick and a goal by Charlton, things looked bleak for Sporting. In the return leg in Lisbon, Law hit the post early, and then in his own words, "the roof fell in." Sporting once again went crazy, winning the game 5–0. Law said United played "like drains," and Sir Matt Busby, their legendary manager, is said to have given them a "bollocking" which was as intense as it was rare. To this day, Sporting's victory is United's worst ever UEFA defeat.

Sporting raced on to the final, where Mascarenhas and Figueiredo once again scored to salvage a 3–3 draw against MTK Budapest; the replay, two days later, ended 1–0 to Sporting, via a goal direct from a corner by midfielder João Morais.

It was to prove the highlight of Sporting's history. Another memorable moment in the club's story also involved Manchester United, though Sporting's fans probably remember it with sorrow.

The back of his green-and-white-hooped shirt read "Espirito Santo, 28, Ronaldo" and he ran rings around the lauded visitors in red. The boy's highly motivated haircut displayed "breeding plumage," as one wag put it: a wisp of lighter locks flopping with insouciance over his brow. He seemed to know that one day he'd be the best player in the world. The post-match report from the *Guardian* newspaper read, "[Barthez, Man United's keeper] did well in the 20th minute to parry a blistering shot from 18-year-old Ronaldo, one of the hottest prospects in Portuguese football."

Cristiano Ronaldo, at the tender age of 18, found himself playing for Sporting Lisbon, against the mighty Manchester United, in an exhibition game in August 2003, to inaugurate the newly built, but same-named, Estádio José Alvalade. Ronaldo didn't disappoint, already utilizing his trademark stepovers, fades, drag-backs, and ankle-shimmies, all in order to dislocate the hips of opposing defenders. Gary Neville, watching at home in Manchester, says he sat upright and realized he was watching something special.

The rest of the club noticed, too, and Ronaldo would move to United that summer. Once there, he would fill out physically and become one of the two best players on the planet before moving to Real Madrid, where he would score umpteen highlight-reel goals. Sporting Lisbon hardly knew him.

Probably the low point in Sporting's history was being chosen to host the final of the 2004–05 UEFA Cup at the Estádio José Alvalade. It should have been an honor, and Sporting conspired to reach the final at their own ground. Sadly, after taking the lead on a brilliant 25-yard curler by Rogério, Sporting missed a bunch of chances, including an unfathomable goal-line miss by their goal-scorer. They then managed to play like Denis Law's "drains," leaking three second-half goals to CSKA Moscow. The stadium that future megastar Ronaldo had helped to open was, just two years later, shrouded in near silence, except for one young man pictured sobbing as the CSKA players mobbed the huge UEFA trophy and punched the stifling Lisbon summer air.

Location	Bucharest, Romania
Established	1947
Nicknames	*Roș-Albaștrii* ("The Red and Blues"), *Militarii* ("The Army Men"), *Vitezistii* ("The Speedsters")
Current stadium	Stadionul Ghencea (28,000 capacity)
Home colors	Blue and red
Leading goal-scorer	Anghel Iordănescu (1968–82, 1985–86), 146 goals
Most appearances	Tudorel Stoica (1975–89, 1990–91), 370 appearances

The first penalty save was a relatively easy one: the ball hit at head height, right where goalkeepers like them. The second save was one of the greatest you'll ever see.

It was the 1986 European Cup final, played in Seville, Spain: Barcelona versus the Romanian side Steaua Bucharest. The game had been European Cup final-dull, the staunch Romanians keeping out a Terry Venables-managed side that, though it featured no real superstars, was still Barcelona. Now, the whole thing would come down to who could score from 12 yards.

Perhaps it's no surprise that Steaua Bucharest were defensively-minded; they are Romania's army team, after all. Established in June 1947, they went through a number of name changes—ASA Bucureşti (Asociaţia Sportivă a Armatei Bucureşti); CSCA (Clubul Sportiv Central al Armatei); and CCA (Casa Centrală a Armatei), before they settled on CSA Steaua in 1961. *Steaua* means "star," and the original crest featured a red one, for Communism, though it morphed into yellow by the time the name Steaua stuck. In 1951, Steaua won their first Romanian title, and they have added 24 since.

Steaua's greatest decade was the 1980s; not only did they win the league five years in a row, 1985–89, but they also reached two European Cup finals, the most by any team from Eastern Europe.

In that 1986 final, they faced Barcelona in Spain, seemingly a thankless task. But Steaua put up bulwark after bulwark against the Spanish side, who didn't find the wit to break down the Romanians. Steaua were hardly star-studded, either, except for then 22-year-old playmaker Marius Lăcătuş, a.k.a. "the Beast," who would go on to shine for 17 seasons and become the greatest player Bucharest ever had.

More famous in 1986 was Romanian goalkeeper Helmuth Duckadam, and he shouldn't have even been playing. For weeks before the final, Duckadam had noticed a soreness in his arm, but not wanting to miss Steaua's greatest moment he had kept it to himself. As the penalties began, Duckadam stood stock still, then bent at the waist, ready to pounce. The first kick, from Alexanko, was the relatively easy one, Duckadam diving to his right. The second, from defender Ángel Pedraza, was brilliantly struck, low to Duckadam's right, but somehow Duckadam turned the ball around the post, falling to his knees to pump fists and celebrate. So amped was Duckadam that when a security official tossed him the ball he'd just saved, he spun and punched it away in what looked like excited disgust. The Barcelona players must have feared the worst—Duckadam was on fire. But Steaua also missed their first two penalties, and coming up to take their third was the 22-year-old Lăcătuş.

Steaua needn't have worried. Lăcătuş hit his penalty so hard that the keeper, diving the wrong way, heard it hit the bar but didn't see it hit the back of the net, and, thinking it had come straight down, dove to punch it away. It was as good a penalty as Duckadam's second save had been; asked about it later, Lăcătuș told UEFA.com, "I was a crazy boy... If I had been older, I wouldn't have dared take a penalty."

And so it went back to Duckadam, and once again he dove low to his right, to make another fine save, this time from Pichi Alonso. Jumping up, he grabbed the ball and kicked it skyward before looking apologetically at the referee and clasping his hands in supplication and excitement. Gavril Balint then scored for Steaua, meaning that Barcelona's Marcos had to make his penalty to keep the game alive.

Marcos seemed to take an age to spot the ball correctly, then wandered back to the edge of the box. His penalty kick was relatively weak, and, diving down low to his left this time, Duckadam pushed the ball away. He had saved all four penalties—the first keeper to ever do so in an official game, and a feat for which he entered the Guinness Book of World Records—and his team were the champions of Europe.

In December that year, Steaua lost 1–0 to Argentina's River Plate in Tokyo in the Intercontinental Cup. In goal that day for Steaua was Dumitru Stângaciu, not Duckadam. After the European triumph, Duckadam had gone on holiday to the Black Sea, but the pain in his arm had gotten worse. He was rushed to hospital where a blood clot was found, and though doctors were able to save his arm, 26-year-old Helmuth Duckadam would never play football again.

Three seasons later, Steaua Bucharest once again made the 1989 European Cup final, but the less said about their 4–0 thrashing by a rampant A.C. Milan, the better. Not even the inclusion in Steaua's team of Romania's greatest ever player, Gheorghe Hagi, could stem the tide of Milanese brilliance that day, as Rijkaard, Donadoni, van Basten, Ancelotti, and Gullit ran riot in front of a back line of Tassotti, Maldini, Costacurta, and Baresi, a foursome that might well have been the best ever assembled in one team.

In December of that year, the Romanian Revolution brought to an end the reign of the dreadful Ceaușescus, Nicolae and his wife, Elena, two of the more odious twentieth-century dictators. In soccer, the revolution led to an opening of Romania's borders such that Hagi would move to Real Madrid, Lacatus to Fiorentina, and a number of other players to top European clubs. It was the best of times for Romania, but the worst for a team, Steaua, who would finally, in 1998, rid themselves of army connections and become, once and for all, F.C. Steaua Bucharest. Since 2010, Steaua's president has been their former goalkeeping hero, Helmuth Duckadam.

Location	Swansea, Wales
Established	1912
Nicknames	The Jacks, The Swans
Stadium	Liberty Stadium (20,750 capacity)
Home colors	Black and white
Leading goal-scorer	Ivor Allchurch (1947–58, 1965–68), 166 goals
Most appearances	Wilfred Milne (1920–37), 586 appearances

The first half was the Michu Show, as a player at the height of his powers made one goal and scored the other. The second half was more Michu, too: a double dummy made the third goal, and a neat pass inside the defense lead to a penalty for the fourth. Michu had nothing to do with the fifth, but by then the cup was won.

It was February 24, 2013, and Wembley Stadium was (mostly) filled with two sets of City fans, Bradford and Swansea. And though the League Cup has always been the unloved third child in Britain, after the Premiership and the FA Cup, the tournament still retains a sense of romance, primarily these days because the big teams tend to field their second-string players, leaving the competition open for "lesser" clubs to be competitive. And so it was in 2013, when second-tier Bradford City faced a small club from Wales. But that small club from Wales had recently made it to the Premiership and were starting to build a very fine team indeed.

For much of their long history, Swansea City were Swansea Town, until the town became a city in 1969. Founded in 1912, the first Swansea players ran about on a cabbagey herb called vetch, which would later lead to their first stadium being called Vetch Field. But Swansea would struggle in this rugby-mad corner of Britain, spending plenty of time in the second, third, and fourth levels of English football. An odd quirk of European football meant that winning the Welsh Cup, as they have done 10 times in their history, gave them access to the Cup Winners' Cup once it was established in 1960. They have appeared in the Cup Winners' Cup seven times, though they've never advanced beyond the second round. (That second round came after a first, in 1982–83, in which they beat Maltese side Sliema Wanderers by an aggregate score of 17–0.)

Despite these European adventures, Swansea City have struggled, at times, to stay alive. The same season Swansea thrashed those unlucky Maltese, they were relegated to the second tier of English football, having finished sixth in the First Division in 1982, and in 1984 they went down again, this time to the third tier. Two seasons later, they finished rank bottom of the Third Division, though to ease their pain somewhat, their archrivals, Cardiff City, finished third bottom; both were relegated to the basement division. Swansea had almost gone out of business; money was tight, and it would get worse. In 2003, they faced a last game of the season against Hull City. Win, and they'd remain in the Football League. Lose, and it was bye-bye to the big time, and maybe to the club altogether.

Nearly 10,000 fans turned out for that final match. A young Leon Britton, who has gone on to star for the team in the Premiership, was at the time on loan from West Ham United, and played right midfield, and it was he who would be tripped for a penalty after just six minutes. James Thomas buried it, but two defensive errors later and, 2–1 down, Swansea faced the abyss. The Vetch was silent; when Thomas missed an easy chance to level the game, the silence turned into groans of distress. More chances for Hull came and went.

Then the soccer gods smiled on Swansea. Justin Whittle, playing at the back for Hull, was said to have handled the ball in the penalty area, though he mimed to the referee that it had hit him in his man parts. Thomas scored his second penalty, and at half-time the game was balanced at 2–2.

Ten minutes into the second half, and Swansea went ahead when Lenny Johnrose nudged a ball into the net after a Roberto Martínez cross, and James Thomas completed his hat-trick to keep Swansea City in the league. The Welsh fans were utterly delirious.

Less than a decade later, Martínez was managing Swansea. A fine tactician and super-decent man, Martínez would bring Swansea to the second tier in 2008, which was their third season at the new Liberty Stadium. Two seasons later, after Martínez left to manage Wigan Athletic, Brendan Rodgers guided Swansea back to the Premiership, where they remain. But Rodgers, like Martínez, got a feel for the bigger time, and both former Swansea managers now work in the city of Liverpool: Rodgers for the Reds, and Martínez for the blues of Everton.

To replace Rodgers, Swansea turned to one of the greatest players to grace the game, Michael Laudrup. It was he jumping up and down on the sidelines in 2013 as Michu's masterclass brought Swansea its first major trophy, the League Cup. Bradford had been annihilated, 5–0. Little Leon Britton was all growed up and running the on-the-ground passing that has endeared the Swansea style of football to so many fans. Swansea City were finally in the big time, and they looked set fair to stay, though Laudrup was fired in February 2014. Wales wasn't just a rugby country anymore; two of its teams, Swansea and hated rivals Cardiff City, were in the top flight of English football, together, for the first time in history. *Hwrê i Cymru!*

TORINO

Location	Turin, Italy
Established	1906
Nicknames	*Il Toro* ("The Bull"), *I Granata* ("Maroons")
Stadium	Stadio Olimpico di Torino (28,140 capacity)
Home colors	Claret (maroon) and white
Leading goal-scorer	Paolo Pulici (1967–82), 172 goals
Most appearances	Giorgio Ferrini (1959–75), 566 appearances

Poor, ruined Xico Ferreira—death is terrible for those left behind. And how could he not blame himself? Francisco "Xico" Ferreira was a much beloved Portuguese midfielder, a stalwart of a fine mid-twentieth-century Benfica side of Lisbon. Oddly, he was also a favorite player of Ferruccio Novo, president of the Torino football club, who played some 1,300 miles away in northern Italy.

In early May 1949, Torino—who at the time just happened to be the greatest club team in the world—flew to Portugal in midweek to play a charity game against Benfica in Xico Ferreira's honor. Honoring him was easy: he was a man known to castigate his own teammates for bad fouls. Ferreira had been told by his original team, Porto, that he was a scoundrel for asking for more money, so he moved to archrivals Benfica because he'd made a solemn promise to do so after Porto's betrayal; he played more than 500 times for this most storied of Portuguese teams, and was planning one final move, to Turin, to play for Ferruccio Novo's team of superstars. Not a scoundrel—the opposite. And yet he was to become poor, ruined Xico Ferreira . . .

It was a little after 5 pm on a day of thunderstorms when the plane carrying "*Il Grande Torino*," as they were known, approached Turin following their charity game in Portugal. The game itself had been a memorable one—a 4–3 victory for Benfica—but never mind the loss: what mattered to Novo and Torino was that the great Xico Ferreira would soon grace the Italian team with his moral midfield abilities in the coming seasons.

And what a team *Il Grande Torino* was, a side for the ages when the ages were so bleak. Italy desperately needed a new beginning. The war had sullied their world standing, and poverty was rampant. Football became a welcome respite from the shame of Fascism and the pressure to rebuild. A man like Xico Ferreira would bring even more moral fiber to a team that was already considered to be, in the words of Italian journalist Gianpaolo Ormezzano, "all full of the sentiment to represent Italy in some new way." It wasn't as if they needed help on the playing side. As recently as 1947, in a match between Italy and a great Hungary side, all ten outfield players for Italy were culled from the Turin club ("Italy" won 3–2). Up front, the great genius Valentino Mazzola could, again in the words of Turin native Ormezzano, "in every time of the match . . . change the result in favor of Torino." A Lionel Messi for his time, this *mezzala* (what we now call a "false number 10") called Mazzola had helped Torino win the Italian league in 1943 and then again in 1946, 1947, and 1948. In 1949, with just four games to go, Torino had already sewn up the league once more, and with the trophy in the bag had headed off to Portugal for that charity match for Ferreira.

That run of championships straddling the war was an astonishing achievement. Torino had beaten Milan by 13 points in 1946 and by 16 points two years later, a record that still stands. There were any number of records, in fact. In 1948, they scored an astonishing 125 goals; in 1949, they dropped one point at home all season. Yet despite all this local brilliance, Italy as a nation still hung its head. Wasn't the chance of bringing a man of Ferreira's standing—a man who'd put an arm around the shoulders of a teammate whose tackle had been too stringent—to Italy worth a brief trip to Lisbon between league games?

Fog rolled all over Turin on Wednesday, May 4, 1949. Hidden behind the swirling clouds stood Superga, a mountain upon which stood the famous Basilica di Superga. The Basilica was the result of a solemn promise made by the Piedmontese to the Virgin Mary if she'd help them beat back Louis XIV in 1706. We may presume the Blessed Mother did indeed help, because, with the French vanquished, the church of thanks was built. There it stands still, an eighteenth-century Baroque masterpiece, 3,000 feet above the city of Turin, with views of the city below and the snowcapped Alps beyond. Filled with the tombs of the dead of the Savoy family (the Italian royals), the Basilica di Superga is a favorite of day-tripping Torinesi and tourists alike, but that day nothing of it could be seen behind the pea-soup weather. The only option for the pilots bringing the Turin club back to their city was to descend and fly by sight, but something went horribly wrong in the navigation and the radios were faulty—the good graces of the Virgin Mary nowhere to be found. The plane carrying *Il Grande Torino* crashed full-on into the back of the Basilica, high up on Superga. The result was catastrophic—everyone on board perished. Gone was Valentino Mazzola, considered to this day one of Italy's greatest ever players; gone was his illustrious striking partner, Croat Ezio Loik; gone were the Ballarin brothers, Dino and Sergio; gone were 14 other players, five officials (including Leslie Lievesley, a British-born coach who once played for Manchester United), three journalists, four crew members, and an organizer.

And gone as a footballing powerhouse was Torino F.C. Unlike Manchester United, who suffered a devastating plane crash in 1958 in which a number of top players perished but who went on to dominate British and European football, the Torino club has prospered only fitfully since 1949. It took them until 1976 to win the league once again, pipping their hometown rivals, Juventus, by two points. But this seeming renaissance didn't take. Though they finished runners-up the following season (to Juventus), that was effectively the end of their great successes. (They did reach the UEFA Cup final in 1992, having knocked out Real Madrid in the semifinal, but lost to Ajax.)

Torino have recently bounced back and forth from Serie A to Serie B (they were even barred, disbanded, and reformed in the mid-2000s after a financial scandal), while Juventus dominated the Italian scene in the early 1980s and the late 1990s, and won Serie A in 2012 (not to mention winning two European Cups since Torino last won anything). These days, though Torino are back in Serie A after a recent three-year run in Serie B, they are a club thoroughly overshadowed by their illustrious city-mates.

And Xico Ferreira? His transfer to Torino never happened. He stayed at Benfica, broken-hearted, for three more years until he retired at the age of 33. He died on Valentine's Day, 1986, at the age of 66. Poor, ruined Xico Ferreira is still considered one of Portugal's finest ever midfielders.

TOTTENHAM HOTSPUR

Location	London, England
Established	1882
Nicknames	Spurs, The Lilywhites
Stadium	White Hart Lane (36,240 capacity)
Home colors	Navy blue and white
Leading goal-scorer	Jimmy Greaves (1961–70), 266 goals
Most appearances	Steve Perryman (1969–86), 854 appearances

Imagine this all-time team, organized in a 4–4–3 formation: Pat Jennings would be in goal, a late-career Dave Mackay sweeping, and Steve Perryman, Sol Campbell, and Gary Mabbutt as a fluid back line. The midfield would feature legends all: Paul Gascoigne, Glenn Hoddle, Osvaldo Ardiles, and a recent superstar, Gareth Bale. Up front, two of the greatest strikers Britain has ever produced would bang in the goals: Gary Lineker and Jimmy Greaves. The rest of the squad of 22 would sparkle with stars: Clive Allen, Martin Chivers, Teddy Sheringham, David Ginola, Alan Mullery, Danny Blanchflower, Cliff Jones, Luka Modrić, Ron Burgess, and Jürgen Klinsmann. Available for sale, given that there's no more room in the squad, would be Alan Gilzean, Darren Anderton, Ledley King, Ted Ditchburn, and Martin Peters.

The problem for Tottenham Hotspur is that, except for a few golden moments, they've never been able to put together a team that has quality in all positions. And at the managerial level, they've had altogether too many bosses. In the last 20 years alone, 17 separate coaches have been and gone (one of them, David Pleat, got the job three separate times in that span). The result is that, even though Spurs have been the landing place for so many greats of the game, their trophy haul is meager for a top British club. Two league titles, the last in 1961, two UEFA Cups and a Cup Winners' Cup is hardly the history they dare shout down the A10 road toward their arch London rivals, Arsenal.

Tottenham Hotspur began, like so many teams in England and elsewhere (especially South America), as a cricketing club. The Hotspur Cricket Club was joined by a number of boys from a local Bible class and morphed into the football team in 1882. A picture taken at the time shows massed ranks of young men, many of whom are holding rifles. As a tactic of intimidation it seems to have worked, because in 1901 Tottenham Hotspur, as they had been known since 1884, won the FA Cup as a non-league side (they were still in the Southern League), the only team ever to do so. The first game of the final, against Sheffield United, was filmed by Pathé News, also a first, ended 2–2, and was watched by just shy of 111,000 people at Crystal Palace. The replay, in Bolton, had a fifth as many fans but the same number of goals—though redistributed, Spurs winning 3–1.

By 1910 Spurs were in the First Division, and would be runners-up, and Cup winners again, in 1921. But for the next three decades, Spurs went nowhere except, in 1928, down into the Second Division, where they stayed until the late 1940s. Then legendary manager Arthur Rowe brought a new style of play to White Hart Lane.

"Push and run," as it was called, was a high-octane form of possession football, a kind of primitive tiki-taka. It consisted of a quick pass and a run around a defender to get the return: simple, but very effective. In 1950 Spurs won the Second Division, and the following year they won the First. Future England World Cup-winning manager Alf Ramsey was on that side, as was Ron Burgess, Bill Nicholson, and Ted Ditchburn in goal. But they weren't young men, and the intensity of "push and run" couldn't last. It would be another decade before Spurs won the league—and the FA Cup in the same year—this time on the back of the best team they ever created.

Bill Nicholson was now the coach, and he assembled a wonderful team featuring Blanchflower, Mackay, and, for the 1962 season, Jimmy Greaves. Avuncular, gruff, and one of the best goal-scorers England ever produced, in nine years with Spurs Greaves notched 220 goals. He just missed out on a league winners medal and on the final of the European Cup, as Spurs lost in the 1962 semifinal to Benfica, but he won two FA Cups, in 1962 and 1967, and Spurs', and England's, first European trophy, the Cup Winners' Cup of 1963. (Greaves was left out of the 1966 World Cup final against Germany; his replacement, Geoff Hurst, scored a hat-trick.) Greaves scored twice in the 5–1 hammering of Atlético Madrid in the 1963 Cup Winners' Cup final; one of the other goal-scorers that May night was John White, who was killed just over a year later when he was hit by lightning while golfing.

That great Spurs team slowly fell apart due to age and transfers (and lightning). Nicholson managed them until 1974, during which time he also brought them a UEFA Cup win, in the competition's first year, 1971–72. That tournament featured an extraordinary first-round result: Spurs beat Keflavik, of Iceland, 15–1 on aggregate. In the semifinal, Spurs knocked out A.C. Milan over two legs, and went to the final full of confidence. Awaiting them were fellow English side Wolverhampton Wanderers.

The first leg was a fine game that featured three second-half goals, two by Martin Chivers, to give Spurs a 2–1 lead to take to London. Chivers's first came after an hour when he rose to head home a free kick; the second, canceling out Wolves' equalizer, came with just five minutes to go, and is now legendary to all Spurs fans. Cutting in from the left flank, Chivers hit a rising drive from 30 yards, a shot that future North American Soccer League star Phil Parkes, in the Wolves goal, hadn't a hope of saving. In the second leg, at White Hart Lane, Spurs did enough with a 1–1 draw to take the trophy.

Two seasons later, Spurs again made it to the final of the same tournament, only for their rioting fans to ruin the second leg, as they fell 2–0 on the night, and 4–2 on aggregate, to Feyenoord. The tie had been lost at home, though, as Spurs allowed a late equalizer; Feyenoord's two away goals were always going to be key. Sadly, fans of the North London team didn't take it well, pulling out seats at the De Kuip Stadium and hurling them around like naughty boys. Nicholson, so old school, was horrified, and a few months later he quit.

Since then, Spurs have remained primarily a cup team. In 1984, they once again won the UEFA Cup, on penalties, after both legs against Anderlecht of Belgium ended 1–1. Spurs left it late in the second leg in London to save the tie, Graham Roberts nicking a goal with just six minutes to go. It had been a thrilling passage of play. Ossie Ardiles, the diminutive Argentine genius in the Spurs midfield, had smacked a shot against the bar when it would have been easier to score, but Spurs kept the ball alive and Roberts, a center back, showed sweet feet to turn the ball home after bringing it down on his chest like an Argentine. In the penalty shootout, another keeper called Parks, this time Tony in the Spurs goal, saved Anderlecht's first, but all the others for both teams were scored, leaving Danny Thomas to win the game. But a nine-step runup starting well out of the penalty box, one of the longest ever seen in the history of shootouts, seemed to signal that Thomas wasn't particularly confident, and sure enough Jacky Munaron, in the Anderlecht goal, saved it. (The subsequent chant by Spurs fans that there's "only one Danny Thomas," was, one assumes, sung both to assure the right back of their love and to remind themselves that at least there weren't two.)

Up stepped Arnór Gudjohnsen, father of Chelsea and Barcelona star Eidur Gudjohnsen and a substitute for Anderlecht on the night, to keep the tie alive. But Parks was determined to be the hero and dry Thomas's tears, and made a brilliant save to his right. Spurs were UEFA champions once more.

In recent years, moments like this have seemed to make do for Spurs fans, given that their team have underperformed. Many cite Ricky Villa's goal against Manchester City in a 1981 FA Cup final replay as one such moment, his slaloming run through the City defense still cited as one of the best ever Cup goals. The emergence of Gareth Bale, too, is cherished, especially for nights like the one in

Milan when he scored a hat-trick against Inter, in the 2010 Champions League, to announce himself as heir to Cristiano Ronaldo's silky skills and goal-scoring abilities. The first two goals were almost identical, Bale scorching down the left wing and hitting unstoppable shots across Júlio César in the Inter goal; the third came from the same position, though there was no run beforehand. The world marveled at what Bale could do.

But context is all. When Bale started scoring in the San Siro that night, Spurs were already 4–0 down, with their keeper, Heurelho Gomes, having been sent off after just eight minutes. Bale's final two goals came in the last minute, making them both futile and dangerous, because on the back of his standout performance it was only a matter of time before a major European team came calling. Sure enough, in 2013, Gareth Bale joined Cristiano Ronaldo (and another former Spurs star, Luka Modrić) at Real Madrid, for an almost-world-record fee of around £77 million. As ever, Spurs fans could live on his sweet memory, but the reality? Bale was yet another former superstar who didn't stay long enough to bring sustained success to White Hart Lane.

Location	Valencia, Spain
Established	1919
Nicknames	*Blanquinegros* ("The White and Blacks")
Stadium	Mestalla (55,000 capacity)
Home colors	White, orange, and black
Leading goal-scorer	Edmundo Suárez, known as Mundo (1964–68), 206 goals
Most appearances	Fernando Gómez (1983–98), 552 appearances

The role that chance plays in soccer is often underestimated. For all the tactics, form, player selection, and money spent, there are still moments when the ball cannons off someone's knee and into the net. Or a top player gets hurt right before a big game; or, worst of all, the dreaded penalty shootout ends an otherwise even contest with what is more often than not a crapshoot. (This is especially true of the English national team, which has been knocked out of six major tournaments since 1990 by being crap at shooting penalties.) Chance has dogged Valencia throughout their history, though it was chance that also begat the first president of the club.

Valencia F.C., representing the third largest city in Spain, are the nearly team of Spanish football. True, they have won La Liga six times and the Spanish Cup seven; they have also won a UEFA Cup and a Cup Winners' Cup. But in the tournament that defines European dominance, the European Cup, Valencia reached two finals, back to back, and lost them both.

Valencia F.C. was established in 1919. Its first president, Octavio

Augusto Milego Díaz, beat out one Gonzalo Medina Pernás to the job via the toss of a coin. Soccer had come to this bustling Mediterranean port via citrus exports, the Spanish businessmen coming back from making contact with British wholesalers with news of this roustabout sport. Quickly, Valencia F.C. outshone the smaller teams based in the city, though it would take until 1930 for the club to reach the top flight of Spanish football. Soon after, though, Spain would be wracked by its brutal civil war, during which Valencia's stadium, the Mestalla, was wrecked, and its players scattered.

But love would triumph over hate, in the form of visionary club president Luis Casanova. Casanova had taken over from Alfredo Giménez, an army commander, and this young tycoon set about building a team that could finally win things. And win it did: Valencia's first Copa del Rey came in 1941, and the next year they won the league. By the end of the decade, Valencia had notched three league titles and two cups, though they would have to wait more than half a decade to produce a team as successful as the 1940s' vintage.

In the meantime, the odd trophy came Valencia's way, including two Fairs Cups (the forerunner of the UEFA Cup) in the early sixties, a La Liga title in 1971, and the Cup Winners' Cup in 1980, in which they beat Arsenal in the final after Graham Rix missed Arsenal's sixth kick (an Englishman no good at penalties—who would believe it?). That Valencia team had featured the great Mario Kempes, hot off his 1978 World Cup-winning performances for Argentina. But Valencia could not sustain a domestic challenge, and it would be the new century before they rose again.

When they did so, they would win two La Liga titles, in 2002 and 2004, the year they also won the UEFA Cup, beating Marseille, 2–0. The joy of that banner season was surely a balm for 2000 and 2001, when they managed to reach the Champions League final in back-to-back seasons, and lose both.

The first hurt; the second really hurt.

The loss in 2000 hurt because it came against Spanish rivals Real Madrid, though losing to such a fine squad was no disgrace. Never before had two teams from the same country fought in the final of the European Cup/Champions League, but it wasn't much of a contest. Madrid at the time boasted Iker Casillas in goal, Roberto Carlos at left back, Steve McManaman and Raúl in midfield, and Fernando Morientes and Nicolas Anelka up front. Valencia, on the other hand, were a solid, if not star-studded, team, anchored around captain and playmaker Gaizka Mendieta. Morientes put Madrid in the lead in the first half, but their domination was clear in the second when both McManaman and Raúl scored within eight minutes of each other to complete the near-rout.

The following year, Valencia had to get past three tough English teams—Manchester United, Arsenal, and Leeds United—to make it to the Champions League final. There they faced Bayern Munich, and this time it was closer, and the entire game was made up of the chancy horrors that are penalty kicks.

The first came after just three minutes when a prone Bayern player, Patrik Andersson, was adjudged to have handled the ball, though he knew nothing about it. Mendieta didn't care, and it was 1–0 to Valencia. A few minutes later Bayern got their own penalty, Stefan Effenberg being poleaxed in the box by Jocelyn Angloma. Mehmet Scholl's kick barely displayed a degree off of zero, and Santiago Cañizares made an easy save with his legs. But six minutes into the second half a third penalty was awarded, when pressure from mon-ster-sized Carsten Jancker caused Amedeo Carboni to punch the ball away from goal with his hand. It was another decision that seemed harsh given that Jancker was doing his best to enter Carboni via his back passage. Scholl had had his chance—this time Effenberg slotted the penalty to the keeper's right, and it was 1–1.

The final stayed tied throughout the rest of the game and extra time. Dreaded shootout penalties arrived. It didn't start well for Bay-ern Munich, when Paulo Sérgio put his kick so far over the bar there are some reports that it has yet to reappear. Mendieta scored for Valencia, as did John Carew, but Valencia missed their next two. After the regular five each, the score was 3–3; it was anyone's cup. In sudden death, Effenberg scored for Bayern once again, as did Bixente Lizarazu; Valencia, in turn, scored both of their kicks. In the eighth round Thomas Linke scored for Bayern, meaning that Mauricio Pellegrino, an Argentine center back, had to score to keep the game alive.

Facing Pellegrino was Bayern's man-mountain of a keeper, Oliver Kahn. Boasting an almost perfectly cuboid head, "the Titan," as he is known in Germany, is an imposing figure—never more so than on that night. Pellegrino hit his penalty high to the right, but Kahn was equal to it, springing like a cat—like a huge, Maine coon cat, in fact—to paw the ball away. And then Kahn set off running, like a Maine coon after a mouse, while his teammates bounced up and down on invisible trampolines. Valencia had lost again.

Subsequent money troubles forced Valencia to sell talents like David Villa (to Barcelona), David Silva (to Manchester City), Juan Mata (to Chelsea), and Roberto Soldado (to Spurs). Unlucky, plucky Valencia, making world-class stars for other teams, and dreading penalties like mice dread cats.

Location	Rio de Janeiro, Brazil
Established	1898
Nicknames	*Gigante da Colina* ("Giant of the Hill"), *Trem Bala da Colina* ("Bullet Train of the Hill"), *Expresso da Vitória* ("Victory Express"), *Time da Virada* ("The Comeback Team"), *Cruz-maltinos* ("Team of the Maltese Cross")
Current stadium	Estádio São Januário, offcially Estádio Vasco da Gama (31,000 capacity)
Home colors	Black, white, and red
Leading goal-scorer	Carlos Roberto de Oliviera, known as Roberto Dinamite (1971–92), 702 goals
Most appearances	Carlos Roberto de Oliviera, known as Roberto Dinamite (1971–92), 768 appearances

He might be only 5 feet 6 inches tall, but Romário de Souza Faria has never been short of confidence. Romário, as he is better known to the soccer world, is said to have claimed that when he was born, the "man in the sky" picked him out, saying, "That's the guy." Assuming that the "man in the sky" has nothing better to do, it's hard not to argue with the claim, especially given what the little genius did in his football career. Romário won a World Cup with Brazil; won the Spanish League (he was top scorer, 30 goals in 33 games) with Barcelona; and won the Dutch league, three times, with PSV Eindhoven. Romário was even elected to the Brazilian parliament in 2010. But surely one of the most significant highlights of his career came in the 93rd minute of the 2000 Copa Mercosur final, playing for Vasco da Gama.

Vasco da Gama are named after the Portuguese explorer who opened up India, and thereby the entire Far East, for his country. They were founded by Portuguese immigrants as far back as 1898 as a rowing club; by 1915 the club also played soccer, and quickly set about changing the makeup of the sport in Brazil. Though a number of other influential Brazilian teams kept their squads all-white, Vasco never had a problem including black players. When Vasco took the Campeonato Carioca, Rio's state football league, in 1923, a third of their players were black. Other teams, such as Botafogo, Fluminense, and Flamengo, tried to complain about professionalism or introduce draconian registration rules, but Vasco held firm, and eventually the team led the way, like their namesake, into a brave new world of multiracial soccer in Brazil.

It wasn't just the right thing to do morally—it also brought Vasco five Cariocas before World War II, and seven more before 1960. In 1948, Vasco won the first ever South American Championship of Champions, the precursor to the Copa Libertadores. They swept through the tournament unbeaten.

It would take until 1974 for Vasco to win their first Brazilian championship, and they would have to wait 14 years for another. In 1997, they won their third, and on the back of that win Vasco entered the Copa Libertadores. A cool $10 million was spent on that 1998 team, a *"Projeto Tóquio"* ("Project Tokyo") as it's known when a team in Brazil spends heavily to try to win the Copa and thence the Intercontinental Cup/FIFA Club World Cup. (The Intercontinental final is held in Tokyo.) Vasco won the Copa Libertadores that year, but in the subsequent Intercontinental Cup, they lost 2–1 to Real Madrid on a late Raúl goal. Vasco made it to the same final the following year, held in their home country this time (*"Projeto Brasileiro"* this time?), but on January 20, 2000, Vasco's countrymen, Corinthians, beat them on penalties after a poor final.

The year 2000 proved to be the best, and the worst, in Vasco's storied history. It began with that loss to Corinthians, when Eduardo missed the final penalty. On December 12, 2000, Vasco faced Palmeiras in the third-leg playoff final of the Copa Mercosur. A forerunner of the Copa Sudamericana, the tournament was short-lived (just four seasons), but in 2000 it produced one of the great finals in any competition.

The first two legs were split between the sides which necessitated a third game, and the decider didn't start well for Vasco. By half-time Palmeiras were 3–0 up, and their lead seemed unassailable.

But this is football, and you're never beaten until the final whistle blows. By the 70-minute mark, Romário had scored two penalties, and Vasco's tails were up. A Vasco fan in the crowd, dressed as Santa (the real "man in the sky"?), was pictured jumping up and down in excitement. But with 13 minutes to go, Vasco's Júnior Baiano received a second yellow card and walked. Vasco were 3–2 down, and one man down. Surely there was no way back . . .

With just four minutes left, a hilarious whiff by Romário cannoned off his standing foot and ran in to the path of onrushing Juninho Paulista, who scored. The game was tied. But even better was to come for Vasco.

With 47:38 on the clock, a throw-in on the left wing started a final Vasco attack. A couple of passes and one nutmeg later, the ball was worked into the Palmeiras box, where a shot that was skewing wide was blocked by a defender, and the ball ran to Romário, who kept his cool and buried the ball in the back of the net. With four goals in 33 minutes, two of them scored with just ten men, Vasco had won the cup. The "man in the sky" had looked down and said, "That's the guy," and "That's his team" and "Here's your cup."

A week later, a real disaster struck, one that revealed the ugly inner workings of Brazilian soccer. Facing a final game to secure the national title, Vasco were well placed to win a tournament that was already widely considered a farce. After backroom deals saw Vasco unrelegated, and the Brazilian Football Confederation (CBF) barred from running the league in favor of 20 of the biggest teams, the resulting season saw a massively bloated league lurch from one ridiculous spectacle to another. Of course Vasco made the final game, against sure-to-be-beaten, second-level San Caetano—it was the equivalent of whatever is the opposite of poetic justice. Then things got worse. A disturbance high in Vasco's over-sold-out stadium (some reports suggest there were twice as many fans in attendance as should have been allowed) led to 137 injuries; hurt supporters were laid out on the grass. But not content to let the disaster get in the way of the game, Vasco president Eurico Miranda had the pitch cleared so that the game could continue. The state governor of Rio himself had to call the stadium to have the game abandoned, but Miranda and his team still ran around the shocked stadium with the trophy. (A farcical rematch at the much larger Maracanã, the following January, confirmed Vasco as the "winners.")

Poetic justice would come eventually. In 2008, Miranda was deposed as president of the club, and Vasco were finally relegated for real. Though they returned to the top flight in 2013, Vasco da Gama finished third from bottom and were relegated to Série B once again. No intervention from either the "man in the sky," nor the Brazilian soccer authorities could save them this time.

Location	Buenos Aires, Argentina
Established	1910
Nicknames	*El Fortín* ("The Fort")
Stadium	Estadio José Amalfitani (49,540 capacity)
Home colors	White and blue
Leading goal-scorer	Carlos Bianchi (1967–73, 1980–84), 206 goals
Most appearances	Fabián Cubero (1996–2007, 2008–), 458 appearances

I n the world of crazy goalkeepers, one stands head and shoulders above all others: ladies and gentlemen of the jury, José Luis Chilavert. The list of Chilavert's exploits—some might call them crimes and misdemeanors, though he's not all bad—is long.

On the plus side, Chilavert's tally of 62 first-class goals—yes, goals—as a keeper is second only to that of Rogério Ceni of Brazil. Chilavert was a free-kick specialist and took penalties with aplomb, but he was also one of the best goalies to ever play the game. He made crucial saves in a Copa Libertadores final, and even took a penalty in the shootout. Chilavert showed his political and moral leanings when he publicly criticized his country's entry into the 1999 Copa América, saying the money should have been spent on education instead. He was also the basis of Paraguay's run to the knockout stages of the 2002 World Cup; and he helped turn Vélez Sarsfield, a relatively unheralded Argentine club, into a powerhouse team in the 1990s.

Vélez came into being in 1910, after a rainstorm. Sheltering from the bad weather in the Vélez Sarsfield rail station in Buenos Aires during a pickup game, three soccer-mad men—Martín Portillo,

Julio Guglielmone, and Nicolás Marín Moreno—decided to form a
real team. Originally Club Atlético Argentinos de Vélez Sarsfield,
then by 1913 Club Atlético Vélez Sarsfield (their current full name),
they initially bummed around in the lower reaches of amateur
Argentine football. Once the professional era came to Argentina,
Vélez finally adopted their blue-chevron-on-white-shirt kit (it was
originally an abandoned rugby uniform, Argentina being a rugby
outpost in South America) and joined the newly formed Primera
División, but in 1940 they were relegated. The game that sent them
down, a 6–4 win by Atlanta over Independiente, was 6–0 at half-
time, a suspicious scoreline if ever there was one. Vélez lost their stadium, and their best player, Victorio Spinetto, was later seen walking
down the street in tears.

Spinetto would become Vélez's coach two years later in their new
stadium, and, like Chilavert, he was a man with significant pluses and
minuses. On the positive side, he turned Vélez into a fine team, bringing them back to the top flight and making them sturdy, solid, and
above all tough, like their manager. On the negative, Spinetto wasn't
afraid to call his players "queers" at half-time, or remind them that
they were the sons of mothers who might have something to say about
their offspring's failings. It should be noted that Vélez's second-half
performances were often better than their first, and in 1953, under
Spinetto's leadership, they came second in the league, a great effort for
a small team.

Vélez's first championship, in the Nacional, came in 1968, but they
were unable to capitalize, and nothing else came their way until the
1990s, when Chilavert got between the goalposts. Three Clausuras
and an Apertura in that decade were a sign that they were now a team
to be considered among the best Argentina had to offer.

Vélez Sarsfield were certainly the best in South America, and
then the world, in 1994. That year they made it to the Copa Libertadores and the Intercontinental Cup finals. In the Libertadores final, a
tense first leg in Buenos Aires against São Paulo ended 1–0 to Vélez on
a goal by Omar Asad, their Lebanese/Syrian striker, known as "*El*

Turco." Back in Brazil, Müller (the Brazilian, not the German) scored for São Paulo, sending the game to penalties.

Cue Chilavert.

On *his* minus side, Chilavert is not what you'd call a conciliator. He was once banned for four games (reduced to three) for spitting on Brazil's Roberto Carlos in a World Cup qualifying game, and it is no mitigation that Chilavert was merely doing what many other players and fans have wished to do to the endlessly provoking Carlos throughout his annoying career. Giving deep background on the spit, Chilavert claimed that Carlos grabbed his own genitals and called Chilavert an "Indian." In a subsequent interview, Chilavert referred to 5' 5"Carlos as a "dwarf," which though funny, sadly must also sit in the minus column. Before that fated game against Carlos's Brazil, Chilavert had even said that Brazil should hand back some land it took from Paraguay in the nineteenth century (we'd suggest that's probably a plus-column comment).

Chilavert has also punched journalists, and Colombian forward Faustino Asprilla, after both were sent off for squaring up to each other in a World Cup qualifying game in 1997. As Chilavert walked off, he swerved toward Asprilla, who was already sitting on the bench, and the punch, a fine left jab to the bridge of Asprilla's nose, instigated a melee in which cops with plastic riot shields weighed in calmly and rationally.

Through it all, though, Chilavert consistently made big saves and scored big and important goals. There was none "bigger" than the one Chilavert notched against River Plate in a league game in 1996, smashing a free kick from five yards inside his own half that swerved with the wind and soared over the despairing hands of the River Plate keeper as he fell backward into the net.

And there was none more important than the penalty Chilavert scored in the Copa Libertadores final against São Paulo. After saving São Paulo's first penalty, he buried his own kick to make it 2–0. Unable to save the next one, from André Luiz (who would go on to play for the San Jose Earthquakes), Chilavert got into a jawing match with the

Brazilian—no surprise there. The rest of the penalties went to form, leaving Roberto Pompei of Vélez with a chance to win it for the Argentines; he didn't disappoint. Vélez were champions of South America.

In the subsequent Intercontinental Cup final, Vélez overcame a star-studded Milan side, 2–0, on goals by Roberto Trotta and, once again, Omar Asad. The little team that could, with the craziest goalkeeper of all, were world champions.

The new century saw Vélez clinch three more Clausuras, an Inicial, and the 2013 Primera División, which if nothing else proves that Argentine football loves a complicated paradigm for its leagues. The short of it is that Vélez Sarsfield, whose shirt features a "V" on the front, now knew how to notch victories. As for Chilavert, he has gone on record as wanting to be president of Paraguay.

Location	Bremen, Germany
Established	1899
Nicknames	*Die Werderaner* ("The River Islanders"), *Die Grün-Weissen* ("The Green and Whites")
Current stadium	Weserstadion (42,100 capacity)
Home colors	Green and white
Leading goal-scorer	Marco Bode (1988–2002), 101 goals
Most appearances	Dieter Burdenski (1972–88), 444 appearances

I t all started with a game of tug-of-war, up in the handsome port town of Bremen, in northern Germany.

In 1899 a team of schoolboys won the war, and they were rewarded with the prize of a football. And though footballs had been coming through this "key to Europe" port for a number of years, thanks to its regular trading status with Britain, this time the sport stuck, and F.V. Bremen came into being. They played as such until 1920, when they changed their name to Sportverein Werder Bremen von 1899.

World War II came, and though they played through the conflict, before the end of the war Sportverein Werder Bremen von 1899 was shuttered by the Nazis. The rump was amalgamated with two teams also once banned by the Nazis (TV Vorwärts and Freie Schwimmer 1910), and became the unwieldy SV Grün-Weiss 1899 Bremen. Good sense eventually prevailed, and SV Werder Bremen came into being in 1946.

By 1964 Bremen had done well enough in the Oberliga Nord to be admitted to the first Bundesliga, which they won the next season. But it proved to be the first of just four league titles, though Bremen did contribute to the introduction of aluminum goals after one of their players, and one from Borussia Mönchengladbach, collided with the post in a game at Borussia on April 3, 1971, and the whole darned thing collapsed, causing the game to be abandoned.

In 1980, Bremen were relegated, and the club knew something had to change. It did, in the form of coach Otto Rehhagel. Rehhagel took over Werder Bremen in 1981 and stayed until the mid-nineties. In that time he transformed the club into Germany's second-best team. Though Bremen never quite ousted Bayern Munich, their two German championships (1988 and 1993) came via fast attacking football backed by a stingy defense. Rehhagel also had an eye for talent, bringing on Rudi Völler, Mario Basler, Karl-Heinz Riedle, and Frank Ordenewitz, a man unique among footballers for once admitting to the referee that he'd handled a ball in the penalty box, thereby giving up a spot kick (Bremen lost 2–0 that day, but Ordenewitz won a Fair Play Award from FIFA).

In 1992, Rehhagel's Bremen finally won in Europe. Though most of the earlier Bremen stars had moved on, Rehhagel was still able to forge a classically German team, full of hyper-fit, hardworking, and often very large players. Bremen faced A.S. Monaco in the Cup Winners' Cup final, and with five minutes to go in the first half, 35-year-old striker Klaus Allofs reacted quickly to a knocked-down free kick, smacking the ball into the back of the net and accidentally kicking the Monaco defender Roger Mendy in the crown jewels at the same time.

Ten minutes into the second half, one of the least likely players ever to appear in the Bundesliga made the game safe for Werder Bremen. Wynton Rufer is half Swiss, half Maori, but the New Zealand native became, with Alofs, a cornerstone of this Bremen team. Alofs won the ball, and set Rufer free; he rounded the keeper brilliantly and buried his shot, bringing Bremen its first European trophy.

Rehhagel would move to Bayern Munich, where he never fitted in. He eventually took over the Greek national team, and somehow got one of the most limited sides imaginable to win the 2004 European Championship, though the less said about how Rehhagel actually got them to play—it was basically "nick a goal, then put eleven men in defense for the rest of the game"—the better.

As for his old club, Bremen won their sixth German Cup in 2008–09, and that team, featuring a young Mesut Özil in midfield, took Shakhtar Donetsk to extra time in the UEFA Cup final, but a goalkeeping error by Tim Wiese gave the Ukrainian side the 2–1 victory. Özil would move on to Real Madrid in 2010, and then Arsenal in 2013; Werder Bremen have yet to fully recover from the loss of his languorous midfield skills, and in the three seasons since Özil left have become a stolid, mid-table Bundesliga side, finishing 13th, ninth, and 14th. They need a new Rehhagel, though preferably one that believes in winning games with style.

WOLVERHAMPTON WANDERERS

Location	Wolverhampton, England
Established	1877
Nicknames	Wolves
Current stadium	Molineux (30,852 capacity)
Home colors	Gold and black
Leading goal-scorer	Steve Bull (1986–99), 306 goals
Most appearances	Steve Bull (1986–99), 474 appearances

A team once so proud, so successful, are now a pale, if still golden-clad, shadow of their former selves. How do soccer clubs go from triumph to irrelevancy in the space of just a few years? In the case of Wolverhampton Wanderers, the blame lies at the feet of the town itself; an economic downturn brought on by a country that no longer cared for its heavy industries; and a club that, financially speaking, couldn't organize a school raffle.

Parts of Wolverhampton slip into an area that is known in Britain as the Black Country, a section of the Midlands known for its mining, iron foundries, quarries, car production, and, in Wolverhampton's case, bicycle manufacturing. It is not a pretty part of England—heavy industry can tend to make a place look utilitarian at best, and some even claim that Mordor, the grim "Land of Shadow" from Tolkien's *Lord of the Rings*, is based on it. But at the height of its industrial power, the Black Country, through the auspices of Wolverhampton Wanderers, produced one of the finest teams England had ever known.

Wolves, as they're most often called, were first established in 1877 as St. Luke's, after Harry Barcroft, the St. Luke's School headmaster, gave two of his star pupils, the Johns Baynton and Brodie, a football. In 1888, the team, called Wolverhampton Wanderers since 1879, was one of the founding members of the football league—in fact, the first ever league game was between Wolves and local rivals Aston Villa. These were the days before two points for a win, one for a draw, had even been considered (it took nearly three months to decide on that formulation). But the league was up and running, and Wolves would finish that first season third, as well as being losing finalists in the FA Cup. Wolves won the FA Cup in 1893 and again in 1908, but by then they were a Second Division team. In 1923, Wolves slipped down yet another division for one season, but a decade later they were back in the First Division, and right before World War II Wolves finished second twice in a row, in 1938 and 1939, the year they lost yet another Cup final.

Once the war was over, Wolves started to build a fine team under new manager Stan Cullis, winning their first FA Cup in 1949, beating Leicester City, 3–1. Their captain, Billy Wright, had taken over after the war from legendary Stan Cullis the player (he had captained both Wolves and England). Wright, who was handed the trophy in 1949 by Princess Elizabeth (she was four years shy of becoming Queen Elizabeth), also went on to legendary status at Molineux, Wolves' stadium, playing nearly 500 games for Wanderers, as well as more than 100 for England, 90 of them as captain.

But it was Cullis who brought Wolves to the peak of their history. Between 1953 and 1961, Wolves dominated the English football scene, finishing third, first, second, third, sixth, first, first, second (and FA Cup winners), and third once again. It was an astonishing run, built around Cullis's vision of soccer as a simple game of long passes and crosses, getting the ball as quickly as possible into the attacking area of the field. Cullis loved an attacking winger slinging balls into the box, and would have had no time for Barcelona's tiki-taka. His was a particularly English style of football, and that's no compliment. But it worked, at least at home.

Wolves also exploited the beginnings of international club football, welcoming teams to Molineux to play at night under newly installed lights. One such visit, from Hungarian team Honvéd—featuring a number of players who had recently starred for their national team in humbling England, 6–3—led to Cullis claiming his team were "the champions of the world." His ridiculous boast led indirectly to the formation of the European Cup, though Wolves' hit-it-and-hope style was no match for the sophistication of teams like Barcelona, who in the 1959 European Cup quarterfinals beat Cullis's team 4–0 in Spain and 5–2 in the Midlands.

Cullis was fired from Wolves in 1964, and the club has never been the same. A mixture of mismanagement, financial and otherwise—they have nearly gone out of business numerous times in the last three decades—as well as the breakdown of the area's traditional manufacturing base, has set the club back on its heels. Wolves reached a European final in 1972, but lost to fellow Brits Spurs in that year's UEFA Cup. In 1980, Wolves opened a new and vast seating area, the Molineux Street stand, which was built about half a mile from the actual pitch; sitting in it to watch a game, as this writer did, was like watching the match on a very distant television.

Unlike at the founding of Football League, Wolves were not part of the Premiership when it was established in 1992. They reached the top flight in 2003, for one season, and again in 2009 for three seasons, but relegation was never far away. As of 2013, they were back once again in the third level of British football, though they would win the League in 2014 and head back to the second tier once again. But bicycles are no longer made in Wolverhampton.

MAJOR DOMESTIC LEAGUES
AND CUP COMPETITIONS

England

English Premier League (before 1992, the English First Division); the Championship (second tier), League One (third tier), and League Two (fourth tier) (before 1992, Divisions Two, Three, and Four).

The FA Cup (knockout tournament open to all professional teams)

The Football League Cup (currently also known as the Capital One Cup, open to members of the Premier League and the Football League [tiers two through four])

Scotland

The Scottish Premiership, Scottish Championship (second tier), Scottish League One (third tier), Scottish League Two (fourth tier) (before 1997, variously the Premier Division and/or Scottish League Divisions One, Two, Three, and Four)

The Scottish Cup

France

Ligue 1, Ligue 2

Coupe de France

Spain

La Liga

Copa del Rey

Germany

Bundesliga (before 1963, various regional leagues existed)

DFB-Pokal (Deutscher Fussball Bund-Pokal, a.k.a. the German Cup)

Italy
Serie A, Serie B, Serie C
Coppa Italia

Brazil
Campeonato Brasileiro Série A, Série B, Série C (after 2009, also Série D). Various state championships. (Teams generally play in both the national campeonato and their state tournaments.)
Copa do Brasil

Argentina
Primera División, Primera B Nacional; below these two levels, football is played on a state level

Note: South American leagues tend to split their yearlong seasons into two halves, usually referred to as "Apertura" and "Clausura." Relegation and promotion is often predicated on aggregate performances over a number of different seasons, rather than just one as in Europe.

USA
Major League Soccer, split into Western and Eastern conferences; top team by record across both conferences is awarded the Supporters Shield. Top teams qualify for post-season home and away playoffs, leading to a final MLS Cup game. There is no promotion or relegation.
Lamar Hunt US Open Cup (founded in 1914 [!], and open to all teams affiliated with the United States Soccer Federation)

MAJOR CONTINENTAL AND INTERCONTINENTAL CLUB TOURNAMENTS

CONTINENTAL

UEFA Champions League

Organized by the European Football Association, features the top-ranked sides from the major European leagues, initially in qualifying rounds, then a league system, after which the tournament heads to a final via home-and-away knockout rounds. Established in 1956 as the European Champions' Club Cup (more commonly called the European Cup), the tournament was, until 1992, restricted to the league champions of various countries. After 1992, when it became the Champions League, teams in second, third, and sometimes even fourth places in certain domestic competitions were invited to join.

Copa Libertadores

Organized by the South American Football Confederation (known as CONMEBOL), features the top-ranked teams from South American domestic leagues (plus one spot for the winner of the Copa do Brasil), initially in qualifying rounds, then a league system, after which the tournament heads to a final via home-and-away knockout rounds. Established in 1960, it was initially restricted to champions of domestic leagues; by 1966, other top-ranked teams were included. In 1998, the tournament was opened to Mexican club teams.

AFC Champions League

Organized by the Asian Football Confederation, the AFC Champions League features teams from the domestic leagues of the top ten ranked Asian countries only, initially in qualifying rounds, then a league system, after which the tournament heads to a final via home-and-away knockout rounds.

CAF Champions League

Organized by the Confederation of African Football, the CAF Champions League features teams from the domestic leagues of the top-ranked African countries, initially in a preliminary stage, then two knockout rounds, then two groups of four, then semifinal and final.

CONCACAF Champions League

Organized by the Confederation of North, Central American and Caribbean Association Football, features top teams from the member countries' domestic leagues, initially in an August–October group stage, then a knockout phase held each March–May.

OFC Champions League

Organized by the Oceania Football Confederation, features the top ranked teams from Oceania initially in a group stage, then playoffs.

UEFA Europa League

Organized by the European Football Association, features the highest-ranked sides below Champions League entrants from the major European leagues, as well as some domestic cup competition winners, initially in a group stage (added after 2004), after which the tournament heads to a final via home-and-away knockout rounds. Established in 1970 as the UEFA Cup, it became the Europa League in 1999, when it merged with the now-defunct UEFA Cup Winners' Cup.

UEFA Cup Winners' Cup

Organized by the European Football Association, featured the winners of domestic cup competitions, pitted against each other in a straight knockout tournament. Established in 1960, it was made defunct via a merger with the UEFA Cup in 1999.

Copa Sudamericana

Organized by the South American Football Confederation (known as CONMEBOL), features the South American teams ranked below those who qualify for the Copa Libertadores, in a straight knockout tournament. Established in 2002, it replaced a number of earlier tournaments, including the Copa Mercasur, Copa Merconorte, and the Copa Conmebol.

INTERCONTINENTAL

Intercontinental Cup
Accredited by both UEFA and CONMEBOL, and held from 1960 to 1979, it was a home-and-away, two-game final, played between the winners of the European Cup and the Copa Libertadores (though some years Europe sent the European Cup runners-up instead). From 1979 to 2004, it was a single-game final held in Japan and called the Toyota Cup. Now replaced by the FIFA Club World Cup.

FIFA Club World Cup
Organized by the Fédération Internationale de Football Association, the FIFA Club World Cup brings together the winners of a season's UEFA Champions League and Copa Libertadores, along with the winners of the Asian Champions League, the Confederation of African Football Champions League winners, the CONCACAF Champions League (of North America), and the Oceania Champions League. The host nation's national champions are also included, and all play toward the final via a one-leg knockout tournament.

ACKNOWLEDGMENTS

I would like to thank the following people for their succor and support:

Josh Benson, of *Capital New York*, Frank Foer, of the *New Republic*, and George Quraishi, of *Howler*, have each published my soccer pieces; without their kindness, I would not have thought to write about a sport I love so much. (Two of Josh's sons, Sam and Joe, look like very tasty players, too—remember the names.) Tom Bingham beautifully illustrated an article I penned for *Howler* and then had the kindness to send me the original piece of art—it hangs in pride of place in my house. David Hirshey and Clive Priddle have taken me for lunch and let me gloat about my team's victories, of which there have been so many, and unduly enjoy their team's woes, of which, etc. Laura Tucker kindly helped me track down a story about Yogi Berra, though it didn't make it through the editing process.

Robert Rich, Jr., a.k.a. Lord Bedlington, a.k.a. Lord Bubba, gave me the chance to play for four minutes of a friendly for the Bedlington Terriers, in their 2011 pre-season game in Canada. Bob will never know how many times I lie awake at night, replaying every one of those 240 seconds of that dream come true (spoiler alert: it's every night).

Kris Dahl, at ICM, has been both a wonderful agent and a kind friend; her assistant, Caroline Eisenmann, is ever receptive. Matt Weiland, whose idea this book was, is an extremely talented editor and a wonderful cheerleader; his son, Enzo, has the good grace to not follow his father in supporting Doncaster Rovers, and seems destined for a storied career as an American Lionel Messi (remember the name redux). Matt's unflappable assistant, Sam MacLaughlin, also did a superb research job on the club facts sections, as did Erin Fortenberry and Emily Injeian. Allegra Huston fixed my wonky copy. (I have received nothing but good vibes and kindness from other folks at Norton.) My brother, Simon Dempsey, has read early drafts of this book and not thrown up, or so he claims.

I have had four constant companions throughout the writing of *Club Soccer 101*:

One, Buddy Pandowski, a Belgian Shepherd, has sat at my feet for pretty much every word of this book. (I'm fully aware that Buddy will never read nor understand this acknowledgment, but he's a good boy anyway.)

My beloved daughters, Lily and Amelia, have not only put up with their middle names (Solskjaer and Cantona [sic.]), but also my obsessive watching, and writing about, football. They are ridiculously fabulous people.

Elizabeth Stein, Buddy's female human, is she about whom grateful folks like me get to say, "without whom." Besides being BFF with whom I share many an LOL, she has never once asked me to turn a soccer game off, never once looked bored as I've bored her with yet another "fascinating" anecdote from the footy world. I am fortunate to know her: today, and every day.